T0212390

Disorder and the Disinformation Society

This book is the first general social analysis that seriously considers the daily experience of information disruption and software failure within contemporary Western society. Through an investigation of informationalism, defined as a contemporary form of capitalism, it describes the social processes producing informational disorder. While most social theory sees disorder as secondary, pathological or uninteresting, this book takes disordering processes as central to social life. The book engages with theories of information society that privilege information order, offering a strong counter-point centred on "disinformation". *Disorder and the Disinformation Society* offers a practical agenda, arguing that difficulties in producing software are both inherent to the process of developing software and in the social dynamics of informationalism. The book outlines the dynamics of software failure as this impinges on information workers and on daily life. It investigates why computerized finance has become inherently self-disruptive. It explores how digital enclosure and intellectual property relations generate conflicts over cultural creativity and disrupt informational accuracy and scholarship. Finally it shows how social media can extend, but also distort the development of social movements.

Jonathan Paul Marshall is an anthropologist and senior research associate at the University of Technology, Sydney.

James Goodman conducts research into social change and global politics and is an Associate Professor in the Faculty of Arts and Social Sciences at the University of Technology, Sydney.

Didar Zowghi is Professor of Software Engineering, and the Director of the research centre for Human-Centred Technology Design (HCTD) at the Faculty of Engineering and IT at University of Technology, Sydney.

Francesca da Rimini is an Honorary Associate at the University of Technology, Sydney (Faculty of Engineering and Information Technology).

Routledge Research in Information Technology and Society

Disorder and the Disinformation Society

The Social Dynamics of Information, Networks and Software

Jonathan Paul Marshall,
James Goodman, Didar Zowghi
and Francesca da Rimini

Routledge
Taylor & Francis Group

LONDON AND NEW YORK

First published 2015
by Routledge

2 Park Square, Milton Park, Abingdon, Oxfordshire OX14 4RN
52 Vanderbilt Avenue, New York, NY 10017

*Routledge is an imprint of the Taylor & Francis Group,
an informa business*

First issued in paperback 2020

Library of Congress Cataloging-in-Publication Data
Marshall, Jonathan Paul, 1956–
    Disorder and the disinformation society : the social dynamics of
information, networks and software / by Jonathan Paul Marshall, James
Goodman, Didar Zowghi and Francesca da Rimini.
        pages cm. — (Routledge research in information technology and society ; 17)
    Includes bibliographical references and index.
  1. Information society.   2. Information technology—Social aspects.
3. Information networks—Social aspects.   I. Title.
    HM851.M3727 2015
    303.48'33—dc23
    2014048749

ISBN: 978-0-415-54000-1 (hbk)
ISBN: 978-0-367-59934-8 (pbk)

Typeset in Sabon
by Apex CoVantage, LLC

Contents

Introduction
Information Society and Disorder

Disruption and disorder are essential in the dynamic composition of contemporary 'information society'. We argue that the ordering structures, processes or forces in information society produce disorders, and that these disorders contribute to social dynamics and the further ordering and disordering of that society. In this view, disorder is not an irrelevant residue, evidence of breakdown, a temporary product of transition between one order and the next, or to be located only in a 'periphery' or in areas that are not 'connected up'. On the contrary, disordering and dislocation is intrinsic and vital to the understanding of social, economic and political processes in the heartland of informationalism itself. Looking at information society in this way brings the unintended and unplanned consequences of human action, and the ways that people deal with those consequences (or fail to deal with the consequences), into the centre of social theory. We assume that social life is always in flux and thus exceeds ordering efforts, while the imposition or cultivation of a dominant order only serves to further the flux. This allows the investigation and theorisation of the dynamics of the 'order/disorder complex', and strengthens the power of sociological explanation.

We will argue that all human societies experience inherent disorders within processes of 'information' and 'communication', and that these are necessary for communication to work. In the information society disorders also arise from, or are intensified by, the extensive networking of people and information through software. The disordering networks of the information organisation, in turn, disrupt software construction. Disordering problems generate attempts at solutions, which in turn generate new problems and disorders. We use the term 'informationalism' to refer to capitalist information society and argue that capitalism, when joined with information networks, produces a 'disinformation society'. This is a realm in which devaluation of 'knowledge', failure of understanding, disorder of networks, disorder of property, disorder in financial institutions and continuous disruption of daily life is common, expected and arises within its successes.

BOX 1   OPENING A WINDOW: THE OLYMPICS

Networked globally through commercial television channels, the Olympics display a disordering template of global information capitalism. At the symbolic apogee of sporting endeavour, the Olympics constitute a remarkable digital *enclosure* (or appropriation) of recreational life. The International Olympic Committee, the IOC, constructs and represents a global sporting order. As a non-government organisation under Swiss law, it constitutes an 'Olympic Movement', pursuing 'Olympism' aiming to "place sport at the service of the harmonious development of humankind" (IOC 2013: 11). Defined as a "competition between athletes in individual or team events and not between countries", the Olympic Games claim to unify the world's supposed five continents, as symbolised by the five interlinked Olympic rings (IOC 2013: 10, 23). At the same time, the IOC claims the Olympic Games as its "exclusive property" (IOC 2013: 22). Through this legally enforced and recognised claim, information, symbolic power and puissance, aiming at harmony and 'sportsmanship', is converted to, bound to and disrupted by, financial power through brand control and advertising revenue.

Since the 1984 Los Angeles Games the IOC has sold exclusive rights of various types to a small group of broadcasters and sponsors. For example, access is restricted by selling monopoly free-to-air broadcast rights to an organisation in each nation, and commercial sponsors get 'sole status', as when Coca-Cola becomes the sole soft drinks provider. Over the four-year period from 2005 to 2008, which includes the Beijing Olympics of 2008, broadcasting netted US$2.5 billion and sponsorship US$1.6 billion, which massively exceeded ticketing income of US$0.27 billion (IOC 2012: 6). Little of the IOC money goes to athletes: multiple medal winners can pick up sponsorship deals, but most athletes do not.

> Only 50% of American track and field athletes who are ranked in the top ten in the nation in their event earn more than $15,000 a year in income from the sport, according to a survey conducted by the USA Track and Field Foundation. . . . "There is an incredibly steep drop in earning power from the elite of the elite athletes to individuals who are just slightly lower ranked", said Jack Wickens, who conducted the survey.
>
> (Riley 10 July 2012)

Exclusive intellectual property rights imply prohibition and restriction. Brand exclusion is heavily policed: for 28 days athletes are banned from publicly associating with companies not sponsoring the games; any evidence of the existence of non-sponsoring companies is removed from events (including the torch relay, which covers a lot of public ground); and IOC inspectors look for any unauthorised use of Olympic terminology and symbols. Athletes are not allowed to mention non-official sponsors during the games, or appear in advertisements for such sponsors. For the London Olympics, special legislation was introduced to enhance brand protection, and a 300-strong 'Brand Protection Taskforce' was employed to enforce it. The ordering and enclosing process eradicated spontaneous celebrations, such as preventing a local butcher making a representation of the Olympic rings in sausages (Longman 24 July 2012). Large groups of spectators were not permitted to wear clothing 'visibly branded' by non-sponsors, and there were strict limits on what food and drink could be brought into the event, to protect on-site fast food sponsors (ironically despite health concerns). Information disappears as part of commercial life.

Commercial ordering imperatives contradict the apparently intrinsic altruistic, sporting and unifying motivations. Competition is increasingly shaped by the availability of sponsorship deals for those that win the medals as individuals, rather than by any broader 'Olympic Spirit'. Countries do explicitly compete with each other to show worth and dominance. Much national coverage focuses on the home countries' athletes alone, to increase ratings, reinforcing national separation and limiting information about what counts as world sport. Viewers of the games are presented with little choice of monopoly providers and are assailed by specific advertising. Those who seek to attend in person are excluded from major events by corporate block-bookings.

The games claim to champion health and fitness, yet they are a 'winner-take-all' event connected with national pride. In countries such as Australia pressures arise to cut funds from 'mass' sports and put them towards elite athletes, especially when the medal count is lower than expected (Tillet 18 June 2012). Meanwhile, the IOC itself, and its national committees, are beset with corruption and bribery scandals, further undermining the whole exercise (Jennings 1996; Daley 1999; Lenskyj 2008). The corruption is not confined to the IOC. In 2013 it was alleged that "Russian businessmen and officials close to President Vladimir Putin have stolen up to $30 billion from funds intended for preparations for next year's Sochi Winter Olympics" (de Carbonnel 30 May 2013). Jean-Claude Killy, who heads the International Olympic Committee's coordination commission for the Sochi Games, was reported as saying: "I don't recall an Olympics without corruption" (Vasilyeva 30 May 2013). Despite protests, the IOC would not defend gay athletes against Russian legislation targeting gay visibility (Lally 28 September 2013). Continuing corruption, and violation of ideals, becomes a normal social process, not an aberration. The IOC's Olympic spectacle usually leaves behind abandoned facilities and public debts. The cost of private profit, waste and detritus is shifted onto taxpayers, who can then face cuts to vital services. It has even been suggested that the Athens Olympics could have contributed to the Greek financial crisis (Georgiakis & Nauright 2012; Gatopoulos 3 June 2010).

Commercial enclosure, exclusive rights and brand protection conspire with national grandstanding to transform the sporting event into a highly ordered global spectacle. As an exercise in informationalism, the Olympics disrupts its stated purpose of inspiring the "harmonious development of human kind". The disorders and unintentional effects cannot be separated from its orders.

Informational capitalism generally tries to solve its problems by vainly displacing disorder 'downwards' and 'outwards' while (equally vainly) attempting to corral security, capital and power in the 'high centre'. Subordinated classes, including many in the so-called class of knowledge workers, experience radical insecurity to enable these orders of profit flow and privileged 'security' (Marazzi 2011). As implied by the fate of athletes, in the order of informationalism only a relatively few 'star' knowledge workers command large salaries; for the rest, knowledge work is insecure and deskilled, as their labour can be distributed widely, outsourced or automated through ICT (Frank & Cook 1995). They are as largely disposable as industrial workers. This mass insecurity, produced by attempts at providing security for accumulation, threatens both the relative social stability and the large-scale consumer spending that capitalism has previously depended upon for its success. Hiding the costs, dangers and wastes of production by transferring them to others, or onto future generations, can erode the very foundations of life. In these contexts, the impulse to re-enforce order can be profoundly counter-productive.

OUTLINE OF THE BOOK

This book is a provocation highlighting the embedded dynamics of informational 'disorderings', so as to help reassess the information order, and provide evidence of its intrinsic self-disrupting processes. We open up the analytic possibilities of positive disorder, suggesting that what (some) people call disorder is not always to be classified as negative or to be crushed. Disorder may herald an opening, either into a new social life, or into a new way of learning about that life: no one can learn without facing the disorder of being wrong. No politics can be democratic, or functional, if it steers away from the areas in which disorder announces the unexpected consequences, or failure, of that politics. Recognition of disorder is vital to dealing with, or adapting to, reality.

The book asks readers to consider the need for 'disorder theory' to generate a theoretical perspective that can reveal unnoticed social dynamics. We focus on Information and Communication Technology (ICT) as a source of an order/disorder complex, and as providing the key context for informationalism, largely because 'information society', 'post-industrial' and 'network society' theorists ground many of their claims for the advent of informationalist order in the emergence of information technologies. Rejecting technological determinism, we insist that technologies are embedded in disharmonious capitalist/managerial (and other) social relations, and soaked in acts of power, resistance, conflict and information disruption. In technologies and their applications, we find antagonisms, conflicts, disarray and a permanent incapacity to establish ordering fixity. These conflicts and failures of information then affect the writing and performance of the software that underlies the society.

First we sketch an outline of the problems with 'order theory', that is, theory that searches for and privileges ordering mechanisms, while presenting some of the heuristics and terms we will be using. Chapter 2 criticises information society theory from this perspective. Chapter 3 establishes the fundamental importance of disorder in computer programming and computer networks. Chapter 4 looks at the disorders and hierarchies of networks in general. Chapters 5 and 6 give an account of some patterns of disorder in information generally, and under capitalist informationalism in particular. These disorders normalise information disruption in social life and turn the information society into the 'disinformation society'.

The second part of the book explores key sites of disordering in informationalism. Chapter 7 is pivotal. There we address the ways that software and requirements engineers have sought to deal with the inherent difficulties of producing software and the way that the social, informational and managerial orders of information organisations disrupt that work. Software is a social system that is used to ensure ideal social orders, or engineer processes of change. As such it runs into problems with the complexities of organisations, the unpredictability of future actions, political relations between organisational players and routine structural failures of knowledge within the organisation. Chapter 8 examines everyday failures in software arising through failures of production and maintenance, or through the ways in which computer networks break previously functional social boundaries. Chapter 9 extends the analysis into the realm of finance where an arms race aiming at faster, deeper and broader financialisation has system-wide consequences.

Chapter 10 explores the realm of cultural consumption, and its commodification. We track resistance to the enclosure of cultural life for profit, through online 'peer-to-peer' sharing of digitised cultural artefacts, highlighting the conflict between profit and ease of distribution. Chapter 11 moves into the heartlands of intellectual engagement, the academy, where the capture of ideas for profit has advanced so far as to potentially undermine the intellectual process and produce an awkward resistance. Finally, in Chapter 12 we discuss how global social movements have engaged in a process of reappropriation, deploying informational technologies in struggles against corporate globalism and encountering the disordering limits of ICT-mediated social agency, as ICT acts back-on and constrains their own forms of organisation. The Conclusion draws these cases and themes together, returning to re-assess the opening provocations, and chart agendas for future investigations.

The key message of this book is that disorder is produced in the heartland of the capitalist 'information society': disorder is not simply a by-product or its dialectical 'other'. While the disorders of informationalism may enable forms of opposition, the source of disorder lies inside its own systemic processes.

In a book that celebrates and recognises the existence of disorder, it only briefly needs to be stated that the authors cannot agree on everything (especially given they are from different disciplines). Whenever we say 'we', we are implying a disordered unity; one that hopefully can cope with that disorder productively. Despite our differing perspectives, we embarked on this study of disinformation society to develop concepts that can be used in different contexts. Specifically, we attempt to develop a conceptual framework for understanding and explaining both informationalism and the ongoing crisis of disruption in software. We argue that being able to face disorder is vital if our society is to have any capacity to address the informational and social problems we are facing. For reasons of space we are largely ignoring the problems produced by the interaction of disinformation society with ecological reality; that is a topic for another book. Similarly, we only mention in passing the conflict between disinformation and science, self-disorderings of government, disorder in international relations or the problems generated by and affecting the military. This book is an exercise in speculation and provocation, designed to open up avenues for inquiry, not an attempt to be fully comprehensive. The next chapter (Chapter 1) explores ideas of disorder and social theory in more detail.

1 Disorder and Social Theory

WHAT IS 'DISORDER'?

We do not posit the existence of a completely ordered, exact and 'abstracted' *definition* of 'disorder', which then applies in all circumstances. Disorder can be socially, and often personally or positionally, subjective. One person or group's 'order' is another person or group's 'disorder'. These differences of opinion can drive politics and social action. Disorder is that which is *perceived* as disorder by some group, or is manifested in events that escape their expectations, models and ordering systems. As Gregory Bateson (1972: 3–8) argued, socially approved order has a limited number of ways that it can manifest, while disorder has an infinite number of ways to appear. Therefore people may often agree on the existence of states of disorder, while intensely disagreeing over what is the best order. The more complicated the system and its social ordering, and the more 'items', types of items, and interactions and relationships between them it involves, the more likely it is that the system will fall into a state that can be labelled disordered by some group, requiring recurring forms of remedial action to maintain the ideal order. As Joseph Tainter argues, the cost in work and resources of maintaining complex societies in their order is unrelenting. Eventually the costs are likely to exceed the returns. "Sociopolitical organisations constantly encounter problems that require increased investment merely to preserve the status quo" (Tainter 1990: 195), and this has to be balanced with the resources, effort and re-organisation needed to solve new problems as they appear. Disorder will always appear and always has a politics.

As well as examining the politics of disorder, we can also investigate to what extent an example of disorder arises from an external 'disruption', or a perceived external disruption, or the way in which internal disorder is projected onto some scapegoated figures in the 'external world'. Disorder that emerges internally from the ordering system, we term '*self-generated disorder*'. We can investigate where what is labelled as disorder occurs, whether it is localised or spreading, how it relates to patterns of ordering, whether it apparently benefits anyone and whether it is necessary for the collection of systems to work at all.

Recurrent patterns of disorder are part of the social order, and may produce stratified benefits and losses; creating order for some, at the expense of disorder for others, and thus feeding social antagonisms—even if those who benefit are not aware of the disorder produced elsewhere. For example, the order that business has tried to impose on information as 'property' can conflict with other social ordering principles that regard information as 'commons', as enabling 'innovation' or as shared 'culture', as is expressed by some peer-to-peer 'pirates' and by members of the academy, amongst others. What one person sees as the essential order of property, another sees as a disorder of culture or communication, or further as an obstruction to knowledge. Both sides are likely to argue that the perceived disorder *threatens* their particular and fundamental values of property, profit or free communication.

However, disorder can also be functional and adaptive. To use an analogy, evolution, which is the central process of life itself, operates through massive excess, failure and inefficiency; through what might be called disorder. It depends on the trillions of creatures who don't survive to reproduce, genes that are not replicated identically and environments that constantly change and exert new pressures, often through the actions of unexpectedly successful organisms. This disorder produces the apparent order of the living world. This suggests, as do our cases, that neither 'order' nor 'disorder' exist as separate processes, with one dominant and the other secondary. They do not form a simple opposition: the two are entangled together in a mutually implicated order/disorder complex, which then drives social, political and creative action. In complex systems, modes of ordering produce disorder. Not all modes of order may be equally productive of what some of those using them will call disorder, but the tendency remains. Social groups respond to disorder as a problem by ignoring it, tidying it, preparing to repair it, persecuting it, treating it as waste, removing it and so on. In informationalism, social groups almost always see recognised disorder as a result of external or intruding factors. Again, naming something as disordered is often a political act, geared to a project of reordering. Consequently, we can explore to what extent ordering impulses are embedded in social conflict, and produce what others consider disorder.

Disorder is primarily of social interest when it is repeated. For example, the introduction of a new software system could be expected to produce temporary disorder as people learn new procedures. However the marked and lengthy (as opposed to temporary) recurrence of disorder, with the new procedures constantly being found inadequate to the work required, and the repeated failure to deal with these problems, suggests a disorder that is a permanent part of the system. Indeed we could suggest that this potential disorder is wilfully ignored in major information technology upgrades, even though the possibility is high that they will be burdened with time over-runs, escalating budgets, technical glitches and disruption to vital work. This is part of the essential workings of 'information society' and should not be ignored.

ORDER/DISORDER AND THE SOCIAL SCIENCES

While it is not correct to imply that all social theorists have ignored disorder, and we refer to many who have influenced our argument, historically most social theory has positioned disorder as a secondary residue or as a result of the breakdown of order. The threat of social disorder has often been used to justify order, of almost any type. For political theorists Jean Bodin (1530–1596) and Thomas Hobbes (1588–1679), the desire for firm order was fundamental, and order was more important than 'justice' or 'rights' (King 1974). Karl Marx (1818–1883) argued class conflict generates crisis and social change, and positioned the end of exploitation, in communism, as ending the disorders of capitalism. Expectations of order and difficulties in defining 'really existing' communism seemed to make it difficult for some Marxists to recognise post-revolutionary dictatorship and struggle. Emile Durkheim (1858–1917) thought anomie was to blame for suicide, and sought to prevent disorder in general, although he was happy to consider some forms of disorder (such as crime) as normal if the rituals around it restated the importance of order (Durkheim 1982: 85 ff; Marks 1974). Max Weber (1864–1920) argued that we should construct unambiguous 'ideal types' to do our analysis (Whimster 2004: 387ff.), thus deleting disorder, and those things/events that escaped this ideal, by making them secondary. However, those excluded disorderly events may be vital to the social dynamics being analysed. Even Anarchists talk about spontaneous order, and rarely investigate disorder itself: Proudhon (1809–1865) supposedly declared that 'anarchy is order' (P. Marshall 1992: x; although possibly the remark should be given to Bellegarrigue 1850/2002). Social Darwinists praised the orders imposed by the elite because they arose from 'victories' in the struggle for existence, and thus expressed real, natural and superior order. Conflict theorists tend to see conflict as a failure of ordering, or as a means of maintaining, or applying, order, say, the order of stratification (in Collins 1975), or structure and personality (as in Ross 1993), not as a product of ordering, or as attempts to extend particular orders.

Arrighi et al.'s *Chaos and Governance in the Modern World System* (1999) demonstrates several failings of not taking disorder seriously, despite the implications of its title. While the book recognises that: "the increase in the volume and dynamic density of the system outgrows the organizational capabilities of the particular hegemonic complex that had created the conditions of the systemic expansion" (1999: 34), new complexes fortunately restore order. While mentioning other players, the book ultimately takes the monolithic and integrated State as the firm basis of power. Its consideration of chaos is limited to a review of the contradictions of Western colonial policy in Asia, and suggestions that financial and military power are no longer congruent with State-based territory. A new Asian hegemony will offer a more sustainable path in the future. The authors view chaos as a product of hegemonic crisis or breakdown, rather than as the unintended results of particular orderings by States or financial organisations.

More usefully, Beck claims that what he calls 'first modernity' is disordered by virtue of its own success in ordering, not because of its failures (2009: 8; Beck & Lau 2005: 526). Beck suggests that with the decline of first modernity, our problem-solving techniques either become hesitant or nostalgic for this lost success (Beck & Lau 2005: 531). Ordering institutions of the 'first modernity' depended on firm boundaries and modes of linear control, while the current world system faces interlinked challenges with multiple feedbacks and consequences, and with events appearing out of control. As a result, "Science is itself developing into a source of uncertainty, lack of knowledge and categorical ambiguity" (ibid: 529). This is vital, and we shall discuss disruption and vagueness of boundaries regularly. Beck also points to knowledge creating irreducible non-knowledge, and hence to a politics of non-knowing: a struggle over "who acquires the public power of definition over what is not known" (Beck & Wehling 2012: 34). In his account Beck distinguishes between risk and uncertainty arguing that risk is calculable and uncertainty is not (2009: 18–19). While recognising contemporary world society has to deal with the uncertain and disordering effects of human action (which it tries to convert into calculable risk), his concept of 'risk society' encourages analysts to turn away from uncertainty, by implying quantifiable risk is more significant. Our approach explicitly recognises that while risk is important, disorder and unpredictability are always present and socially vital.

UNPREDICTABILITY AND COMPLEXITY

Disorder can appear to arise when people think that social knowledge should be accurately predictive. In complex systems accurate prediction of social process and results of actions is largely impossible, especially over a long enough period of time (Lorenz 1993: 10–12, 102ff.). This unpredictability is magnified because all social action exists within complex interactive systems that involve and interact with other complex interactive systems, including the world's ecologies. The greater the number of linkages, feedback paths, participants and types of participants (assuming we could count them), and the more that participants can modify themselves in response to events, the greater the uncertainty. As social theorists, we do not have to be concerned as to whether social systems are 'ontologically unpredictable' in their inherent causation and nature, or whether they are 'epistemologically unpredictable' in that theoretically they are predictable, but we can never have enough information to model what will happen: the effect is the same (Eigenauer 1993; Glennan 1997). In this book, we incline to the more conservative position of epistemological unpredictability. That humans can reflect upon the actions (and possible actions) of others and try and second-guess them, adds to unpredictability (Soros 2010). We should also note that some non-self-reflexive physically interactive systems, such as the weather, or planetary systems, are also non-predictable over enough time (Eigenauer 1993: 458; Peterson 1993). Nobel Laureate in Chemistry, Ilya Prigogine, writes that, given this view, "the future is no longer determined by the present" (1997: 6). Hence, "[c]hance, or probability, is no longer a convenient way of accepting ignorance but rather part of a new, extended rationality" (ibid: 55).

The ongoing unpredictability of human and non-human contexts means that people's efforts at producing order in the future are constantly disrupted, and that a significant part of everyday social life involves dealing with, or recovering from, the resulting disorders. Attempts to restore order may generate further disorder, further disputes, further attempts to manipulate the orders and further solutions or failed solutions. For example, in derivatives markets, attempts at insuring against the future become overwhelmed by the speculative betting against the future that is enabled by those markets. This changes the ways markets work and their underlying values. Attempts to make order and security (and take advantage of it) generates further disorder and indeed, system-wide crisis. Society is always in a process of flux with relations between changing agents, no matter how stable it or its 'units' may appear. If uncertainty in complex systems is fundamental, then the calculability of risk is also uncertain. People cannot accurately predict the future distribution of events and they cannot estimate the risk, extent or cost of catastrophes that have not previously occurred. Recognising complexity does not mean that social theorists cannot theorise about trends, regularities, patterns of interaction or the general dynamics of the social world, any more than recognised complexity stops scientists theorising about the weather, ecologies or likely results of actions. However, ignoring unpredictability can be counter-productive in any attempts to deal with the future.

For example, the mainstream discipline of market economics, in general, failed spectacularly to predict or prevent the 2008 financial crash. Market economics had apparently been successful from some points of view. Important professionals in the field helped create the problems by believing that most major economic problems had been solved, that markets were predictable, well-informed and self-correcting. After the crisis, most economists apparently continued as usual, blaming the problems on individual greed, or supposed extraneous factors, such as State regulation, rather than on the market. Assumptions about correct order generated perceptual constraints. This reflects the seductiveness of shared ordering models, and the ways they screen out unwanted information and 'exceptions' that challenge the rule. Paul Krugman (2 September 2009) suggested that economists "mistook beauty, clad in impressive-looking mathematics, for truth"; that is, they liked ordered models. While defending economists from the details of Krugman's attack, and defending neoclassical market economics in general, Colander writes

> Professional economists have been unwilling to admit that the economy is far too complex to be captured by any unified model. In private

discussions among ourselves we recognize this complexity, but we don't add the appropriate warning labels to our models when they are discussed in public. There, we pretend we understand more than we do.

(2011: 20)

Difficulties were not broadcast. Maintaining the appearance of ordered knowledge, and the status that goes with it, was more important than accuracy of information. As we shall see, this appears to be a fundamental dynamic in information society.

Bezemer (2009) points out that some people did indeed predict the crisis (see 35ff. for names). However even if this was the case, those in authority either did not hear them, or claimed afterwards that nobody saw it coming. That may be because those in power wish to defend their faith in market-based equilibrium or efficiency models, but also because institutions can be more geared to assigning blame, to justify what we call their 'solution set' and their continued existence, than in finding counter-information. Power can shield a group from knowledge (Tierney 1999). If counter-information existed, then that information was not distributed. Even after the collapse, the response was not to embrace different models but to reaffirm the virtues of markets, bail out the 'unfortunate' financiers and impose restraint and austerity on those with less status or power. This serves to demonstrate that corporate free markets are never 'free' to other solutions, or open to the circulation of information, and that some ideological modes of understanding are not falsified by reality (Mirowski 2013).

BOX 2   ECONOMISTS AND THE QUEEN OF ENGLAND

In November 2008 the Queen of England, while on a visit to the London School of Economics, asked why economists had failed to predict the crash. Six months later she received an open letter from the British Academy signed by 33 people (bankers, economists, professors, MPs etc.) that sought to answer the question. The letter emphasised the mythology of risk 'securitisation'. It states that 'most' people believed:

> that the financial wizards had found new and clever ways of managing risks. Indeed, some claimed to have so dispersed them through an array of novel financial instruments that they had virtually removed them.

(Besley et al. 2009: 2)

The letter points out that bankers and governments propelled this wishful thinking. It seems that those who should have identified the problems were making significant money out of the delusion, or identified with those making the money, and hence were reluctant to challenge that delusion. People were even praised for removing rules that might have helped stabilize the process. Those in positions of power were dismissing, or not receiving, any information contrary to that they wanted to hear, illustrating the paradoxical role information plays in information society. Market order was expected, rather than seen as temporary, or liable to self-disruption. Ignorance was collectively bolstered and rewarded.

The Academy's attempt at a response to these systemic risks, interconnections and imbalances, is telling. Their letter stressed the gulf between financial players and the financial system. Everyone seemed to be doing their own job competently, and by the approved measures of success, they were performing well:

> The failure was to see how collectively this added up to a series of interconnected imbalances . . . This, combined with the psychology of herding and the mantra of financial and policy gurus, lead [sic.] to a dangerous recipe. Individual risks may rightly have been viewed as small, but the risk to the system as a whole was vast.
>
> (Besley et al. 2009: 3)

Rather than addressing 'the system as a whole', the failure of information in markets, inherent unpredictability or the effects of trying to 'free' markets, the Academy resolved, reassuringly, that it would develop its forecasting, making "a new, shared horizon-scanning capability so that you never need to ask your question again" (ibid: 3). What is remarkable here is the gap between an apparent apprehension of the problem's systemic nature and the failure to imagine how the problem could be addressed. The metaphor of 'horizon-screening' is unimaginative, as well as impossible to guarantee in complex systems. If an investor could see the future then they would always profit from investment, and no doubt try and hide this knowledge from others. However almost by definition, humans cannot see the future.

The terms used in the letter imply also that 'everyone' was to blame, and suffering little individual risk, which may have been true for financiers, but was not true for those who lost their homes and their life savings by following advice from financial experts (from which advice the experts profited). So the economists reaffirm a class, or 'information group' (see later), focus on affirming 'acceptable order' and rendering disorder negligible; thus avoiding any need for a wider rethink and diffusing responsibility through distribution. The systemic tendencies remain embedded, and, if anything, as outlined in Chapter 9, are intensifying.

This rigidity is not confined to economists. Tetlock (2005) researched the predictions of 284 experts in various social fields, finding that they generally could not predict the future more accurately than non-experts. Predictions from some experts were even less reliable than random choice. Ironically, the better known and more quoted the experts, the less reliable were their predictions, another example of how information 'works' and is distributed in informationalism. Furthermore, experts tended not to change their minds when their predictions failed, apparently valuing their conceptual order more than they valued adjusting to reality. Interestingly Tetlock found that those who held one position strongly, and saw the world totally in that position's terms, tended to do worse than those with a more encompassing approach who tolerated ambiguity and paradox. The more experts reduced the world to packaged order, the less likely they were to predict accurately. Too much ordering, even in theory and approach, is deleterious. Therefore, we can recognise the benefits of tolerating ambiguity and not seeking full explanatory order. In the social field we can recognise a strong relationship between power, expertise and ignorance in establishing and perpetuating crises.

ANALYSING DISORDER

Recognising that contingency, paradox, disorder and flux are sociologically important does not prevent explanation. Unpredictability does not imply that events are inexplicable, nor that relatively few and simple principles cannot generate complex and unpredictable events. Shifting patterns, flows, orders and patterns of disorder do emerge. We can posit principles, and can draw attention to the way order and disorder are made, some of which will depend on the social intention of groups and some not. We can look at the way modes of ordering do produce disorder, and then look at the effects of those disorders. We can observe the various groups ('classes', 'information groups', etc.) that do form, and ask how much uniformity they can construct, while wondering how they coordinate themselves, what effects coordination has and how they fracture themselves.

Following on from this basic position something needs to be said about our use of terms. Our use of the term 'system', for example, does not imply harmony or integration, or that something is 'systematic'. It just recognises that a complex group of processes interact with each other, often in unpredictable ways. Systems tend towards flux; we can only see moments of that flux. The term 'mesh' is used to deal with this integration or lack of integration between systems or parts of systems. Something is 'well meshed' if the two systems interact smoothly, and 'badly meshed', if the systems interact disruptively. There can be degrees of mesh and interference between these systems. The term 'conform with' is used when one system is supposed to be dominant over another. Software has to conform to its hardware environment, but whether the social system has to conform to the software or vice-versa, is a subject of contestation. Different social systems of technology, knowledge, organisations of production, organisations of distribution, organisations of profit, organisations of power, structures of communication (which may not be nameable in advance), may mesh either well, badly or too well. They can disrupt each other or produce forms of overdevelopment, destroying any previous balance. Parts of a system that meshed at one time can later on disconnect and gain their own life, changing the degree of meshing and 'harmony'. The point here is that institutions, groups and technologies do not always interact smoothly, even if they have done so at other times. We are not just emphasising failure: overly well-meshed systems can be disruptive, as their one-sided dynamics become magnified.

Issues of meshing mean that technology is not simply an expression of society or "society made durable" (Latour 1991), it can be both an expression of society and a disruptor of that society; it can serve one part of a society well, and damage another part. As already stated, meshing can be, and often is, highly conflictual and disruptive. With a disruptive mesh 'locked in', there may be permanent production of disorder, with society becoming disorder-prone. Because of the possibilities of innovation and accident, this potential for lack of mesh, disruptive mesh or excessively 'good' mesh, is ongoing. Technological innovation or implementation is often a source of unexpected meshing effects, and always opens the possibilities of unintended systemic effects. Jeremy Rifkin's (1995) argument illustrates this point. He suggests that in previous economic and technical 'revolutions' new economic opportunities offset the loss of jobs, and this may lead people to implement change in a certain way. However the changes of the informational revolution may mesh with the economic system differently. Automation of the workplace dispossesses workers; the knowledge sector can't absorb everyone (1995: xvii), new production is highly automated only requiring a few workers (ibid: 288), and it dispossesses knowledge workers as well. He claims the "road to a near-workerless economy is within sight" (ibid: 292). This process affects both the industrial sector and the 'knowledge work' sector. If correct, this could obviously produce social and economic disorderings, as widespread unemployment lowers the demand for products and services, putting further people out of employment, thus further flattening demand. Under capitalism, solutions that free people from wage labour cannot be countenanced. We can also argue that the 'new' technologies of computing and communication mesh awkwardly with information distribution when that information becomes commoditised, as the tools that make and distribute the information become the tools by which it is 'pirated'. Nothing suggests that these general tensions can be resolved in a harmonious order, revolution or not.

The idea of 'slack' (Demarco 2001) derives from meshing. When an organisation is extremely well meshed and efficient, it has no unnecessary or redundant processes, and no 'slack'. This lack of slack, lack of inefficiency or redundancy, not only tends to leave workers exhausted, but lowers the organisation's capacity to absorb shock, loss or sudden change in its environment. Its efficiency makes it vulnerable. Slack is the 'disorderly' excess that helps resilience: "the degree of freedom that enables reinvention and true effectiveness" (ibid: 2). Ordering by efficiency drives and cost-cutting exercises almost always reduces slack.

We use the term 'model' to refer to an explicit understanding of how reality fits together and works. Models may be formal and mathematical and be expressed in software, but not necessarily. By their nature, models simplify complex reality and hence diverge from it, and, being applied, distort it, having unintended but often reflexive effects, as actors try to achieve conformity with the model, or deal with the distorting effects of the model. People in a complex system, especially at different places, will model that system differently, not necessarily more accurately. Models will be subject to conflict. When models are applied to a complex human situation they often change the behaviour of people in the system and the results of behaviours in that system, so that even if they were initially accurate they become less accurate as they are applied. Due to broad societal reflexivity, the more people apply the models, the less likely it is that the models will be accurate. Thus if a group uses a financial model that enables them to exploit the financial system, then the results of behaviour in that financial system will change (previously successful action will be less successful and so on, new loopholes will open, etc.), and other people will begin changing their behaviour, and the system will work differently. If everyone starts applying the model, then the system will definitely change. New models will be introduced to try and second-guess this behaviour and the system will change again. Accepted social models can change the reality they model. Used to introduce order, they constantly disorder themselves.

'Complexity' occurs when the system is too difficult to be understood as a whole by any one person or group. Each event in a complex system might be unique, and non-replicable, and thus be rendered unimportant, or vitally important, no matter what its effects. Complete modelling of complexity is difficult, and modelling the system requires simplification and deletion of information. As previously stated, we understand complexity primarily in epistemological terms, although complex systems, like society, seem to form complicated interactive networks in constant flux, with each temporary state feeding into the next, with people's understandings of society's workings feeding into those workings, and into the way people approach problems. As argued earlier, acting in complex situations is likely to produce unintended effects.

The term 'problem cycle', suggests that societies develop, congeal and institutionalise '*solution sets*' for particular recurrent problems (the 'problem field'), whether ecological, cosmological, military, nutritional, reproductive, communicational and so on. As a result, we can have information groups forming around particular institutionalised, or organisational, solution sets that can include technological, organisational, economic or other processes. The groups that congeal around solutions relate to each other in contested patterns of power and privilege, which may destabilise the solutions. Economist Thorstein Veblen (1857–1929), for example, suggested in the early 1900s that there was an ongoing conflict between business people and engineers, partly because they were wedded to different kinds of solutions, and occupied different places with respect to technology. While business remained emotionally tied to old solutions, engineers favoured new solutions that were efficient or 'interesting' from their point of view (Coser 1977: 266–8). Similar conflicts can occur today around software. Problems and their solutions may affect different parts of the population differently, which leads to different perceptions of the problems and their possible solutions or even to the perception of different problems. These groupings around solution sets, institutions and technology both make and express social differentiation and the groups' differing 'interests'. This is then is translated into patterns of alliance, conflict and power struggle. Relations between groupings, and between groupings and their solution sets, may create feedback loops that generate further conflicts. Important problems may be created by other solutions. If the problems change, it may be hard to change the solution sets, or the relations between the groups associated with them, causing further disorder with problems being made to conform to the solutions on offer.

The tendency for a dominant mode of order, its models and problem-solving techniques to become more intense and rigorously applied in areas of its dominance, we call 'intensification'. While marking success, this can also mark an area of resistance. Intensification usually also implies 'extension', in which the mode of order and its models are extended to modes of life that were previously largely free of its influence. In extension the modes of ordering or problem-solving are extended from places where they may have worked well (for some), into areas where they are *at best* dysfunctional, as when corporate styles of management are extended into other domains with different problems.

DISORDER, SUCCESS AND WASTE

Intensification and extension demonstrates that disorder is not only produced by failure, but by success. For example, the success of computer production and distribution leads to new levels of toxicity in waste and refuse, and new highs in energy use. Production of technical waste not only affects the countries most informationalised but is also exported, displacing its main impacts elsewhere, making things appear to be 'tidy' from within (Grossman 2006; Slade 2006). As Maxwell and Miller (2012) argue, one good reason for ignoring the claims of disembodiment common in cyber-theory is the amount of physical and chemical waste produced in the manufacture and use of ICT; a waste that is further compounded by the relatively quick obsolescence of the technology to generate continuous profit. However, Maxwell and Miller appear to assume that this problem can fairly easily be ordered away, from inside the system, by better accounting procedures.

BOX 3   'IMMATERIAL' COMPUTING

The continual introduction of new products leads to vast quantities of working information machines, or 'e-waste', being thrown out. In 2013, the Australian Bureau of Statistics suggests that in Australia alone "17 million televisions and 37 million computers have been sent to landfill up to 2008" and less than 10% of the computers dumped in 2007–8 were recycled (ABS 2013). The Environmental Protection Agency in the U.S. estimated that in 2011 the U.S. produced 3.41 million tons of e-waste, disposing of 142,000 computers and over 416,000 mobile devices each day (EPA 2013: 67–72). The *Economist* (24 April 2011) predicts that by 2020, Europeans will be producing 12 million tonnes of e-waste annually, and to "make matters worse, authorities do not know where half of it ends up. At current capacity only one-third of waste electrical and electronic equipment . . .is safely discarded". Some is smuggled overseas. Businesses can complain about the cost of taking responsibility for the clean up, and even when they do claim responsibility are often vague in the information they provide to allow public evaluation of their 'green' claims (Greenpeace 2012).

Computers and e-waste usually contain toxic heavy metals such as lead, cadmium, mercury, arsenic, beryllium or brominated flame-retardants. These poisons tend to leach out from the dumps into the environment. Much of the waste from the U.S. is exported and dumped elsewhere, although other industrialised countries are supposed to recognise the Basel Convention on the Control of Transboundary Movements of Hazardous Wastes and their Disposal. Often the waste is processed in largely impoverished places like Agbogbloshie in Ghana, Delhi in India, or Guiyu in China, where:

> children pile e-waste into giant mountains and burn it so they can extract the metals—copper wires, gold and silver threads—inside, which they sell to recycling merchants for only a few dollars. In India, young boys smash computer batteries with mallets to recover cadmium, toxic flecks of which cover their hands and feet as they work. Women spend their days bent over baths of hot lead, "cooking" circuit boards so they can remove slivers of gold inside . . . [I]n the United States . . . the Federal Bureau of Prisons has kept inmates busy processing e-waste.
>
> (Acaroglu 4 May 2013)

One writer remarks that they recently visited the Agbogbloshie recyclers' markets in Central Accra, where they saw people dismantling and melting electronic and mechanical goods.

> The toxic chemicals released are spread throughout the area when it rains and of course spread to the homes each evening . . . the path of the toxic smoke . . . floats right into the food market. So whatever doesn't get into your lungs can now settle onto the food supply.
>
> (Caravanos 2010. See also Hugo 2010).

Claims also arise that criminal gangs buy access to disposed-of hard disks "which they mine for bank details, credit card numbers and account passwords" (O'Brien 2 October 2011), indicating other fears of disorder arising from removal of disorder. This waste and pollution and its concealment is not incidental to information society, but is part of the way it operates.

Waste and disorder are produced by all systems; perhaps systems can be defined by their waste and the way they process it. The question is whether such waste is a threat to existence, or the basis for transformation. Not all waste is inherently destructive, for as Darwin (1882) pointed out, much life on the earth's surface depends upon the waste products of earthworms. In informational capitalism waste tends to be excessive, poisonous and destructive; it is put to one side rather than re-integrated into the system, with the producers of waste apparently sheltered from the consequences and costs. The waste is not fertile.

Successful modes of ordering can also 'freeze' the society, or parts of society, into particular solution sets, even when its problem field has changed, thus preventing adaptation to new problems. Reflecting this, it is often proposed that markets have to be the solution to problems in information society, or that we have to solve all problems of climate change through spontaneous technological innovation. In this situation, the more that modes of ordering and solution sets for problem solving have been previously successful, the more they are likely to become institutionalised, intensified, extended, made resistant to change and embedded in what is perceived as class interests, and the less likely they will adapt to new problems or the problems generated by their own success.

We can expect that the more intense the ordering system, the more it will classify unwanted things or events as disordered or even criminal, and attempt to alter them, or ban them from visibility. The greater the flexibility of the ordering systems, the less will be classified as disorder, and the more adaptive the system. However, as well as an ordering system becoming too rigid for its own good, it could also become too flexible to carry out its aims.

DISORDER AND POWER

Disordering can be essential to attempts to entrench an established order, as when military regimes produce chaos so that people will turn to them for safety (Ferrara 2003), or when laws seem to be changed on a whim to stop Occupy demonstrators (Graeber 2013: xi-xii). Disordering can, more obviously, undermine and even destroy the sense of beneficial order. Disorder and disordering can further provide 'spaces' for the emergence of new creativity and challenges to existing modes of ordering, as when people operate in ambiguous zones, or zones not entirely subject to a particular authority; producing what Michael Mann (1986: 15, 363ff., 537) calls "interstitial emergence" or "interstitial surprise".

Power is central to any order/disorder complex. While there are many types of power, we see power as a set of relations, an ongoing struggle, not a singular possession (Elias 1978). It is best seen as a "multiplicity of force relations" (Foucault 1979: 92). Power usually marks an attempt to impose, intensify or extend a model of order, and depends on an easily triggered network of responses. Power always risks contestation, disruption, failure or unintended consequences, every time it is used. The meaning or legitimacy of an act of attempted power, like other events, depends upon the context and framings brought to it (see the following). Power also disrupts information flows, through what we shall term the 'power/ignorance nexus' (Graeber 2004a: 72–3), which leads powerful people to become more disruptive and ignorant the more intense or self-protective their power becomes. The general pattern of power in informationalism we call 'distributed governance', because in complex networks governance is, or appears, to be dispersed and no longer has relatively clear outlines, boundaries or unchallenged central points. However, while rigorously defined and clearly located hierarchies may become rare, hierarchies still exist powerfully. Responsibility for events is hard to locate, and people tend to shift that responsibility away from themselves if possible and, given the distribution of power, this often is possible. Distributed governance points to the realisation that unexpected or uncontrolled reactions and consequences are inherent in a networked system of power. Efforts at influencing other people and their actions often do not have the results intended and resistances may be found that were unexpected. This may help explain the feelings of powerlessness felt by all social groupings and classes (see Chapter 4).

A successful solution set, resulting from the problem cycle, can always result in a particular group becoming relatively more powerful than the rest and more insulated from the problems the group generates. Once this happens, the dominant group may try to remove or prevent solutions to the problems that it, or its favoured solution set, generates. This is both a positional and institutional folly, expressing the power/ignorance nexus, and breaking the possibility of corrective feedback. A group may then become 'revolutionary' to the extent that it proposes new solutions, can carry them out, build the appropriate technology, persuade others of their virtue, form alliances to oppose vested interests or take advantage of the disorders generated by the elite group. The success of this revolution will be affected by the kinds of problems those new solutions generate. In responding to the disorder they have generated, victorious revolutionaries may replicate the stabilising structures of the old regime, as with Bonapartism or Stalinism.

In informationalism, transformatory action may take a viral, non-programmatic 'swarming' form, carried through interactive information networks. Given the distributed means of engagement, mobilisation may be rapid but highly episodic and fragile. Attempts at sustaining leverage may be difficult; by the same token, attempts at maintaining civil order may be rendered highly contingent. We may find ourselves in a field of possibilities, but with little to show for the potential revolutionary fervour, as appears to have occurred with the Occupy movement. However, as revealed by peer-to-peer communication, discussed in Chapter 10, practices disrupting the prevailing information order may not be driven by a revolutionary purpose, but can reflect broader social responses, which when aggregated (or swarmed) can prove highly disruptive (albeit largely unintentionally).

CATEGORY ORDER/DISORDER AND 'CLASS'

The tools we use in social science tend to assume that order and ordering is both more important and more natural than disordering. Taking disorder seriously requires us to rethink these tools, particularly our categories and the way they can distort attention, by leading us to assume that all members of a category are the same in some simple and stable way. Category members can be included in a category in many different ways, having what Wittgenstein famously called 'a family resemblance', sometimes resembling each other in the shape of their nose, in other cases by the structure of their jaw, or even by their behaviour (1958: §65–71). The shifting resemblances arise because things are classified together socially and practically, rather than being classified together because they absolutely resemble each other. Human category membership also shifts in social usage as a result of exploration, alliance, conflict, argument and context (Taylor 1989; Lakoff 1987; Marshall 2006b, 2007). Social categories are not normally fixed but politically dynamic.

Through using fixed categories, social theory often understands society as being composed of relatively stable units that interact with each other, rather than imagining the 'units' as being in flux themselves. While removing the appearance of internal 'disorder' from the categories, this order may simplify excessively, directing attention away from flux, and processes and events that do not fit the abstractions. A named 'society', for example, is a loose collection of 'processes', it is not a 'thing' or an enduring object. It is in flux, and, in the contemporary world, its boundaries and processes are rarely firm and distinct, but blend into other societies. It may be composed of what could equally be called 'societies'. Calling something 'a society' is always an abstraction or simplification, however necessary we may find it (cf. Strathern 1988: 11ff.; Barth 1992). Our expectations of ordered categories can lead us to ask meaningless questions that suppose the categories deployed have 'eternal' essences, 'such as what are the themes of American history?', when 'American history' has been many stories, many views and many narrowly won or lost conflicts. Indeed the disunities, and marginalised people, may have driven American history and culture as much as, if not more than, the unities and supposed mainstreams (Russell 2010; Graeber 2013: 61ff., 81–2). Looking for unity can suppress awareness of cultural dynamics.

In other words, in normal usage, we define category disorders as irrelevant, or as taboo or dangerous (Douglas 1969). Categories need to be applied for us to understand processes, but can be used to do more or less violence to the data. Ordering tools, like categories, also disorder, but they are both necessary and unavoidable. Disorder theory directs our attention to the limitations, exclusions and disruptions produced by these categorical ordering processes, so we are moved to examine what we might normally consider unimportant empirical complexities, namely trivialities, trash, exceptions, shifts, inconsistencies and statistical oddities. Ever-present disorder should not be assumed to be unimportant.

The concept of 'class' is an important example of these problems of order in analysis. Informational capitalism is undoubtedly a 'class-based society', but the processes and people that 'class' attempts to refer to may be imprecise, messy and in flux. Different and shifting alliances, changes of patterns of inclusion and exclusion, are relevant both to the functioning of class and to transforming class. We do not have to think that every member of a class or group is a member in the same way, or has the same interests, or perceives everyone in that group to be a member in quite the same way, or even perceives each other as a member. The different and sometimes incompatible ways that a person can be included in a class, or achieve (perhaps temporary) membership in another class, or be expelled from a class, are pertinent to analysis, as are the frictions and conflicts (implicit or explicit) within classes.

If we expect every member of a category to be similar in the same way then we suppress the differences between members in favour of their similarities, when it may be the differences and frictions that drive group dynamics and people's experience of their lives. Yet again, if we argue that because there are confusions in the term, 'class' does not exist in any sense, we are also using expectations about the importance of order in categories to dismiss a useful analytic device.

'Class' should here be understood not as a form of stratification, in which divisions between classes are clearly defined and class categories are relatively stable. Rather, it should be understood as a changing social relation between categories. Class position, membership, consciousness and agency are always relational to others, and fluid; a class rarely constitutes a fixed, stratified, block or category. Class is more like a 'social movement' that builds unities, affiliations and differences, inclusions and exclusions, wins or loses struggles with other groups, and tries to occupy particular places in the sociotechnological solution set or in the battles over accumulation and property. Class is active and 'self-making', as much as it is made by others or by circumstances. To make itself, or to give members a degree of unity, it also has to become an 'information group', or set of compatible information groups; that is, its members need to share some information, understandings, modes of interpretation and sources, in order to act as a group.

If, as we are arguing, there are changes in the ways that accumulating, producing and problem solving generally have been enabled or restricted, then we would expect to find a period of struggle, with a process of class disordering, reordering, reshaping, reassertion and further disordering. If we acknowledge these disruptions to established class structures, then we would expect to see movements of people between and across classes, and we would expect the experience of these changes to be important in the way that people think of, use and, with others, make their class position in the world. Class may be riven by, and unified by, power differences and by social complexity generally. Disorder and variability in class affiliation by no means suggest an end to class categorisation, but on the contrary, they affirm affiliation and potential loss of position as part of the process of class contestation, exclusion and construction.

Given the ongoing processes of social action and social flux, similar analytic problems arise with other important social categories such as 'information', 'money', 'public/private' and 'property', and these problems are again central to the functions, roles, understanding and effects of such categories in society. Some of these terms are dealt with in other chapters.

DISORDERS OF INFORMATION

As the volume of information increases, making the information overwhelming to navigate, it produces what we call 'data smog', where socially useful information becomes hard to find (Shenk 1997). In order to filter this smog, people tend to belong to 'information groups' or loose, often relatively uncoordinated, collections of people who are marked by allegiance to particular types and sources of information, to particular modes of problem perception and solution, and to particular ways of disregarding information, simplifying information and making sense of the world. Belonging to an information group saves time. Such groups form loosely imagined communities not necessarily tied to a nation, as in Ben Anderson's original (1991) formulation, but are often linked in opposition to other such groups. The information group can become an identity category (particularly a negative category: "I'm not one of them", pointing to another group) although people can belong to more than one information group, with varying degrees of commitment or awareness of their occasionally contradictory nature. Information groups generate fractures of knowledge and grouping, allowing us to trace the intertwining of power and ignorance, where a group becomes able to impose a solution set that may be destructive of themselves and others, or find themselves displaced and superseded by their own solutions. As suggested above, gaining the characteristics of an information group is one way that classes gain agency and self-identity. A temporary, more rapidly fluxing information group we call a 'swarm', adapting the term from the peer-to-peer file-sharing lexicon. Swarms tend to focus on a particular temporary information source or activity. They have low levels of social interaction, stability or consistent membership. They are vulnerable to the disruption of their focal source, but can easily appear around another similar source.

'Sources' are what we call formalised emitters of information. A source provides a mode of framing the information, telling the consumer or information group whether the information is likely to be agreeable and conform to expectations. Information from a recognised and 'trusted' source will spread more quickly through a network of similar information groups, and have greater apparent value than more accurate information from an unrecognised source. In many cases, sources intensify their group members' normal explanations and hence ignorance of, or hostility to, other ways of perceiving the world. Conflict with other groups is likely to make for easy rejection of the information they could provide.

In these circumstances, projected fantasy can become dominant, producing degrees of what we call 'information paranoia'. This is a way of making sense of (and reducing) information, by assuming that others are out to deceive you. It can lead to an active doubting of all sources of information, especially non-valued sources. This helps protect the integrity of information groups and their identity, and the identity of its members, amidst the data smog and allegations of falsified information. It also intensifies conflict.

'Disinformation' is usually defined as the intentional dissemination of false information, while 'misinformation' involves its unintentional dissemination. However, because information has many social functions, a source's intentions are hard to access directly, and the 'accuracy' of information can be socially contested or difficult to determine (especially in the data smog), we use the term 'disinformation' to express the way information becomes distorted, disrupted or disordered by the processes of transmission and interpretation in informationalism. As information becomes the key ordering device and means to power, it can never be taken at 'face value', as by definition there is always a subtext. With this generalised scepticism, sources become increasingly mistrusted, disinformation becomes expected and information paranoia becomes even more widespread.

'Structural secrecy' contributes to a climate of disinformation as information flows accentuate boundaries between groups (especially information groups), which then leads to misinterpretation, and lack of both shared knowledge and accurate knowledge about the other. Important factors increasing structural secrecy include: rivalry, hierarchy, prospects of punishment or reward and different cultural fields or information groups. In hierarchy, the 'power/ignorance nexus' is activated when the threat of punishment or the lure of reward persuades people to tailor information in ways that are pleasing to those who control that threat or reward. In the other direction, people dominant in the hierarchy tend not to give those below them all the information available in order to keep inferiors vulnerable and to hide the results of their own mistakes or vulnerabilities. Everyone in the hierarchy then acts on fantasy and supposition. Hierarchy can become a breeding ground for disinformation and information paranoia.

We use the term 'culture' for the socially developed life of meaning, art and understanding. Culture is not uniform; differences and unstable replications are among its dynamics. Culture involves habits, actions and artefacts (which can include technology), so it is not an ideal or immaterial process. Cultures are tied to information production and interpretation and hence to information groups. Culture enables communication, and produces barriers to communication. Cultural producers tend to resist 'enclosure' *by others* (although they may try to enclose their own works). Enclosure occurs when boundaries are put around something to mark it out, prevent access by some others and to make it (or frame it as) private property. Enclosure, as an exercise of power and claim to ownership, is often contested. In the abstract, all exploitation involves enclosure, as it makes something that was a collective production (whether emerging directly from a group's work or from a cultural tradition), belong to limited numbers of people only. Yet, in a capitalist society enclosure becomes a livelihood necessity for all producers. Enclosure is the sole means of meeting daily needs.

DISORDERS OF CAPITALISM

Capitalism intensifies distortions in information exchange. We look at how the drive for increasing profit in capital accumulation and commodification produces its disordering ill-effects as well as how it produces its wealth-ordering benefits, without seeing them as separate. For just this purpose, nineteenth-century thinker John Ruskin coined the term the '*ill*th', to denote the social ills generated by the accumulation of *weal*th (Ruskin 1907: 171; emphasis added): rather than a common-wealth, we have the common-illth. We can investigate how certain forms of illth are institutionally entrenched within informationalism. We may even interpret globalised informationalism as quintessentially a system of displacement, of socialising costs or 'ills', and privatising gains, where illth (waste, insecurity, disorder and injury) are shifted into the public domain and onto the relatively less well off, while monetary wealth in the elite private domain is concentrated to an unprecedented extent. This concentration is itself, in Ruskinian terms, a form of illth, as it is no longer used productively, but channelled into specu-lation, depriving the general populace of weal (general good or welfare), even at the cost of informationalism's survival (Oliver-Smith 1996; Tierney 1999). Concentration of wealth, and the extension of commodification into previously free areas, may also produce wealth and illth in the same action.

Pro-capitalist theorists tend to ignore illth and argue that capitalist order, beneficence and wealth arises from spontaneous random individual 'selfishness', often referring to Adam Smith's single passage, in his *Wealth of Nations*, on the 'invisible hand' (1982: I, 456). As examples we can instance the fantasy of market efficiency proposed in Krugman's (1995) *Self-Organising Economy* or as assumed in neoclassical and Austrian economics and perhaps first argued by Mandeville in the three parts of his *Fable of the Bees* (1705, 1714, 1732). However, contemporary corporate markets are neither a spontaneous order, nor a beneficial anarchy, but result from an imposed order, which has involved the capture of the State by corporate interests, particularly since the late 1970s. Spontaneous disorder, in fact, arises from attempts to produce or enforce more 'free market' order.

Capitalism is not under-regulatory, and makes demands on people for them to survive, and to prosper. As Philip Mirowski writes: "'deregulation' always cashes out as 'reregulation' only under a different set of ukases" (a 'ukas' being a Tsarist edict; 2013: 57). The 'freer' the market, the more protection and regulation the corporate sector gains in its favour, the more policies are imposed by in return for its favours, and the less liberty workers have (Ferguson 2012; Galbraith 2008; Harvey 2005). This includes copy-right ownership; skewed distributions of income; rewards for failed execu-tives; punishment for unvalued workers; regulation of workers; diminution of responsibility for working conditions; cheaper worker injuries; regulation of unions, strikes or protests; shifting tax burdens onto the middle class; government transfer of taxpayer monies and property to the corporate sec-tor through contracting or public asset sales; taxpayer-funded support for failed financiers; shifting of responsibility for regulation onto the industries being regulated; shifting of costs and wastes onto the commons, and so on. Even if capitalism was anarchic, rather than compulsively ordering, then by encouraging huge divergences of wealth and power, it creates elites who will team together to organise a State to prevent others from impinging on their greater rights, power and wealth. Political ordering, power and advantage getting, is part of the corporate market, not extraneous to it.

As this capitalist ordering appears successful, it intensifies and extends, enforcing its order over an ever-wider previously free terrain, commodifying and privatising ecological, social and civil commons, from the atmosphere, to social communication, to public services. Rosa Luxemburg (1871–1919) proposed that capitalism requires areas of life that are non-capitalistic in order to work and provide increased surplus value (Luxemburg 1972: 55–61). However its mode of working turns all such relations into capitalistic monetary relations, so that the system no longer works in the same way and ultimately reaches its limits of expansion. For example, capitalism requires non-commercial trust, but tends to make trust a commodity, and therefore less trustable; as Marx and Engels say (1968: 38) even kinship ties tend to become commercial. Similarly Geoffrey Hodgson discusses what he calls the "impurity principle" whereby "every socio-economic system must rely on at least one structurally dissimilar subsystem to function" (1999: 126), with the implication that a system that becomes total is headed for collapse. Hodgson suggests, as an example, that people in the workplace must develop some autonomy from their managers, to overcome the failings of that management (1999: 131). Similarly, information society requires culture to function, but culture has other functions than just profit, so as culture becomes incorporated into the market, its generative richness may be constrained. Social media flourish because of people's need to informally network and keep in touch with a widespread group of others, and this could be undermined if people feel *all* their contacts are being exploited so that someone else can make money from them; a realisation that has continually seemed to plague Facebook (e.g. SMH 19 Jan 2011). Functional non-totalism is a form of slack, and easy to perceive as inefficiency or disorder.

Furthermore, this capitalist order does not necessarily lead to the best of all possible worlds, even for the 'dominating groups'. While there are indeed system-wide collective capitalist interests, the 'capitalist class' is not a unified social movement. There is no collective capitalist, no necessary unity, and no necessarily well-informed and knowledgeable capitalists; there is competition, rivalry and strategic information distortion. Self-seeking behaviour, ostensibly 'rational' at the level of acquisitive individualism, can produce profoundly irrational and disordered systems, as the United Nations' negotiations on climate change make clear (Marshall 2011). Similarly the struggle over resources that results in upper-level wealth may also mean that heavily rewarded work does not generate income, and so fewer people become producers of income. For example, the scientists and engineers who produce the technological innovation capitalism benefits from, may receive considerably less reward and status than the accountants, lawyers and managers who administer the profits of that innovation. In this context, the number of technical knowledge workers may decrease. Similarly, wage labour and appropriation may conflict with human propensities for personal 'gift' exchange and, in particular, with the traditions of collaborative exchange between the programmers who built the internet.

Moves to control and extend commodification also have disordering consequences, because if capitalism is innovative and efficient it is only because businesses that fail are allowed to fail, and new ones that are better adapted take over—although 'better adapted' may mean more ruthless rather than more virtuous. Both with and without this failure, capitalism has an in-built tendency to concentrate economic power in the hands of fewer and fewer corporations and people. Historically the only hope for capitalism has been the periodic collapse of those companies that are too big and that distort the market, allowing smaller companies to compete, innovate and fill in the gaps. Likewise, the periodic collapse of the economy, and widespread crisis, leading to massive write-downs, enables renewal. Crisis is functional for capitalism as a system, but not for the individual capitalists who face ruin and seek to shore-up their power principally through the State. However, with the institutionalisation of corporate power, established powers do their best to prevent this disorder from reaching them. The government and taxpayers often 'have' to bail these corporate powers out, protecting the incompetent, inefficient and disordered from penalty, so that disorder accumulates in the system and becomes potentially more destructive. Such bailouts burden the State with debt, and generate the moral hazard of extending privileges to those that are considered 'too big to fail'. But then again, other capitalists may object to these bailouts, because they prevent opportunities for them to increase profits, or get cheap labour. With no 'capitalist in general' capable of maintaining the complex system, there is a permanent conflict between the system-wide requirement that companies collapse, and the 'orderly' interests of particular users of the system.

The problems are intensified as while the market is supposed to provide information feedback that allows corporations to adapt, high-level managers are generally insulated from the effects of the feedback. Even if dismissed for incompetence, or if they send the company into disaster, they receive high rewards. Simultaneously, through its power and mobility, the corporate sector often supports and uses quasi-legal channels for the exchange and transfer of money (for instance to enable tax evasion and bribery that helps corporate success), while at the same time enabling the funding of terror and organised crime (Robinson 2003; Palan 2003; Naim 2006; Napoleoni 2008, 2010; Deneault 2011). Importantly, the corporate world then fails to fund the State they need to support their claims to property, legality, the orders of contract and the internal peace that enables trade and appropriation.

Our summarising proposal is that capitalism disrupts information, and that information is central to the functions of capitalism. This will be dealt with throughout the book, but in general we can assert that capitalist production involves information as: first, contained within, and generating of, the technology and 'science' of production; second, enabling the play within markets that requires the generation of advertising to gain sales, 'branding' to distinguish similar products, together with the 'foreknowledge' of prices of components, labour, resources, likely sales and investments; and third, the relaying of instructions, understandings of how to manage organisations and what is going on in the organisation, and responses to challenges, crisis and the predictions of consequences. It is impossible to perform capitalist activities without information. However, information in capitalism is not only disrupted by the normal ambiguities of communication (especially as produced by power and hierarchy), but information is also crucially disrupted by its function in the market. In markets information is used to gain a political or economic advantage or sales effect, which generates deceit, and furthermore markets turn information into a commodity that has to be restricted and enclosed out of the public cultural domain (via patenting, copyright, trademarking and secrecy) to make a profit. These restrictions on information turn public goods into private property, making people pay for things that were previously held in common or paid for by taxes on corporate profits. Profitable restrictions disrupt necessary information flows. Money itself is a marker of information and the measure of capitalist value and the heart of commodity exchange; it is therefore affected by all the problems and paradoxes that affect information. This contradiction between 'accurate' information and capitalist profit and security is vital to understanding the dynamics of informationalism (See Chapters 5 and 6).

CONCLUSIONS

All functional systems require and generate what appears to be mess and disorder so they can function. The complex interactive systems that living organisms, including humans, set up are not predictable in detail, and over long enough time are not predictable at all. As a result, attempts to maintain total order imply stasis, rigidity and death. We suggest that informational capitalism attempts to impose a total order of hierarchy, markets, commodification and work, in which 'everything' should both be purchasable and unavailable unless purchased. Given that capitalism operates as, and within, complex interactive systems, then evolutionary, 'revolutionary' and disruptive processes will emerge, some of which appear necessary to support informationalism, and some of which might mutate informationalist orders into new disorderly and functional systems. In this context, and to outline the book again, after a brief discussion of information society theory, we examine the embedded patterns of the order/disorder complex in networks, software and information. We then argue that people using peer-to-peer file sharing are struggling to reveal an existence beyond commodification simultaneously with being parasitic upon capitalism and the orders generated by capitalism. We suggest that academic knowledge work is undermined by informationalism but seems to be trying to find new ways of existence in its collapse, and that social movements can use the tools of informationalism to set up a new emancipatory politics, even as informationalism disorders them and undermines their achieved success

By inverting the order-disorder priority we expose the limitations of a binary attitude to technology, which thinks of technology abstracted from its social relations of existence, and which seeks to 'assess' whether its effects are positive or negative. We argue that technology both enables *and* restricts; it makes some actions easier and some harder, produces some order and some disorder, and the results are not always predictable. Our case studies enable us to explore these processes of enablement and restriction, and ordering and disordering. Indeed, in the order/disorder complex, disorder drives further attempts at ordering, while modes of ordering (and problem solving) produce their own modes of disorder, which people then respond to, forming the 'problem cycle' of informationalism.

We are not arguing that conflict is more fundamental to human 'being' than cooperation. On the contrary, conflict becomes important in social theory precisely because of cooperation. Ironically, people can only maintain and support conflict socially because they can cooperate with others, yet cooperation does not always have its intended effects and neither does conflict; hence sometimes people cooperate in movements that undermine group well-being. Similarly, as is well known, conflict may itself generate some levels of cooperation and integration (Simmel 1955; Gluckman 1960). This illustrates the order/disorder complex in action.

To reiterate, this book is not seeking to suggest that there is no such thing as order, or that all orders need to be condemned. Order is necessary and inevitable. We are suggesting, though, that the potential for social order to be self-destructive, or interact disruptively with other orderings, is sociologically, politically and organisationally significant and probably inevitable. This realisation directs attention to events that are usually considered to be insignificant failures of real order, of marginal value, or mere untidiness or rubbish. These events can offer evidence of the systemic failings of social beliefs about ordering, and hence of arrangements of power and organisation. The application of policy and plans always has to be sensitive to evidence of failure, disordering human responses and conflict, or unexpected interactions, and not to an assurance that continuing with the 'right' policy will produce the results we intend. In order to succeed more regularly, software engineers and social movements need to have some awareness of how their modes of ordering, or protests against particular orders, can be self-disruptive. Human society, and the world, always resists complete control.

BOX 4   THE SOCIAL DISORDERING OF BRIDGES

As an example of how order can produce disorder even in civil engineering, let us consider the London Millennium Footbridge that crosses the River Thames in London and was opened in the year 2000. It is a steel suspension bridge for pedestrians, supposed to be stable enough to support at least 5,000 people. It incorporated a radical new design, and unnamed engineers were reported as saying it was "an absolute statement of our capabilities at the beginning of the 21st century" (Science Daily 3 November 2005). However shortly after opening it was closed due to a strong lateral wobble that arose when people attempted to walk across it. Computer simulations during the design process had not indicated the possibility of any such result, showing the failure of these computer simulations and the modelling even in established engineering (Strogatz 2003: 71ff.). After the event, researchers generally agreed that the supposedly random vibrations of pedestrians set up the sway.

The fact that ordered pedestrian vibrations could cause damage to bridges was well known by the nineteenth century, and soldiers were ordered to break step when marching, as the order of step was destructive and disorder was safer (Taylor nd: 2). A public notice is still in place at both ends of Albert Bridge in London simply stating "all troops must break step when marching over this bridge". The Millennium Bridge presents a more complex case. Steven Strogatz pointed out that the bridge was a flexible structure with a natural frequency close to that of human walking (Science Daily 2005). Although people were not deliberately walking in step, eventually a critical number would unintentionally step in time, generating a slight sway that would make more pedestrians fall spontaneously into step, inadvertently producing order, amplifying the movement and causing more people to walk in step with the vibrations (Strogatz et al. 2005). The bridge engineers comment:

> If the surface we are walking on is oscillating sideways a little we place our feet further apart to stabilise ourselves and our sideways (lateral) force increases. We also find it more comfortable to walk in time with the surface's movements.
>
> (ARUP 2002)

Strogatz and his team simulated people walking over the bridge and found that "as more and more people walk on to the deck . . . there is no hint of instability until the crowd reaches a critical size . . . after which wobbling and synchrony erupt simultaneously" (Strogatz et al. 2005; Taylor nd: 3). That is, everything appears to be working smoothly until there is a sudden change of state; sometimes known as a 'tipping point'. MacDonald (2009) even argues that the coordination of steps was not necessary to produce the effects; that is that random movements of a similar type can produce ordered forces with unexpected and disordering results.

The problem seemed to be that the bridge designers had not factored in 'random' human factors or the feedback effects between the bridge and pedestrians. The British standard code of bridge loading was updated to cover the phenomenon, now known as 'Synchronous Lateral Excitation' (BSI nd).

The bridge was closed for two years and the engineers charged with fixing the problem discussed stiffening the bridge, limiting the number of people allowed on the bridge and active control of the vibrations, eventually deciding on passive dampening (Taylor nd: 4). Dampening disorder is a response that here evidently proved adequate. In other circumstances, especially social ones, such 'disorder dampers' are not so readily available.

While marching over bridges is a simple case of order eventually proving destructive, the Millennium Bridge did not collapse; it simply proved unusable as the vibrations became so strong that many people could not walk across it and hence the effect temporarily stopped. As a thought experiment, we can imagine a case in which the bridge was not so well built, or in which the order of pedestrians was imposed, or in which damping effects were insufficient. In these cases the order, together with its interaction with its environment, or the order generated in the interaction between people and the bridge, could conceivably destroy the bridge or the use of the bridge. There is no necessity, for a 'naturally occurring', or designed, dampening system to either exist, or to produce equilibrium, in all systems in all situations.

2 Robustness and Order in Theories of the Information Society

THE BIRTH OF INFORMATION SOCIETY THEORY

From the 1960s onwards, Western social science underwent a crisis of faith in what had come to be the established model of industrialism. The crisis expressed a perception that new forces were generating a radical reordering within industrialised societies. These societies appeared to be undergoing a radical break with the past, which seemed to be systemic rather than simply a conjuncture of circumstances. People in the social sciences aimed at conceptualising this break as relatively tidy, straightforward and ordered, both hiding some of the complexities, and the resistance of social history to hard-and-fast categorisations.

'Post-industrial' society was first conceptualised as a society liberated from domination by machines. Writing in the early twentieth century, and advocating a post-industrial craft society, Arthur Penty argued that that "the problem of machinery was central in the social problem" (1922: 13) and that "the unrestricted use of machinery has proved to be purely destructive" (ibid: 52). By contrast, machines dominate current day conceptions of post-industrial information society. The machines tend to change with the fashionable technology of the day; 'Nuclear Age', 'Space Age', 'Digital Age', 'Information Age', 'Age of Biotechnology' and so on. In general (although the variants are important), information, and information machines, have been declared to be central and transformative, with debate centring on the character and spread of the resulting transformation and not, for example, on the degree of such transformation, or whether it is more an intensification than a change of state. The idea of a new historical epoch has repeatedly captured the orderly imagination of many, and is often linked with a triumphant assessment of that new epoch's potential. Like 'industrialism' and the supposed inevitability of 'modernisation', we often find ideas of informationalism being used to acclaim, or criticise, the 'birth of the new order' rather than to analyse it.

The range of explanatory models posited to characterise the new period is bewildering, but that variety is not something to dismiss; it is part of what we must analyse. Just to take a brief selection, contemporary society has been characterised in many different ways: as 'network society' (Castells 2000a,b,c, 2001, 2011; Barney 2004; Van Dijk 2006), 'risk society' (Beck 1992, 2009), 'managerial society' (Burnham 1941; Pound 1990; Wolin 2008 and implied by any number of books on management), 'post-industrial society' (Touraine 1971; Bell 1976), 'programmed society' (Touraine 1971), 'control society' (Beniger 1986; Mulgan 1991; Deleuze 1995), 'surveillance society' (Lyon 1994; Surveillance Studies Network 2006), 'Empire' (Hardt & Negri 2000, 2004, 2009) and as 'knowledge' society or 'information society' (Drucker 1969, 1993; Bell 1980; Masuda 1980; Toffler 1980, 1984; Lyon 1988).

It is hard to order these various theorists into neat categories, and there are cross similarities. For example, the programmed society might perhaps be considered a more technocratic version of managerial society. However, many of these models share the assumption that the exercise of power, meaning, value and organisation itself, has changed from that found in industrialised societies. They thus point to the 'new' and, hence, to a new 'problem cycle'.

Some of these positions arise because analysts want to either applaud or denigrate current developments, rather than address those developments as both enabling *and* restricting, with likely beneficial *and* harmful tendencies. Certainly, there is a tendency to construct an account of what is assumed to be the new (or coming) dominant order, and in the process, minimise disorder as passing. Yet the range of theories, and the ways they contradict each other, may be said to express a significant range of disorder, and indeed this disorder is perhaps where we need to look. The theoretical disorder is characteristic of informationalism and the need for marketable originality. At the most, the ideas express parallel counter-tendencies in a society that was encountering new uncertainties and new possibilities. In these uncertainties, and the dynamics they reflect, we find further ground for different ways of theorising.

A tendency to construct the new and separate it out from the old makes the analysis too tidy and schematic. Apparent continuities are positioned as hangovers of the past, soon to be overwhelmed by the favoured prefigurative forces, no matter how marginal those coming forces may seem today. Continuities simply become detritus to be thrown away, while differences are exaggerated to make the separation of categories clear. By directing attention away from previous trajectories and conflicts, these models have society emerge, not in continuity and struggle, but as a transformed object, stripped of its past (in a sense positing a complete 'break' with that past, as with the early Foucault). Against this claim, industrial and informational societies are not discontinuous modes: informationalism still depends on industrial mass production of technologies, mass production of food, mass production of clothing, and is embedded in the growth of wealthy corporations, and the displacement of most workers from relatively secure labour. Hence, we join Schiller (1999) and Dyer-Witheford (1999) in arguing it is vital to recognise the importance of the continuities of capitalist history. However, we also insist on the apparent disjunctions; it is not just the same old capitalism. Castells, while perhaps downplaying economic (dis)organisation, and implying a degree of smoothness, also states that "Informationalism presupposes industrialism" (Castells 2004: 8).

TENETS OF 'INFORMATIONALISM'

Despite the diversity we have pointed to, by the 1980s a series of key claims had emerged within theories of information society. Such claims are also outlined in a number of accounts, including Dyer-Witheford (1999: 22–6), Castells (2000a: 60–3, 69ff., 176ff., 232ff.) and Toffler (1980, 1990). We are not alleging that every theory shares all of these points, but that most theories share at least one of these points, often more than one. We are, for the purposes of contrast, simplifying and ordering the varieties of theory, rather than attempting to be exhaustive, or making firm claims about similarity.

In summary, there are five standard claims:

1) The use of digital information technology, or ICT, is changing society, usually for the better—making it more adaptive. ICT makes an orderly infrastructure.
2) There is a shift from an economy based on manufacture and exchange of goods to an economy based on exchanges of information. Orders of information, knowledge and culture are central to this new economy.
3) So called 'knowledge workers', 'information workers', 'immaterial labourers', etc. become increasingly important or dominant. Their labour is central to the society.
4) Networks are orderly and adaptive. Network power lowers hierarchy, distributes power, helps democracy and produces flexibility.
5) While there is frequently an ambiguous relationship to capitalism, it is often held that capitalism is improved by informationalism. Networked speed and responsiveness fosters this improvement.

These points tend to merge with each other.

We engage with these and related claims throughout the book, and attempt to qualify them or refute them. In Chapter 3, 7 and 8 we primarily look at the disorders produced by ordering by computers and software. In Chapter 4 we look at the disorders of networks and the ways this interacts with computers. Chapters 5 and 6 look at the way the informationalism distorts communication, knowledge and information. Chapter 11 touches on the devaluation of knowledge workers. Chapter 9 looks at the way networks and computerisation disorders and orders finance and financial information, while Chapter 10 looks at disorderly relations between digitisation and networked property.

While we assert that information society is not discontinuous with its past, neither is it the same; rather ICT allows a potentially disruptive *intensification* and *extension* of capitalist orderings (particularly of accelerated and extended commodification), creating unintended and disorderly consequences. While informationalism has gained traction as a 'solution set' arising from attempts to extend corporate, military and political power, it also disturbs that power and its solutions.

Let us first turn to a central postulate for almost all the theorists we have mentioned, namely that computers and software underlie information society, its information and communication networks, and that society is relatively stable and robust due to this fact.

COMPUTING AND SOCIAL THEORY

Before large-scale public consciousness of computer networks, Daniel Bell wrote of people:

> living in a vastly enlarged world that is now tied together, almost in real time, by cable, telephone and international satellite, whose inhabitants are made aware of each other by the vivid pictorial imagery of television, and that has at its disposal large data banks of computerised information.
>
> (1980: 525–6)

Bell made a direct connection between popular consciousness and connectivity enabled by, in this case, electronic rather than digital media. As Duff (1998) argues, when compared to other writers in the field, computers were not central to Bell's general theory. What was more important was the claim that mass engagement with communication technology, interactive as well as broadcast, was reconfiguring the world as 'vastly enlarged'. The implications for analysis of social change were manifold. With the advent of digital technology this became a definitional characteristic. In his introduction to network society theory, Darin Barney states that one of two fundamental characteristics of network society:

> is the presence in those societies of sophisticated—almost exclusively digital—technologies of networked communication and information management/distribution. [These] technologies . . . form the basic infrastructure mediating an increasing array of social, political and economic practices.
>
> (Barney 2004: 25)

His other rather tautological point is that network societies are organised into networks. Tautology is not an unusual practice amongst observers of information society, reflecting the expectations of radical change driven by technology. Whether deliberately, or not, the 'basic infrastructure' becomes seen as primarily technological or 'informational', rather than social. This leads analysis into a model of social change in which change derives from a unified technology, rather than from social power, struggle, misunderstandings and unexpected consequences. Any disorder is simply seen as resistance and passes away.

Justin Rosenberg observed a similar tendency amongst globalisation theorists, many of whom believe that the dissemination of communication technology was explanation enough for the social transformations wrought by globalisation. The term 'globalisation' functions as a vacuous explanation, in the same way that terms like 'information society', 'network society' and so on function in 'information society' theory: "Globalisation as an outcome cannot be explained simply by invoking globalisation as a process tending towards that outcome" (Rosenberg 2000: 2). For Rosenberg, what is needed is a 'theory of globalisation' that explains the phenomenon, rather than a 'globalisation theory' that merely restates what is being observed.

> What presents itself initially as the *explanandum*—globalisation as the developing outcome of some historical process—is progressively transformed into the *explanans*: it is globalisation which now explains the changing character of the modern world—and even generates 'retrospective discoveries' about past epochs in which it must be presumed not to have existed.
>
> (ibid: 3)

The parallels for information society theory, as opposed to theories of information society, are instructive. In their analysis of 'Empire', Michael Hardt and Antonio Negri appear to embrace the confusion of 'explanandum' and 'explanans', and the resulting non-explanation. At one point they write (without evident irony) that:

> The development of communication networks has an organic relationship to the emergence of the new world order—it is, in other words, effect and cause, product and producer. Communication not only expresses but organises the movement of globalisation.
>
> (Hardt & Negri 2000: 32)

Hardt and Negri continue their explanation of the transformation produced by technology:

> The computer and communication revolution of production has transformed laboring practices in such a way that they all tend toward the model of information and communication technologies.
>
> (ibid: 291)

Everything is made mono-causal, loosing the struggle and disorder, which allows them to propose a kind of 'class' harmony arising among information workers in common cause with a wider populace, to form the 'multitude'. However, the networks neither organically mesh nor provide a general unified class basis for revolt, especially not a dominantly democratic leftist one. There are many forces opposed to capitalist informationalism and the multitude is fractured. The Tea Party in the U.S. has probably had more immediate effect than Occupy, apparently taking over a major political party, bringing the U.S. government to the edge of default on several occasions with its messy alliance of 'elitist' wealth, popular protest and electoral engagement (Eidelson 18 October 2013; Stolberg & McIntyre 5 October 2013). U.S.-based David Wasserman of the Cook Political Report asked: "When else in our history has a freshman member of Congress from North Carolina been able to round up a gang of 80 that's essentially ground the government to a halt?" (Stolberg & McIntyre 5 October 2013). Likewise, in the context of a continuing European fiscal crisis, both the nationalist far-right and leftist anti-institutionalist parties attracted voters in the 2014 European elections (McDonald Gibson & Lichfield 25 May 2014). The multitude is not united.

When discussing network power, Manuel Castells, who might be considered the leading and most referenced theorist writing about the 'information age', similarly makes information technology the centrepiece of explanation: there is little to no consideration of the forces that developed the technologies, brought them into play in the social field or how they work or don't work. He defines the network society as "a social structure made of information networks powered by information technologies characteristic of the informationalist paradigm" (2001: 166). Thus, "informationalism is the technological paradigm that constitutes the material basis of early twenty-first century societies" (Castells 2004: 8). Elsewhere he adds, "What is new in our age is a new set of information technologies" (Castells 2000d: 10). In this respect the analysis is surprisingly linear, and teleological. Writing in the same year as Rosenberg, and Hardt and Negri, Castells argues that a "technological revolution centered around information technologies" has begun to "reshape, at an accelerated pace, the material basis of society". This technology has reshaped economies, by making them globally interdependent (which to an extent they had been for a considerable time), while "Capitalism itself has undergone a process of profound restructuring, characterized by greater flexibility in management; decentralising and networking of firms" (Castells 2000a: 1).

Castells moves on to suggest that information technology is tied to the production of good information, which has its own self-expanding volition:

> What is also characteristic of this technological paradigm is the use of knowledge-based, information technologies to enhance and accelerate the production of knowledge and information, in a self-expanding, virtuous circle.
>
> (Castells 2000d: 9–10)

Here Castells implies that knowledge improves along with networking, and that increasing distribution of accurate knowledge is fundamental. The idea of a 'virtuous circle' seems to rest on the idea of positive feedback loops being good for you, so that a 'positive' change in one social field induces positive change in another linked field, and vice-versa. There is no sense that an information technology could, equally, enhance and accelerate the production of disinformation, or that positive feedback loops can spiral out of control—producing massive amounts of 'noise' and blocking information transmission. Furthermore, in Castells's formulation the virtuous 'circle' appears to be internal to information technology and its 'paradigm'; there is no break, no disordering. Consequently, he can claim such societies "organize their production system around the principles of maximizing knowledge based productivity" (2000a: 219) and that informationalism rests on "the augmentation of the human capacity of information processing and communication" through computers and software (Castells 2004: 28). The validation of this process as 'virtuous' appears without any sign of doubt and the outcome is positioned as unambiguously superior and virtuously ordered. However, as we suggest in Chapters 5 and 6, this may not be the case.

For all societies, digital communication, and the software and technology that drives it, represents nothing less than "a revolutionary change in the material conditions of their performance [and] affects the entire realm of human activity" (Castells 2004: 9). These new technologies supposedly allow systemic management of complexity, and give:

> an unprecedented combination of flexibility and task implementation, of co-ordinated decision making, and decentralized execution, which provide a superior social morphology for all human action.
>
> (Castells 2000d: 15)

Informationalism offers an improved and robust capitalist society because:

> networked organisations outcompete all other forms of organisation, particularly the vertical, rigid, command-and-control bureaucracies. . . . Companies that do not or cannot follow this logic are outperformed and ultimately phased out by leaner, more flexible competitors.
>
> (2004b: 222)

This is a recurring theme:

> networks are complex structures of communication constructed around a set of goals that simultaneously ensure unity of purpose and flexibility of execution by their adaptability to the operating environment . . . Their structure evolves according to the capacity of the network to self-configure in an endless search for more efficient networking arrangements.
>
> (Castells 2009: 21)

Networks from this perspective are always adaptive and efficient. It appears that for Castells computer networks allow superior order, superior decision-making and superior adaptability, with flexibility as an untrammelled good. Castells implies an increasing coherence in this society, writing of "the growing *convergence of specific technologies into a highly integrated system*" (2000a: 71; emphasis in the original) and the "shared logic of information generation" (ibid: 72), without apparently wondering if the absence of difference can also produce disorder, or whether all 'information' is beneficial, or accurate.

Importantly, though, for Castells, informationalism never subsumes society. For him informationalism as an exercise of power, always produces its opposition: regardless of how efficient or effective it may be, power exercised over people always produces what he calls 'counter-power' (2012). Earlier, Castells argued that sharp social divides open up between the 'space of flows', where networks are privileged, and the 'space of places', where people live (Castells 2000a: 453ff.; 2005). Network power is seen as severing the institutional linkages between elites and their subordinates, accentuating powerlessness. In this context, legitimating identities, which engage with existing political institutions, are superseded by 'resistance' identities. The dialectic between order and resistance is seen as producing new 'project' identities capable of superseding the status quo. Resistance, here, is driven by exclusion and marginality from informationalism, not by its internal contradictions and crises. Informationalism is seen as coherent, on its own terms, and counter-power as in the first instance a battle for "the autonomous construction of meaning," as the basis for more pre-figurative 'projects' of counter-power (2000c: 73ff; 2009: 422). In *Communication Power* (2009), Castells documents the stratification of informationalism, as a power structure, one where information rationality is deployed as a mode of domination. Here, any disinformation is cast as deliberate spin rather than as being produced by the internal disorders of informationalism (2009: 196ff., 204ff., 224ff.). This ensconces the ruling class as prime manipulators, able to exercise power in the absence of instability and crisis, not themselves in any sense confused and caught-up in a power/ignorance nexus. This, we argue, gives too much credit to elites, and to their system, and marginalises 'counter-power' as an external challenge to an internally stable and coherent entity.

In criticising notions of 'information society' through a disorder-focused approach, we co-opt and deploy the terms 'informationalism', 'capitalist informationalism' or 'disinformation society' in order to question the information society thesis, especially the idea that accuracy of knowledge is a vital component of this society. We assert that, embedded within information capitalism, there are deep contradictions that validate ignorance and proliferate disinformation. Informationalism and information embodies attempts to order people as much as attempts to inform. Our focus on the systemic disorders of information and networks challenges the idea that information networks are relatively robust, integrated and seamless, and we dispute assumptions that this society produces an informed democracy. We argue that informationalism is structurally self-disordering, with potentially fragile patterns of domination and control, and that the counter-movements arise within these disordered fields, and may also disorder themselves. Disorder is not 'outside' informationalism, arising from social movements, or the marginal world, but is present at its core.

We also argue that informationalism introduces new disorders, through its dependence on information and information technologies. Information is itself disorder-prone, as is information transmission and interpretation; the cultural power of information as a set of meanings, framings and instructions is inherently unstable. In sum, we argue that capitalism partially based in information, when joined with information networks produces what we call 'disinformation society', although the success and efficiency rhetoric of its theorists suggests otherwise.

The weight of systemically generated disinformation (largely produced by management and media structures, commodification of information and the resulting ignorance and distortion) undermines the society's capacity to solve its self-generated problems. By this formulation, we avoid implying that the generation, or propagation, of misinformation is always deliberate, or that powerful people know what is 'really' going on. The system itself generates inaccuracy and confusion. Actual 'knowledge' or cultural innovation may even decline as information is directed at managing problems of accumulation for those further up the hierarchy, thereby undermining solutions for society as a whole.

Focusing on software, we find failure and precariousness are inherent in the social process of software development, and the imposition of supposedly good managerial order. 'Information disorder' and social conflict are expressed in, and disrupt, software design and installation processes. Conversely, as software acts as a mode of ordering for organisational and social control, even when it 'works', software produces disruption by extending inappropriate modes of ordering into previously functional areas, extending the reach of incoherence and allowing previously unimaginable forms of feedback, resistance and gridlock, all of which have disruptive social consequences.

As nearly all information society models place digital technology at their centre, we address this issue in the next chapter. We then deal with some of the instabilities of networks, and in the subsequent two chapters, examine the ways capitalism intensifies communicative distortion.

3   Computers, Systems, Instability and Failure

Accounts of informationalism often assume that information technology helps produce a resilient and efficient form of social ordering. This implies, as ICT sales representatives suggest, that ICT invariably performs as intended: that it increases efficiency, reduces duplication and improves communications, while improving data capture and processing. These ordering accounts suppress the experience of repeated failure and difficulties with computer software, including upgrades and new implementations. These disorders cost significant amounts of money, time, emotional pain and frustration, and constitute an important part of social experience under informationalism. In this chapter we look at some of the data behind this sense of disorder. The next chapter extends the argument by suggesting the networking of ICT further adds to disorder and disorientation.

RECURRENT FAILURE AND DISRUPTION

The recurrent failure of software implementation is well known in the industry. In 1995 the Standish Group estimated that in the U.S. alone "at least $185 billion is wasted on development projects that fail, often because the software does not satisfy user's needs" (Hickey et al. 2003: 279). In 2004–5 the same organisation estimated that 30% of all software projects were cancelled, nine out of ten came in late, almost half ran over budget, and 60% were considered failures by the organisations that initiated them (*Economist* 27 November 2004). In 2009 Standish declared that 24% of projects failed, 44% were challenged and 32% succeeded (Dominguez 2009). The 2009 report also reportedly claimed that "projects over $10 million only have a 2% chance of coming in on time and on budget, and represent a statistical zero in the success column" (Sessions 29 October 2009). It is worth noting that the Standish reports are produced for sale, and that the authors of this book have not read them, and it would seem that most people quoting the figures have not read them either. This is not rare with such reports, as they are costly and hence confined. These figures have often been disputed, as they are so high, are not reproduced in the personal experience of critics, and are generated by people who make money out of software management and who benefit from increasing the perceptions of difficulty (Sauer, Gemino & Reich 2007). However, figures from other sources also suggest a sense of widespread disruption. Saran (27 May 2003) writes that in:

> a survey of 450 IT directors across the UK, Germany and France, 73% said they had suffered major faults in their IT systems. Respondents said the lack of quality in software had a direct impact on their business. [36%] reported that IT failures had led to 'considerable reduction in turnover', and 43% said poor software quality led to a substantial drop in staff productivity. [45%] said poor software quality had damaged the company's image among clients and prospective clients.

A survey by Chris Sauer and Christine Cuthbertson, of 1,500 IT project managers in the UK across all industry sectors, found that only 16% of the projects "hit all their targets (budget, schedule and scope/functionality)", 45% of projects ran over time and 59% were over budget. Furthermore, "54% of projects failed to deliver on the planned-for functionality" while 9% were abandoned. On the whole "55% of projects come within 5% of their schedule, 5% of scope and 4% of budget". This was considered to be "pretty good" (Huber 4 November 2003).

A European Services Strategy unit specifically looked at 105 large out-sourced public sector ICT projects that had widely known difficulties and reported that:

- Total value of contracts [was] £29.5 billion.
- Cost overruns totalled £9.0 billion.
- 57% of contracts experienced cost overruns.
- The average percentage cost overrun [was] 30.5%.
- 33% of contracts suffered major delays.
- 30% of contracts were terminated.
- 12.5% of Strategic Service Delivery Partnerships . . . failed.

(Whitfield 2007: 3)

Joe Harley, Chief Information Officer of the British Department for Work and Pensions, said in 2007 that only 30% of government IT projects were successful. He claimed failure rates in the private sector were similar and that the British government spent over £14 billion per year on IT, which was unsustainable (Espiner 18 May 2007). A public service clarification said that "Only projects which were on time, on budget and exactly to specification were deemed a success. If they never saw the light of day they were deemed a failure. Anything in between—around 63% of the projects—was deemed neither a success nor failure" (Collins 23 May 2007). This still might not be considered a rousing success. John McManus and Trevor Wood-Harper (2007) conducted a study on behalf of the British Computer Society between

1998 and 2005 and claimed "only one in eight information technology projects can be considered truly successful (failure being described as those projects that do not meet the original time, cost and quality requirements criteria)". A survey by Dynamic Markets Limited (2007: 4) for the TATA consultancy states that 62% of projects overran on time, 49% overran on budget and 47% had higher than expected maintenance costs. They report that 16% of those surveyed "say the implementation of their new IT system has had a negative impact on existing IT systems" with 73% of IT managers saying that "they personally have been affected in a negative way as a result of IT projects not going according to plan". El-Emam and Koru report on their two years of web surveys:

> If we consider overall failures (cancelled projects plus delivered projects with unsuccessful performance), the most up-to-date numbers indicate that 26 percent to 34 percent of IT projects fail.
>
> (2008: 90)

However, despite revealing that more than a quarter of IT projects failed, they concluded that these figures did not provide evidence of a "software crisis", which perhaps reveals industry expectations of failure. An over 25% failure rate in most other 'engineering' fields would probably be unacceptable. A 2008 report of a survey for IAG consulting of over 100 companies with an average project size of US$3 million concluded that:

> 68% of companies are more likely to have a marginal project or outright failure than a success due to the way they approach business analysis. In fact, 50% of this group's projects were "runaways" which had any 2 of:
>
> - Taking over 180% of target time to deliver
> - Consuming in excess of 160% of estimated budget
> - Delivering under 70% of the target required functionality.
>
> (Ellis 2008: 1)

Cast, another research company, analysed 365 million lines of code in 745 software applications submitted by 160 organisations "located primarily in the United States, Europe, and India", involving finance, energy, insurance, retail, IT consulting, government and so on (Cast 2011: 1–2). In analysing problems in the programs, Cast uses the term 'technical debt' to represent "the effort required to fix problems that remain in the code when an application is released". They estimate an average cost of US$3.61 per line of code to fix the mistakes, so that programs of about 300,000 lines long will, in general, cost over one million dollars to fix (ibid: 18). Bill Curtis, Chief Scientist at Cast, pointed out that nearly 15% of the projects examined had over a million lines of code. He also stated that "over one-third (35%) of the violations discovered in the study result in damage to business by adversely affecting the security, performance and uptime of application software" (Cast 8 December 2011). Technical debt also diverts money and effort from innovation into repair (ibid), and thus increases the difficulties of adaptation. Cast quoted David Norton of Gartner saying that technical debt "doesn't go off with a bang, it's more a slow burn. Change starts to take longer . . . and opex [operating expense] costs start to spiral—it will not be a single cataclysmic event, it will be death by a thousand cuts" (ibid).

Another survey of 200 organisations in North America and Europe performed for CA Technologies, a software management company, claimed Information Technology (IT):

> outages are frequent and lengthy . . . 50% of organizations said IT outages damage their reputation. 18% described the impact on their reputation as 'very damaging' . . . 44% of respondents believe IT downtime damages staff morale, and 35% said it can adversely impact customer loyalty.
>
> (CA Technologies 2011)

In other words, IT may be essential to business but also disorders reputation, staff and customers.

The experience of such ongoing disorder can produce pessimism in information workers. A Geneca Consulting survey of "596 individuals closely involved in the software development process" reports that "75% of respondents admit that their projects are either always or usually doomed right from the start . . . [and] 80% of these professionals admit they spend at least half their time on rework", that is, in trying to fix systems that do not work properly, and 78% "believe that the Business is usually or always out of sync with project requirements" (Geneca Consulting 2011: 3–6). IT workers expect projects to be difficult and disruptive, and to require extra work to keep them going.

BOX 5   2012 SOFTWARE FAILURES

IT workers tend to collect lists of large software projects that don't work or have suffered significant failures. This is a list of projects voted by consultants for Software Quality Systems. One article (Jowitt 14 December 2012) comments that according to SQS, the annual survey "has exposed the ongoing problems within the financial and banking sector, which has dominated the software glitch top ten lists over the past three years".

10) "**Leap Year bugs hit banking and healthcare payment systems**". The extra day caused a leading multinational corporation to suffer a cloud computing service outage, affecting governments and consumers. The bug also disrupted a payment system used by the health

industry in Australia, preventing 150,000 customers from using private health care cards for two days.

9) **"Utility billing nightmare"**. Thousands of customers of an Australian energy company were sent late payment charges for bills they didn't receive. A German utility company overcharged 94,000 of its customers for exit fees. This cost the energy supplier $2.24 million in settlement payouts.

8) **"Gambler loses winnings to computer virus"**. An online gambler who had his winnings reported as $1 million, was told by a High Court that this was due to software error and, as this was covered in the game's terms and conditions, he had no legal claim.

7) **"Teething problems for new revenue service software system"**. The U.S. Internal Revenue Service upgraded its software and revenue service system, at an estimated cost of $1.3 billion, to promote e-filing of tax returns. The result: 85% of refunds were delayed by over 23 days.

6) **"Security staff shortage at major international sports event"**. A computer miscalculated the number of security staff required for the London Olympics. Members of the armed forces had to stand in.

5) **"Airline glitch strands passengers"**. A U.S. airline and its passengers suffered hundreds of delayed domestic and international flights across the U.S. and internationally due to software problems. This was the third such incident that year.

4) **"US elections vote glitch"**. During the 2012 U.S. elections voting machines automatically changed votes from one candidate to another without allowing the voter to correct the error.

3) **"Social networking giant IPO trading glitch"**. Problems in a share trading system affected a major IPO causing up to 30 million share trades to be "processed incorrectly if at all".

2) **"IPO withdrawn because of technical failure"**. A stock trading business launching its own IPO on its own trading system was forced to cancel after serious technical failure stopped trading before it had even begun.

1) **"Software glitch costs trading firm $440million (£273m) in 45 minutes"**. A share trading firm lost $440 million in 45 minutes using a flawed trading algorithm in its newly installed high frequency trading software.

(Jowitt December 14 2012; Codd 17 December 2012; SQS 2013). Other such lists for the year are available.

General opinion, anecdote and experience tend to back up this impression of disorder. Charette writes:

Most IT experts agree that such failures occur far more often than they should. What's more, the failures are universally unprejudiced: they happen in every country; to large companies and small; in commercial, nonprofit, and governmental organizations; and without regard to status or reputation.

(2005: 43)

Freedman (1 July 2005) quotes software engineer Joseph Goguen from the University of California at San Diego as saying:

More than half the large custom systems that are started never reach users . . . Usually they're just cancelled, but sometimes they're declared a success and then not used . . . The developers end up designing and building the wrong system . . . and they don't realize it until they're almost through.

Freedman adds that Goguen notes only about 20% of the costs of failure are related to technical problems, while close to 60% of the costs arise because of the organization's failure to explain, or know, what it requires.

Firoz Dosani, vice president of Mercer Management Consulting Inc, is quoted as claiming that:

When the true costs are added up, as many as 80% of technology projects actually cost more money than they return . . . "It's not done intentionally", he says, "but the reality is, the costs are always underestimated and the benefits are always overestimated".

(Scheier 14 May 2001)

The costs of these disruptions can be hard to estimate. In 2002, the American National Institute of Standards estimated that straightforward computer bugs "cost the U.S. economy an estimated $59.5 billion annually" (Newman 2002). McManus and Wood-Harper claim that "the cost of project failure across the European Union was 142 billion Euros in 2004" (2007: 38). Towards the end of 2005, Charette wrote that over the previous five years he estimated:

that project failures have likely cost the U.S. economy at least $25 billion and maybe as much as $75 billion. . . . that $75 billion doesn't reflect projects that exceed their budgets—which most projects do. Nor does it reflect projects delivered late—which the majority are. It also fails to account for the opportunity costs of having to start over once a project is abandoned or the costs of bug-ridden systems that have to be repeatedly reworked.

(Charette 2005)

Michael Krigsman, an IT journalist and CEO of consulting and research firm Asuret, asked Gene Kim and Mike Orzen "two qualified experts to re-assess the worldwide economic impact of IT failure" (10 April 2012). They:

> calculated the global impact of IT failure as being $3 trillion annually . . . [saying] when we analyze the value streams of almost all processes across all industries, we discover over 80% of the effort creates no value in terms of benefit to the customer.

They thought that a fair proportion of the wasted costs were consumed by maintenance:

> If we conservatively estimate that 50 percent of global IT spend is on 'operate/maintain' activities, and that at least 35 percent of that work is urgent, unplanned work or rework, that's $980 billion worldwide of waste!

Such cost figures, if correct, are not trivial.

Computers and networks not only face disruption when they are being built and installed, but during their daily operation. Natural disasters can affect networks. In Chapter 8, we show that in January 2011 flooding in Queensland, Australia, resulted in widely reported breakdown of computers, computer networks and phone networks—although the internet as a whole stayed up. Storms in California in that January and the previous month seriously disrupted AT&T's internet networks and produced less heavily reported breakdowns for Verizon and Time Warner. In the Californian case cutbacks in technical staff may have caused a tardy response to the emergency, and lack of service to the wires. Capitalist rationality undermined the slack, stability and resilience of the networks that underlie the economy. In that same month of December the internet phone service Skype broke down for varying amounts of time depending on the source the story, and Microsoft accidentally deleted numerous Hotmail accounts during an upgrade.

BOX 6   THE FAILURE OF THE 'OBAMACARE' SOFTWARE

While we were writing the final version of this book U.S. President Obama launched his health care scheme on 8 October 2013 and the software failed spectacularly. It is much too early to analyse the failure of www.healthcare.gov properly, especially on the technical side, but some common social factors can be pointed to that illustrate disinformationalism in action. In this case explicit politics, or the fracturing between information groups, plays into and, plays up, software disruption. Such splits can occur within, or between, organisations; with the patterns of disorder repeated. Information warfare and disorder is inherent in both informationalism and software installation.

a) *Rivalry and conflict.* The launch was bound in with political turmoil. There was a tight information group determined to undermine or sabotage the software project's success, and portray it badly, and another such group that depended on its success for its operational future. Information about the crash was not unbiased or accurate by default. Exploitation of the tension worked for the Republicans in that a poll taken between 17–20 October reported that 56% of Americans thought the website problems were indicative of broader problems with the law (Craighill & Clement 21 October 2013).

b) *Imposed deadlines.* There was a political need to launch by a certain date to counter-attempts to prevent the system being launched, rather than a plan to launch by program readiness and after proper testing (Pear et al. 12 October 2013).

c) *Funding cuts.* The funding for software construction was reduced by the ongoing politics.

d) *Size compounds problems.* Republican states were reluctant to build their own systems, so reduced funding coexisted with a bigger than expected project.

e) *Specification creep.* Specifications and rules for the project kept changing as the project developed.

f) *Too many groups involved.* Fifty-five different private contractors were used to write the software, almost certainly leading to coordination and communication problems.

g) *Competition in blame.* Companies were motivated to put the blame elsewhere (Pear et al. 12 October 2013: Kliff 24 October 2013).

h) *Conflicting understandings.* The more organisations involved, the greater the number and differences in understandings that are likely to arise about what is needed, expected and when it is due. Information does not flow.

i) *Understaffing.* The government's project administrators were suffering overwork and cuts in staffing, so planning and control declined (Klein 4 November 2013). Leading up to the launch, many of the government's coordinators were on 'furlough' because of the Republican-generated shutdown of the government. This increased problems (Shear & Pear 8 October 2013).

j) *Power/ignorance.* It appears that the White House and top administrators were not well informed as to the state of the software during the project. Information flow was disrupted (Klein 14 October 2013).

k) *Distributed governance.* Connection (mesh) between the system and the computer systems of the health insurers was poor. When data did get through to the insurers it was incomplete. Lack of coordination when the insurers were getting their systems ready for the new connection probably increased the problems (Arit 8 October 2013). Many participants may have expected the project to be delayed and hence were behind schedule themselves.

l) *Unexpected usage compounds problems.* The number of people using the system on the first day was massively underestimated, and the system could not cope. When people tried to log back in, or correct errors, the user load increased. The more it failed the more it was over-loaded. Both the interest in the program, and the need for it, helped produce its failure (Andrews et al. 1 October 2013). This continued over the next week. The White House claimed that more people visited the site in the first four days than they had expected to sign up in total (Mullaney 6 October 2013). When the insurers tried to use the system to deal with their incomplete data they further overloaded the system (Eilperin et al. 9 October 2013).

m) *Helplines were unhelpful.* All people on the helplines could do was report that the system was overloaded and there was nothing they could do. This did not reduce frustrations (Cunnigham 8 October 2013).

n) *Sabotage and paranoia.* There were later reports that, presumably politically motivated, hackers attacked the website in order to bring it down. Government spokespeople denied these attacks were successful (Isikoff 13 November 2013).

o) *Politics of blame.* The Senate investigation was more interested in allocating blame in a political struggle for informational dominance than in uncovering the problems.

Repeatedly we can see that there was very little slack in the arrangements—everything had to come together with maximal efficiency, in a socially tumultuous environment, for it to work properly. This only occurs rarely, but is often hoped for.

NETWORK DISRUPTION

While it is hard to give useful figures on internet disruption, we can discuss phone disruptions, as the internet makes great use of phone lines and connections, and this gives us some idea of the problems and responses. In October 2011 it was reported that millions of users of the wireless handheld BlackBerry devices, "all over Europe, the Middle East and Africa", who were "served by a RIM data centre in Slough" were cut off. Users were "unable to browse the web . . . [use] instant messages, or access other internet services such as email" (Williams 10 October 2011). For the company, RIM, this coincided with increasing pressure from competitors, failure to meet profit and sales targets, while soon after their product was blamed for helping promote riots in London (ibid; Williams 11 October 2011b). The day after RIM declared the problem fixed, the network crashed again with the same spread (Williams 11 October 2011a). Information was not readily available. RIM "only acknowledged yesterday's crash after millions of users had been without services for several hours and it has made no statement on the cause" (ibid). This is not unreasonable, as the company itself may not have known what was happening, but expresses both the expectation that information will be concealed and the preference people have for some information rather than none; which increases the pressure for information to be issued, whether accurate or not.

The crisis spread, and reports claimed "users in India, Brazil, Chile, and Argentina joined those across Europe, the Middle East and Africa in the blackout". RIM eventually apologised for the 'inconvenience', stating that:

> the 'delays' were 'caused by a core switch failure within RIM's infrastructure. Although the system is designed to failover to a back-up switch, the failover did not function as previously tested. As a result, a large backlog of data was generated and we are now working to clear that backlog and restore normal service as quickly as possible.
>
> (Williams 11 October 2011b)

That the tests had failed to show the problem, emphasises the problems generated by complexity of networks.

The crash also showed the sharp edges of dependency. Lord Alan Sugar, previously a British computer entrepreneur, commented:

> In all my years in IT biz, I have never seen such an outage as experienced by BlackBerry. I can't understand why it's taking so long to fix . . .
>
> All my companies use [BlackBerries], every one so reliant on getting email on the move, people don't know if they are coming or going.
>
> (q. Williams 12 October 2011a)

Many users, including a member of the UK Parliament, used Twitter to announce that they would be getting another kind of internet phone, because their demand for constant contact and information made even a short disruption feel disastrous (Williams 11 October 2011a). Stories appeared of companies losing email contact with the world, and of people missing emails that needed urgent business responses. Later still it was revealed that RIM's "backup system also failed . . . for reasons that remain obscure" (Williams 14 Oct 2011). The article's author resolved the obscurity by claiming the failure resulted from a network upgrade "specifically designed to prevent outages". This claim has verisimilitude because it is a commonly known source of problems. The accuracy of the information and its sources are vague:

> it was initiated after a North American BlackBerry outage in December 2009. Work in Britain was completed only two months ago, sources said. . . .

[At] an unknown point, following the switch failure, the Egham data centre's Oracle database, a bespoke and heavy-duty communications data storage application, was corrupted. This database is effectively the 'brain' of the BlackBerry Internet Service, handling messages and forwarding data to users.

(ibid)

While the outage only lasted three days, it demonstrates the emotional and commercial reaction to short-term disruption. Commentary on the articles also alleged that the quality of BlackBerry phones had declined as extra features were added and, in keeping with the expected paranoia, suggested that the crash was the result of hacking from Apple or related to unrest in the Middle East. One commentator remarked that the internet had been designed to stop failures at specific points from disrupting all communication, however businesses generally preferred centralised distribution, which gave them more control while making their services more vulnerable. Some complained about lack of compensation. Others reported their machines were working during the crash, while others claimed their machines were not working even after the outage was supposedly fixed. Again this demonstrates the complexity of information breakdown, as networks can appear to work partially.

Similar loses are present in other networks. Meng et al. (2007) report a delivery failure rate of 5% for SMS messages with much higher drop outs in high traffic situations. In June 2011 customers of the Sprint mobile phone network complained of "long delays in receiving SMS text messages" lasting hours or even days, texts that "did not arrive at all" or jumbled or incomplete texts (Isaac 7 July 2011). The problems occurred across multiple devices, and the company gave no indication of when the problem would be resolved. In addition to network issues, specific phones and operating systems can generate problems, as was the case when Apple released the mobile operating system iOS 7 in September 2013. Customers complained of iMessages "failing to be sent or received from their iOS devices" (Slivka 2013). The relentlessness of hyper-consumerism and built-in product obsolescence/waste that typifies informationalism and its rapid reiterations of itself makes technological and social disorder inevitable.

COMMUNICATION LOSS

Email is generally reliable, although estimations of loss in the U.S. of email vary from as high as 40% (Langa 2004), through 20% (Return Path 2009) to as low as 0.71–0.91% (Agarwal et al. 2006: 2). Lang (2004) found that his Australian university accounts were not good enough to test email reliability. He also discovered that accounts were wildly variable in their loss rate, with one account losing 65% of its email (Lang 2004). Despite the low average loss rates they report, Agarwal et al. state that:

> [the] authors have themselves experienced and/or are aware of multiple instances of silent email loss recently, including that of a funding proposal and a job recommendation letter email sent to a company, a conference program committee invitation email sent from a company, a decision notification email for a major conference sent to an author in the U.S. from a server in Australia, and possible loss during a recent IMAP server upgrade at a university.
>
> (Agarwal et al. 2006: 2)

Some of this loss may arise from the ways that anti-spam tools, which are supposed to produce order in inboxes, inevitably remove genuine mail.

Generally reliable internet mail software also creates problems and, given the typical absence of information, fantasy and supposition arise. For example, Google's Gmail collapsed badly in December 2006, with much mail being unrestored. At least one report alleged that Google had no backups of the mailboxes (Gottipati 2006). It appears that Google never explained their inability to restore mail and, as usual, most of what can be learnt about the effects of, attitudes to and conflicts around such events comes from reader commentary and speculation, appended to articles. The unreliability of the commentary compounds the confusions.

Some of the commentators on Gottipatti's article argued that as the accounts were free, people should stop whining and not use the service for storing any important records, but, of course people *had* relied on it. If something is generally reliable, then its failure is significantly more disruptive than if its potential for failure is obvious; it is difficult to maintain suspicion of something that generally works. Consequently, the loss can be correspondingly significant. Academics and small business users often use Gmail because its storage capacity and search facilities are far better than those provided by their universities or workplaces, and thus it becomes important where email is a record of business and research. This again is not a marginal group of people.

In the absence of information, some commentators on the Gottipati's article suggested Google did have backups that were wiped and lesser backups reloaded, and that this collapse had probably affected more people than had actually noticed their lost mail, as it would be hard to notice. Given the lack of real, findable information, fantasy fills the gaps and information paranoia suspects the worst case. Others claimed that email deletion was relatively common, not a one off; and indeed the chain of comments on the article lasts for several years, with people freshly reporting lost mailboxes.

In early 2011, Bosker (20 January 2011) reported that: "Twitter is full of complaints from Gmail users who have noted sluggish performance from Google's webmail service. . . . So far, no outages or issues have been noted on Google's App Status Dashboard". The problem was reported more quickly than the service itself announced it. Some of those commenting on the article stated they had not had any problems, while others stated that (for them) Gmail had been slow for weeks to months. Network effects complicate observation as they are not always evenly distributed and are therefore hard to uncover. By the end of February 2011, another crash had occurred with some people losing their accounts. This time Google said it would back up the lost mail from tape (Weintraub 28 February2011a, b). Weintraub estimated the stack of tapes Google would have to keep to do these backups would, if piled on top of each other, be 4 kilometres high, although this drew sceptical responses from his readers (28 February 2011a). Dislocation and disillusion amongst users was noted, with users reported as tweeting remarks such as "I feel like google has betrayed our trust and is trying to pretend that everything is back to normal" and "I do not trust Google with my e-mail anymore" (Lee 1 March 2011), while others complained about not knowing what was happening or the projected time span of repairs. One person is quoted as writing "I really feel completely invalidated by the fact that none of my support emails, like i was advised to send, have been responded to" and another remarks on the distribution of blame: "The 'fail' messages haven't been about technical failures, but have almost all originally implied that we violated terms of service, etc" (Lee 3 March 2011). Often users seemed to be expecting instant explanations, when Google workers may themselves not exactly know what is happening. One problem for Google is that the size of its customer base (apparently unspecified, but supposedly large) means that even a disruption of a small percentage of the total number of accounts becomes significant in terms of protest.

A cursory use of Google's search engine produced internet media reports of other Gmail crashes in August 2008, February 2009 (AP 24 February 2009; Beaumont 24 February 2009), September 2009 (CNN 24 September 2009), October 2009 (Huffington Post 17 October 2009), June 2010 (Huffington Post 29 June 2010), September 2011, November 2011, April 2012 (Kanalley 17 April 2012; BBC 18 April 2012), May 2012 (Zdnet 29 May 2012), December 2012 (Whittaker 10 December 2012; Leach 12 December 2012), April 2013 (Wolf 17 April 17 2013), August 2013 (McAllister 17 August 2013), September 2013 (Aguilar 24 September 2013) and January 2014 (Weis 24 January 2014; Holowka 25 January 2014; Bouc 26 January 2014). These crashes also point to the necessity for ongoing and speedy maintenance. While it is to be hoped that the maintenance staff have the time, the on-the-job experience and incentives to continually improve the program, this is not always the case and it is frequently recognised that maintenance is difficult, especially given staff turnover.

Canfora and Cimitile write that problems in maintaining and comprehending programs are:

> frequently compounded because the maintainer is rarely the author of the code (or a significant period of time has elapsed between development

and maintenance) and a complete, up-to-date documentation is even more rarely available.

(2000: 96)

Bennett and Rajlich also point to inevitable losses of staff and the result-ing degradation of knowledge, writing: "most research has ignored address-ing the staff expertise" (2000: 10). Ahmed adds that maintenance difficulty is increased because it is often outsourced, with multiple contractors, little stability in the workforce that might allow continuation of knowledge and experience, and the production of insignificant or inconsistent documen-tation (2006: 450). Similar complications may arise because the software depends upon 'legacy' systems, either hardware or software, and nobody remaining in the organisation knows how they work or interact with each other. Bennett and Rajlich suggest that cost and urgency (with little slack) also factor.

Changes are often made on the fly, without proper planning, design, impact analysis, and regression testing. Documents may or may not be updated as the code is modified; time and budget pressure often entails that changes made to a program are not documented and this quickly degrades documentation. In addition, repeated changes may demol-ish the original design, thus making future modifications progressively more expensive to carry out.

(ibid: 5–6)

So not only does system architecture and coding tend to degrade over time with the code becoming more and more convoluted and disconnected from any kind of systematic presentation and coherence and thus more prone to breakdown, but information about the program tends to become less and less accurate or useful. The program becomes harder to fix. Change is often rushed and knowledge labour outsourced. This adds to pressures to start the whole process of rewriting the software again. Informationalism only functions at all because people constantly keep tending systems to keep them going, and ease of this maintenance is often undermined by the structures of work, or by financial organisation and managerial pressures. This necessary labour of maintenance and its failure is largely unrecognised and unstudied by the social sciences, despite being vital to life in informationalism.

Political events can also disorder communication. In 2004 Ladar Levi-son set up Lavabit, an encrypted email service, as a response to the U.S. Patriot Act (Mullin 14 August 2013). In August 2013, in the wake of Edward Snowden's revelations about the massive internet surveillance by the National Security Agency, Levison abruptly shut down Lavabit because he could no longer guarantee the 410,000 users' privacy (ibid). Regimes intended to order information, propel innovative counter-orders, which in turn are disordered by further ordering attempts. As Snowden had been a Lavabit user, commentators have speculated that the NSA or FBI had demanded Snowden's account details be handed over. Information paranoia is opened due to lack of information. Levison has been gagged from discussing these issues, but did publicly announce that if he had not terminated Lavabit he would have "become complicit in crimes against the American people" (Hill 9 August 2013). Consequently many users lost their data, although two months later in October 2013 Lavabit briefly reopened to allow users to download their stored communications, in a temporary reordering of a disturbed information-order.

Soon after Lavabit terminated, another well-known internet site that used many anonymous tip offs and commented on issues of internet law, Groklaw, also closed down. Pamela Jones, the site owner, wrote:

> The owner of Lavabit tells us that he's stopped using email and if we knew what he knew, we'd stop too.
>
> There is no way to do Groklaw without email. Therein lies the conundrum . . .
>
> no matter how 'clean' we all are ourselves from the standpoint of the screeners, I don't know how to function in such an atmosphere. I don't know how to do Groklaw like this.
>
> (Groklaw 20 August 2013)

Jones is responding to the gaps in information and assuming the worst. She continues by quoting Janna Malamud Smith's book *Private Matters: In Defense of the Personal Life*:

> The totalitarian state watches everyone, but keeps its own plans secret. Privacy is seen as dangerous because it enhances resistance. Constantly spying and then confronting people with what are often petty transgressions is a way of maintaining social control and unnerving and disempowering opposition. . . .
>
> (ibid)

And concludes:

> Oddly, if everyone . . . leap[t] off the Internet, the world's economy would collapse, I suppose. I can't really hope for that. But for me, the Internet is over.
>
> (ibid)

In keeping with the paranoia, many commentators on an article on *The Guardian* website accused Jones of not really existing, of naivety, of plotting something and of having a deficient business model and using the surveillance story as an excuse to close down (Comments on Arthur 20 August 2013).

The successful and increasing 'digitisation' of social life and political action leads to increasing and conflicting potentialities for disruption, feelings of powerlessness and a sense of surveillance from both commerce and the State. In 2014 Google was being sued by numerous people for auto scanning their emails, ostensibly to target advertisements, but people suspected other uses (Oreskovic 15 April 2014). There is increasing digital paranoia as, in leaving a digital record, whatever you do may be used against you. In the wake of the revelations leaked by Edward Snowden, that the U.S. authorities had been routinely collecting and mining digital records, concerns at the implications for political life and for privacy have been voiced at all levels, including for instance the Chancellor of Germany, Angela Merkel, who herself was subject to digital surveillance. One obvious response, proposed by many engaged in the debate, including Edward Snowden himself, is to shift into encryption (Rusbridger & MacAskill 18 July 2014). However, as key forms of interactivity go 'underground', the benefits of public engagement are lost and the potential for disordered, paranoid, interventions are greatly heightened. This ongoing order/disorder complex intensifies positive feedback loops in the surveillance and escape relationship, with a high likelihood of unexpected and disordering side effects.

CONCLUSION

There is a recurrent sense of software failure, and software project failure, which is backed by figures from the field. The costs of these failures appear to be significant. In a context in which people depend for social life and even survival on ICT, disruption, even of relatively small magnitudes, can appear to menace their daily existence. Maintenance is essential for ongoing functionality but difficult given its informationalist context. As these types of failure and disorder in software and electronic communication have occurred regularly over a 50-year period they are not trivial. They are an ongoing part of the social fabric, and must be considered fundamental to the social processes of informationalism and to result from, and generate, the regular disruptions and disorders of social and work life in that society.

These ICT disruptions are magnified by networking, as even the smallest disruption can, through intensive interconnection, threaten to push the whole system into instability. The next chapter develops this point by looking at the instabilities of networks.

4 Networks, Disorder, Unpredictability

Informationalism is heavily networked, technologically and socially, and this chapter points to the disorders arising from intense networking, where interconnection and unexpected linkages lead to systemic repercussions. The chapter begins by discussing the paradoxes of network governance (or distributed governance), in which the distribution of power through networks apparently reduces centralism but sharpens hierarchy and widens inequality. The order that arises in networks also concentrates power in nodes, hubs and connections, which lead to vulnerability. The connection of different networks may increase instability and unpredictability. These factors undermine any simple assumptions about equitable networked social order.

DISTRIBUTED GOVERNANCE: NETWORKS AND CONFUSION

One of Hardt and Negri's more interesting (although more unfortunately named) ideas is that of 'Empire'. The terminology generates difficulties, as argument about the dynamics of what they call 'Empire' becomes sidetracked by arguments based on the normal meanings of the word. By 'Empire' Hardt and Negri mean that:

> [in] contrast to imperialism, Empire establishes no territorial center of power and does not rely on fixed boundaries or barriers. It is a decentered and deterritorializing apparatus of rule that progressively incorporates the entire global realm within its open, expanding frontiers.
> (Hardt & Negri 2000: xii)

Negri defines Empire as "the transfer of sovereignty of nation-states to a higher entity", but not to a World Nation, or to an existent nation like the U.S. (Negri 2004: 59). More importantly, it is "a network power" (Hardt & Negri 2004: xii), even though one country may have temporary dominance.

They argue that Empire is an artefact of 'information society', dependent on ICT, although they skip the problems of ICT in their analysis. Empire "takes form when language and communication, or really when immaterial labor and cooperation become the dominant force" (2000: 385). What they call 'immaterial labour' is contrasted with the labour of industrial workers and is defined to include communicative labour, the interactive labour of symbolic analysis and problem solving, and the labour in the production and manipulation of affects (ibid: 30). Empire is produced through the ICT-supported networks of governments, corporations, NGOs and others, which stretch beyond any particular country or organisation, and is undoubtedly reinforced through the concomitant intensive globalisation of people, politics and trade, in which everything has the possibility of interacting with everything else through some pathway or another.

As a result, centres of authority and patterns of resistance are harder to localise than they once were. Empire is "a plurality of poles and a flurry of activity constructing assemblages of state and non-state actors, establishing new forms of authority, and determining new norms and practices of regulation and management" (Hardt & Negri 2009: 227). Because of the arguments provoked by the term 'Empire', we use the term 'distributed governance'. In this system, governance is dispersed, diffuse, without relatively clear outlines, boundaries or unchallenged central points. Responsibility is hard to locate, and people tend to shift such responsibility elsewhere.

Distributed governance embraces the idea that unexpected or uncontrolled reactions and consequences are inherent in a networked system of power. Power 'centres' may be nomadic, as cultural activists Critical Art Ensemble (1994: 11ff.) argued some 20 years ago with both their location and sites of resistance resting "in an ambiguous zone without borders". Such ambiguity opens up possibilities for disturbances that, unlike traditional forms of subversion, might resist being co-opted too rapidly. Despite the differences in scale and military power, groups like Al-Qaeda ("the Base", which paradoxically, has no physical base, being constituted entirely of ideological and social nodes) can have significant impacts on how global political antagonisms and conflicts are framed. Thomas Rid emphasises fracturing within this part of the 'multitude' writing that the "global jihadi movement has dismantled and disrupted its own ability to act as one coherent entity" (2010: 47), but "the jihad's new weakness is also its new strength" (ibid: 42). It is not coherent but is still disruptive. However, Fawaz Gerges (2011) while suggesting that Al-Qaeda is relatively weak and largely operationally unsuccessful, argues that it is kept alive as a force in the world's imagination by the actions of its opponents, anti-terrorist organisations and networks that need it to justify their ordering efforts and budgets. The disorder is maintained by attempts at ordering.

Despite the change, older centres and understandings of power may try to reassert their relative dominance, as distributed governance disrupts their sense of sovereignty. Hardt and Negri regret that the U.S.:

> denied and repressed the novelty [of 'distributed governance' or 'Empire'], conjuring up specters from the past, forcing dead figures of

political rule to stumble across the stage and replay outdated dreams of grandeur. . . . It took only a few years, though, for these ghostly figures to collapse in a lifeless heap.

(2009: 203–4)

Contemporary weaponry (or even an ordinary item like an aeroplane) magnifies the difficulty of maintaining control as significant and spectacular attacks can be made by very few people, and it may not be clear precisely who is making the attack: it is easy to destroy, but much harder to preserve gains in terms of dominance or ideology. The U.S.-led wars in Afghanistan and Iraq drifted on, with little resolution, and little to show for the time, death and expense, except to display concretely the difficulty of imposing order, and the dangers of 'blowback' (Johnson 2004, 2008). Power was risked and, in that risking, its threat was disrupted and diminished: "the United States is imperially overstretched: its strategic commitments exceed the resources available to support them" (Layne 2011: 153). Pathways of power were broken and unintended consequences had more effect than intended ones. Such apparent weakness is likely to encourage other forces, like the so-called Islamic state, to take military action and stretch the U.S. even further on multiple fronts. War expenses also affected the U.S.'s capacity to deal with its own economic problems, leading to further disruption.

Clearly "nation states, major corporations, supra-national economics and political institutions, various NGOs, media conglomerates, and a series of other powers" remain (Hardt & Negri 2009: 205). However, the complexity of distributed governance increases with the huge and multiplying number of independent, conflicting actors and different information groups. There were 51 member states in the UN in 1945; there are 193 in 2014 (UN 2104). At least 25 U.S. corporations have revenues greater than the GDPs of UN member states (Trivett 28 June 2011). The Yearbook of International Organizations lists over 67,000 *international* non-profit organisations in 2014 (UIA 2014). These multiplying 'old' style institutions can find themselves unable to shape outcomes in this dispersal of power and independent action, as appears when none of the dominant players were able to achieve their aims at the UN's Copenhagen Climate Change Conference in 2009, unless failure was indeed the aim. Chinese representatives seemed to retreat into theories of conspiracy, or 'information paranoia', when China's expected power block broke up (Marshall 2011: 18). As David Victor argues the climate meetings' strength of involving all UN nations, plus many NGOs, adds to the difficulties of agreement as not only do we have superpower rivalries and histories but "talks are often held hostage to the whims of even small players—as happened in Copenhagen and Cancún [with] Sudan and Bolivia and a few other nations whose emissions of warming pollution are tiny" (Victor 4 April 2011). Indeed the network can become an excuse for doing nothing, as everyone waits for others to act first to avoid being taken advantage of, and blames the actions of others rather than themselves. In this world, minority interests can appear to hijack a state, as with Tea Party Republicans in the U.S., and parties with extremely small numbers of initial votes in Australia who won seats through complex, unexpected and entirely legal distributions of electoral preferences (Green 13 September 2013)

While state integrity is threatened by distribution, states may also find it hard to tax mobile corporations that blur territorial boundaries and distribute their existence. Apple, for example, has been accused of shifting "billions of dollars in profits away from the U.S. and into Ireland, where the maker of iPhones and iPads has negotiated a special corporate tax rate of 2 percent or less" (Guglielmo 21 May 2013). Indeed the initial U.S. Senate report claimed that distribution was so exploited that:

> Apple Operations International [AOI], which from 2009 to 2012 reported net income of $30 billion, but declined to declare any tax residence, filed no corporate income tax return, and paid no corporate income taxes to any national government for five years.
>
> (Levin & McCain 2013: 2)

However AOI's board meetings almost always take place in California, often without the sole Irish director attending, and its assets are managed by an Apple subsidiary "Braeburn Capital, which is located in Nevada. Apple indicated that the assets themselves are held in bank accounts in New York. . . . no AOI bank accounts or management personnel are located in Ireland". AOI has no direct employees (ibid: 22). Information disorder was also exploited as "Apple told the Subcommittee that it is unable to locate the historical records regarding the business purpose for AOI's formation, or the purpose for its incorporating in Ireland" (ibid: 21). The head of the U.S. Senate committee investigating the issue said that "While Apple paid almost $6 billion in taxes last year, the company also shifted $36 billion in taxable earnings away from the U.S. in 2012 and avoided a payment of $9 billion", or a total of $44 billion between 2009–12. Apple claimed that it was likely the largest corporate income tax payer in the U.S. (Guglielmo 21 May 2013).

> Only 21 of the top 100 publicly traded companies [in the U.S.] disclose what they would expect to pay in taxes if they didn't keep profits offshore. All told, these companies would collectively owe over $93 billion in additional federal taxes. [This] represents close to the entire state budget of California and more than the [U.S.] federal government spends on education.
>
> (Smith 2013)

The U.S.-based Citizens for Tax Justice looked at 12 well-known U.S. corporations for the years 2008 to 2010 and concluded: "Had these 12 companies paid the full 35 percent corporate tax, their federal income taxes over the three years would have totaled $61.2 billion. Instead, they enjoyed so many tax subsidies that they paid $63.7 billion less than that" (CTJ 2011). As a group, these companies received a tax subsidy.

This massive tax avoidance leaves States underfunded in their attempts to protect corporate rights and privilege, generate peace (of a sort) and educate their workforce for knowledge work. Few corporations can compete successfully against tax avoiders without also engaging in tax avoidance, and this sets up a 'virtuous' feedback loop that further lessens the income and capacity of States, making the situation worse. It seems probable that if States cannot extract tax from companies they will find them difficult to regulate in other ways as well.

To some extent this confusion in power is not new, as power always involves some degree of distribution. Political scientists discuss the 'balance of power', which implies there is never completely uncontested (or undisrupted) power and that power arises in 'ratios', to use Norbert Elias's term. Elias claims that power ratios "are bi-polar at least, and usually multipolar" (1978: 74–5, 131). Even dictators and absolute monarchs are not completely free to act, being constrained by the activities of others (Elias 1983: 277ff.). Power ratios are an expression of the dynamic patterning of human coaction. Those patterns, which are easily activated, express and enable the established modes of power. What is different in the contemporary world is that many of these power ratios operate, and splinter over almost the whole planet simultaneously, rather than being almost confined to particular areas. It is hard to avoid them completely.

CONNECTIVITY AND DISORDER

That a fulcrum point for control may no longer appear to exist, may help explain the diffusion of feelings of powerlessness evident across all social categories. Even at the height of post-Cold War self-confidence, there was little sense that CEOs, for example, knew what was going on, or felt in control as shown in Garten's (2001) interviews. Holstein begins his book on media management for CEOs by writing: "Chief Executive Officers are losing the battle for how Americans perceive them and the companies they lead" (2008: 1). He gives examples of CEOs being attacked for salaries, bonuses and payouts (even when their companies collapsed owing a great deal of money). Corporations such as Wal-Mart failed to avoid scrutiny over their treatment of women and minorities, and unions won PR battles (ibid: 1–12). The same lack of managerial control seems evident at the World Economic Forum (Lapham 1998). As Pigman (2007: 152) states:

> Crucially the multi-stakeholder model of global governance supported by the World Economic Forum is one of the central forces challenging the notion of markets and firms ruling untrammelled over other social forces and interests.

British conservative MP Rory Stewart describes his experience:

> in our situation we're all powerless. . . . The politicians think journalists have power. The journalists know they don't have any. Then they think the bankers have power. The bankers know they don't have any. None of them have any power. . . . This is the age of the wizard of Oz, you know. In the end you . . . finally meet the wizard—and there's this tiny, frightened figure. I think every prime minister has sort of said this since Blair. You get there and you pull the lever, and nothing happens.
>
> (q. Aitkenhead 4 January 2014)

Even the most powerful can feel hampered, threatened òr in contra-dictory spaces. The crisis in information reaches to the highest levels. No organisation, or person, can act without the possibility of unforeseen conse-quences, unknown connections being activated or contestation being felt. As we have suggested before, in the network of distributed governance, due to the spread of competing factions, resistance and unintended consequences, it is not clear where responsibility lies. Either no one has responsibility, or responsibility is always deniable. There are always other factors involved or appearing to be involved. That there is no unambiguous point of blame furthers the information disorder, and informational paranoia. To quote cultural commentator Kirby Ferguson, conspiracy theories are a "dramatic expression of a uniquely modern anxiety: the sensation that you are trapped within the invisible design of a greater power" (Armitage 31 October 2013). Distributed governance not only renders this feeling common but causes a problem for revolutionaries as the direct adversary can seem to have disap-peared (Negri 2004: 92). All Negri can counsel is withdrawal and "refusal" (ibid: 93). Activist and academic David Graeber writes:

> [I]t was the enemy's very disorganization that was our worst foil . . .
> At the summits, all [the global Elites] did was bicker with one another. What's the radical response to confusion? How on earth were we able to come up with a response to their evil plans if they couldn't even figure out what those were?
>
> (2012: 3)

Networked power may also be more abstracted from specificity, from dimensions of place, class, time and identity. There is no base to strike against, and as such, this kind of power may be profoundly demobilising and disempowering. Rather than simply helping to unite people, or creating a new force for a pluralistic but united counter-power (which, as mentioned earlier, some writers have called the 'multitude'), distributed governance and networking can equally enable fragmentation and ignorance.

At the same time as fragmenting, bringing people into contact through newly arising networks can generate conflict, as despised difference becomes visible. Events that would have been localised and largely unheard of, can be manipulated locally and produce (probably unintended) global political effects. A good example is the way that cartoons of the prophet Mohammed in a small Danish paper became a political resource, used to provoke clashes and provide justification for the intensification of difference all over the world (Klausen 2009). This clash demonstrates the fragility of information. The fact that something is said to be the case by supposedly multiple sources, reinforces its appearance as truth, and reinforces the clashes between parties ready to blame the others, particularly when the information groups (Muslim and non-Muslim) are already pre-disposed to believing what they are told by trusted sources and friction between them already exists; "the cartoons and the protests against them confirmed existing prejudices on both sides" (ibid: 3). Information paranoia is centred in the willingness to believe negative stories about those defined as others. Furthermore if the newspaper had:

> not published the cartoons in the paper's online edition—and kept them there—only regular subscribers would have seen them. And when the crisis reached its zenith six months later the offending pages would have been composted and available only in a few libraries in Denmark.
>
> (ibid: 4)

However, the scandal and conflict did not require people to see the images, just for the actors to be linked to each other, and to people who could use the 'fact' of scandal for a political effect.

Linkage can lead to other unexpected side effects. Adding connections, or generalised integration, can further increase the ease with which disaster spreads and multiplies. Useful and restraining boundaries are destroyed. For example, rather than simply distributing risks so as to lessen them, as the theory of financial derivatives incorrectly suggests, the links can help distribute crisis. Unexpected risk can come from any quarter and spread elsewhere rapidly. People can look for, and use, areas of lowest regulation or containment, thus making a small pocket of risk (or fraud) globally significant, and in the long term destroying market trust and stability. While such behaviour may be hard to find, its effects may spiral outwards and be uncontained. 'Sub-prime', and fraudulent, mortgage deals in the U.S. were not sequestered from the world's financial system due to the globalised trading of complex bundled debt instruments. "The collapse of the subprime mortgage market led to the collapse of one market after another in quick succession because they were all interconnected, the firewalls having been removed by deregulation", and we might add, by networking (Soros 2010: 40). Many people were vulnerable to what could otherwise have seemed like localised corruption.

These hidden but consequential linkages further the likelihood of inaccurate knowledge about the system being distributed through the system, as people seek the most favourable areas for their activities. People can bypass those controls that might dampen and stabilise system behaviour. Another factor generating the U.S. mortgage crisis was that the internet allowed mortgage suppliers to find mortgage appraisers who would give them what appeared to be the profitable sales response and approve bad debts. A petition signed by 10,000 appraisers "charged that lenders were pressuring appraisers to place artificially high prices on properties. According to the petition, lenders were 'blacklisting honest appraisers' and instead assigning business only to appraisers who would hit the desired price targets" (FCIC 2011: 18).

Mortgage suppliers either directly or indirectly could bypass safeguards and scrutiny. This provided the incentive for more reputable appraisers to also decrease levels of scrutiny to keep in business, which pushed standards down further. Trust was bought, and the information provided was what the customers wanted to hear, rather than accurate.

Greater efficiency or speed of connection also increases the risks. Efficiency, by definition, means there is less drag or friction to slow the transmission of effects, whether desired or not. Efficiency, especially cost efficiency, can also mean there is no waste, redundancy or slack to support the system if it starts to disintegrate. Infrastructure systems are built so that the pathways are not much more sufficient than they are expected to be, they are not expensively redundant, and hence are soon on the verge of overload. Everything is always at the limit. This intensifies problems when traffic and speed is always increasing.

All of these factors multiply the possibilities that use of power will trigger rapid unintended effects throughout the system.

NETWORKED HIERARCHY

Distributed governance might seem to point to a lowered distinction in power, perhaps creating horizontalised power structures and producing a new potential for democracy and freedom (Friedman 2005). However, there is no reason to assume all networks are inherently egalitarian and non-hierarchical (Buchanan 2002: 119–24, 130–2). Even if internet networks do produce organisations with low hierarchy, removing hierarchic layers can intensify difference. Paradoxically, the social relations developed can enable more forceful and effective compliance than can deep hierarchic power structures, as these flattened hierarchies can allow less space for the lower levels to conceal their actions from the upper, and intensify their need to report what they think those above them crave to hear. There is less ability to adapt to local circumstances without being exposed.

Empirically, the order of informationalism separates the few from the many, bringing into being a world where, unprecedentedly, (and with some argument over estimates) 1% of the population now owns half the wealth of the planet (UN 2011; Credit Suisse 2013). An Oxfam report states that the richest 85 people in the world own as much as the bottom half of the world's population and the wealth of the upper 1% amounts to $110 trillion, which is 65 times the total wealth of the bottom half (Oxfam 2014: 1–5). Information on the distribution of wealth, especially at the high end, is not clear as is common with information in the information society. The authors of a Credit Suisse report on the world's wealth observed that finding out about high levels of wealth "requires a high degree of ingenuity because at high wealth levels, the usual sources of wealth data—official statistics and sample surveys—become increasingly incomplete and unreliable" (O'Sullivan & Kersley 2012). Despite, or because of, these difficulties, they estimate that in the world 29,300 people are worth at least 100 million U.S. dollars. Of these 2,700 have assets above 500 million U.S. dollars. More than two thirds of the world's adult population have wealth valued at less than 10,000 U.S. dollars (ibid). These divergent effects have increased along with informationalism. In the U.S.:

> Including capital gains, the share of national income going to the richest 1% of Americans has doubled since 1980, from 10% to 20%, roughly where it was a century ago. Even more striking, the share going to the top 0.01%—some 16,000 families with an average income of $24m— has quadrupled, from just over 1% to almost 5%.
>
> (Beddoes 13 October 2012)

Adjusted for inflation, median household income in the U.S. in 2011 was less than in 1996, and the median share of U.S. wealth fell 40% between 2007–10 (Stiglitz 2012: xii). As Robert Reich pointed out:

> In 2005, Bill Gates was worth $46 billion; Warren Buffett $44 billion. By contrast the combined wealth of the bottom 40 percent of the United States population—some 120 million people—was estimated to be around $95 billion.
>
> (2007: 113)

Effectively, 120 million U.S. citizens own about the same as two men. The family of the Wal-Mart founder was probably worth almost as much as Gates and Buffett, at a total of $90 billion (ibid).

In this hierarchy, attempted 'control' is concentrated. A study by Vitali et al. looking at the transactions of 43,000 transnational corporations, suggests:

> nearly 4/10 of the control over the economic value of TNCs [Transnational Corporations] in the world is held, via a complicated web of ownership relations, by a group of 147 TNCs in the core, which has almost full control over itself. The top holders within the core can thus

be thought of as an economic 'super-entity' in the global network of corporations.

(Vitali et al. 2011: 6)

Actually-existing capitalist network society has produced a gross sharpening in global hierarchy. Industrial society saw national publics mobilised, and the State activated to redistribute income and ameliorate the ravages of capital. Informationalism has seen the disaggregation of publics into information groups, and the corporate harnessing of State power to enable a rapid sharpening in class divides, writ large across national borders. Yet the deepening divides create their own crises and disorders, and do not entirely benefit the "one percent". The concentration of global wealth creates new risks, not least in the ability to identify the existence of the 'one percent' who now control most of the globe's wealth (see Chapter 12). There is also the resultant underconsumption, and its corollary, a decades-long upsurge in financialisation, which has radically destabilised global accumulation (see Chapter 9). Simultaneously, new dispossessions generate unprecedented ecological exhaustion, and capitalism still depends on the 'natural systems' it destroys.

A central informational side-effect of growing global inequality is the apparent capture of the political process for global elites, and the resultant severing of meaningful correction processes within national polities. Growing and massive inequality ensures that political and economic priorities are further skewed to imposing even more strongly the order of dominant institutions and their problem-solving techniques. Useful spontaneous or compensatory linkages tend to be repressed, or deliberately put outside, rather than listened to. Informational disorder strips away the capacity of the dominant few to be informed about what is going on, as completely as it does for anyone else. Increasing inequality destroys smooth levels of consumption, any efficiencies in markets and even the capacity for markets to function in a moderately ordered way (Stiglitz 2012: 104ff; Oxfam 2014: 10–22). Extreme inequality furthers the effective separation of networks, prevents talented outsiders ascending to the upper ranks and lessens the chance of people outside those ranks getting a good education as inequality increases "the benefits to affluent parents of reducing the chances of the competitors of their children" (Osberg 2014). As Pareto argued (1901/1968), in such a case, society faces becoming bound to dead ideas and practices championed by a small and restricted elite. Extreme hierarchies and small elites subvert the virtuous flexibility claimed for networks.

SMALL ELITES

The 'small world' thesis, in which almost everyone is connected to everyone else through a relatively small number of links, is relatively well known. However these small worlds are not necessarily linked to 'larger worlds' as strongly as they are linked to each other (Watts 2003). They may form separated clusters with weak and rarely used links. Network vulnerabilities may therefore arise because of the relatively small numbers of well-connected people who sit on corporate boards in the Western world. Davis et al. (2003) argue that the corporate elite constitute a small world, and that this is an "endemic property of social and other networks" (2003: 303). While elite firms and directors and the ties between them are subject to significant change over time, the hierarchy remains fixed (ibid: 315). In the U.S.:

> [l]ess than one-third of the largest firms in 1999 were among the largest in 1982, and less than 5% of the directorships were constant across this time. Moreover, less than 2% of the ties among firms that were created by particular shared directors in 1999 could be traced back to the beginning of the 1980s. Yet in spite of the rampant turnover among boards and directors, and nearly complete turnover in ties, distances among the corporate elite remained virtually constant.
>
> (ibid: 321)

This indicates that class membership is variable (perhaps even precarious), but the 'structural' presence of the class is not. Similar connections are likely between high-level executives of other types. More significantly, these high-level executives and directors choose each other and tend to form a relatively closed 'club' at any one moment, however the members may change. They may restrict competition and 'new blood', even if unconsciously. They tend to "end up being disproportionately represented in policy organizations, in the governance of non-profits, and in government service. They become, in a sense, the political vanguard of the corporate community" (Davis et al. 2003: 308).

This closeness helps appropriation. Around 2005 a group of Silicon Valley elites, top executives from three companies, successfully rearranged the info-order of tens of thousands of their employees by making clandestine "gentlemen's agreements" to artificially lower wages by "sharing salary data" and not recruit each other's workers. Apple, Google and Pixar led the way, later "bullying" Adobe, Intel and Intuit into joining what has been called a "wage-theft pact" (Ames 23 January 2014). Months before formalising the new arrangement Apple CEO Steve Jobs had warned Google co-founder Sergey Brin that if Brin hired "a single one" of Apple's Safari team "that means war". Aware of information's propensity to escape boundaries, Google CEO Eric Schmidt "instructed his Sr VP for Business Operation Shona Brown to keep the pact a secret and only share information 'verbally, since I don't want to create a paper trail over which we can be sued later'". This "secret and illegal pact" helped to keep the wages of information workers relatively low while pushing up stock prices, executive salaries and bonuses. Possibly it also contributed to the 'incestuous' relationships characterising the boards of directors of these companies, epitomised by Eric

Schmidt serving on Apple's board until 2009 when Department of Justice (DoJ) anti-trust investigation "pushed him to resign". A 2010 DoJ investigation exposed the larger new order, triggering a class action suit against what court documents called "an overarching conspiracy", thereby propelling a new cycle of disorder/order (ibid).

While this ability to conspire with, and reinforce one another, gives these groups strength, even if their positions are temporary, it also leads to vulnerabilities. The smallness of elite networks means that 'the rulers' are easily traced by websites such as 'They Rule' (www.theyrule.net), created by software artist Josh On in 2001. They Rule is a network visualisation software program that uses publicly available data about the membership of the boards of "some of the most powerful U.S. Companies", noting that some people sit on the boards of "5, 6 or 7 of the top 1000 companies". In 2011 They Rule joined forces with LittleSis.org (http://littlesis.org), "a free database of who-knows-who at the heights of business and government" maintained by a "community of obsessive data miners" who have formed a "grassroots watchdog network connecting the dots between the world's most powerful people and organizations". As of June 2014 the LittleSis database had over 2,185,025 citations and 725,012 relationships, ranging from corporate lobbyists and think tanks to politicians and business leaders. Open source cultural projects such as They Rule and LittleSis exemplify the possible power of what we might call 'slow networks,' or even 'swarms' where spatially dispersed human nodes (casual users/activist/researchers) with weak ties casually add content and analysis. Over time this data aggregates into a comprehensive knowledge base for counter-hierarchy.

Other vulnerabilities for a close-knit elite are self-evident; with such a tightly defined class, contagion can relatively easily take hold, up-turning the prevailing order: "it is literally true that an especially contagious airborne virus would spread quite rapidly through the corporate elite" (Davis et al. 2003: 322). Furthermore, the short distances, and close ties in similar conditions, may decrease the elites' ability to innovate, think independently or for their companies to have the varied structures and workings suitable for different environments. They will tend to make procedures, practices and ideas consistent, rather than varied and adaptive (to help their movement from one place to another), and most of their solution sets will come from others in their small world, who they know or wish to emulate. Information available to such boards is likely to be very restricted and uniform. Bad ideas or 'fads' can take hold, spread quickly and overwhelm perceptions of reality. There is no ordering salvation in, or for, the elites.

LINKAGES LEAD TO VULNERABILITY

Clearly, hierarchies are entrenched and institutionalised in the network. One relatively obvious fact of networks is that as they grow, some hubs become better connected than other hubs. The best-connected hubs then tend to accumulate even more connections. There is currently, in terms of size, only one Google, one Facebook, one Amazon, one YouTube. These dynamics entrench relations of power and success.

> The expansion of the network means that the early nodes have more time than the latecomers to acquire links. Thus growth offers a clear advantage to the senior nodes, making them the richest in links. . . . Because new nodes prefer to link to the more connected nodes, early nodes with more links will be selected more often and will grow faster than their younger and less connected peers.
>
> (Barabasi 2002: 87–8)

BOX 7   HUBS, CABLES, SURVEILLANCE

One vulnerability that arises from the tendency of networks to gain hubs and marked pathways is that because most internet traffic goes through marked routes (usually marked by physical cables under the oceans), it becomes relatively easy to attempt total surveillance. Thus it can be alleged that information revealed by Edward Snowden has shown that the British Government Communications Headquarters is:

> collecting all data transmitted to and from the United Kingdom and Northern Europe via the SEA-ME-WE-3 cable that runs from Japan, via Singapore, Djibouti, Suez and the Straits of Gibraltar to Northern Germany.
>
> (Doring 29 August 2013)

As Australia connects to SEA-ME-WE-3 through a link from Singapore to Perth, it seems logical to assume that the interception gathers a fair amount of Australia's telecommunications and internet traffic with Europe (ibid).

It is also possible that 95% "of long distance international telecommunications traffic" is carried by these channels. This concentration arises because of the concentration of ownership. The international consortium owning the cable includes British Telecom, SingTel Optus, Telstra and "other telecommunications companies across Asia, the Middle East and Europe" (ibid).

The leaks by Snowden apparently allege that British Telecom, and Vodafone, "are passing on details of their customers' phone calls, email messages and Facebook entries" to the spy agency (Ball et al. 3 August 2013). Later leaks suggest that the NSA and its partners only need to tap the lines at 20 points in the world "to 'trace anyone, anywhere, anytime' in what is described as 'the golden age' [of] signals intelligence". The tapping also involves the governments of Singapore and South Korea and the use of strategically placed military bases in the Middle East (Dorling 24 November 2013).

Confirming some of these suspicions, and motivated by the "significant public debate about the transparency, proportionality and legitimacy" of "widespread government surveillance and data 'harvesting'" that Snowden's allegations had triggered, Vodafone published their "inaugural" 'Law Enforcement Disclosure Report' in June 2014 (Vodafone 2014: 61). This 20-page document provided a "country-by-country analysis of law enforcement demands received based on data gathered from local licensed communications operators", an endeavour that had "not been without risk" presumably to the corporation's ability to be allowed to continue its business in certain territories as laws governing such "disclosure" are sometimes "unclear" or prohibitive (ibid: 61–2). The corporation acknowledged the "potential for confusion" when individual operators rather than governments take responsibility for providing transparency in data surveillance practices, citing recent "law enforcement disclosure reports" published by German and Australian operators that were not always "comparable" to Vodafone's aggregated statistics due to methodological and local political factors. Secrecy had been paramount, both between the operators and its customers, and even within the organisation, creating further informational disorder, and perhaps even increasing workplace stress:

> There are wide-ranging legal restrictions prohibiting disclosure of any aspect of the technical and operating systems and processes used when complying with agency and authority demands. In some countries, it is unlawful even to reveal that such systems and processes exist at all . . . Vodafone employees familiar with the systems and processes involved are prohibited from discussing details of these with line management or other colleagues.
>
> (ibid: 65)

Networks and the confluence of corporate and government action help justify, or unwittingly create, more information paranoia.

Because so much traffic goes through the big hubs, when one breaks down it can have widespread ill effects, pushing traffic onto other hubs that may already have heavy traffic, and thus be prone to collapse if more traffic arrives, compounding the effect. If networks are well meshed, and there is no slack, then when collapse occurs it tends to occur catastrophically. As a result, we may hypothesise that big organisations (when tightly networked internally with little slack and well connected to the system), may suffer worse effects than organisations that are less integrated and efficient. They also transmit the disruptions to those others who are connected to them. Their size also means that they are obvious points of attack, and vulnerable to attacks from many directions. "It has been long known that many networks show resilience to random node removal, but are fragile to the removal of the hubs" (Onnela et al. 2007: 7336). Networks can also collapse "after a phase transition" if the much rarer ties that connect areas of high interconnection are removed (ibid: 7336). Given that in commercial hubs the amount of traffic can determine profitability, then in addition to the 'natural' tendency of visible hubs to attract connections, there may be further conscious attempts to consolidate a hub's position, and to prevent other hubs and pathways becoming established to challenge that profit, further rendering the whole system vulnerable.

If there is an attack, or spreadable cause of collapse, then:

> Because each hub is linked to a very large number of other [nodes], it has a high chance of being [re-]infected by one of them. Once infected, a hub can pass on the virus to all the other [nodes] it is linked to. Thus highly linked hubs offer a unique means by which viruses persist and spread.
>
> (Barabasi 2002: 135)

When originally separate networks come together more problems arise. Singh and Sprintson (2010) point to problems with electricity with the integration of generators, transmission lines, power electronics, computing and communication. Such networks have many sources of failure: failure in components, software, networks and human mistakes:

> However, the contemporary power system reliability literature is focused almost entirely on the failure of physical system components, i.e., the current carrying part. There have been a few publications in power systems attempting reliability analysis of cyber-physical systems.
>
> (ibid: 1)

Thus in a multiply connected system such as this, a failure of computerised control of power distribution, or failure of communication between computers, can lead to a failure of power distribution, which can then affect components elsewhere, in a cascade. While each system might be robust, when connected together they may become vulnerable. Buldyrev et al. (2010: 1025) point out that networks are becoming increasingly dependent on one another:

> infrastructures such as water supply, transportation, fuel and power stations are coupled together . . . owing to this coupling, interdependent networks are extremely sensitive to random failure, such that a random

removal of a small fraction of nodes from one network can produce an iterative cascade of failures in several interdependent networks.

Combining distributed governance with the disordering effects of complex computer networks points to further possibilities for destabilisation and self-generated disorder. Computer and risks researcher Peter Neumann writes:

> Distributed control of distributed systems with distributed sensors and distributed actuators is typically more vulnerable to widespread outages and other perverse failure modes such as deadlocks and other unrecognized hidden interdependencies (particularly among components that are untrustworthy and perhaps even hidden), race conditions and other timing quirks, coordinated denial-of-service attacks, and so on. Achieving reliability, fault tolerance, system survivability, security, and integrity in the face of adversities in highly distributed systems is problematic.
>
> (2007: 112)

BOX 8   STUXNET WORM: THE SPREAD OF NETWORKS AND CYBERWARFARE

The Stuxnet worm (a self-replicating computer virus transmitted via the internet) is an exemplar of the instability and vulnerability in networks. Gross (2011) writes that the worm was searching the world for programmable-logic controllers, which are small computers that:

> regulate the machinery in factories, power plants, and construction and engineering projects. . . . [They] perform the critical scut work of modern life. They open and shut valves in water pipes, speed and slow the spinning of uranium centrifuges, mete out the dollop of cream in each Oreo cookie, and time the change of traffic lights from red to green.

The worm used the network to spread and to hide and endanger common operations. It appeared to be aimed at Iran's nuclear programme. An article in the *New York Times* (Broad et al. 15 January 2011) alleged that the virus "appears to have wiped out roughly a fifth of Iran's nuclear centrifuges and helped delay, though not destroy, Tehran's ability to make its first nuclear arms". One part of the code sent centrifuges spinning out of control, the other played normal signals back to the people observing the controls.

Ralph Langer, a German security expert who decoded Stuxnet, saw it as a new form of industrial warfare, and one to which companies in the U.S. were vulnerable, as they use similar computers and software to control all kinds of processes (Broad et al. 2011). Because of networks and interconnection, the weapon cannot be localised to specific targets. Richard Falkenrath, former Deputy Homeland Security Adviser to President George W. Bush, also points to the unpredictable consequences of the attack, as many untargeted computers across the world were affected:

> This kind of collateral damage to the global civilian realm is going to be the norm, not the exception, and advanced economies, which are more dependent on advanced information systems, will be at particular risk.
>
> (Falkenrath 26 January 2011).

He also implies that the worm defines "the shape of what will likely become the next global arms race". While cyberwar cannot be contained, the spread of consequences is magnified when the attacker knows they cannot be identified and may face no retribution. Retaliation will be based upon suspicion, and that can be manipulated. Knowledge of the worm's development is vague, but suspicions, or information paranoia, flourish. It is possible Stuxnet may have been a co-project with the U.S., as the U.S. national intelligence knew of "well hidden" holes in programs sold to Iran by the German company Siemens, which were exploited by the worm. However, "[m]any cyberwarfare and intelligence experts, such as Sandro Gaycken of the Free University of Berlin, say [that the signatures used to identify Israel in Stuxnet] are so obvious that they could well be 'false flags', planted to mislead investigators and complicate attribution" (Gross 2011). Joseph adds "The cyber-world where Stuxnet lives is so murky, so hard to know the truth about, that some experts still question certain elements of the public story". Iran could even have used the discovery of the worm for its own disinformation program. Some commentators alleged that the worm was badly designed and infected too many hosts for a targeted attack, as this increased the chance of its detection (Leyden 19 January 2011b) while others disagree (Gross 2011).

Despite this inevitable uncertainty, rather than suggesting more caution, Falkenrath argues that Congress should grant the U.S. president broad authority to wage offensive information warfare, presumably using murky intelligence. He further points out that Siemens gave the U.S. the information to help the U.S. ward off cyber-attacks, not make them, and asks "Will Siemens and other companies think twice next time the American government calls?" Such warfare may split companies into camps supporting some governments and supporting attacks on other governments. So the unity of the net can produce splits of interest as people attempt to protect themselves by separation.

British computer scientists have announced that: "It is unlikely that there will ever be a true cyberwar". They think it is more likely that online war will be conducted alongside offline war, but they also point to disordering network effects. "The effects of cyber attacks are difficult to predict—on the one hand they may be less powerful than hoped but may also have more extensive outcomes arising from the interconnectedness of systems, resulting in unwanted damage to perpetrators and their allies" (Sommer & Brown 2011: 6). However, they claim that there are substantial risks of local disruption and loss resulting from attacks on computer and telecommunications services. As well, "reliable Internet and other computer facilities are essential in recovering from . . . large-scale disasters" (ibid: 5).

> Catastrophic single cyber-related events could include: successful attack on one of the underlying technical protocols upon which the Internet depends, such as the Border Gateway Protocol which determines routing between Internet Service Providers and a very large-scale solar flare which physically destroys key communications components such as satellites, cellular base stations and switches.

In other words disasters easily compound with linkage.

As only a few corporations make most of the software and computers in use, systemic vulnerability is increased "through a monoculture effect". Networks can lower variability, and concentrate power. Vulnerability is further increased because "[n]etwork effects in information markets create a first-mover advantage that encourages suppliers to rush to market rather than spend time fully testing the security of new products" (Sommer & Brown 2011: 48). As capitalist informationalism encourages hurriedly written and probably faulty software for sales advantage, the whole system is at risk.

CONCLUSION

Networks confuse the location of power, and complexify the use of power through distribution. They help mobile people and organisations to avoid responsibility and taxation. They weaken the representative potential of States, and the ability of States to attempt to perform useful functions for most people. Networks open the possibility for disruptions, and bad information, to be speedily spread through the system. It becomes harder to wall off parts of the system, thus protecting them from fraud or lack of correct maintenance. Network effects lead to extreme concentrations of power, of wealth, of connectivity and so on, which lead to systemic vulnerabilities. If major hubs, or concentrations of elites, suffer disruption, then the whole system risks disruption. Distribution can lead people to feel that everything is unpredictable and out of control. No matter where they are in the social system it feels like they are vulnerable. Networks may be many things but they do not necessarily add stability or adaptability in themselves, and network instability may be accentuated when the networks depend upon unstable computer networks and software, and interact in unexpected ways with other networks.

Having established that software is unstable and hard to implement properly, and that networks are not always adaptive, efficient or democratic in nature, we move on to consider the disorders of information.

5 Disorders of Information

A central claim of information society theory is that the economy has shifted from being centred on the industrial production of 'things' to the production and manipulation of symbols, information and culture. Additionally, the idea of the 'information society' evokes ideas of the 'knowledge society', which implies a growing rate of accurate knowledge. Politicians and international organisations pronounce the importance of "this knowledge-driven economy", claiming that: "Knowledge and the ability to innovate . . . are the raw materials of this revolution" (Blair 1999). An OECD 'Global Forum on the Knowledge Economy' was established in 2011 by four Committees of the OECD Directorate for Science, Technology and Industry (OECD 2012). In business, discussion of 'information management', 'information science', 'knowledge management', 'knowledge ecologies', 'knowledge brokers' and 'working smarter not harder' is common.

'Knowledge industries' have been discussed since Fritz Machlup (1962) stressed the importance of Research and Development, education and information services in the 'new economy', arguing that "all information in the ordinary sense of the word is knowledge, though not all knowledge may be called information" (1962: 15). Economists Linde and Stock write that 'knowledge society' and 'information society' are "viewed as more or less quasi-synonymous" (2011: 3). Many formulations about the 'new society' explicitly echo this idea:

> What has now become decisive for society is the new centrality of theoretical knowledge, the primacy of theory over empiricism, and the codification of knowledge into abstract systems of symbols.
>
> (Bell 1971: 4–5)

We have already mentioned Castells's idea of the 'virtuous circle'. He also writes:

> What is specific to the informational mode of development is the action of knowledge on knowledge. . . . [there is] a virtuous circle of interaction between the knowledge sources of technology and the application

of technology to improve knowledge generation and information processing . . .

[I]nformationalism is oriented towards technological development,
that is to the accumulation of knowledge and towards higher levels of
complexity in information processing . . . [T]he pursuit of knowledge
and information . . . characterises the technological production function
under informationalism.

(Castells 2000a: 17)

Elsewhere Castells argues that industrialism failed because it "could not
manage the transition to *knowledge-based productivity growth* by using
the potential unleashed by information and communication technologies"
(2004: 15; emphasis added). The basic work of informationalism is when
workers "find the relevant information, recombine it into knowledge, using
the available knowledge stock, and apply it in the form of tasks oriented
towards the goals of the process" (ibid: 26). The "key factor for productivity growth in this knowledge-intensive, networked economy is innovation"
(ibid: 29). Linde and Stock write:

The knowledge society is concerned with all kinds of knowledge, but scientific and technical knowledge reaches a particular significance . . . as
production is heavily driven by scientific-technological results . . . and
the population's opportunities in life are dependent upon the levels of
science and technology reached by society.

(2011: 82)

Contrary to this reassuring order of 'real knowledge' the category of 'information' is itself not an ordered, easily definable analytic category (Floridi 2010,
2011; Levy 2008) and this is important for analysis. Information, as category,
encompasses many different things with very different applications and effects.
The term not only has a specialised meaning in mathematics (Shannon &
Weaver 1949), but is also applied to: instructions, data about anything, music,
films, pictures, diagrams, scientific theories and research, software models,
financial projections, product design specifications, misunderstandings, public relations spin, deceit, propaganda, sports trivia, random combinations of
letters and so on; many of which may have nothing to do with 'accuracy' or
'knowledge' in its normally understood sense. In informationalism these different types of information are made to be equivalent in two ways; first by being
transmuted into digital format, and second by being valued according to how
much people or organisations are prepared to pay for them. This latter move
turns information into a 'product' or 'commodity' that is valued by commercial 'appeal' or strategic effect, with wide-ranging consequences.

Treating 'information' as unproblematic, or implying it is based in
'knowledge', and ignoring the instabilities in its meaning, relegates disorders

into background noise, dissolves disruptive variety into singularity and fore-grounds ordering effects to produce a narrative of unending social progress and knowledgeable adaptability. However, the problems inherent to the cat-egory of 'information', in the production of data smog, in the process of communication itself, in the construction of information as commodity, in the connection between information and power relations and in the dynam-ics between information groups, are vital to understanding social processes. These disordering processes are intensified by capitalism, and further the distribution and production of 'inaccurate' information, at all levels. Conse-quently, we are not sanguine about the ability of informationalism to knowl-edgably solve, or adapt to, its own problems within the current ordering of its problem field.

These next two chapters develop these themes, shedding light on the case studies that follow. As usual, our aim is to derive some components for a theory of informationalism that forces disorder into the foreground as both vital to the system's functioning *and* to the system's crises. Our basic supposition is that knowledge, information and computing do not easily explain the form of society, as they are also formed by society in a complex self-disruptive system.

INTERPRETING INFORMATIONALISM: A TWO-PART SCHEMA

Our first challenge is to characterise the disorders that are embedded in information and communication themselves, and analyse the resulting dynamics in 'information society'. The second task is to demonstrate how these disorders are intensified and played out in the context of capitalist social relations. This broad two-part schema is conceptualised by staying with the order/disorder complex and emphasising a series of mutually rein-forcing 'informational disorder tendencies', and recognising that both the categories of capitalism and communication blur. We begin, in this chapter, with the unavoidable ambiguities of information as a social relation, and the ways that humans attempt to contain, generate and exploit those ambi-guities. At this level, the tendencies may be considered to be generic as they reflect the ways in which information is defined, mobilised and distorted through social communication. In Chapter 6 we examine, more specifically, the ways that capitalism and the commodification of information intensi-fies these 'paradoxes' and confusions while creating new ones. Elsewhere we examine how information disorder grows out of and affects the 'com-puterisation' of society. Through the case studies we explore how sites of digitisation, networking and computerisation are sites of disorder, disrup-tion, repeated failure and contestation, not sites of integration, harmony or resolution.

'INFORMATION' AS SOCIAL PROCESS

Information is tied to communication. Anything that *may* be communicated is information. In this formulation accuracy is not primary. While types of knowledge may exist that cannot be communicated via symbols, and this may further disorder informationalism, we are simplifying. As information and communication are joined, the first and most important feature of this order/disorder complex is that orders of communication and information are always entangled with interpretation, misunderstanding, strategy and noise, and always occur in a social context involving persuasion, building or severing relationships and building relative power or status.

Order/Disorder

Since Shannon's classic article "A Mathematical Theory of Communication" (in Shannon & Weaver 1949), meaning has been associated with disorder and a degree of unpredictability. A message that is entirely predictable, so that interpreters know exactly what comes next, can contain little information. In a technical (although not always in a practical) sense, the more unpredictable a message the more information it contains. The distinction between practical and technical arises because strings such as "apriyhiuw fhgpov anetoins" potentially have a lot of unpredictable order and hence information in this sense. To transmit, or receive, a long chain like this correctly might be quite difficult. However, it may not mean anything; exact interpretation may be impossible. Furthermore, in any transmission of a message, error, noise or disorder may creep in. If the message is predictable to a degree (has 'redundancy' to use the technical term) then it is often possible to correct the error, as we usually do with misprints. If the message has such a high level of information, and low level of redundancy that it is impossible to predict what follows, and thus to detect error, high levels of inaccuracy in transmission and reception could be expected. On the other hand, a message that appears to be easily resolvable may have slight but important variations that are removed during an error correction process that only perceives the expected order and ignores the disorder. Consequently, all communication results from an interplay between ordering and disordering factors that risk upsetting each other. There is a permanent tension between intention, expectation, transmission, interpretation, response and the way these factors feed into ongoing communicative events.

Interpretation

Added to this particular interplay of order and disorder, meaning in communication and information is unstable, subject to accident and varied interpretation (Derrida 1973, 1988; Steiner 1975; Ellis 1993). As information only becomes information within a social context, it is immediately contingent;

founded on the nature of that context, the conflicts between intention and interpretation, the flexibility of categories, the interpretive framings brought to it, the previous histories of argument and (mis)understanding, power relations, group differentiation and so on. Information is not simply transmitted from one mind to another (with or without error); it is entangled with politics, hierarchy, persuasion, relationships, misunderstanding, lying, obfuscation and establishing and protecting group boundaries, from the beginning. To approach relatively accurate communication and mutual understanding takes considerable work, awareness of failure and good intentions over time (Dervin & Foreman-Wernet 2003). Most communication is probably 'good enough' for mutual action, rather than completely accurate, but always has the possibility of accumulating divergences. While the information and its excess produce further information and effects, they are not necessarily those intended by the original source.

Framing

Messages arrive in a context of other messages, and within a history of messages, alliances, oppositions and actions, and this affects their interpretation. A more general way of expressing this is to claim that meaning depends on the framing or context that people bring to messages, whether making or interpreting them (Bateson 1972: 184–92; Snow & Benford 1988; Tannen 1993; Mclachlan & Reid 1994; Marshall 2007: 18ff.; Lakoff 2010). Different framings change the meanings and implications of the messages. Thus even a simple, apparently irreducible, statement like '1 + 1 = 2' can have different consequences and implications if it is emitted in a basic lesson in arithmetic or a lesson in language. It may be used as a casual statement of basically assumed truth, something to puzzle over in mathematics or philosophy, a piece of rote learning, a mystical mode of enlightenment, or even something to be shown to be differently represented in binary where 1 + 1 = 10. Self-referentially, framing and context is also information so the perception and interpretation of information is structured by other information. Messages may themselves affect the framing, as their information provides further framing for interpretation. As a result, framings can be unstable; embedded within the sociopolitical process, as when different groups compete over the framings allowed, or brought into play, or seem unaware of differences in the framings they bring to dialogue. People also frame, interpret, judge or assimilate new information by what they already 'know', through the models they have of the world and through loyalties. Thus a person who trusts science might tend to dismiss those who criticise the global warming thesis, even if they themselves do not understand the science. As such, the perception and interpretation of information is itself structured by other information and by group allegiance. Politically, framing processes act as group attempts to understand the problems under discussion, justify their own actions and to render other actions invalid.

Information Groups

A major part of framing involves putting other people into social categories, as this influences the ways their messages/information are understood, or even ignored. Thus, for example, 'extreme' Republicans in the U.S. may dismiss anything said by a Democrat as false or underhand, and call those Republicans who do attempt to engage in dialogue 'Republicans in Name Only' to try and enforce the boundaries of information group categories, and frame any divergence from their own views as coming from a non-trustable information out-group. Information acts to indicate and maintain group membership and define a group's opponents. Placing people into groups (either trustable or not), or treating them as types, is part of the way that 'information groups', their framings and their differences, are constructed.

Information becomes more persuasive depending on its source and whether that source is placed in a group that is valued or not (Turner et al. 1987: 27–8, 155, 160; van Knippenberg et al. 1994; Haslam et al. 1996; Hopkins & Reicher 1997). New or challenging information is often rejected, especially if it comes from a person or organisation categorised as unreliable, immoral, politically suspect or wedded to an unacceptable solution to problems. Political valuations of the source frame perceptions of information quality. Information flows are used politically to sustain group identity or a sense of group community, and sharpen disconnection with other groups, emphasising differences even if there is much in common. Information groups often polarise, or move away from, positions identified with opposing groups (Sunstein 2009). On the other hand, information (or the suppression of information) may also be used to persuade different information groups that they are indeed allied with other groups, in opposition to still other groups, when they may have relatively little in common. The apparently successful alliance between libertarian capitalists and authoritarian Christians in the U.S. Republican Party is an example of such a move.

Such information groups are imagined communities bound together by apparently shared sets of framings, shared sets of 'exemplars' of membership, shared sets of valued sources of information and common modes of categorising self and others such that it is relatively clear who is *not* a member of the grouping. We reiterate the 'shared *sets*' to emphasise that people do not have to share all items in the sets, just some. Information groups act as a way of filtering excess data smog and discrediting information from other groups; as a result they operate as informal but bounded political formations. Group membership and/or rejection will affect a person's sense of who they are, as well as how others place them.

Powerful and populous information groups can be completely invisible to members of other information groups, as appears apparent in David Freedlander's article (19 October 2013) about right-wing radio host Mark Levin, where the main point of the argument is that the reader (in Freelander's information group) will not have heard of Levin who has a regular audience of seven million in the U.S. Fear may be implied by the article. Opposed information groups rarely interact. This closure furthers other political uses. In a Senate report on the lobbyist Jack Abramoff (Committee on Indian Affairs 2006), it was revealed that Abramoff had persuaded the owners of a casino in Louisiana they were threatened by a casino that might be opened across the border in Texas. For a sizable sum, he offered to mobilise opposition amongst Christians in Texas. His associate Michael Scanlon produced a document in which he wrote:

> We plan to use three forms of communications to mobilize and win these battles. Phones, mail and Christian radio. . . . Our mission is to get specifically selected groups of individuals to the polls to speak out AGAINST something.

It is apparently easy to raise negativity, but:

> Simply put we want to bring out the wackos to vote against something and make sure the rest of the public lets the whole thing slip past them.

Information groups were both considered powerful and unlikely to leak information to other groups. The lobbyists actually defrauded the organisation they were working for, knowing that they would not communicate with other information groups either, but they did set up fake 'grassroots' organisations (Committee on Indian Affairs 2006: 249–51). In a similar case they used Ralph Reed, the former executive director of the Christian Coalition, who boasted that he had "on file over 3,000 pastors and 90,000 religious conservative households [in] Alabama that can be accessed in this effort" (ibid: 24. See also pp. 144–6). In this case political views of information groups, and their disjunction from other information groups, are being manipulated for monetary gain, so capitalism plays some part in fostering such groups.

As we shall argue later information groups often share limited sets of sources, thus limiting the information they perceive or discuss, and magnifying the sense of truth of their models of reality. Information groups are not necessarily internally harmonious; they will argue over a range of ideas, however this range of ideas will be limited, with unusual variation leading to the 'paranoid' suspicion that the emitter of such ideas must not be a true member of the group. Hostility between different groups also limits what can be discussed internally, and what information is considered valuable.

Models as Frames

Models, by their nature, simplify reality and hence diverge from it, and, being applied, distort it. Models are essential to planning (and perhaps for any explicit human understanding), but are themselves social: they arise and spread through power relations, structures of communication and previous knowledges, rather than solely by their supposed usefulness or accuracy.

Problems with models can intensify and widen into systemic disjunctures once they are incorporated into software that organises what people can do, or defines how reality should behave, when reality and people behave differently. Software models are usually hard to challenge as they are based on preconceived socially placed orders (usually of those in authority), and are often invisible to those they affect. Models in software can place people into categories to predict their behaviour, frame their behaviour and direct or frame behaviour towards them (whether beneficial or otherwise). This procedure Henman calls 'targeting' (Henman 2004). While some targeting is used for marketing, the kind of targeting Henman discusses tries to pre-empt, or predict, behaviour (such as cheating or terrorism) by supposedly violent or suspicious outgroups in society, and therefore has a built in tendency for paranoid projection that tends to increase the hostility and separation between groups and produce further miscommunication. The disorder created then justifies the ordering system. It also restricts the actions of workers on the ground. Whether intended or not, computer programs can concretise policy with unintended effects, and the programs become political players themselves (Henman 1997). With such built in categorisation, people can be excluded from some social benefits or participation, and hierarchy can be hardened through strict definitions of access and denial. The insurance industry relies on such targeting categories, as do credit providers, producing data-based structural exclusion on a grand scale (Gill 1995). Once categorised, a person's life can be indelibly influenced, and it may be exceedingly difficult for them to uncover their category status, or alter it. It may be hard to alter the models without significant reprogramming, so the models enshrined in software may continue their disruptive effects even if the model is 'consciously' abandoned in the wider society. This is especially likely if the model affirms social hierarchy, or its perceived interests. Imposing a model through software can be a form of social violence as well as a creator of disorder through ordering.

On the other hand, when IT systems add complexity and connection they can disorder those standard models of organising that depend upon simplification and boundaries (Kallinikos 2005; see also Chapter 8). For example, IT can have effects on the private/public boundaries that operate to restrict information flow, to allocate property, and determine the difference between the intimate and the commercial, the domestic and the political. This boundary has become part of the way that property, power and space have functioned under capitalism. However, divisions between public and private realms are permanently contested. Shifts in this information flow change what can be kept private, and change the ways people are perceived by others (Meyrowitz 1985). Nowadays people leave permanent data trails that are publicly available, so that in theory an occasional expression of the 'wrong idea' or 'wrong behaviour' could lead to permanent exclusion from higher-grade employment, as employers check up those trails, just as careless remarks can lead to people losing jobs (Steiner & Coster 13 April 2010). Surveillance can be built into daily life, so that no one escapes their past mistakes, and all protest can potentially be dangerous (Swain 8 August 2013). In such cases the disorder of messaging can lead to the creation of an order hostile to the person who made the messages. Again, this will probably be influenced by hierarchy.

Hierarchy and Management as Sources of Disorder

Placing people into groups to frame their messages, the responses made to them and the behaviour they are allowed, implies that information and communication are never free of power relations. All human 'messages' are in some respects political, in the sense that they aim at producing some kind of expected response in, or from, others (Peckham 1979). Similarly, any intention to speak 'truly' implies the possibility of deception. When combined with the notion that communication aims to produce an effect, it becomes apparent that impression management, manipulation, deception, force and awareness of the possibility of these occurring, are fundamental to communication and cannot be ignored as accidental. Any accuracy of information can be 'disturbed' by the aim for strategic effect. We may instance the way that many of those who dismiss climate science as unproven, and hence challengeable, rarely if ever, say the same thing about 'free-market' economics, which involves considerably less 'consensus', testing or proof.

We have previously indicated that hierarchy is fairly extreme in network society and this also frames information. Power relations occur within, and create, hierarchy (even if unstable) and are influenced by group boundaries and identities, which both pattern and break the flow of information. The anarchist and magician Robert Anton Wilson pointed to this through the second of his 'Celine's Laws', which can be summarised as 'Accurate communication is possible only between equals' (Wilson 1980: 118–25). Hierarchy, almost automatically, ensures the spread of 'bad', partially false or misleading, information when there is the possibility of punishment for telling the truth, or of reward for telling superiors what they want to hear (Prendergast 1993). Similarly, the people 'higher up' tell those 'below' them what they think they need to hear to obey. The tendency to 'protect' other people from information is probably less dependent on the depth of the hierarchy, than on the power and threat differences between levels, thus complicating the common idea that removing levels of hierarchy produces democratic efficiency. We may hypothesise that in a hierarchy with large power and threat differences, very few people 'actually know' what is going on, and gaps in information are filled with conjecture and psychosocial projection. This increases tendencies to suspicion, and may accentuate hostility between the groups, as those below hide what they do and think, and fantasise about what is happening above, tailoring information to those fantasies and to observed responses. 'Information paranoia' runs through hierarchy and disrupts its functioning.

Management researcher William Starbuck reports that managers have a grossly inflated sense of their own effectiveness in making decisions and planning, usually based on information received from their underlings (Starbuck 1992; Mezias & Starbuck 2003). Starbuck found that the majority of corporate heads of finance could not even estimate their companies' sales volumes, stating "the perceptions of executives are usually terribly wrong . . . sometimes it's truly ludicrous" (interview in Abrahamson and Freedman 2006: 43–4). It becomes highly probable that lack of reality in the information affecting decision-making, destabilises the efficient functioning of corporations and other hierarchical organisations. Those who argue the market acts as an antidote to ignorance dispute such claims (Block 2001), but the market supports what works in the market and, in the short-term, that does not have to be accuracy, or long-term survival. We might also suspect that the 'market pressures' that lead to insecure and devalued knowledge workers would increase the probability that knowledge workers would tailor the information they produce to meet the perceived biases of management and keep their jobs. There is little to generate mutual trust.

The presence of information paranoia in management is shown in management texts, such as Albrecht's *Crisis Management for Corporate Self-Defense* (1996), which suggests that everyone, especially your employees, *are* out to get you. Employees are portrayed as incompetent, exploitative, drunken, sex-mad thieves. The book recommends that they must be controlled. If something bad, from a manager's point of view happens, then the manager and the organisation must spin things correctly or they and the organisation are sunk. If external protesters protest against company actions or policies, the advice is to ignore them, get the media on the company's side and tell a good story; not check out whether the protesters have a point or if something needs to be remedied. Maintaining established appearance is ultimately everything, and bad messages, if possible, should be ignored or dismissed as intrinsically malevolent. The aim is total information control, and hence suppression of displeasing and possibly accurate and useful information. In a similar guidebook Furnham and Taylor (2004) appear to take corporate legitimacy so much for granted that they see insider reporting of business corruption as simply another example of employee betrayal along with theft, hacking and sabotage. In these models, 'good management' produces informational disorder by dismissing or attacking anything that threatens the corporate image, or the correctness of management. This inability to communicate across a hierarchy of rewards, punishment and suspicion is a prime cause of the power/ignorance nexus, and of the managerial creation of disorder.

Communication can also become confused in a hierarchy through the use of jargon. Some jargon depends on specialist knowledge maintaining information group barriers unintentionally through shared specialist practice, but people often voice suspicion that management-speak aims for opacity or expresses stupidity.

BOX 9   SOME REACTIONS TO MANAGEMENT LANGUAGE

Humorous or scathing websites about management language are common. See:

'the handy dandy management buzz word generator'

www.stickings90.supanet.com/pages/buzzword.htm

'The Corporate B.S. Generator'

www.atrixnet.com/bs-generator.html

'The Ridiculous Business Jargon Dictionary'

www.theofficelife.com/business-jargon-dictionary-A.html

'MBA Jargon Watch'

www.johnsmurf.com/jargon.htm

As well as giving a list of "the most annoying pretentious and useless business jargon", *Forbes Magazine* ran a twitter playoff, for its readers, between annoying pieces of jargon

www.forbes.com/sites/groupthink/2012/01/26/the-most-annoying-pretentious-and-useless-business-jargon

www.forbes.com/special-report/2012/annoying-business-jargons-12.html

No one appears to approve of such language, but it seems to be always used.

Much of such language serves other purposes than informing. David James, a former management editor for *Business Review Weekly* and editor of *Management Today* gives three such purposes.

a) To convey a sense of expertise. "If you cannot understand what they are saying, then they must be clever and worth the exorbitant fee".

b) It "marks a manager's entrance into a privileged elite".

,c) It euphemises and furthers self-deception about decisions that hurt others. It depersonalises employees by depicting them as 'human capital' or 'knowledge resources', rather than as "thinking, feeling humans. It is no accident management jargon is a lexicon of things and objects" (James 13 July 2013).

Words like 'downsizing' and 'letting go' blur actions for the utterers, but hardly for those being sacked. The speaker attempts to avoid and distribute responsibility away from themselves, while the audience is left bemused and distrusting. Economist John Kay remarks of a particular manager, that he:

> cannot describe what he and co-colleagues are doing because they are not doing anything: their time is spent in office politics and in diverting the resources of the company to their own interests. The popularity of the joke[s about management language] reveals that most employees of large organisations recognise some reality in this account. Less venally, a senior executive is unwilling to talk substantively about corporate strategy but too vain to remain silent. And so he rambles on, repeating long words and exhausted phrases.
>
> (Kay 12 July 2005)

Such language is not confined to business; it has also spread to the now managerialised and corporatised universities (Bode & Dale 2012). Hierarchy, in information society and elsewhere, is often justified by claims of knowledge and talent. As implied by James (above) one way this claim can be displayed (and membership announced) is by showing mastery of the current, rapidly changing, jargon. It also avoids giving away information to underlings, which might weaken the secrecy required to maintain the hierarchy and its opacity, while protecting the speaker from being held to have argued a particular position, allowing them some safety space when the situation changes, as it will. Furthermore, underlings can be blamed for misunderstanding directives, giving even more safety to the speaker in the uncertain environment of distributed governance in which actions always have unexpected consequences. Similar processes are involved in management fads. Embracing the latest fad places a manager in an information group, and not only gives the manager something to do, and something that can be seen to be done, but gives them an air of control, of adapting to change, solving technical problems and of being up to the minute in an uncertain and confused environment. However these actions then continually place the workplace under upheaval, as organisations and workers' positions are continually restructured and their behaviours and responsibilities changed in accordance with the latest fad or status game. However, if effectiveness was produced, then it would be eliminated with the next fad. Institutional fads produce victims and workplace cynicism (Best 2006: 19).

Best suggests that management fads tend to spread through networks and apparently solve ambiguous badly understood problems, newly recognised problems or the repeatedly found difficulties of complex unpredictable systems (2006: 47–9, 56–7). Fads become part of the way managers desperately try to impose order in their favour, as modes of ordering break down, before complexity and new problems. Miller and Hartwick argue that fads need to be simple and easily conveyable to spread, but being "suited for a simple world, they have limited utility in the real one". Fads tend to be overly optimistic, said to apply to all situations (overly ordering), focus on concerns of the moment and rarely challenge power or hierarchy: "what makes them so popular is what undermines them" (2002: 26–7). There is an industry devoted to promulgating these fads, so promulgation of this 'information' has commercial motives (Huczynski 1993). Businesses such as consulting firms, management writers, business media and business schools compete to define and sell new management techniques:

> Fashion setters who do not participate successfully in this race . . . will be perceived [framed] as lagging rather than leading management progress, as being peripheral to the business community, and as being undeserving of societal [and financial] support.
>
> Swings in management fashion, far from being cosmetic and trivial, are in fact deadly serious matters for business schools and the scholars staffing them.
>
> (Abrahamson 1996: 255)

Managers may be pressured to imitate fads and techniques used by others in their particular sector of the economy, as there are few ways of rationally determining what produces success, especially given the dubious information from other firms (Perkmann & Spicer 2008). Best also points out that it is hard to tell the difference between a fad and a real innovation during the development phase (2006: 7–8).

This has consequences for computer software, as rapidly changing in-group management language may make it hard for computer engineers to understand what is required, as well as cover managers' own lack of understanding of what the workplace needs. As the fads affect models of organisation, they affect the way software for the workplace is designed, and may lead it to conflict with later fads as well as reality.

The ordering of hierarchy has the potential to distort information in other ways. Laurence J. Peter and Raymond Hull famously proposed a direct relationship between hierarchy and incompetence in *The Peter Principle*. They argued that "in a hierarchy every employee tends to rise to his level of incompetence" (Peter & Hull 1969: 15). If a person is competent they get promoted, and when they are no longer competent at their work, they tend to stay in that position. Hindle (2000: 171–2) counter-argues that in 'de-layered' organisations, with less hierarchy, "much of the incompetence has disappeared". This is doubtful, as 'distributed' modes of administration obscure responsibility, removing the limited accountability for incompetence that can arise with deeper hierarchic models. If incompetence seemingly disappears it is because responsibility disappears. Even so, in a shallow hierarchy incompetence might have a greater effect, because there are fewer competing and competent modules compensating for that incompetence. It is again not the number of levels in the hierarchy that is important, but the degree of inequality between those levels, and the capacity to exercise arbitrary power with impunity.

The advent of distributed governance also dovetails with the increased 'portability' of management (in)capacity. Generic managers become interchangeably incompetent in the hierarchy. Satirist Scott Adams points out that in 'the old days' the structure of promotion meant that a manager had once been competent at something connected to the organisation's business. With the emergence of a discernible manager class, managers can be imported from outside the organisation and be promoted to incompetence "without ever passing through the temporary competence stage" and having no experience of the work they administer (Adams 1996: 12–13). Likewise they will have no trusted contacts in the organisation who might give them accurate information. Given that it is now expected that managers will move on, they may gain further promotion elsewhere without having to encounter the longer-term consequences of their mistakes, and thus never learn to avoid such mistakes, so that their incompetence accumulates.

People who are incompetent at fulfilling their positions are probably less likely to recognise or reward competence, and hence encourage incompetence in others. They are also less likely to be able to relay information accurately, or recognise accurate information. Their main aim may become directed towards hiding information that reveals their inability. Lazear argues that the more that rewards focus on transitory effects "that may reflect measurement difficulties, short-term luck, or skills that are job specific", or the more information is filtered by short-term focus, the more likely a Peter effect becomes (Lazear 2003).

Generalising the issue, Vaughan argues that when information crosses social boundaries (up and down the organisational hierarchy, or travelling between different departments) the risk of misunderstanding, mistransmission and misinformation increases. The result is that "structural secrecy" forms between groups; "an informal network that excludes certain knowledge claims, perpetuating partial understanding and the possibility of unexpected negative outcomes" (Vaughan 1999: 277). The groups become different information groups, within the same organisation, and the organisation is defined by its patterns of ignorance and structural incompetence.

There are many cries that boards of directors often seem to have been ignorant of what was going on in the company. Like Lawrence Mitchell (2005) we suggest that this is a recurrent disorder promoted by the structure and independence of boards, which severs ties with the rest of the organisation and tends to limit the information the board receives to that provided by the CEO or other senior management. These structures of communication mean that boards are easily kept in the dark by the very people they are meant to oversee. Given that the senior management may not have much idea of what is going on either, as discussed above, the problem compounds. Directors may also be chosen for virtues that do not include knowledge of the business they are supervising; ignorance is not rare. Similarly, given the small networked world of the elite the directors likely know one another, form a closed information group, are reassured by each other and by the custom of not rocking the boat. They may also use each other to get further directorships, which furthers groupthink. In the U.S., they are largely protected from liability and responsibility. It is rare for directors to be successfully and punitively sued by shareholders, so they have no incentive to push investigations, and if they do so may get a name as troublemakers or break friendships, risking a loss of income and advancement. They are also frequently unknown by shareholders and meet in private; which also protects them from outside information and comment, and hides their responsibility or its lack (Gillespie & Zweig 2010: 2–6).

BOX 10   MERRILL LYNCH: HIERARCHY AND STRUCTURAL INCOMPETENCE

Merrill Lynch was one of the most famous financial companies in the U.S.; "It had offices in every nook and cranny in America, where brokers stood at the ready to sell middle-class Americans the stocks and bonds they needed to put their kids through college and build their retirement nest eggs" (McLean & Nocera November 2010). However, from the late 1990s onwards it was repeatedly accused of not giving its customers correct information. In 1998 they agreed "to pay US $400 million to Orange County, Calif., to settle claims that [they] . . . helped push the affluent county into bankruptcy . . . with reckless investment advice". Orange County lost $1.6 billion (Pollack & Wayne 3 June 1998). Memos had circulated within Merrill Lynch saying that Orange County was badly exposed and "recommended halting sales of risky securities to Orange County. But the firm never did so"; the rewards were too great. When the county purchasing officer "became concerned that rising interest rates would undermine his investments", the seller "produced a Merrill economist to quell his fears" (Wayne & Pollack 22 July 1998). Between 2001–7 the company was successfully sued in 26 cases for issuing biased research, having to pay out a total of $164 million (Graybow 5 September 2007). In 2005, the company was convicted of not supervising financial advisers "whose market timing siphoned short-term profits out of mutual funds and harmed long-term investors" (ConsumerAffairs 15 March 2005). In 2008 New York State's Attorney-General "threatened to sue Merrill Lynch for misrepresenting certain debt investments as safer than they were" (BBC 16 August 2008). There are other such cases, indicating some regularity. It is impossible to say whether the board of directors were troubled by these events.

Stanley O'Neal became President of the firm in 2001 and CEO and Chair in 2003. "O'Neal had never worked as a stock broker and had no particular affection for the business that had long been Merrill's heart and soul" (McLean & Nocera November 2010). Despite having a deal with his Executive Vice Chairman and Head of Institutional Banking and Securities in return for their supporting him to become CEO, he had them removed. He destroyed the culture of job security for knowledge workers, and moved into the Collateral Debt Obligation (CDO) market based on housing loans that many say were too complicated to understand and blame for the 2007–8 financial crash. For example, Janet Tavakoli, head of a finance consulting firm, is reported as saying they allowed "dicier assets to be passed off as higher-quality goods, giving banks and investors who traded them a false sense of security". CDOs depended on computer software for the overly complex carve up of debt. The profit in selling them to others was large (Morgenson 8 November 2008). At least some employees who openly opposed this move were dismissed. O'Neal "insisted that the company's executives speak only to him about their businesses and not with one another", breaking chains of communication and knowledge flow (McLean & Nocera November 2010). He "rarely asked for input when making a decision. And under no circumstances did he want to be challenged once he had made up his mind" (ibid). People who were reluctant to take on high levels of risk were dismissed. People who were aggressive and risky and agreed with the policy were hired and promoted inside areas about which they knew little. These people helped remove competence, for example they got "rid of Merrill's most experienced mortgage traders". The risk management section was demoted from front office to back office and its information chains ('spy networks') with the trading desks were broken. At least some managers claimed that "the firm had very little exposure to subprime-mortgage risk" (ibid). "Amazing as it sounds, the C.E.O. of Merrill Lynch really didn't have a clue" about the extent of the CDO exposure (ibid).

O'Neal picked eight of ten outside board members, and they had little financial experience (Gillespie & Zweig 2010: 6). The board were not informed of how much risk he was pushing onto the company books. The February 2007 annual report claimed 2006 was the most successful year in the company's history and the board paid O'Neal $48 million for that year. Ten months later the company had a third quarter loss of $2.3 billion and a writedown of $8.4 billion on bad investments. Eventually shareholders lost up to $60 billion (Gillespie & Zweig 2010: 7–10).

When O'Neal finally told the board how bad the situation was, their reaction implied they had no previous understanding at all (McLean & Nocera November 2010). The board ousted O'Neal later that year, but there was no internal successor as many credible people had been removed. In April 2008 the head of the board's audit committee was asked why the board did not notice the $40 billion exposure to CDOs, replying that the "CDO position did not come to the board's attention until late in the process" (Gillespie & Zweig 2010: 7–10). Information transmission was broken everywhere.

After the immediate crisis was over, when taxpayers' money was supporting the company, just before Merrill Lynch was sold to Bank of America and after another $27 billion loss, $3.6 billion was distributed as bonuses to 700 top employees (de la Merced & Story 11 February 2009). Bank of America argued the information as to who received what was "private and should remain private to protect the rights of the individuals and the competitive position of the company". The payments were made before the closing of the books for the year, and with an underestimation of the year's loss by $7 billion (Story 23 February 2009). Expectations of secrecy and reward were deeply ingrained:

> "These are private sector workers, and people do not expect that their salaries and bonuses are going to be in the newspaper", said Gary Phelan, a lawyer with Outten & Golden. "It's suddenly a crime to make money, it seems".
>
> (Story 18 March 2009)

This distribution and encouragement of ignorance and breakdown of information throughout the organisation is not an accidental sequence of events, but based in the power/ignorance nexus, the building of structural incompetence and boosted by the appearance of short-term profit. It displays a pattern that capitalist information organisations are prone to.

Given these disorders of information in hierarchies, and the overt presence of inequality, we cannot assume dominant classes or groups know what they are doing, or that they are unified. CEOs may constitute a relatively powerful, but rivalrous, information group, but like all such groups they will display patterns of ignorance, which need to be investigated as much as their patterns of communication and influence.

Data Smog and Filtering

Another factor disordering communication in information society is the sheer volume of information. Eric Schmidt (2005) of Google cited a study indicating there were "roughly five million terabytes" (i.e. roughly 5×10^{18} bytes. One terabyte equals 1,024 gigabytes) of information in the world, and he estimated that only 170 terabytes, or 0.0034%, was searchable. Hilbert and Lopez (2011) argued that, in 2007, humankind was able to store 2.9×10^{20} "optimally compressed bytes". The Library of Congress Web Archiving FAQ (2013) states: "As of January 2013, the Library has collected about 385 terabytes of web archive data. . . . The web archives grow at a rate of about 5 terabytes per month". Worldwidewebsize.com (7 February 2013) estimates the size of the World Wide Web as "at least 13.32 billion pages". The figures indicate the massive amounts of information in circulation, and the impossibility of reaching all of the relevant material on any subject.

The easier it is to create information, the more information will be created, reaching a point of 'data smog' where too much information is generated to be humanly processed or navigated (Shenk 1997; Levy 2008). At this point it becomes impossible for anyone to judge or read everything relevant to them, and the amount of information available lessens the chance of finding particularly 'good' information. Similarly, the more information can be obtained, the more it is likely to be collected. This increases the amount of administration, as more and more data, on finer and finer points, can be collected and analysed. There is no limit to the amount of information that can be collected, or the work that can be devoted to that gathering. Indeed, the more data 'needs' to be observed and administered, the less energy and resources may be devoted to the actual services that are supposed to be being supplied.

The more data is collected, the less people are able to review the information that is available. Consequently, people are more likely to make judgements according to what they, or their information group, already 'know', by their habitual framings, and by their relationship to the group from which the information appears to come. Information groups act as filters limiting information and allowing people to steer their way through the data smog, and evaluate data, by their attachment to the group and disjuncture from information out-groups and other information. While collection of information may increase when people face social uncertainty, it may be more directed at confirmation of bias and group membership, than at discovery. These problems may be intensified if the filtering models are built into software, so that the contrary data never appears.

Information that is socially popular with information groups will tend to be repeated and occur often, and confirm itself through the repetition, much like rumours and 'secrets'. Easily found information is likely to be simple and conform to people's easy emotional responses and their existent models and framings, and this may be engineered deliberately in an attempt to make it repeatable and well transmitted. This realisation is emphasised in the formal politics of information society. Politicians frequently seem to be required to explain a situation in 'sound bites' or repeat the same formulation robotically in response to any question, so that the same sound bite will be repeated on as many news channels as possible. In a lecture to the Australian Parliament researcher Sally Young (2010) commented:

> Analysing primetime TV news stories, I found that the average election-news story is only two minutes long—and during this story, the reporter and host speak for more than half the time while politicians speak only in 7 second soundbites. The average news story about the 2007 election devoted less than 30 seconds to letting politicians speak in their own words. For example, on the 12 November, the day of the Coalition's campaign launch, John Howard delivered a speech for 42 minutes but that night on the evening news, voters heard only 10.4 seconds of it. We know from American research that the soundbite has shrunk over time, keeps on shrinking and that they have less soundbites on their news compared to ours.

The perceived inability to be simultaneously complex and heard may encourage officials and sources to embrace the Platonic/Straussian theory of the 'noble lie', as they feel they cannot tell the truth and be understood. Hierarchy reinforces this tendency, with the result that the audience gains a reciprocal expectation of being lied to, manipulated or patronised. This, joined with the tendency to see things in terms of socially validated bias, fantasy and projection, furthers the information paranoia in which all information that does not confirm a group's biases is treated with suspicion.

BOX 11 MAKING GOVERNMENT AN INFORMATION GROUP

The information group is part of the process that creates a power/ignorance nexus. In Australia, the new (late 2013) right-wing government under the Prime Minister Tony Abbott proceeded to destroy all independent government bodies that might give it information it did not want to hear, building walls around their information group. Amongst their first actions after the election, but before Parliament had met, they decided not to have a science minister (for the first time since 1931), the science portfolio now being submerged in industry (Porter 17 September 2013). They abolished the Climate Commission "which had been established to provide public information on the effects of and potential solutions to global warming" and proposed to shut down the Climate Change Authority, which was looking at ways of reducing carbon emissions, and the Green Energy Fund, which was looking to develop alternate modes of energy (Arup 19 September 2013).

As part of its priorities, the government announced procedures that removed a quarter of the jobs at Australia's top science body, the CSIRO. Later Mr. Abbott said that sackings were up to CSIRO management. They also immediately scrapped the following advisory committees: Australian Animals Welfare Advisory Committee; Commonwealth Firearms Advisory Committee; International Legal Services Advisory Committee; National Inter-country Adoption Advisory Council; National Steering Committee on Corporate Wrongdoing; Antarctic Animal Ethics Committee; Advisory Panel on the Marketing in Australia of Infant Formula; High Speed Rail Advisory Group; Maritime Workforce Development Forum; Advisory Panel on Positive Ageing; Insurance Reform Advisory Group; and the National Housing Supply Council (Towell et al. 8 November 2013). The head of the Advisory Panel on Positive Ageing stated that the group had almost finished its work and cost probably about $100,000 a year. Similar remarks on cost were made by the High Speed Rail Advisory Group.

New positions, such as the board of the Commission of Audit whose mission was to eliminate 'government waste', were filled with people with very clear 'rightist' ideological positions and, in one case, large-scale contracts with the government. No union, community, charity, research or environmental representatives were appointed to the Commission (Allard & Kenny 24 October 2013), thus ensuring that little in the way of opposing views would be heard. The opposition shadow finance minister commented "There's a principle that the Government doesn't seem to be able to handle which is there are other people who have expertise too" (Yaxley 8 November 2013). The Australian government has since cut more funding for science, for advisory bodies that it might disagree with and for public education.

In the context of growing social insecurity, ease of communication can increase the possibility of disruptive social panic, as information that produces panic is easily spread and produces the motivation to spread it. Chain emails warning of viruses are a good example, where unwitting, well-intentioned people perpetuate the computer virus hoax, or even a virus, by forwarding the message to their email contacts (for a list see Urbanlegends nd). Mass engagement becomes highly episodic and affective, leading to what some have characterised as 'emotional movements' rather than 'social movements' (Waldgrave & Verhulst 2006). When these events encourage information paranoia, ongoing states of panic become part of social life, and the conditions are reinforced because there is always the possibility of disruptive events happening.

CONCLUSION

'Information' is only meaningful as part of the social process. It is necessarily unstable, ambiguous and political or manipulative. It is embedded in past attempts at communication, in forging group membership and reinforcing hierarchy. It is also influenced by assumed or imagined social categorisations. As a result, as well as being necessary for cooperation, information always involves the possibility of breakdown, misunderstanding and misappropriation. As digital technology massively increases information flow and eases attempts at communication without diminishing the problems of divergence, noise, framing, understanding, interpretation, self-reference and group relations, it also increases the incidence of misinterpretation, reinterpretation or conflicted communication, therefore increasing the potential for disruption and conflicts. These unintentional effects are spread system-wide through the networks. In the process, boundaries are superseded, realigned or reinforced in a disruptive flux that is generative for some but destructive for others. Framing, which is important for the resolution of meaning, tends to invoke group cultural identity, and so devalues information from other groups, and increases the power of the information group as a form of information filtering and dismissal. Hierarchy is entrenched and because of its framing effects and boundaries, tends to disrupt accuracy and transmission of information. Vague jargon and lack of managerial clarity becomes an essential part of generating status and power in an information hierarchy, where the end of information is not to inform, but to attempt control, diffuse responsibility and confuse the 'enemy' or the outgroup. This magnifies the ineffectiveness and confusion of managerial action. Constantly changing organisational fads spread because of informationalism's complexity and hierarchies, because of the industry dependent on selling solutions and because of the relatively easy transmission and replication of slogans, when compared to intricate and laboured thinking. This further disrupts the capacity of organisations to deal with problems. However, as we will see elsewhere in this book, the effects of these disruptions may be fertile as well as oppressive.

6 Capitalism and Disinformation

Moving from the general disruptive properties of information as a social process to the relationship between capitalism and information, the potential for disorder, generative or otherwise, dramatically increases. The primary intensifying factor is that, in information society, 'information' becomes a key commodity, which is produced or acquired, and sold or rented to make a profitable return. However, the disorders that we have just discussed, plus the social role of information and communication in the making of culture, present major problems and disorders for profit, and for capitalist social functioning. Alvin Toffler, an early advocate for information society theory, pointed to an important problem for information capitalism. Toffler argued that information was a difficult concept for capitalist economic theory because information is a potentially unlimited resource unlike labour, capital or land (Toffler 1984: 21–2). As Wark also remarks: "information need not be subject to the laws of scarcity at all. My possession of some information does not deprive you of it" (in Christopher 2003: np). To make profit out of information, and give it a purchase value, information must be restricted through 'informational enclosures'. Barriers have to be set up to keep people out. Consequently, accurate free information, under capitalism, is almost valueless when compared either to hidden information that people think might be useful, or inaccurate free information that gives a financial, propaganda or political result. Restricting access to 'privileged' information, or providing inaccurate but saleable information, becomes a key tool for competitive advancement and profit.

The second problem for informationalism is that information is not destroyed as it is 'consumed'; indeed it is needed to generate, or be developed into, more information. Put together, there is a fundamental contradiction between: first, the free exchange of information required to plan action, deal with other information, create satisfying culture, enable system survival, innovation or adaptation; and second, the necessity, under capitalism, for information to be privatised for accumulation and profit. Once distributed, information always has the possibility of being shared again, requiring either constant effort to enforce the enclosure, or the constant generation of new and restricted information with the devaluation of old information (even if accurate), to keep up the incoming profit.

INFORMATION AS CULTURE OR ENCLOSURE

Enclosure is difficult, as information, in all its varieties, is social and cultural in nature. Culture itself arises from shared information and traditions, and from conflicts over understanding that information and traditions. Information never exists *sui generis,* isolated from all other information or other people's cultural or intellectual productions. It exists in a relation of mutual dependence, and is not easily isolated to make saleable property. Even the great original discoverers and innovators, as Isaac Newton famously said, 'stood on the shoulders of giants', making use of information and ideas that preceded them, surrounded them or engaged them (including the very phrase about giants, see Merton 1993). Without those ideas, and information from others, Newton would not have been able to make his discoveries. Development of knowledge would have been set back.

Enclosing information, so as to make it units of sellable property, severs its sociality and is even more problematic than putting fences around fields as there are no easy natural boundaries around information from which to make commodities. Enclosure depends on a political consensus, or more often on the use of force (police, courts, penalties etc.) whether framed in legal terms or not, which can continually expect to be challenged. Coercion and struggle is never far from informational commodification.

One method of restricting information is to claim ownership through patent or copyright claims, which define a regime of legal and illegal use. The limits and boundaries of these forms of property are often in dispute, requiring defensible definitions of uniqueness and non-derivation from existing information property owned by others. The vagueness of boundaries means that the legal system is constantly used to enforce or dispute property claims. 'Patent trolling' can result, when people take others to court over dubious intellectual property (IP) claims hoping that the difficulty of establishing IP boundaries may mean that victims prefer to pay user fees, to the cost and delay of court cases. Lawyers for Apple wrote:

> Apple is the firm most targeted by [trolls]. Over the last three years alone, Apple has faced. . . allegations of patent infringement in 92 separate matters. 57 of these cases have been resolved. Apple has rarely lost on the merits. But victory figures as small consolation, because in every one of these cases, Apple has been forced to bear its legal fees. . . the threat of fees often forces an undeserved settlement. . . despite its success in litigating the merits, for business purposes Apple has agreed to a settlement in 51 of the 57 closed cases.
>
> (Rosenkranz et al. 2013: 2)

This has considerable impact and becomes part of normal activity. Bessen et al. (2011) state that in 2010, U.S. companies found themselves in trolling cases "2,600 times, over five times more often than in 2004" and that "[o]ver the last four years, the loss of wealth exceeds $83 billion per year". In this situation, it becomes strategically valuable to make patents as vague as possible to catch later innovations in their ambit rather than simply protecting the inventor's own device. While some corporations buy rafts of patents in the hope of extorting money, others fight patent cases to delay the sale of competing products. The U.S. state of Vermont launched the first ever government lawsuit against patent trolling in May 2013, to counter-act a case in which a company demanded money from businesses using scanners (Mullin 23 May 2013).

Innovation is also blocked as new ideas and products depend upon inter-locked previous 'events' or discoveries that are walled off as private prop-erty. Demands for high fees restrict usage and social benefit. If the patent holders ask too much, the patented advance may not be used during the life of the patent, by those who could benefit or develop innovations. The greater the number of owners involved, the greater the potential gridlock as each owner has the right to block other people's use of that combined resource (Heller 2008). Locking-up information into patents has a stagnat-ing effect on the wider society, undermining the innovation patent law was supposed to encourage. Corporations rent out the patents they already own, rather than innovate. Thus, according to Heller, while the number of pat-ented medical processes and discoveries has increased, the number of new 'life saving' drugs decreased (q. Allemang 23 August 2008). Gridlock inten-sifies as the ordering process of private ownership is extended into fields where it has previously been marginal.

Copyright has had a similar effect, inhibiting cultural development and elaboration, and ironically undermining the conditions for originality, as for example when the cost of sampling music means that contemporary hip-hop is likely to use fewer combinations of other records, meaning that the dependence on 'original' tracks is more obvious and less modified by other tracks. Information society requires culture to function, but the profit nexus destroys that culture's generative richness, so that the more that capitalists live off renting ideas to make money from what other people may do with those ideas, the less actual production and innovation occurs. This is not a situation of maximally efficient competition, but rather a model of collapse, where there are no ultimate winners. The process of domination becomes driven not by production so much as by dispossession of information and culture (Harvey 2005).

SOURCE EFFECTS: SOURCE RULES

In markets of over-plenty and data-smog, the sorting and filtering of informa-tion by various corporations (either news or 'data mining') becomes a major site of information power. Faced with a plethora of unreliable sources, users turn to news aggregators that rely on a highly concentrated set of sources.

Mass communication though social media appears to concentrate content by replication. A government study in Australia found that the bulk of communications content circulating in Australia, including though the internet, could be sourced to just 13 providers (Department of Broadband, Communications and the Digital Economy 2012). Curran et al. (2013) researched internet news and found that it heavily focused on the nation, tended to come from established media companies (as independent sources found it hard to survive) and featured the voices of State actors, those people defined as 'experts' and voices from business; "In short, news websites do not stand out as citadels of empowerment, amplifying the voice of the people" (2013: 887). Ease of communication does not produce a proliferation of production houses, but instead accentuates dependence on what are seen to be reliable sources. This replicates network effects in which a very few nodes come to dominate the transmission of information.

A source provides a mode of framing the information, telling the consumer or information group whether the information is likely to be accurate, agreeable and conform to expectations. Information from a recognised and 'trusted' source will spread quicker through a network of similar information groups, and have greater apparent value than more accurate information from an unrecognised source. The source's value, then, depends on whether they are able to become an exemplar for a set of information groupings, or are otherwise able to generate trust. This implies that a source will become the more valuable the more it confirms and exalts the existing biases used to interpret and spread its messages. The income of the source depends upon its prior reputation for an information grouping, and its capacity to deliver an audience (perhaps to advertisers). Hence the tendency of information to become political and pleasing, rather than accurate, is reinforced. Here, bad information drives out good when it is profitable or strategic. Power relations come into this process, but the process can, in turn, grant power. This further affects accuracy, as sources tend to deny, or downplay, their own failures in order to retain status. Admission of information failure becomes a measure of information hazard, not of informational accuracy. As a result, sources have an incentive to deny error. Maintaining reputation and status becomes more important than accuracy. This does not mean that everyone will value the source equally; there will be contestation over sources, for example over the relative value of *Fox News* or the *New York Times*. Because of information group loyalties, and data smog, different groups will value different sources and be largely unaware of what is said elsewhere, further closing off the groups from each other.

Profit seeking means that sources will see a virtue in trying to diminish the status of other sources (particularly those contrary sources known as members of other information groupings) so they gain more influence and a bigger audience. The main message a source may give out is not to trust other sources, especially if other sources attempt to correct them. David Frum (2011), once a speech writer for U.S. President George W. Bush, notes that cultivating information groups and hostility between them, has a business function:

> The business model of the conservative media is built on two elements: provoking the audience into a fever of indignation (to keep them watching) and fomenting mistrust of all other information sources (so that they never change the channel).

Yet again the economics of information profit leads to distortion. Sources and information groups cultivate a sense of information paranoia and distance from information outgroups.

HIDDEN DRIVERS OF DISTRIBUTION

A well-documented technique of spreading information is to blur the 'interestedness' of the source, thus attempting to avoid the information paranoia directed at outsider sources. Forms of this practice can be called: 'guerrilla marketing' (Levinson & Levinson 2011) 'stealth marketing' (Kaikati & Kaikati 2004), 'viral marketing' (Rayport 31 December 1996; Rushkoff 1996) or buzz marketing (Thomas 2004), etc. Such advertising aims to overcome the data smog of other advertising that people have trained themselves to ignore (Kirby & Marsden 2006; Leung 11 February 2009). It involves making advertising either surprisingly visible, or indistinguishable from news or normal events, often by using apparently neutral (but paid) people to spread information, or by persuading people to pass on the message by themselves. In these cases, the interaction or apparent word of mouth, makes the recommendations seem personal and therefore valid (Katz & Lazarsfeld 1955; Smith et al. 2007), or indeed motivated by the 'mark's' own interests. Commodification leads to a major independent filter of information being disrupted. The techniques can take advantage of the hub effect in networks; some people are exceedingly well connected, thus if you 'infect' them with the information, they will spread it throughout the network (Katz & Lazarsfeld 1955; Goldenberg et al. 2009). Given small world network interconnection effects, the messages can in theory reach everyone, relevant to the marketing. Of course, if people can be convinced to convey the message to others for nothing, the cost of the advertising can be quite cheap.

Known examples of such marketing include Procter & Gamble's Vocalpoint promotion, which reputedly rewarded 600,000 women who had large social networks to promote its products in ordinary conversation (Berner 28 May 2006). Sony Ericsson ran a campaign to launch their camera phone by employing 60 actors in ten cities to ask passers by to take a photo of them with the phone and engage in a conversation about how good it was (Leung 11 February 2009). BlackBerry, according to an actress involved, paid "a bunch of hot girls and we would just walk into bars, whip out our

BlackBerries and try to get guys to look at them by flirting" and by asking them to enter their phone number for the promise of a date (Osterhout 18 April 2010). One company even paid actors to attend the local courthouse and talk to people about a nearby furniture sale (Vranica 9 February 2005). The latter may sound trivial, but it shows the permeation of ordinary life with commercially biased information.

Given that it is easy to hide identity online, it is rarely going to be clear whether messages of praise or criticism are genuine, paid for or both (Dellarocas 2006; Gregory 29 January 2010). "Companies often hire marketers to post positive reviews of their products on appropriate message boards or in chat rooms without revealing their affiliations" (Osterhout 18 April 2010). It also becomes unclear how many apparently different people repeating the message are the same person using different names, thus backing their arguments up with 'sock puppets' as they are known. The same happens in politics with wealthy organisations either trying to get popular support for political arguments, or setting up fake grassroots organisations ('astroturfing') (Quinn & Sweney 8 June 2013). The Chinese government reputedly hired over 300,000 people to write in support of its positions (Fareed 22 September 2008). Even the U.S. military is reputedly studying the field so as to spread the messages it chooses through terrorist (or other?) networks (Estes 21 September 2013; Technology Review 17 September 2013). Faked information becomes even more strategically important, politically and commercially.

Information can also be given potency or cogency by getting many people (paid for, otherwise motivated or sock puppets) to talk about the same issues in the same way, making them widespread 'talking points'. This repetition and volume not only spreads the information far and wide, gets more people repeating it, but also generates the appearance of truth, as whatever is said by many people 'must have' some validity, otherwise it would not be so popular. This can include spreading messages that are completely false, but believable to the target audience. A good campaigner may pay attention to what parts of the message take off, learning from this what has appeal and what should be repeated.

Many argue that such methods of spreading information also spread distrust. Berner quotes Commercial Alert Executive Director Gary Ruskin as warning of the danger of the "basic 'commercialization of human relations', where friends treat one another as advertising pawns, undercutting social trust" (Berner 28 May 2006). The practice could harm digital social networks in general (Millar 7 June 2011). Perhaps somewhat exaggeratedly a writer in *WIRED* predicts:

> Anyone with a video blog is, potentially, just one irresistible offer away from becoming a corporate stooge, a sock puppet, a product placer, an astroturfer, a shill. An industry that once confined itself to Madison Avenue is now operating from your town, your street, your

bedroom. . . . What's real, what's make-believe? Who to trust, when it's precisely those not yet suspected of advertising who attract advertisers?
(iMomus 8 May 2007)

At the least the practice tends towards ensuring the possibility that common beliefs and discussions have little basis in any reality other than corporate profit or political fantasy, and this will affect people's responses to other information by the framings introduced, and by increasing the probability that disbelieved information will be dismissed as false. For the advertiser, there is the possibility that the information can get out of their control and customers can lose trust in the brand when they discover the deception (Brandt 1 November 2001), but this can probably be lessened by 'paid for' people keeping discussion on track. Paranoia may be increased, as much of the research into this kind of marketing may not be published, because keeping it secret adds to the apparent ability and money-making capacity of marketing companies, or to the political power of other organisations.

Another technique that relies on information apparently coming from independent sources, is when corporations, or others, sponsor think-tanks who then produce research that supports their points of view. As the head of the Australian Institue of Public Affairs said at an inquiry: "We've got about 4000 funders . . . there are occasions when we may take positions which are somewhat different from those of the funders. Obviously that doesn't happen too often, otherwise they'd stop funding us, but it does happen occasionally" (Swan 31 May 2012). Think-tanks provide the required supposedly independent news items and comments for easy dissemination, backing up, and helping to form information groups with arguments and data, often removing complexity from analysis. There are allegations that many members of the U.S. Congress now tend to get their research done by various think-tanks rather than by the more neutral office of Congress. This not only provides the results they want, but allows them to question the need for organisations like the Congressional Research Service, therefore challenging the existence of more neutral information at all (Bartlett 14 December 2012). Prominent members of U.S. think-tanks also work as professional lobbyists for commercial interests (Williams & Silverstein 10 May 2013; Bender 11 August 2013). Think-tanks may even have supposedly independent lobbying arms, to maintain their 'charitable' status, and allow political action. Thus the American Heritage Foundation has an affiliate called Heritage Action for America, the Bipartisan Policy Center has the BPC Advocacy Network, the Center for American Progress has the Center for American Progress Action Fund and so on (Williams nd). This also increases general information paranoia and distrust of information not accepted by one's own information groups, as the potential bias is not something people are unaware of.

Think-tanks of similar persuasion reinforce each other and help pull together alliances. Many sources hostile to recognising the environmental crisis come from 'conservative' think-tanks (Bonds 2011; Brulle 2014). For example, Jacques et al. (2008) found that of 95% of 141 books that were sceptical of environmentalism published between 1972 and 2005 were associated with such conservative think-tanks. Corporately sponsored think-tanks were the breeding ground for the initially small (Crockett alleges less than 50 people in the UK pre-Thatcher) but elite social movements that supported neoliberal ideas and 'unrestrained' markets, and recruited members by political allegiance (Crockett 1994: 2; Mirowski 2013: 71). The known bias of think-tanks helps them attract funding, as the funders know exactly what they will be getting for their money. This generates another 'virtuous circle', which increases bias and inaccuracy, disturbing the difficult to observe relations between applied policy and results. Problem solving, or even recognising problems, becomes more difficult, and this is inherent in the informational system.

Working in tandem with the commodification of social networks and ideas, public information can increasingly be hidden when 'commercially sensitive'. Here, the public sector is becoming increasingly immersed in private secrecy. For example, public services are contracted out to private companies and the contractual terms are secret or 'commercial in confidence'. Consequently, the contract cannot be criticised or even evaluated for its effectiveness. Political journalist Josh Gordon writes (22 November 2012) "The more public money that flows to private contractors, the less scope there is to scrutinise how it is being spent", a point also made by the Auditor General for the Australian state of Victoria who remarked that "his ability to scrutinise taxpayer-funded projects has 'diminished rapidly'" (ibid). The Victorian government did increase oversight of the Audit Office, but did not increase its ability to track corporate acquisition of public money.

When joined with distributed governance, corporate power and information restriction, governance overall may become more secretive. Joseph Stiglitz (2013) commented on the inequality of information flow in the supposed free trade agreement, the Trans-Pacific Partnership (TPP):

> The decision to make the negotiating text secret from the public (even though the details are accessible to hundreds of advisors to big corporations) makes it difficult for the public to offer informed commentary.

Julian Assange, founder of Wikileaks, is reported to have said:

> "If you read, write, publish, think, listen, dance, sing or invent; if you farm or consume food; if you're ill now or might one day be ill, TPP has you in its cross hairs", . . . If instituted, TPP "would trample over individual rights and free expression as well as ride roughshod over the intellectual and creative commons".

> (Pesak 21 December 2013)

Releases through Wikileaks claimed that the agreement would extend patent and copyright terms, lower the standards for granting patents on medicines, place citizens under surveillance for information piracy and increase damages for patent and copyright infringement (Wikileaks 2013). Other leaks suggested that the agreement contained provisions to allow corporations to sue States for having environmental or health regulations that cause loss of profit (Martin 9 December 2013, 10 December 2013). In Australia such fundamental changes might normally require a referendum with open discussion (Fraunce 4 January 2014). Allegations surfaced that the then recently victorious right-wing Australian government was trying to remove clauses that would stop tobacco companies from suing it over mandatory plain packaging (Martin 13 December 2013), displaying either information paranoia in the reports, or an openness to corporate influence in the government. While the TPP involves a reaction to mass pubic infringements of what corporations view as their right to profit from information, that reaction in turn produces counter-reactions, as discussed in Chapters 10 and 11.

INFORMATION AND CAPITALIST MARKETS

For all of these reasons, information, particularly accurate information, offers capitalists an unstable vehicle for realising profit and control. While the value of information is determined by money, at the same time the value of money is determined by information. Information is again evaluated by reference to other information, none of which may be accurate.

Trading generally depends on information, but the restriction of information is a tool for competitive advancement, so capitalist competition greatly magnifies information disorders. For example, a declining share price gives the message the market is abandoning a company and the value of the company is thereby affected (See Drucker 1993: 183ff.; Soros 1994). Therefore, it is in some people's interests to hide information that may affect price, so they can profit from using that information. This is especially evident in financial markets, which are now the largest markets in the contemporary world. In 2004 the estimated turnover on the Forex markets was 1.9 trillion U.S. dollars a day, of which 95% was probably speculative, and on derivatives was 1.2 trillion U.S. dollars per day (BIS 2004). In 2012 the Bank of International Settlements wrote that the "notional amount of outstanding over-the-counter (OTC) derivatives fell by 8%, to $648 trillion, in the second half of 2011" (BIS: 2012). The World Bank (2014: 16) estimated, that at that time, the world GDP stood at $72.68 trillion, which is about 12% of the notional value of the derivatives. The speculative economy overshadows the value of conventional trade or the events being insured against, and makes the 'regular' economy parasitic on chaotic speculation or gambling. The disorder of gambling becomes the primary order of the economy.

In such a speculative system, if information is equally distributed then nobody has a market edge. As businessman Mark Porat argues, "merchants live off imperfect information" (Burstein & Kline 1995: 419). It is also in traders' interests, in this system, to issue or pass on false or confusing information to mislead others or take advantage of them. Alexis Goldstein, an ex-worker at Merrill Lynch and Deutsche Bank, is quoted as saying:

> "That's how you make money. You make it so complicated the clients don't understand what it is they're buying and selling, or how much risk they're taking on". . . . The more complex the product, the higher the commission you can charge, and the less likely it is that there will be copycats driving down your profit margins with increased competition, she explained. In other words, complexity "isn't a side effect of the system—it's how the system was designed".
>
> (Edwards March/April 2013)

Concealment and special knowledge are part of the game, not openness and dissemination of accuracy. The capacity to mislead, to distribute false information or to maintain commercial secrecy becomes a prime strategic resource, and so all commercial information is suspect.

BOX 12 'DON'T TRUST US'

In 2013 the U.S. Department of Justice charged the ratings agency Standard & Poor's (S&P) with giving safer ratings than deserved to investment products to win more fees from issuers, and with not downgrading collateralised debt obligations despite knowing the securities were in decline. In defence S&P argued that the government's case should be dismissed as no federally insured financial institutions were affected and because "its own statements about the independence and objectivity of its ratings were 'puffery' that could not be taken at face value" (Stempel 17 July 2013; 3 September 2013). In other words S&P seem to be insisting that people in the market should not trust the information they issued, even if they set themselves up as the arbiters of financial truth. A court case in Australia had already found that S&P misled local councils who had bought supposedly AAA rating investments. The judge wrote: "S&P's rating of AAA . . . was misleading and deceptive and involved the publication of information or statements false in material particulars and otherwise involved negligent misrepresentations" (Schimroszik 6 November 2012).

Networking intensifies the problems. Accounting firms and credit ratings agencies, which supposedly guarantee or evaluate the financial soundness of organisations, may not only be paid by those organisations they are evaluating, but may have mutual shareholdings, investments, directorships, rivalries and so on, all of which may or may not affect the accuracy of information, or the accuracy of the perception of the information, they give out. We can expect that in a functioning capitalist economy, accurate information about the economy, the market or about economic behaviour will be restricted as part of the dynamics of that economy and market.

In neoclassical economics, information, as present in market prices, is assumed to be perfect across all fields—this is the key condition that allows the construction of imagined market efficiency, where *all* means of production and consumption are deployed as effectively as they can be. This free market fantasy shapes much of economic analysis and public policy—as a visionary model to be aimed for—yet the disorders of information show it to be a fallacy. Information by definition is never a pure asocial 'signal' ensuring private motivations are correlated to spontaneously produce public good. The money and price system is manipulated at many points, to convey strategically 'favourable' messages about value, worth and ability to supply. The market is never asocial or apolitical, and it has nothing driving beneficial information. Money is also an information problem.

Money, as a signal, is not external to, or independent of, the system, acting as a mere marker of value; it is subject to the same disorders as other information. Just as words are affected by other words and acts of power, money is affected by other information (from relatively accurate, or deliberately misleading sources), by models, by the framings brought to it and by the relative power of issuer. The value of a currency both depends on perceptions of, and gives information about, the relative economic (and possibly military) strength of its authorisers. In currency trading money itself becomes a commodity evaluated by other monies, in an endless play of signs, and its fluctuations are the information that determines its temporary value, which also depends on divinations of its future value. Money is subject to propaganda, persuasion, manipulation and misinterpretation. It depends on mob guessing about how others see the strength of those issuing the money. This is not changed by such conventions as a gold standard, because we can only estimate and guess whether a currency can really be exchanged for gold and at what rate, or how valuable some unit of gold really is in terms of other goods, or even what the supply of gold might be like in the future. Money inevitably involves 'games' of perception and trust between the issuer (or source) and the user, the information in circulation and the models of the world deployed. Therefore in information capitalism, money is not an abstract medium of exchange, or neutral information carrier (or price signal) that efficiently reflects demand and distributes production, as is usually alleged in neoclassical economic theory. Money is a disorderly social relation, founded in potential distortions of communication, which produce the uncertainty that allows it to be traded. Encouraging uncertainty may encourage trade.

If misinterpretation and misunderstanding is normal, people are overwhelmed with information, people engage in and expect strategic distortion, people are grouped by bias and useful information can be enclosed, then only imperfect information exists. The dream of perfect open information is directly contradicted by the necessity to enclose information to recast it as private property. Capitalism subverts the information flows it needs to function.

COUNTER-MOVES

As already implied, the normal course of the development of ideas, information and culture is firmly embedded in collective sharing with reward coming through status and recognition. This kind of informational sociality was clearly manifested in the traditions of collaborative exchange between programmers that enabled the building of the internet (Hauben & Hauben 1997; Gilles & Cailliau 2000). This continues online in such ventures as free/libré and open source software (FLOSS) (Moody 2001; Coleman 2012). Social exchange of this kind can implicitly, or explicitly, challenge information commodification as a form of production. With free exchange, people can strive for informational accuracy. In this context, accuracy as a recognised value (even if disputable), is relevant to status and can be judged by the found social effectiveness of the product. However, while this is a form of knowledge development recognising that knowledge has to be shared to be developed; such free exchange does not necessarily overcome capitalism or hierarchy (Marshall 2006a). Many open source groups are necessarily elitist hierarchies (meritocracies), and the software produced (or 'premium' versions of it) is often expropriated for sale, to support continued development. Such informal online economies of collaborative exchange often only exist because people can make their living elsewhere, and are generally not dependent on that exchange for their livelihood (notwithstanding that some sectors have spawned new economies around them, such as FLOSS support services). This may render them a relatively weak and parasitic alternative, dependent on the forces that they challenge for their survival. The moves may be self-disordering.

Furthermore, commerce can re-monetise and appropriate freely given labour, as when authors are required to pay to be published in open access journals (see Chapter 11), or when companies gain free 'fan' labour to improve or market their products. On the margins of informational capitalism the 'underground' or alternate economies of swapping and 'piracy' become relatively normalised (Botsman & Rogers 2010; da Rimini & Marshall 2014). But how significant these economies will become is hard to predict.

Running counter to the process of enclosure, digital information may be relatively easily replicated, reappropriated and redistributed and hence decommodified. Product that escapes exists as a leak on accumulation. The tools of information capitalism, which allow the appropriation of the workers' ideas and the generation of information, are also the tools that allow people to 'steal' and modify information property and circumvent restrictions of ownership (see Chapter 10). At a corporate level, industrial espionage and ambit court cases over escaped information become everyday methods of trade. Ease of replication and distribution directly affects minor players who are unable to find other sources of income or enforce their property rights. The challenge disrupts many levels of information society, not just a segment.

As we discuss in Chapter 10 digital platforms that rent their space and services to users and advertisers rather than selling information products are complicit with this 'pirating'. Internet Service Providers (ISPs), for instance, have strongly opposed legislation that would make them responsible for the online copyright violations committed by their subscribers. Yet by 2013 ISPs had "been ordered to block users' access to copyright infringing sites in a total of 12 countries" (IFPI 2013: 29). However technology news portals report the rapid appearance of 'proxy sites' enabling entry to prohibited search engines like the Pirate Bay, rendering techno-legal enclosures useless, until at least those proxies themselves become 'blocklisted', and consequently superseded by new proxies in a seemingly endless cycle (Ernesto 3 June 2013).

THE PARASITIC INFO-COMMODITY

Finally, viewing the world through the model of the information economy distorts informationalism itself, as the focus on what is constructed as 'immaterial' diverts attention from the 'material economy' that is necessary for survival. It requires suppression of the question of 'how do you eat by only exchanging information?', denigrating the processes that support informationalism's existence. In other words, the information society is vitally dependent upon 'material' processes such as power stations, factory farms, mining, manufacturing, manual labour, garbage processing, physical maintenance of 'infrastructure', a healthy ecology and so on, which are devalued by its ideology. People do not work in immaterial workplaces, they are situated, and 'materially' present somewhere. They too are doing physical work, whether it be typing on a computer, or creating art, or standing in front of an audience, and this can harm them. While workers or commodities can be contingent (expressing displacement, disconnection and info-instability), they are never immaterial and they require materiality. Similarly, information itself always has a physical body or form, whether it is sound waves, display devices, fibre optic cables, texts or image. Under informationalism, the industrial economy does not disappear but becomes 'offshored' out of the Western world, transferred to places with the fewest restrictions on manufacture, pollution or worker's conditions, that are compatible with making the actual product. The mess of production is exported out of sight, but still affects the precarious workforce of informationalism. It seems likely that the open, accurate and improving exchange of information can only exist where some people gain their livelihoods from other sources than selling that information.

CONCLUSIONS

Only one of the functions of information is 'to inform'. As well as the normal errors and ambiguities that are essential to communication, there are other functions to information that involve producing action, announcing group membership, gaining political advantage, diminishing another group's political advantage and hiding actions or advantage. These functions can then be intensified when information becomes a restricted commodity and/or marker of status, and a tool in the market. The combined effect of informational disorders outlined in this and the previous chapter is that information society dynamics counter-act the production of useful and freely available knowledge. When profit and power is involved, false information is likely to drive out, or drown out, accurate information. As Jacques Vallee points out, data does not become information, or become useful, outside of a purpose, and it is the purpose that creates the value of that information (1982: 46). It follows that social purposes, social groupings, social relations, structures of communication, conflicts, power ratios, the power/ignorance nexus and institutional modes of problem-solving or limiting problems, tend to define the importance of information either in terms of its market value or capacity to exert influence. This affects public knowledge, as with greater collaboration between State and corporate players, public information is increasingly privatised, as 'commercial-in-confidence' and hidden. Meanwhile, the digitisation of social life enables State and commercial surveillance on a scale never before imagined. In the new info-era public and private are messily reconfigured; there are new fields of 'private' information and simultaneous wide-scale loss of personal privacy. Privatised information is only the latest extension of the appropriation of collective labour. It represents an intensification and extension of capitalist processes into the whole of the intellectual and cultural world. At present this extension looks like it has no limits or no boundaries. Yet its order, enforced by law and implicit violence, appears to disorder those fields of production and distribution it depends on.

The information, in information capitalism, which moves people to spread that information and act on it, will (as marketeers argue) tend to be information that is tied to high motivators, such as 'fun', profit, the perceived interests of the powerful, payment, fear, anger, widespread bias or emotion (Dobele et al. 2007). This marketing can increase the possibilities of what might be called a 'sensationalist' or 'emotional' politics, and the planting of warped or faked information into the public realm. In this world, information expresses a pre-existing or threatened bias, and is aimed primarily at generating effect and affect. This can occur at all levels in the hierarchy, and a position near the top is only differently informed to a position near the bottom, not more accurately. As a result, any 'rational' and 'calm' consideration of data and policies is in decline, while the lack of trusted information leads to the increased possibility of psychological projection, and distress. Information society may routinely tend to generate a politics of information paranoia and projected conspiracy. In this case, we may ultimately end up with a situation in which only a very few people actually support the political process while most people are suspicious of it. Again, the system relies on publicly available informational 'signals' to adapt to reality, yet simultaneously, as a commodity, information is tailored to pleasing expectations and biases, or shutting down access to alternatives, rather than to accuracy. As a result, the information economy erodes the conditions of its own existence, destroying the information flows on which it relies.

In sum, informationalism is caught by the paradox that the information society requires free and easy distribution of information in order to make new products and carry out new explorations and adapt to changing conditions, while at the same time requiring restrictions on information so that property can be constructed, artificial shortages created, profit made and hierarchies preserved.

The factors of hierarchical management, ignorance, differences in information groups, inaccurate communication, commodified and enclosed knowledge and the broader context of ongoing change and complexity, all affect the construction of software, as we shall demonstrate in the next chapter.

7 Software Development

INTRODUCTION

Software is an artefact both produced by, and helping to produce, informationalism. Informational capitalism is becoming increasingly dependent on software, and its need for software to *always* work, efficiently and correctly, continues to rise. As we have shown, despite the accomplishments and accumulated experience of the Software Engineering discipline, a considerable proportion of software projects fail to be delivered on time, within budgetary constraints or working as expected. Like the larger systems of power in which software is embedded, software can often be unstable, uncertain, unpredictable and prone to disruption and failure. Yet each new software development project carries the hopes of users for order and certainty; offering a technological solution that will supposedly solve a specific problem or support an activity. No matter how often software might fail, or underperform, software users remain optimistic that 'this time it will be different!'

This chapter explores the reasons for problems in, and difficulties with, software as depicted by software engineers (and particularly by requirements engineers), which remain neglected by information society theorists. These include problems intrinsic to software itself, and problems resulting from the social and communicative life in information organisations.

REQUIREMENTS ENGINEERING I

Whatever software development methodology or process model is used to engineer software (and we shall talk about some of these later in the chapter), development commences with investigating, exploring and analysing what to build. This stage of the software development process is referred to as Requirements Engineering (RE). Requirements engineering is critical in all software development methodologies, because it is the stage where information about the purpose, functionality, scope and boundaries of the software should be fully identified, analysed, defined, documented and agreed-to. It is at this stage that software development most directly faces the social disruption of information and the difficulties of complex systems. Without an accurate, consistent and complete requirements specification, it is very difficult to develop, modify and maintain software. Almost 25 years ago Fred Brooks, in a landmark paper, stated:

> the hardest single part of building a software system is deciding precisely what to build. No other part of the conceptual work is as difficult as establishing the detailed technical requirements, including all the interfaces to people, to machines, and to other software systems. No other part of the work so cripples the resulting system if done wrong. No other part is more difficult to rectify later.
>
> (Brooks 1987)

More recently but similarly emphasising the importance of RE, Fowler suggests that "everything else in software development depends on the requirements. If you cannot get stable requirements, you cannot get a predictable plan" (Fowler 2005). However, such stability is not easy. Rather infamously, back in 1982, McCracken and Jackson argued that is *impossible* to know the complete requirements in advance:

> systems requirements cannot ever be stated fully in advance, not even in principle, because the user doesn't know them in advance—not even in principle. To assert otherwise is to ignore the fact that the development process itself changes the user's perceptions of what is possible, increases his or her insights into the applications environment, and indeed often changes that environment itself. We suggest an analogy with the Heisenberg Uncertainty Principle: any system development activity inevitably changes the environment out of which the need for the system arose.
>
> (1982: 31)

Bergman et al. (2002: 154) also point out that it:

> is virtually impossible to find optimal solutions to complex problems in a reasonable amount of time due to the inherent limits of human information processing. At best, such problems are amenable to 'satisficing'—solutions that are satisfactory but not optimal.

In other words, it may be the case that the needed information is largely unknown and changes as it is gathered and applied.

Problems associated with capturing, analysing, specifying and managing software requirements are widely recognised as among the major reasons for software project failures in which the end product does not meet the real needs of the users (Davis 1993; Jackson 1997; Thayer & Dorfman 1997; Sawyer et al. 1998; Bano & Zowghi 2013). Errors in requirements specifications can also have a major impact on software costs and on the time spent in software development, particularly during its use and maintenance phase. Early detection and correction of potential problems during requirement analysis may alleviate many much larger problems later on during testing and maintenance. Several independent analyses provide evidence that the later in the life cycle an error is detected and corrected the more costly it is (Boehm 1976; Daly 1977; Boehm 1981; Faulk 1997; Nurmuliani et al. 2005). Boehm and Papaccio (1988: 1466) state that "the cost of fixing or reworking software is much smaller (by factors of 50 to 200) in the earlier phases of the software life cycle than in the later phases". They claim that if people in software projects invested more effort up-front in verifying and validating the software requirements and design specifications, then those software projects would harvest the benefits of reduced integration and test costs, higher software reliability and easier maintainability. Similarly, by examining project failures resulting from requirements problems in U.S. defence systems, Faulk (1997) observes that requirements-related problems are persistent, pervasive and costly. One older estimate is that 40% of requirements need rework during the course of the software development project (Hutchings & Knox 1995). Requirements problems are present to a certain degree on almost all projects despite the many techniques aimed at addressing them (Cheng & Atlee 2007). In many cases RE processes fail to effectively manage requirements knowledge and information, or deploy the most appropriate technique for the particular situation (Sawyer et al. 1998; Davis et al. 2006).

Evidence gathered over the years reinforces the need for software developers to do a substantially better job of performing requirements analysis and specification than they have been doing (Boehm & Papaccio 1988; Jeffery 1992; Davis & Hickey 2002). In other words, it is recognised that failure of requirements specification is normal, despite the best efforts of requirements engineers, and presumably the best efforts of organisations. This is partly because RE is a social as well as a technical activity and disordered social dynamics affect it directly (Bano et al. forthcoming). All the factors that structure and drive distributions of ignorance through an organisation will hinder accurate information, where it exists, from being conveyed to, and modelled accurately, by requirements engineers and programmers, whether they are insiders, or brought in to build the software. These factors then interact with the inherent difficulties of software engineering.

SOFTWARE ENGINEERING

Difficulties in requirements engineering are not the only difficulties in software projects. Software development processes remain poorly understood, and constitute a substantial area of research in their own right. Software engineering is the discipline concerned with designing, constructing and maintaining reliable, cost-effective software. Many definitions for software engineering are given in the literature (e.g. Sommerville 2010), however the following definition expresses the multifaceted nature of the discipline, and provides a comprehensive description of what software engineering is about.

Software Engineering is that form of engineering that applies

- a systematic, disciplined, quantifiable approach,
- the principles of computer science, design, engineering, management, mathematics, psychology, sociology and other disciplines as necessary
- and sometimes just plain invention,

to creating, developing, operating and maintaining cost-effective, reliably correct, high-quality solutions to software problems.

(Berry 1992: 7)

The term *software engineering* was first used at two conferences organised by the NATO Science Affairs Committee in 1967 and 1968. These conferences were held to discuss what was, even then, referred to as the "software crisis"; that is that the quality of software was generally unacceptably low and deadlines and cost limits were not met. The conferences endorsed the claim that building software is similar to other relatively orderly engineering tasks, and concluded that software engineering should use the philosophies and paradigms of established engineering disciplines. That the software crisis is still with us, 45 years later, clearly indicates that even if software construction processes resemble traditional engineering, they have their own unique properties and problems.

DIFFICULTIES IN SOFTWARE ENGINEERING

Frederick Brooks (1987) gave one of the most comprehensive explanations for the difficulties in software engineering. Brooks argued that the very nature of software makes it fundamentally different from other engineered products and hence it requires special techniques and methods. Moreover, it is highly unlikely that a "silver bullet" will be found that will miraculously solve all the difficulties that arise. Brooks divided difficulties in software construction into two categories: essential problems unavoidably inherent in the intrinsic nature of software, and accidental problems that are extrinsic and not inherent to software construction in itself, such as apparently happenstance events like coding errors. The four 'essential' aspects of software production that make it intrinsically difficult are: 'complexity', 'conformity', 'invisibility (un-visualisability)' and 'changeability'. Adding to these essential factors is the social nature of much software, as we emphasise throughout the chapter. We now examine each of these aspects in turn.

Complexity

Software complexity means that the intended product is usually too difficult to be understood as a whole by one person. Simplification is difficult as "descriptions of a software entity that abstract away its complexity often abstract away its essence" (Brooks 1995: 183). However, modelling the system requires simplification, deletion and distortion. Only rarely are the parts of the project absolutely alike; if they are, then they can be made into a subroutine, but much of the project will be specific and different (ibid: 182). Furthermore, although an organisation normally uses its own generic development process model, the specific life cycle of each software product is unique. This uniqueness may increase the difficulties of generalising the learning that has arisen in one situation to another. As complexity affects the process of software construction, it increases the difficulty of managing the process. People in the complex system, especially at different places will see it differently, not necessarily more accurately. Similarly, communication amongst team members in different parts of the process becomes increasingly problematic as the work goes along and product complexity increases and knowledge diverges. Loose ends become a problem. Any personnel turnover creates more difficulties in terms of knowledge loss. Finally, lack of full understanding of the product makes its maintenance very hard, and maintenance typically takes two-thirds of the total effort in software development. Social dynamics add to the complexity, and since requirements engineering is the most communication-intensive activity of software development, complexity will strongly affect the process and product. Generating major and predictable changes to complex systems, in an orderly manner, is always difficult.

Conformity

Software is forced to conform to, or mesh with, an existing environment with which it is going to interact. Complexity increases because the environment the software has to conform to is a unique product of the social and contingent history of the organisations involved. At the least, software has to conform to the hardware and other systems' interfaces, which can vary enormously from site to site. The degree of conformity is usually decided and agreed upon during the requirements stage and hence it is ideal if the stakeholders in software construction are able to develop a full understanding of the extent of conformity needs at that time. However, this may be difficult as the modes of conformity to task, environment or structure, may be an unconscious, tacit, unspoken or even denied part of the background of organisational life, and not noticed or not understood by all vital participants; relevant information may be unknown or hidden. While software has to conform to its hardware environment, it is not always certain as to whether the software has to conform to the social environment, or the social environment to the software. Changing the social environment can result in ongoing struggle, especially when software is used to extend power, or increase workloads.

Invisibility

Invisibility, or the un-visualisability of software, also causes difficulties in software development. It is not that people cannot visualise software; it is just that it is hard. This difficulty distinguishes software engineering from other engineering disciplines where geometric abstractions, maps or plans are very powerful tools for problem understanding, solution development and conceptual testing. Invisibility is related to inconceivability.

> The reality of software is not inherently embedded in space. Hence, it has no ready geometric representation in the way that land has maps, silicon chips have diagrams, computers have connectivity schematics. As soon as we attempt to diagram software structure, we find it to constitute not one, but several, general directed graphs superimposed one upon another. The several graphs may represent the flow of control, the flow of data, patterns of dependency, time sequence, namespace relationships. These graphs are usually not even planar, much less hierarchical.
>
> (Brooks 1995: 185)

Although software engineers have found ways to represent specific views of the product, mainly using different forms of diagrams (for example the Unified Modelling Language, UML 2012, suite of diagrams), these tools do not make the software visible in the same way that geometric representations make other more tangible engineering artefacts visible. It would seem likely that this inability to easily represent software, and the resultant change in the organisation, diagrammatically leads to problems in sharing models. This increases hidden incomprehension or miscommunication between the users and developers, especially when there are structural or organisational borders between these groups. In a related vein, Luqi and Goguen (1997) contrast software engineering with other engineering disciplines by pointing out that in other engineering fields much of the formalisation of the application domain is already done, generally accepted and understood, and that the engineer only needs to apply the methods or formulae. Non-existence of such formalisation increases the difficulties.

Changeability

Change in requirements and its effective management is a core problem of software engineering (Boehm & Papaccio 1988; Luqi & Cooke 1995). Such changes are not just accidental results of poor process management.

The mere fact that when a system is installed in the world it will inevitably change that world will, in turn, bring about changes to the system itself. In effect, the business 'problem' and business organisation, or the new organisation being attempted, initially defines the nature of the technical 'solution' that is desired, but the solution itself changes the characteristics of the business processes and the problem space, resulting in new problems and new possible solutions. In other words, the business environment and processes drive the definition of the system needs and problems and are, in turn, fundamentally changed by the new system forming a problem cycle. Changes frequently arise as a result of the user's increased understanding of the software capabilities and available technology, and the requirements engineer's deepened understanding of the problem and the business environment.

> [A]s a software product is found to be useful, people try it in new cases at the edge of, or beyond, the original domain. The pressures for extended function come chiefly from users who like the basic function and invent new uses for it.
>
> (Brooks 1995: 185)

Hence systems and business processes, solutions and problems, co-evolve.

Sociality

Social factors intrude because gathering information is a social activity, and because software organises and distributes work, organises the communications between groups of people, provides an environment in which actions occur and is performed within the shifting politics of the organisation. Structures of work, structures of communication and environmental factors are all important aspects of social life. Changes in any of these aspects can disrupt people's strategies of livelihood and upset the expectations they may have about the social world and thus may be resisted. Social complexity is added to technical complexity, and social change to requirements change. The different groups being serviced by the software may have different and even conflicting requirements and needs, and yet, due to power and visibility issues, not everyone gets to have a voice in the decision-making about what needs to be done, or gets to be heard when the engineers prioritise and process the problem fixes. What suits one group may not suit others. Similarly the dominant groups may try to use their input into the project to disadvantage the less dominant groups (Marshall & Zowghi 2010: 288). This may not be clear to the software engineers, who even if they did know, may feel that attempting to resolve the issue could get them into complexities they would rather avoid.

Patterns of managerial ignorance may also be important, when people influential to the project do not understand how the organisation works, or the field the organisation works in. One obvious boundary of ignorance arises as people in business and people in programming can have very different cultures, aims, understandings of the world, problem fields and solution sets. It is sometimes hard to cross those barriers, although project managers are supposed to. One unintended consequence of project management could be that it lessens the interaction between programmers and business people, and thus reinforces the incomprehension. An example of a cultural distinction that could cause problems, is that made by software engineers between functional (FR) and non-functional requirements (NFR). As Mairiza et al. (2010: 315) note, NFRs listed in the literature include: accuracy, compatibility, correctness, debuggability, durability, effectiveness, installability, safety, testability, usability and viability. Mairiza et al. write that:

> NFRs are often neglected, poorly understood and not considered adequately in software development. . . . NFRs are not elicited at the same time and the same level of details as the FRs and they are often poorly articulated in the requirements document.
>
> (ibid: 311)

This might surprise those ordering the new system, who might think of what programmers see as 'non-functional', or relatively unimportant, like accuracy or usability, as being vital.

Social dynamics also affect software development because software development is not instantaneous, and ordinary work must go on alongside the development. Unless people are allowed time to participate, then they may find themselves burdened with extra work, such as providing requirements, or training, on top of what they already have to do. This may interfere with smooth and informed development process as well as disrupting normal work. The longer the time taken the more disruption might become normal. The sense of disruption will be even higher if the new system, or parts of the new system, are installed before they are working smoothly, and to some extent it is only possible to be sure whether the software is working as planned after it is fully implemented. Users may find that newly installed parts of the software no longer work the way they used to, or that they have to learn new techniques. If the software deadlines interact with business deadlines (as when an Australian bank installed a major new system at the end of the financial year when its customers needed to access their data), then disruption and panic is magnified. Deadlines can propel hasty and incomplete finishes without proper testing, but without deadlines it becomes hard to make sure that the project is ever finished, as software can always be improved.

Another social difficulty arising in software development is that we have few (if any) generally agreed measures of software quality. Quality is a complicated phenomenon and it is essentially defined by a combination of many characteristics. Hence the notion of quality is normally captured by models that attempt to illustrate the composite properties and their relationships

(Fenton & Pfleeger 1997). In such models, the focus is typically on the final product (usually executable code), and the key attributes of quality are identified from the perspective of different users. These key 'quality factors' are usually high-level external 'non-functional' attributes like "reliability", "usability" and "maintainability". These quality factors are often assumed to be at too high a level to be meaningful, or to be measured directly. Similarly, the apparent quality of software can depend on one's position in the organisation, the tasks one has to carry out on it and the expectations one had for it. From one perspective the code may be brilliant, but from another the program may appear unusable. Finally, our understanding of what software *failure* really implies varies considerably depending on how we perceive failure within different contexts or how little we know about the way computers operate. Whether we consider software that exhibits a slow response time or has an unintuitive user interface as a failure is entirely dependent on arguable human judgement. There will always be defects that need to be identified and fixed, but this cannot always be directly attributed to the standards of software quality or the process that was followed to develop it, or even the competency and skills of the software developers and managers. Naming the result as failure can become a tool used to attack other parts of the organisation, which might be held responsible for the problems, in a political contest. In other words, quality judgements around software are often social, partisan and subjective and may depend on the relative strength of factions in, and between, organisations.

These factors make the products of software engineering fundamentally different, and more socially implicated than other engineering products, and consequently software engineering differs from other engineering disciplines. We now move on to look at the ways in which software engineers have attempted to deal with the problems and make the process orderly.

Software Development Processes

The software development process, or software development life cycle, consists of a group of activities, methods and practices that practitioners use to design, construct and maintain software along with its associated products such as plans, models and documentation. The overall aim of a software development methodology is to describe nearly everything that must be carried out in a successful software development process, so as to deliver a high quality, reliable and cost-effective software product. As already remarked, such completeness may be almost impossible to attain and the requirements for the completed software may be modelled or communicated badly. Since the 1960s, many different models of the software development process have been proposed and, in the space available, it is not possible to cover all the methodologies that have been described. We shall outline the methods known as 'Waterfall', 'Rapid Prototyping', 'incremental models', 'Spiral' and 'Agile', showing some of their problems. Arguments over which method is best are often fierce, and this demonstrates the difficulties of the field, and the difficulties of reaching agreement on method.

A software development process usually begins when a need is expressed for a software product by someone from the problem owner's organisation. This need may arise from the inadequacy of the organisation's current software due to changes in the environment (including other software systems the organisation has to interact with), or the fragmentation of software during maintenance. It may also result from events that have nothing to do with failure in the existing software, but are primarily located in social action, understanding and status maintenance or extension, such as changes in management, takeovers or the perception of new opportunities for improvement or cost savings. With Commercially Off-The Shelf Software (COTS), this need can derive from the marketing activities of the vendors rather than from the needs of the organisation itself. Vendors may, for example, announce that they will no longer offer support for earlier versions of the software; consequently organisations that cannot guarantee to keep the software maintained and functional will be forced to upgrade or move to new software. Indeed the point of the vendor not providing support may be to force organisations to buy its upgrade, so it can stay in business. Levinson (2001) writes:

> In reality, CIOs [Chief Information Officers] are lucky if they can get three years out of a product before vendors release entirely new versions of their software. Vendors [put] further pressure [on] CIOs to buy those new releases by threatening to stop supporting previous releases—a tactic they often take both to cut their tech support costs and to get CIOs to pay again and again for what is essentially the same product.

Once the 'need' is established, there is usually a series of development phases. Typically, (and similar processes happen with the customisation of COTS), requirements are obtained, a software product is specified, designed, built or implemented and fully tested before its use; although it is sometimes impossible to fully test software outside actual use. Once the software construction is complete, if the project sponsors are satisfied with the product, or think it is good enough or that there is no time or money left, then the software gets installed. Then, while the software is in operation, the project shifts into the maintenance phase, which focuses on fixing defects that are discovered during use, and designing and implementing new and emerging requirements. Pressures on time, budgets and staffing, together with periodic crises of failure, often force operators to introduce changes on the run during maintenance, without much planning or record keeping, which undermines both the programme structure and information about the programme. This eventually produces pressures for system replacement (Canfora & Cimitile 2001). When the software finally approaches the end of its usefulness, it is either fully, or partially decommissioned, and replaced by new software. The process is cyclical: perceived problems generate attempts at solutions, and those solutions eventually present problems themselves because the environment has changed, the solutions generate problems themselves, or repair errors accumulate.

It is now well understood that software construction is an iterative and often incremental activity, and is more appropriately referred to as "software evolution" (Lehman & Ramil 2003). It has to deal with ongoing, situational and unavoidable flux, and software is always changing or being developed. In information society there is little respite from software change and the resulting disruptions.

The diversity of contemporary process models, together with the tools that support them (Garg & Jazayeri 1994) is a clear indication of the numerous ways in which different phases of software development work may be viewed and the lack of general agreement. The primary concern is constructing a model to represent the evolving nature of software, as specifically applied to the software requirements. Early models of the software and systems life cycle, such as the Waterfall model (Royce 1970) and the Spiral model (Boehm 1988), were primarily plan-based, acting as managerial tools, and were not very effective for, or accurate in, representing actual development practices (Davis 1993). More recent models emphasise *process* in addition to abstract description of the ways in which software is developed, adding details about the nature of the relationships between agents, their activities and their products. There is growing, but still marginal, recognition of the need to understand the internal politics of the organisation involved (Bergman et al. 2002; Milne & Maiden 2012).

We will now describe the more commonly used software development life cycle models, so as to clearly identify the central role of requirements engineering in all the models and to demonstrate some of the problems that arise in using them. The first set of software development methodologies we describe are considered to be plan-driven. Plan-driven software development uses structures and plans to mitigate and control risks. Plan-driven methodologies attempt to gather as much information about the software and its requirements at the beginning or for each stage of development, before the next stage starts. For example, in the requirements phase, analysts elicit requirements from customers, attempting to produce a complete software requirements specification document. Software architects use this document in the next phase to develop the software design, and so on. This planning structure is intended to prevent any kind of unexpected and undesirable changes arising (Markus 2010). It aims for predictability.

Waterfall

Reflecting this plan-driven approach, the *Waterfall model* (Royce 1970) suggests a linear, systematic and sequential model for software development. Royce himself criticises the model and complicates it. However, in an example of the way information disorder occurs, his work became primarily known for formalising the idea, and it was the simpler version he attacked that was generally adopted. Martin blames this on a U.S. Department of Defense Document (DOD-STD-2167) that set standards for software construction in the military (Martin 2010; cf Brooks 1995: 266). The name of the method was also given later, but Royce still became known as the 'father of waterfall' (Fairley 2009: 56). The acceptability of the model finds its origins in the manufacturing and construction industries where there are highly structured and well understood physical environments, where changes are progressively more costly and sometimes even impossible. In the early years of computation, this product-oriented model was used by default. The process begins with requirements definition and progresses through analysis, design, coding, testing and maintenance.

The Waterfall model has been criticised for representing an unrealistic model of software construction, as real projects seldom follow the smooth sequential flow that the model depicts. Although this linear model can cater for iteration, it does so only indirectly, and this results in confusion when changes need to be made. Furthermore, as already suggested, 'problem owners' are rarely able to state all their system requirements explicitly at the outset, and requirements are discovered as the work progresses or as the system is used. However, the Waterfall model requires or assumes such initial competence and understanding, and has problems accommodating the uncertainty, or even conflict, that exist at the start of and during almost all software projects, and the resulting need to manage changing requirements. Waterfall perhaps seems good for managers, as it makes the software process look predictable, orderly and controllable within managerial conventions yet, as it distorts the process, it may make it harder to manage. We could suggest that the Waterfall model mirrors the general (erroneous) perception that the information society and its problem-solving techniques are orderly, predictable and well-informed.

Rapid Prototyping

The rapid prototyping model was introduced to overcome the problem of lack of feedback and proper iteration in the Waterfall model and to improve activities around requirements capture. The prototyping approach commences with preliminary requirements gathering. Then a rapid design around the apparently mandatory requirements takes place, focusing on those parts of the software that are visible to the problem owners. This design leads into the construction of a *prototype*, which is a working model that is functionally equivalent to a subset of the final product. The prototype is presented to the problem owners for validation and is used to refine requirements for the next stage of development. Brooks points out that in practice most prototypes get thrown away (1995: 116, 264–6). This further shows the difficulty of gathering requirements explicitly and accurately, and implies that people using this model have to be prepared to dispose of the results of labour and money with only indirect result. Another problem arising in this system is that it is very easy to overlook the overall software quality, or its long-term maintainability, in the rush to get the prototype working. Developers also often make implementation compromises in order to get a prototype working rapidly. This may result in inappropriate design trade-offs and inefficient algorithms. When such issues are pointed out to the problem owners, and it is explained that the product must be rebuilt so that a higher level of quality can be achieved, problem owners frequently find this unacceptable (Pressman 2005; Sommerville 2010). The 'rush' is usually generated by social issues, such as: curtailing cost, internal politics, changing environment or perceived immediate need. In this case, the race to get a seemingly orderly system up becomes counter-productive.

Incremental

The iterative process of prototyping can be combined with the Waterfall model to form the incremental model. The incremental model applies the Waterfall model in a staggered fashion as calendar time progresses. Each application of the Waterfall model produces a deliverable referred to as an increment. The process flow for any increment can incorporate the proto-typing approach. Like the prototyping approach or any other evolutionary model, incremental development is inherently iterative. Unlike prototyping, this model aims to deliver part of the final software product with each incre-ment and is specially suited to situations where the required staff are not available for a complete implementation by the deadline (Pressman 2005). A requirements change management process is not explicitly represented in this model but it can be incorporated more effectively with the delivery of each increment.

Spiral

The Spiral model aims to combine the best features of the waterfall and pro-totype models and add to them the element of risk analysis. Boehm's (1988) Spiral model aims to minimise risk by using prototyping and other means. To simplify, this is a Waterfall model with each phase preceded by a risk analysis in which an attempt is made to control or resolve the risks identi-fied. This is, in effect, another attempt to create order, and predict the future of a complex interactive system that may not be practicable. If it is appar-ently impossible to resolve all the significant risks at that stage, then project termination becomes an option. It also may not make sense to perform risk analysis if the cost of this analysis is comparable to the cost of the project itself. Most of the risk analysis may have to be performed before the devel-opment contract is signed, as legal issues may arise if the contract is suddenly terminated, and neither profit nor result is guaranteed for either side of the transaction. This makes its implementation difficult. Cost and allocation of resources are a constant pressure on the production of good software. Yet, because of its precautionary elements, the Spiral model is perhaps best for internal development of large-scale software.

Plan-based approaches emphasise formal (and often written) communication and control. They depend on the accuracy of the models and estimates employed and the accuracy with which they are communicated, all of which can be normally disrupted. Using these models, software engineers attempt to define and contract obligations, so that everyone should know what is expected, and what they should deliver. Furthermore, plan-based development provides for iteration between different stages of development (e.g. requirements, design, implementation, test) using specialised teams or groups. Again, we should emphasise that selecting an approach for software development is situational and depends upon many factors such as organisational needs (for all the groups involved), problem complexity, team skills and capabilities, and the ordering or managerial conventions of that workplace. These variants may not always be recognised or understood.

Structured planning is difficult to organise. It is often undermined by social complexity, social innovations, unexpected changes, unexpected results, business environment change, communication failure, misunderstandings, overestimation of ease of the project, overestimation of the results and internal politics. This is especially likely if consideration of social activity is deleted by the engineers. The orders of software planning and simplification may disrupt software writing and implementation.

Agile

In response to the difficulties with these predictive and disruptive methods, in the mid-nineties a group of new adaptive software development methodologies were introduced becoming known as agile methodologies. These new methodologies criticise many of the assumptions made by plan-driven methodologies. Instead of rejecting change and trying to control it with rational processes and documentation, agile methodologies 'embrace change' and focus on 'continual feedback' from the customer. The agile approach is largely unafraid of disorder and the unknown, and expects it.

In 2001, 17 software developers, methodologists and practitioners of agile methods met and subsequently wrote what is known as the *Agile Software Development Manifesto* (OMG 2001), saying they had come to value:

- Individuals and interactions over processes and tools
- Working software over comprehensive documentation
- Customer collaboration over contract negotiation
- Responding to change over following a plan

They state:

> The growing unpredictability of the future is one of the most challenging aspects of the new economy. Turbulence in both business and

technology causes change, which can be viewed either as a threat to be guarded against or as an opportunity to be embraced.

Rather than resist change, the agile approach strives to accommodate it as easily and efficiently as possible, while maintaining an awareness of its consequences. Although most people agree that feedback is important, they often ignore the fact that the result of accepted feedback is change. Agile methodologies harness this result, because their proponents understand that facilitating change is more effective than attempting to prevent it.

The hope is that by recognising change they can produce order. The ideas underlying agile methods were reasonably common even before the manifesto. For example, Larman and Basili (2003) give examples of software development from several decades previously with short iterations and high degree of customer involvement.

The agile approach to software development emphasises continual informal communications and an ability to react to changes and uncertainty. Agile methodologies utilise short iterations and a high degree of frequent feedback from customers, users and stakeholders. Developers can implement software in small parts and negotiate with customers about the completeness of what has been produced before they move on to the next part. Typically customers provide a preliminary list of general requirements, which is then negotiated and prioritised in communication with the developers. Through frequent interaction with the stakeholders, the development team's understanding of what customers consider the most important parts of the software functions and, hopefully, the customers' understanding about what is technically possible within the budget, are expected to increase. Like all the other approaches it assumes that the official stakeholders understand what is required at the workface, which may or may not be the case, and that accurate communication occurs relatively easily. Once an iteration cycle is completed, the working software is demonstrated to customers, showing the customers the state of the project and, hopefully, enabling continuous feedback from those customers. The feedback then determines the next stage of production. This contrasts with the plan-driven models where every requirement is specified at the outset and it is mainly the developers who determine the development tasks and their priorities for completion (Boehm & Turner 2005).

Most agile software development methods attempt to promote teamwork, collaboration and process adaptability throughout development life cycle. Software development tasks are divided into small increments with minimal planning. Iterations are short, typically one to three weeks in duration. Each iteration involves a 'cross-functional team' working in all of the stages of software development: requirements analysis, design, coding and testing. In waterfall style software development, testing is done after implementation and coding is finished, while in the agile approach testing is done concurrently with coding. This style of development is meant to minimise risk and allow flexibility and adaptability to changes. Each cycle of iteration may not have enough functionality to be considered a major release of the software, but the overall aim is to make some working software with minimal defects available at the end of each iteration.

Although the agile approach is claimed to address many of the challenges of software engineering, there is no shortage of criticism in the literature from academics and industry practitioners alike. For example, if programmers do not write comprehensive documentation that can add difficulties during the maintenance phase when the new maintenance staff have to work out how the code works from obscure or sporadic notes. Valuing collaboration over contract may mean that it is harder to hold anyone firmly responsible for anything. As it is complex, agile software development raises new challenges that have to be addressed. For example, agile methods introduce a shift from a command-and-control style of management to leadership-and-collaboration management. This move implies that project managers may have to give up their authoritative role, which may be resisted (Nerur et al. 2005). Agile project teams are usually cross-functional and are expected to be self-organising, paying little attention to the corporate roles of each member of the team, something that may again be difficult, depending on the organisation. Likewise team harmony may be hard to maintain if the members have different departmental loyalties. Formal managerial and authority structures may likewise get in the way of testing and accuracy. Moreover, it may not be easy to involve the cross-functional development team in decision-making, especially if it is distributed. In this style of management, the team members would have to share the responsibility for software development as a whole. It can therefore be challenging for different groups of team members to agree on issues of an organisational, cultural or political nature when there is no project leader with the authority to make the final decision (Cohn & Ford 2003). The method requires that the development team has constant access to the customer, and some agile methods even demand that the development team must have a full-time customer allocated to the team. Experience shows, however, that most customers do not recognise this need, and even if they do, they don't always have knowledgeable people available to join the development team (Boehm & Turner 2005). So the agile method still runs the risk of being disrupted by power relations, communication structures, misunderstandings and ongoing organisational politics. Indeed, some writers have suggested that relatively ignorant managers can adopt agile approaches in the hope that it solves all their problems, or is quick (as the name might suggest), and might be bitterly disappointed as a result (Bell 2012). Ian Evans describes what he claims was a successful large-scale agile project at British Telecom but remarks "the approach taken by BT is not for the faint hearted—it has included a high degree of risk, and certainly a lot of pain" (Evans 2006: 20). Agile can still be undone by changing requirements, as previously programmed modules are asked to do work they were not designed for. Agile may encourage requirements change and what is called 'scope creep' where requirements become more elaborate as the project continues. It may also lead to piecemeal and inconsistent design (Heath 2012). Agile methods may be more suited to small projects, and particularly unsuited where temporary failure would be disastrous. Agile approaches may increase social complexity, which may sometimes be to the good, but may also add to coordination problems. In other words: "Agile and plan-driven methods have home grounds where one clearly dominates the other" (Boehm & Turner 2004: 148, 55), and debate continues over the nature of those home grounds.

REQUIREMENTS ENGINEERING II

We have emphasised the importance of the requirements process at all points of the software project, and stated how important communication and its disruption is to that process. The terms 'requirements' and 'engineering' were first tied together by Alford (Alford 1977) in the development of SREM (Software Requirements Engineering Method). Requirements engineering has been considered as the fuzzy and rather 'dirty' stage of software construction where a formal specification is developed from some possibly vague and informally expressed ideas. Requirements engineering was initially applied to information systems, and hence was oriented towards organisational and application issues. Since the word 'engineering' has been attached to 'requirements', however, the associated research efforts have endeavoured to incorporate an orderly engineering approach to what was traditionally known as systems analysis (Siddiqi & Shekaran 1996). Davis (1993) notes that there is little uniformity in the terminology used to describe requirements engineering and its related activities. Furthermore, we do not have a single term as yet to express the evolutionary nature of requirements from the process of elicitation through to the whole life cycle of the software (Boehm 1984; Van Lamsweerde 2000). Despite significant advances in the last decade or so, the engineering of requirements remains a relatively immature and difficult discipline. Furthermore, when it comes to choosing between methods, languages and tools, disagreement is often found among researchers and practitioners (Zave & Jackson 1997). Because social issues are at the heart of many of the problems in software development and because they cannot be addressed by the currently available technical methods, novel and eclectic research approaches and paradigms need to be sought (Zowghi 1999).

A survey of software developers of 17 European countries in the IT, production and services sectors consistently ranked 'requirements specification' and 'managing Customer requirements' as the most important problems they faced (Ibanez 1996). In that study, requirements specification and management were regarded as significantly more problematic than documentation, testing, quality systems, standards, design, configuration management and programming. Despite this recognition of requirements engineering's importance, in comparison with the rest of software development activities (or its use as a point of blame), relatively little time and effort is usually expended in the initial identification and analysis of user requirements (Davis 1993; Davis et al. 2006). Almost three decades ago, Boehm (1981) reported that only 6% of the total project costs and 9% to 12% of the project duration are dedicated to the requirements phase. It appears that very little has changed over time as Boehm's figures are very close to those reported in Chatzoglou and Macaulay (1996), which stated that 5%–15% of the project costs and 15% of the project duration are assigned to requirements engineering. More recently, Marshall reports of a small series of interviews: "Absolutely none of the people interviewed thought they had a satisfactory requirements process" in the projects that had affected them (2012: 299). Part of the problem here stems from authority and models. If management primarily aims to reform and improve work practices, it may have no particular interest in finding out what people are doing now, or how they do it. Consequently, management may downplay any attempt at interviewing the workers and gaining full elicitation of requirements, especially if workers might be assumed to be threatened by the process. Management may in such circumstances present abstract plans to the requirements engineers, who produce what is asked for but which does not provide what people need to perform their work (ibid: 301).

Evolution, Consistency and 'Completeness'

We have already pointed to Brooks's characterisation of software as inevitably undergoing change, because the people involved in providing and engineering the requirements cannot possibly envision all the ways in which a system can be utilised at the outset and because software is going to be used by different groups of people with differing goals and dissimilar needs. Furthermore, the environment where software is situated frequently changes and so do the software boundary and business rules governing the utilisation of software (Zowghi et al. 2000; Zowghi et al. 2001; Zowghi & Nurmuliani 2002). However the tendency is for requirement's engineers to proceed as if:

> requirements exist 'out there' in the minds of stakeholders (users, customers, clients), and they can be elicited through various mechanisms and refined into complete and consistent specifications.
>
> (Bergman et al. 2002: 154)

Furthermore, requirements engineers assume that there are coherent organisational goals rather than ongoing struggles and disagreement (ibid). Yet, requirements change and development is normal in complex systems as we have already suggested. A study by Nurmuliani et al. (2005: 2) suggests that the "problem is triggered by continuous change in users' needs, disagreement among customers or stakeholders on agreed requirements, and changes in organization goals and policies", that is, by social factors and the problem cycle. As a result of these changing requirements ('requirements volatility'), the design of a software-intensive system may have to change. Consequently, implementation has to be modified to accommodate changes to software design and to fix defects. Most important though, organisational needs should not be taken as being fixed.

The expression of the needs for any new computer-based system is often informal and vague; Jackson (1995a) calls it a 'rough sketch'. Requirements analysts examine this *incomplete* and often brief expression and, based on the available knowledge and expertise, make assumptions, deduce conclusions using default knowledge to transform this rough sketch into a *more complete* set of requirements. The articulated requirements are then presented to the problem owners for validation. As a result, new requirements are often identified that should be added to the existing requirements. Moreover, some of the previously held assumptions and deduced conclusions that the problem owners do not agree with need to be removed from the set. In practice it often happens that revision of requirements comes either from strikingly new and different needs that demand that the conceptual model be revised in order to account for them, or from some unexpected conclusions that are deduced from the conceptual model itself and that may even contradict some of the already known and used requirements (Zowghi & Gervasi 2002). At each step of the evolution of requirements, the set may lose requirements or gain requirements. One of the requirements analyst's critical tasks in this process is to ensure that as far as possible, the requirements set at each step of evolution remains consistent.

The problem of simultaneously managing changing requirements and maintaining the consistency of evolving requirements throughout software development life cycle is one of the most significant issues in requirements engineering. It is very difficult to predict and trace the implications of change and to check for inconsistency due to complexity and change. It is also time-consuming and many organisations are not sufficiently adaptable to routinely check for inconsistencies. It is normally left for the implementation stage and rigorous testing to detect them (Zowghi 1999). Typically, an organisation's "organizational, functional, and team discourse norms may not always agree", which can add to the difficulty of getting technical and design consistency (Adler 2000: 388).

Another important goal for requirements engineering is the need for 'completeness', namely to capture all the relevant relationships and needs. An application domain situated in the real world consists of *a distinct and identifiable set of individuals* and a *finite set of predicates on those individuals* that represent properties of the individuals as well as relationships among them (Zave & Jackson 1993). The process of identifying these individuals of interest and precisely defining their appropriate relationships constitutes a substantial part of requirements evolution. The boundary between the real world and the application domain is necessarily a 'leaky interface' because the individuals and predicates continue to be discovered and captured during requirements evolution and hence this boundary is volatile. Therefore, at any point in the evolution of a system, one cannot claim with absolute certainty that all the items of interest and their relationships have been captured *completely*, because the application domain itself (where the requirements are situated), is indeed an evolving entity (Brooks's change, conformity and complexity). This argument suggests that absolute *completeness* of requirements specifications can never be established and completeness remains only relative measure (Zowghi & Gervasi 2002; Zowghi & Gervasi 2004). Consequently important or relevant factors are likely to be ignored.

Ambiguity in Requirements

Requirements engineering aims to produce a 'software requirements specification' (SRS) document. This document is inevitably imperfect, due to technical, communicative, political, organisational and environmental factors. Almost all requirements specification documents are written in natural language. While flexibility of natural language gives rise to powerful expressiveness, it also introduces the risk of undesired ambiguities resulting in misunderstandings between stakeholders and developers. Goguen notes that:

> much of the information that requirements engineers need is embedded in the social worlds of users and managers . . . at its source, this information tends to be informal and highly dependent on its social context for interpretation.
>
> (Goguen 1994: 165)

This informal social knowledge is hard to communicate across social groups. Ambiguities in requirements specification documents mean that multiple distinct meanings can be assigned to the same requirement (or, more generally, sets of requirements) (Gervasi & Zowghi 2010). Ambiguous specification may result in two or more software developers writing programs whose behaviours may be different or contradictory; they might operate under different assumptions, even though each developer may be confident that she has programmed the correct behaviour based on her interpretation of the specification. Ambiguity has long been considered to be one of the worst defects in requirements specifications, and that its identification and removal should be prioritised, but it is not just a 'defect' that can be eliminated, and if recognised, can help in program development (Gervasi & Zowghi 2010). During requirements elicitation, analysis and modelling, alternative models for the system are elaborated and a *conceptual model* of the enterprise as seen by the system's eventual users is produced. The specifications are validated and analysed against *correctness* properties (such as *completeness* and *consistency*), and *feasibility* properties (such as *cost* and *resources* needed) (Zowghi 2000b). Competing modes of validation may result in further lack of clarity.

Requirements specifications may also become distorted, as the specifications document also has to persuade stakeholders of the work that should, and can be done, by the software development organisation. It is, in effect, not just a technical document but a rhetorical sales document and statement of commitment. Requirements engineers also have to deal with managers from their clients' organisations who have limited technological understanding and may have unrealistic expectations of what can be done within the existing constraints of time, money, general technical capabilities and the current environment. These factors can lead to the specification writers introducing 'strategic ambiguity' in the SRS document. Levels of accuracy and completeness also depend on who will judge the document, their ability to understand it, and the ability of parts of the organisation to communicate successfully with each other and the requirements engineers, and whether those assessing it will follow its recommendations (Adler 2000: 386–7). As the document has to deal with unknown future changes, implications and complexities, it can never be considered to be complete.

Complexity in Requirements

A complex system is composed of a potentially large number of components that interact in a non-trivial way, and is unpredictable. There is a great deal more to be considered in such a complex system than just the sum of its parts (Simon 1981). The complexity of most software and systems-related problems does not allow us to think about the whole problem at once. So, at any one time in order to progress, software engineers may identify an aspect or part of the problem that can be considered separately, and leave the rest aside until later (Jackson 1995b). Complex systems that exhibit any form of structure are usually thought to be better understood if decomposed into subsystems or component parts. Jackson (1995b) refers to this activity as 'separation of concerns', decomposing the complex system into a number of simpler and separate 'partial descriptions' of particular domains, often according to different criteria. There are many different ways of separating concerns into partial descriptions (see for example Alford's list of various ways to apply separation of concerns in incremental development, in Alford 1994).

The particular criteria selected to separate concerns will have a decisive effect on the development project and will determine the structure of every activity in the development process (Jackson 1995b). The goal of such an activity is to allow one to address only issues and concerns that are related to one part, ignoring (or postponing the consideration of) other parts that are irrelevant to the issue at hand. One of the well-known applications of this principle is in engineering requirements from multiple perspectives, referred to as the 'viewpoints' approach to software development (Mullery 1979), where a system is partitioned into several viewpoints. However after separation, successful re-integration can then be a problem. As Chechik and Easterbrook suggest: "It is often impossible to assess properties of the [re]-composed system based only on descriptions of individual concerns" (2001: 1).

POWER, POLITICS AND REQUIREMENTS FAILURE

In discussing power and politics in requirements engineering, Milne and Maiden (2012) argue that we have to view software system development within a sociopolitical context. They then outline six reasons why power and politics are perceived to be outside of the acceptable scope of requirements engineering, as it is currently practised. These include the difficulties associated with uncovering and defining power and politics, the traditions of requirements engineering in which politics is ignored and the time such activities adds to requirements elicitation (ibid: 83–4), all of which are themselves social factors. Some common assumptions used in requirements engineering also eliminate politics, as with the assumption that organisations are unified with common goals, when they may well not be.

Another possible reason for the neglect is practical. Being interested in an organisation's politics could arouse management paranoia or hostility. Requirements engineering can also challenge the official channels of power and knowledge in the organisation, in that the best sources of knowledge about what is needed from a software system may not be the recognised, responsible or easily visible, managerial staff. Engineers and workers report that attempts to communicate accurately with managers about the inadequacies of their software plans can be dismissed (Marshall 2012: 293–6). This is especially so when the main point of the project is perceived by some of its 'victims' (which may directly include those working on the project) as extending the power of management, limiting workplace autonomy or indeed rendering segments of the workforce redundant (ibid: 296–8). Here, the apparent certainty of instructions embedded in software may be intended to substitute for organisational indeterminacy. Such perceptions, or suspicions, may lead to what Rost calls "subversive behaviour" and deliberate or indirect sabotage, which clearly has the potential to disrupt the project. Subversive behaviour does not only have to come from workers, it can come from other tiers of management or other departments (Rost 2004). By participating in such fragmented, and fragmenting, managerial projects, software development teams become political, or a tool of politics, themselves, whether they want to or not. It is also possible that requirements engineers can be caught in, or even captured by, power struggles between different departments or between those who have an alternative vision of change. Such conflicts can subside in favour of those who have the power to ensure their priorities and models prevail, regardless of their merits. The effect, though, may be to erode organisational goodwill, and to ossify hierarchy into software.

The traditional view of requirements as being pre-existing facts that have to be captured from their application domain, to be formalised into unambiguous, complete and consistent specifications, has long been challenged within the research and practitioner communities. Goguen (1996) argues that software requirements are socially constructed and are not just objective facts to be discovered by a requirements engineer. They are perceived to be subject to (sometimes intense) negotiations, conflicts, frequent change, thus are captive to all kinds of manoeuvrings in the power and politics of organisations. Similarly, proposals for 'socially constructed Information Systems' such as those published by Lin and Silva (2005) and Ovaska et al. (2005) consider software requirements not as a reality waiting to be discovered, but rather as elements in a contested and dynamic framing and reframing of understanding. As Milne and Maiden suggest (2012: 85), Lin and Silva elegantly point out that this consideration presents a major chance for the organisational actors to exercise power and politics in order to influence other actors' understanding of reality.

CONCLUSION

There are numerous problems with assuming software development is an orderly process. Some of these arise from the nature of software itself, and some from the fact that software is developed by humans in a social/informational environment that is too complex to specify completely. Software development in organisations is a social and political act because software organises and distributes work, organises the communications between groups of people and provides an environment in which actions occur. Furthermore, it is performed within the shifting politics of the organisation where it can appear to change the balance of power and activity between groups. Software also tends to impose one model of how things are done, often a model that was built in abstract hope or is subject to dispute between groups. The models also risk changing the complex reality they aim to improve, creating unpredictable outcomes. The solution to some problems changes the problem field and generates further problems in a never ending cycle. Requirements engineering also depends on 'good communication'. As such software development is not only disrupted by its intrinsic difficulties, but by the cultural, structural and political forces that disorder communication of information more generally in the 'information society' or 'information organisation'.

8 Software Disorder and Everyday Life

INTRODUCTION

As we have argued, information society depends upon computers and networks to solve the problems and challenges it faces and generates. However, due to the way contemporary organisations are managed and experienced, breakdown (or failure to meet expectations), is often denied or unexplained, with blame and governance distributed and subject to dispute. Use of information technology can also threaten established social boundaries and demarcations. Furthermore, the problems of digital ordering are embedded in a series of capitalist imperatives that cast information itself as commodity and resource to be bought and sold, with image often more important than accuracy. These recurrent processes leave people ignorant, feeling disrupted and/or suspicious that they are not being told what they need to know, generating information paranoia.

This chapter aims to describe software and network-based information disorder as an 'everyday affair' creating difficulties at every level. The social experience is explored through stories of network failures, hacking panics and governmental failure, illustrated by comments from the public demonstrating the spread of information paranoia when people feel under-informed.

The stories we present about these disorders are not absolutely reliable, because information about breakdowns and broken boundaries is often produced in a wider context of maximising sales, excusing faults or protecting image and power, so the information can easily be perceived as biased or as deliberately obscuring other information. Information acts within struggles over competitive advantage, persuasion, marking out information groups or retaining the status of sources, rather than as 'informing'. Indeed, the alarm people feel about software failure and vulnerability may be promulgated by sources that appear to profit from alarm. When a software or security company issues data about hacking, viruses and spam, in the context of marketing its own software, people may suspect the information. The source may be obscured as the information is repeated and spread, but nevertheless there is a lingering doubt as to its disinterestedness, and people will judge by their existing biases or the reputation their direct source has for them.

Uncertainty over information is a social fact, and in informationalism, available data often comes from such potentially biased or uncheckable sources. There is no external objective place from which to assess claims, hence the ongoing presence of strategic doubt. Similarly, when we read people's comments online there is no guarantee that what they state as being their experience or knowledge, is actually their experience or knowledge. However, the remarks are generally quite repetitive, displaying some of the information society's explanatory myths, whether they are true or not.

It should be emphasised that failure of ICT can result in widespread problems because of its general tendency to work, or through people's ability to become accustomed to conforming to the software difficulties. When something works it tends to be taken for granted and people become reliant on it working. It becomes invisible, and only present when it disrupts. Taking ICT for granted may also mean that people pay more attention to the models and computer output, than to their own senses or research. 'Comic' examples of this occur with people driving their cars into fields or lakes because they are looking at their GPS systems and not their environment. More serious examples occur when people rely on malfunctioning machines to tell them about dosages of medicinal treatments that are trusted above the patients' own, more visceral, feedback (Papows 2011; Delaney et al. 2008; Cancer Voices SA 2008). Similarly, financiers and governments may pay more attention to their economic simulations than to the actual economy (Marshall 2013b).

In what follows we track some of these tendencies by primarily using news from a defined and randomly chosen 'normal' period of the recent past, the month of January in 2011. While limiting both the range of events and potential 'cherry picking', it allows us to describe the scope and aggregated social force and experience of software disruption. January may be considered a 'slow' time of the year for news events, at least in the high-income countries of Europe and North America, and 2011 was relatively distant from the 'exceptional' events of the 2007–8 financial crisis. We track events through a survey of internet sources, addressing their particular significance but at the same time building a picture of their aggregate impacts, system-wide. For more reports from the same month see Marshall (2013a).

NETWORKS, MAINTENANCE AND WEATHER

We have already suggested that networks are not always stable or resilient. Networks also cannot be isolated from increasingly unstable ecologies and weather patterns. Thus in January 2011 the Australian state of Queensland suffered severe flooding, which led to the loss of internet services (Chirgwin 12 January 2011) and the failure of at least one banking network (Anon 13 January 2011). Power, telephone, fibre-optic and mobile lines were threatened or collapsed (Jones 12 January 2011a). Brisbane City Council's flood flag map failed due to high demand for updates on road closures and evacuations, and may have been hard to use on mobile devices, even when working. People reported that hoax or inaccurate messages on Twitter and Facebook generated panic that Brisbane was to be evacuated and public transport was shutting down (Chirgwin 27 January 2013, see the comments; Hearn 11 January 2011). The decentralised nature of communication channels helped to spread confusion as well as useful information. These experiences demonstrate how information both helps and hinders, causing system collapse with mass usage, and being intertwined with misinformation whether hoaxes, mistakes or alarm. Despite this double-sided nature, the main report on Twitter usage during the floods only focuses on the positive aspects of communication (Bruns et al. 2012).

A Commission of Inquiry into the floods stated that the flood problems were worsened by run-offs from dams, and that they:

> found non-compliance with the manual under which the dam was to be operated. What should not be overlooked is that the manual itself was ambiguous, unclear and difficult to use, and was not based on the best, most current research and information.
>
> (QFCI 2012: 30)

Information disorder is everywhere. Many officials and corporate representatives seemed relieved that the floods peaked earlier than expected and did not cause greater disruption, but even so: "Carriers say it is too early to calculate the cost of repairs, but is likely to run into tens of millions of dollars" (Battersby 13 January 2011), which implies a burden to the profitability of companies doing repairs or to taxpayers. The Flood Report stressed that in many areas people could not depend upon the internet or mobile phone services for information or warnings, and that these networks were easily disrupted (QFCI 2012: 389, 582). The report also suggested that the communication issues were not addressed afterwards, and that the event could easily have been much more serious than it was. While the flooding clearly caused people more problems and disruption than did the temporary collapse of communication channels, these events indicate that reliability of information and communication, in information society, cannot be taken for granted, especially during a crisis.

Similarly, beginning in December 2010 storms disrupted internet and phone communications across the U.S. This disruption extended well into January 2011. In California AT&T lines were particularly affected with Verizon experiencing "extensive outages" along with Time Warner Cable (Lazarus 6 January 2011). In the absence of open official reports (as far as we can see) we are again left with anecdotes and comments, such as the following:

> Less than a month after having back surgery, 68-year-old K.P. would position herself at the end of her driveway, the only spot at her east

Hemet home where she could get service on a borrowed cell phone. There, she hoped someone from Verizon would hear her.

Her home phone went silent Dec. 28 amid drenching rainstorms that hit Southern California and remained that way for 12 days, she said. Her dial-up Internet was useless too.

(Pierceall 3 February 2011)

About 32,000 other Verizon customers had communication problems, with another 70,000 having problems with AT&T. The AT&T issues also affected other telcos who rented copper lines from them. Some readers of articles about the collapse accused AT&T of not being interested in copper wire services as there was more profit in wireless phones, and it was alleged by others, including some claiming contact with AT&T's workforce, that the workforce had been cut back to the degree that it could not respond to emergencies. It is a common claim outside of business that focusing on profitability and cutting slack can lead to inefficiency or crisis. A Verizon spokesperson said that due to the emergency it had "increased its work force by 73 percent, although he wouldn't say how many workers Verizon started with, and the employees worked 10-hour days, six days a week instead of a typical 40-hour, five-day work week" (Pierceall 3 February 2011). Such comments suggest that telco engineers in the U.S. face patterns of unemployment followed by overwork during crisis situations. This may reflect a lack of corporate interest in dealing with the ongoing costs of maintenance. All costs, including necessary ones like maintenance, are simply burdens on short-term profit and, possibly, to executive rewards. It also suggests that corporate cultivation of just-in-time employment means that some people depend on catastrophe and overload for work. In another context the American Society of Civil Engineers warned of the "increasing congestion and deferred maintenance and age" of that infrastructure, and estimated that less than half the amount needed to maintain it adequately was being spent (ASCE 2009: 5–7). This includes the electricity networks necessary for computer and information networks. Errors and weak points are continually accumulating, so crisis becomes normal, and storms and floods have the potential to create cascading network effects.

Later in the month Verizon customers throughout Virginia had similar problems. "Customers' devices were in a constant state of 'searching for service' during the outage, causing an inconvenience not only for users but for police and Emergency Medical Service workers as well" (Amodio 25 January 2011). A few days later Verizon reported that a major outage was affecting Sprint, T-Mobile, AT&T and other carriers using RIM's non-corporate email service in the U.S. The explanation, after the event, was that system maintenance caused the problem (Hodgkins 29 January 2011). In these situations, maintenance itself can be portrayed as the disruptor. This might also either increase, or express, the reluctance to perform essential maintenance work.

Significantly and repetitively, readers of the articles quoted above complained that companies offered little to no reliable information, and this led to them waiting for repair services that did not turn up, or having to depend upon an inadequate help line with lengthy delays. Information disorder is rife, and if time and information is profit in information society, then an organisation in a position of relative power will have an incentive to increase profit by taking time and informational precision from others with relatively less power. Burdens of failure are shifted on to those experiencing the costs of that failure. Some people also stated that they had continual problems with lines dropping out after rain, implying that small disruptions of these kinds are regular events, as we would expect from ignored maintenance.

Cold weather in January was also blamed for sporadic outages in East-Link lines in Sudbury, U.S. (Carmichael 26 January 2011). Again customers responding to the article display their world view and experience by complaining about the regularity of problems, the slowness of the company's response and the axing of local staff, which was held to both increase the delay, and increase profit. One writes:

> I have been with EastLink now for 4 months and have had to call them more than 10 times, and I've had to have techs come to me 3 times, and each time nothing was done! No credits given to me what so ever.

Lack of compensation for disrupted services was a common complaint, and this also was explained as avoiding cuts in profit. There was either no apparent obligation for the company to provide the services customers were contracted for, or little awareness of such an obligation. Storms in Baltimore left people without power for over three days. The power company said the severity of storms was unusual. The writer wrote: "But for those without power, that's little consolation. Without TV, Internet and cell phones, it can be hard to function" (Fuller 29 January 2011).

Ice storms in Texas in late January produced similar results. Two coal-fired power plants shut down because of burst water pipes, schools and airports were closed, and power was brought in from Mexico. Lt. Governor David Dewhurst said: "Lack of adequate winterization and preparation appear to be a major cause of the outages", which again implies lack of ongoing maintenance (Brown 2 February 2011). One article states that three security guards refused to allow the reporter to speak to the person dealing with the media, because "officials were not doing any interviews" (Plohetski et al. 2 February 2011). Attempts to shut down information flow seem normal.

Other newsworthy outages in the U.S. in that January affected American Airlines departures (Burt 2011), Comcast (Rutherford 20 January 2011) and people more generally in East Florida, South-eastern Illinois, Colorado (Anon 4 January 2011) and New Mexico (Qwest comments 2011). It appears that significant outages and network breakdowns are not unusual, even if they are scattered. The scattering perhaps makes them look rarer than they are, and they become too normal and plentiful to report. Each outage can then be treated as an individual event, rather than as part of the ongoing disorder.

Weather is not the only cause of network failure. Earlier we discussed the Blackberry crash. Similarly, for the last couple of years Vodafone in Australia has been consistently attacked in the press and by its users for its failure to connect people, line dropouts and lack of security. In January 2011 Vodafone faced a possible class action suit from 9,000 customers protesting about failed connections. Vodafone had initially blamed connection failures in 2010 on software bugs, but then admitted that there were serious problems with its network. In early January they announced they were "working to continue to resolve the current network issues which have been affecting some customers" (Grubb 5 January 2011). A commentator on the Grubb article pointed to the information disorder; "its staggering how many people are affected and yet on the vodafone website, under current service conditions, they blatantly advertise that there is no current service outages!" Another wrote:

How about stopping the head of your support teams from arrogantly blaming users and denying problems exist and lying about call waiting times? How about you stop having your phone support staff deny the problem exists?

Again, people expect that information will be false, self-defensive, company propaganda. Almost a year later Vodafone were suing their suppliers for losses due to signal failure and still ambiguous about their responsibility (Battersby 14 November 2011). In June 2013 the company advertisements implied that its networks worked.

Network failures occurred throughout the world in January 2011. "The Government of Chubut in Argentina and residents using its systems have been affected by Internet outages the government said could be caused by equipment problems in the data center" (Jones 12 January 2011b). In Kenya, "mobile operator Safaricom . . . reported major cuts to its fibre optic network that has led to outage of services for customers in parts of Central, Western and Eastern regions". This failure was linked to tales of increasing vandalisation of cables, with the government planning to increase punishments to life imprisonment for such offences (Karanja 2011). These harsh punishments perhaps arose as the actions were threatening the viability of info-capitalism itself in an informationalising nation. Similarly punishments for digital 'piracy' in the informationalised West, often seem relatively extreme as we discuss in Chapter 10. Another report of the events implies that operators and 'authorities' suspected that the lines were being cut by "disgruntled employees or competitors in the industry" (Ratemo 21 January 2011). Whether true or not, this recognises the vulnerabilities of systems to relatively low levels of attack, and the possibility of corporate warfare and worker sabotage destroying the general interest, but paranoia and blame shifting is also is plausible. Safaricom alleged that, as part of this attack, its main competitor was also cutting its price to unsustainable levels (ibid). The CEO of Safaricom said of the competing company that because it "has insignificant market share in Kenya, if they damage their business here it doesn't matter. They can just pack up and go home". Business competition forms part of a way of explaining, and normalising, disruption. The CEO further alleged that these actions would force operators to "stop investing in infrastructure because they are unable to do so profitably" (Editor 19 January 2011). The relatively high cost of networks, and low returns on fixing or guarding them, contributes to not maintaining them, and thus to ongoing problems.

Interactions between network problems, occurring in different parts of the world, also produce disruptions. In mid-January 2011 the Australian ISP iiNet lost 50% of its customers in New South Wales briefly, after a router was upgraded. Close to the same time, repair works disrupted a cable they used to connect to Cape Town in South Africa and this took out their call-centre (and help desks), compounding the problem. Users complained about slow downloads for Google and slow links to Japan, which disrupted games (ARN Staff 21 January 2011).

Disruption can also arise because it may be impossible to test all the possible kinds of interactions between different systems. The more complexity, then the more unexpected interactions and results. "Microsoft . . . told BBC News that it is investigating why some handsets running its Windows Phone 7 software are sending and receiving 'phantom data'". People were complaining that their phones were sending out about 30–50MB of data per day, eating up their phone data allowance, and thus sending them into disconnect or excess fees and potentially overloading phone networks. The phone and software marked Microsoft's entry into the mobile phone market (BBC 10 January 2011). Microsoft later announced that "a third party solution commonly accessed from Windows Phones is configured in a manner that potentially causes larger than expected data downloads" (Eaton 19 January 2011). A similar story surfaced when the Chinese government announced that some relatively new Android phones were making false calls. This time the problem was apparently not a mistake. Zhao Wei, CEO of Chinese security company Knownsec said "The phones make money by silently accessing mobile services operated or linked to the handset maker", thus subsidising the cheap cost of the handsets. "This [fraud] is fast becoming an industry in itself" (Kan 14 January 2011).

Failure, or complications, of information equipment and networks is relatively common, and it seems that some of these failures arise from lack of maintenance, lack of testing, fraud or conservation of profit and, in information capitalism, are unlikely to end. People have to learn to live around these disruptions, but the more dependent they become on the equipment working, the worse the disruption seems.

ICT AND BOUNDARIES

ICT also creates problems by altering previously existing boundaries. These changes and problems become part of information politics, generating paranoia, suspicion and disinformation. When people and groups who were not previously connected, or who were only loosely connected, are brought into contact, problems can arise. In particular mistrust and conflict are likely to be triggered, with people attempting to restore boundaries, or destroy the boundaries of others. Hacking is one well-known and feared violation of boundaries.

Hacking Panics and Practicalities

Particular technological systems enable different types of vulnerabilities, crime and types of panic about crime. So, as Durkheim (1982: 85ff.) suggested, crime, or breakdown of conventions, is *normal*, and cannot be isolated from the social processes that make ordered normality. Crime, its distribution and punishment (or avoidance of punishment), are part of the system. Similarly, a system creates (or opens) particular vulnerabilities, or points of exploitation, even as it defends against them or suffers from the unexpected consequences of its order. New technological arrangements allow new kinds of accidents, and create new stresses. The following cases show the way that ICT has changed conventional boundaries (especially boundaries of protection), and opened people up to each other, without any clear defence. Again we use events reported in January 2011 to limit the field available.

Hacking while generally referring to computer intrusion, is a term that covers many eventualities and thus may include things that some people find relatively harmless; people can still suggest that 'hacking' is an expression that should be used for writing clever software code or solving problems. The Wikipedia article 'Hacker-term' (27 October 2013), states: "In the computing community, the primary meaning is a complimentary description for a particularly brilliant programmer or technical expert", but this shades into clever solving of problems that some other people may not want, or need, solved.

Knowledge of hacking is a part of everyday computing and social networking, although it may be denied or promoted. According to Rachwald (13 November 2008), the Gartner company estimated that:

> organizations worldwide spent $288 billion on information security products in 2007 U.S. companies alone spent $79 billion in 2007. The U.S. government is allocating $7.9 billion in 2009 for cybersecurity, which is $103 out of every $1,000 requested for IT spending—up 75 percent from 2004.

In January 2011 Internet Security company Secunia reported an increase in vulnerabilities to the 'top 50' implementations on Windows XP and Vista of 71% and 75% respectively over the year of 2010. There was a further increase in the number of vulnerabilities they classified as highly critical, with most of the vulnerabilities emerging from third party programs and not from Microsoft itself. The reason, they claimed, was that these companies were not as quick as Secunia was in spreading patches to users (Secunia 2011: 14–15), which of course renders the information suspect as sales pitch. UK-based net security firm Sophos, in an unsolicited report issued in January 2011, claimed that attacks on Facebook users had increased over the past year; something that Facebook representatives denied. Sophos claimed that scams circulated quickly with little effort to stamp them out, and suggested that a remedy might be that only approved developers should be allowed to make apps for Facebook that accessed user information or could post to their walls, but this might disrupt profit (Leyden 21 January 2011). Knowledge of a bug in Internet Explorer that allowed an attacker to crash the machine 'escaped' in January 2011 when details were indexed by Google, or perhaps the information just confirmed what some hackers already knew. Arguments flourished over who was to blame (Goodin 3 January 2011; Cheng 6 January 2011). With so much information it is inevitable that some hidden and possibly harmful information will escape, and it may not be clear who at fault, and this intensifies organisations' attempts to keep information suppressed.

Finding someone to blame is an important part of seeming to control boundaries. A hacker in Adelaide received a suspended sentence for selling software that could capture people's bank details, on what the judge described as an "internet criminal bazaar" (Kappelle 13 January 2011). Another hacker began a one-year prison sentence after entering Vice Presidential Candidate Sarah Palin's email account and posting her emails publicly on the internet. The hacker had faced a sentence of 20 years on one of the four charges (Reuters 14 January 2011; Jacobsson-Purewal 14 January 2011). A few months later, supposedly all of Palin's emails as Governor of Alaska were released publicly by the State of Alaska anyway (Harnden 2011; MacAskill 2011). A company called Seacoast Radiology reported that the security hole that had allowed unknown hackers to hijack their server to play computer games was fixed (Goodin 14 January 2011a). An IT manager at UK retailer Sainsbury's was jailed for setting up accounts and transferring loyalty points worth "almost £80,000" to them (Oates 14 January 2011).

Sony argued that a court in San Francisco should be able to try a person for circumventing Digital Rights Management features in a PlayStation 3, because he had used Twitter, PayPal and YouTube, which are all based in California, and had agreed to their Terms of Service. The Judge indicated the broken boundaries invoked by the prosecution, and reportedly said:

> If having a PayPal account were enough, then there would be personal jurisdiction in this court over everybody, and that just can't be right . . . That would mean the entire universe is subject to my jurisdiction, and that's a really hard concept for me to accept.
>
> (Goodin 14 January 2011b)

Later, after finding the accused's behaviour was possibly a violation of U.S. copyright law, the same judge ordered the hacker to hand over his computers and hard drives, and to stop publishing the tools used to bypass protection on the PlayStation 3 (Goodin 27 January 2011). The judge agreed with Sony that the accused's activities were "purposefully directed . . . at the forum state", which would also seem to mean that a person in any place connected to California could be tried there if they had an effect there, almost exactly what she had previously found troubling (Groklaw 27 January 2011). We may suspect that protecting the boundaries of copyright and property overpowered other considerations.

On the other hand, George Washington School of Law professor, Orin Kerr, claimed that people should be able to do what they like with hardware they have bought and "this is the first case I know of claiming that you can commit an unauthorized access of *your own computer*" (Kerr 13 January 2011). Under older property regimes you can more or less do what you like with something you have purchased. In informationalism copyright and property are extended into new fields, with little theoretical limit to the possibility of an action being defined as violation of, or similar to, someone's conceptual property. Public and private boundaries *within* property relations have been changed by modes of power, communication and boundary vagueness or violation, leaving no clear boundaries in intellectual or computer property, opening up threat almost everywhere.

Hackers were also charged in a U.S. court with obtaining personal details of iPad users from AT&T servers. The hackers were alleged to have used the data to contact board members of Reuters, the *San Francisco Chronicle*, and Rupert Murdoch's News Corp to tell them about the leak and offering to describe the theft in more detail. This perhaps shows the flexible boundaries between hacking and journalism; especially given the ongoing scandal over Murdoch's *News of the World* newspaper using 'phone hacking' to gain information (*The Guardian* ongoing b). Previously these hackers had proposed, on internet chat, to use the data to provide targets for spam. However, their communications were hacked, but in this case the hacking was considered legal. The charge claimed they "perpetrated the breach 'for the express purpose of causing monetary and reputational damage to AT&T and monetary and reputational benefits to the defendants'" (Goodin 18 January 2011). Again whether this confused set of actions is as unambiguously definable as the charge claims is unclear.

An Austrian carbon trading registry suspended its trading after a series of hacker attacks to preserve the security of other EU systems, presumably because of the dangers of linkage and undefined boundaries. Previously an EU Exchange website had been hacked; some blamed green hackers protesting against carbon credits, while others alleged that people opposed to action on climate change were eager to skim money off the exchanges or make them fail (Leyden 19 January 2011a). Ambiguity is inherent, while information paranoia, or what might be called 'caution', directs responses. Several days later the European Commission suspended certain transactions around carbon trading altogether, while stating the "Commission's best estimate is that roughly 2 million allowances, representing a total of less than 0.02 % of allowances in circulation, have been illegally transferred out of certain accounts" (Europa MEMO/11/34). A fairly small level of boundary violation justifies a generalised fear. It was also reported that systems in Austria, the Czech Republic, Estonia, Greece and Poland had been subject to theft over the previous five days. As each trading certificate came with its own serial number it was not clear how the 'thieves' could resell them (Goodin 21 January 2011). It is also not clear whether this was criminal activity or economic or political 'warfare'—again boundaries are ambiguous. However, the lack of clarity leads to suspension, as authorities don't know what the boundary breakers could have done afterwards. Paranoid projection in uncertainty gives unlimited potential to crime and to fears of crime.

Despite this unlimited potential and panic, normally reported computer crime figures are relatively low. For example, the National Fraud Authority in the UK wrote in January that:

> Online banking fraud [in the UK alone] increased by 14 per cent, from £53 million in 2008 to £60 million in 2009, representing an overall increase of £48 million since 2004, the first year in which online banking fraud losses were measured.
>
> (National Fraud Authority 2011: 12–13)

They also report that fraud in online "shopping, auction and application fraud" accounted for half of all complaints (ibid) and that telecommunication fraud was estimated "to cost £730 million a year" (ibid: 24). "Plastic card fraud", which may also involve use of computer networks, cost £440 million (ibid: 35). The Fraud Authority estimated online ticket sales fraud cost people £168 million (ibid: 32). By comparison, although overlapping, identity fraud was estimated to cost £1.9 billion a year, and fraud involving organised crime £8.9 billion (ibid: 26, 32). By comparison, the Australian Payments Clearing Association reported in June 2011 that "card-not-present (CNP) fraud—that is, online, mail or phone-related card fraud—increased by 38%". Over 2010 there were 795,986 transactional frauds, only 1,247 of which were cheque frauds (APCA 22 June 2011). These are clearly small amounts when compared to the total financial traffic in the world. They are also estimations.

Information seems hidden as usual, and real fraud figures may be much higher. An Australian researcher in the fraud field who wished to remain anonymous told us that:

> I worked for two different banks in the past and I found they would have been happy to report all fraud to the police if that were possible, however actual crime statistics produced by the Australian States and Federal Police is dictated by the work processes of those organisations (they only accept a small minority of frauds for investigation and the rest effectively don't get entered up anywhere).

Conflicting social organisations, attempts to balance costs, transfer costs and remove panic also reduces information and lessens attempts to deal with fraud. John Buzzard, an executive at a credit scoring company is reported as saying.

Losses are comfortably in the multimillion-dollar range each year but are incredibly hard to authenticate because of the discreet position that most financial institutions take when asked to assess a loss figure.

(Consumer Reports June 2011)

The article goes on to suggest that security measures in the U.S. are not particularly rigorous because the "losses for banks do not yet exceed the costs of a switch-over, although merchants say that's because they usually shoulder much of the cost burden from fraud" (ibid). Whether this is true or not, it indicates common paranoia and fears that secrecy may be being used to reinforce commercial legitimacy, displace costs onto smaller players, and that fraud is more normal than reported and rarely prosecuted. The British Chief Executive Designate of the Prudential Regulation Authority claimed that it would be difficult to prosecute banks themselves for fraud, because it would be destabilising.

His comments come days after HSBC's record $1.9bn (£1.2bn) settlement with the U.S. authorities over money-laundering linked to drug-trafficking. U.S. assistant attorney general Lanny Breuer said of the decision not to prosecute: 'In this day and age we have to evaluate that innocent people will face very big consequences if you make a decision'.

(Wilson 14 December 2012)

Corporate crime cannot be dealt with because the networked consequences appear too great.

Hacking is not restricted to an underworld, but is found in the State and corporations. While little is available from our time frame, the Chinese and Russian governments are often reputed to sponsor hacking and the theft of ideas. The U.S. Office of the National Counterintelligence Executive stated that: "Chinese actors are the world's most active and persistent perpetrators of economic espionage . . . [and] Russia's intelligence services are conducting a range of activities to collect economic information and technology from US targets" (NCIX 2011: 5). China has accused the U.S., Japan and South Korea of similar activities (Xinhua 20 March 2012). Files from the G20 meeting for 2011 were hacked in Paris, with suspicion pointing to people with an interest in currency valuations, including the Chinese government (BBC 7 March 2011). The organisers of a security conference in Austria in 2009 singled out corporate espionage as a significant problem saying "Stealing products is a lot easier than doing research . . . Industrial espionage is getting a bigger problem" (infosec 18 September 2009). Reports from internet security companies McAfee and Idappcom both claimed that cyber-crime was turning towards 'industrial espionage' (infosec 30 March 2011).

Corporate hacking can also feed into the disruption resulting from illegal distribution of information bounded as commodities. In January 2011 *Ars Technica* reported an academic study from December 2010 that stated that "fake files made up 25 percent of actual user downloads" from peer-to-peer torrent sites. "The study's authors conclude that most of the video content from fake publishers comes from antipiracy groups, but that the software is more likely to be from malicious users out to spread a computer virus or promote a botnet" (Anderson 24 January 2011). Thus by attempting to enforce the order of copyright, companies may well be distributing viruses that then affect the computers of those who are not engaged in piracy themselves but are connected to those who are. Corporate attitudes to 'piracy' also seem ambivalent. Mike Asay, Senior Vice President of Business Development at Strobe and Emeritus board member of the Open Source Initiative, alleges that large software companies have generally been happy to allow piracy of their software in the developing world, because it binds the mass of users to their software rather than providing a chance for freeware alternatives to establish dominance (Asay 21 January 2011). Bill Gates is often reported as saying to an audience at the University of Washington:

> Although about 3 million computers get sold every year in China, people don't pay for the software. Someday they will, though . . . and as long as they're going to steal it, we want them to steal ours. They'll get sort of addicted, and then we'll somehow figure out how to collect sometime in the next decade.
>
> (Piller 2006)

Again the boundaries between theft, loss and good business strategy are not clear.

Networks and Boundary Politics

Networks also present casual and normal data vulnerabilities. These unsure boundaries were indicated by a case involving Google and the State of Connecticut, which in January 2011 was being negotiated rather than settled in court. Connecticut, representing all 50 U.S. States, had demanded that the company turn over the data its Google Maps Street View cars had collected from insecure Wi-Fi networks in the state. Google had refused to hand over the data, which it claimed had been gathered by accident. John M. Simpson, Director of Consumer Watchdog's 'Inside Google Project', was indignant, saying the "biggest privacy breach in history shouldn't be settled in secret" (Metz 29 January 2011) but this seems normal in information society with secrecy accruing to corporate power. As people commenting on the article wrote, the settlement implies that Google is able to keep, or copy, the data and not admit any wrongdoing, even if it has done the same thing many times before. Power is seen as important in establishing which boundaries are recognised, who gets punished and who suffers information vulnerability:

> Google, like some multinational Banks and Media corps and, to some extent, Social media & computer companies doesn't give a toss what Governments in a particular location do or say. They have more perceived and actual power and far better PR machines. Cross them at your expense.
>
> (comment on Metz 29 January 2011)

One person suggested it could be part of a coordinated spying plan with the American states deciding to take a cut, while others stated that if your data was not secure then you could not object to being spied on. This idea of coordinated spying was not just paranoia, but confirmed in 2013 when Edward Snowden leaked records of NSA spying on almost everyone (*The Guardian* ongoing a; Greenwald 2014). The Google case also implies that large amounts of personal data is there for the taking and could lead to accidental disruptive consequences. Do those who had the information skimmed by Google really want their information in the hands of their local government, spy agencies or potential blackmailers either?

As we saw with the Stuxnet worm story, also surfacing during this month, hacking can also affect political relations between States and break the boundaries of warfare. Sometimes the presence of cyberwar, and sometimes the sides involved, are unclear and based in suspicion. Accurate information is suspended within the need to do something, increasing the role of fantasy and paranoia.

This ambiguity about boundaries and panic also applies in domestic politics. In January 2011 in the UK, Sir Hugh Orde, President of the Association of Chief Police Officers, stated that use of text messages, Twitter and Facebook to organise protest campaigns speedily had created "a whole new dimension to public order" (Hill 27 January 2011). People had, for example, been organising online to walk into shops, fill them and do nothing. This effectively shut down the shops. People doing nothing in shops can thus become suspected of trespass and subject to violence; paranoia increases. Orde added that if demonstrations had no leaders or hierarchy, and there was no one to negotiate with, then "our policing tactics will have to be different . . . slightly more extreme", especially given the presence of cyber-crime and protest groups like online hackers Anonymous (ibid).

An example occurred in August 2011, after the London riots, when two young men were jailed for four years for posting messages on Facebook that were alleged to be inciting riots. This was despite no trouble emerging from their posts (in one case the police were the only people who turned up). As a member of the government stated "if [the offenders in question] had committed the same offence the day before the riots, they would not have received a sentence of that nature". The prosecution argued that the posts had caused widespread panic and rumour, despite the lack of turn out. Disorderly 'information' and even jokes, as one of the offenders claimed was the case, can cause panic amidst the authorities as they seek to allocate blame and filter the confusion. The judge said that sentencing guidelines could be dismissed because of the context of the riot, which perhaps shows the broken boundaries of the guidelines. As usual with the mess of information there was some uncertainty about the *official* nature of advice to ignore guidelines and extend sentences. "The judiciary and the Ministry of Justice have denied that they were involved in circulating the advice to justices' clerks last week" (Bowcott et al. 17 August 2011). The threat of networked disorder and ambiguous communication is met with the imposition of more intense orders, which then catch the innocent or ineffective and lead to further disruption and paranoia.

Social networks can also be disrupted by management actions seeking control and order of ambiguity, as when in January 2011 Facebook banned, unbanned, re-banned and finally unbanned a breastfeeding support group. Several members reportedly had their accounts disabled. This is not the first time Facebook has banned such a group because it mentioned breasts and thus supposedly violated Terms of Use, which are ignored in other contexts. The owner of the page received a form message from Facebook stating that:

> Pages that are hateful, threatening, or obscene are not allowed. We also take down Pages that attack an individual or group, or that are set up by an unauthorized individual.
>
> (TheLeakyB@@b 3 January 2011)

Obviously some of these definitions have the potential to be overbroad. Users of the group created Facebook support pages to protest. Responding to protests, Facebook insisted that the company took "action according to our policies, which are designed to ensure Facebook remains a safe and trusted environment for everyone, including the many children (under the age of 13) who use the service" (Belkin 6 January 2011). Facebook is *not* supposed to accept children under 13, but it does (and cannot police this limit anyway), but the informational attitude and its cautions are ambiguous. Facebook was later reported to have claimed this remark was a typo (Ozimek 10 January 2011). Blanket control of information is difficult and causes problems, yet there does not seem to be the same amount of caution with people's personal information when it is profitable to the company to sell it to others.

Networks also allow hacking to be a source of protest. Hacks on social networks can select for celebrity and thus not affect many people, but they become part of the folklore, and pointedly illustrate that no one is safe. French President Nicolas Sarkozy's Facebook page was hacked to display a message that he would not be seeking re-election in the following year (Leyden 24 January 2011). Facebook founder Mark Zuckerberg's page was also hacked to "promote an alternative business plan for the social network site" (Leyden 26 January 2011). Fame attracts attention in unexpected ways, just as it becomes a kind of currency and source of power. A day or so after the hack on Zuckerberg, Facebook offered users the option of accessing the network via secure encryption. Some people alleged that Facebook saved money by making secure login an option, rather than automatic (Metz 26 January 2011). In any case this event could demonstrate that a *visible* hack against the powerful is necessary to make the 'danger' real, especially when 'danger' competes with profits. A *USA TODAY* article suggested that "It will be much harder this year for companies to deflect the rising onslaught of cyberattacks orchestrated to knock them off the Internet". Examples of some 'Denial of Service' attacks include those on:

> the Motion Picture Association of America's website, knocking it offline for 20 hours. The motive: payback for MPAA's alleged efforts to shut down PirateBay.org, a popular site for downloading pirated music and movies . . . Home PCs were [also] behind the December attacks that disrupted the websites of PayPal, Visa, MasterCard and PostFinance, a Swiss bank. Protesters sought to punish them for cutting off services to the WikiLeaks whistle-blower site.
>
> (Acohido 5 January 2011)

Comments on the article demonstrated a range of interpretations. Some people suspected the events were evidence of a government plot to show the internet needed regulation, some suspected that the attacks were continuing as MasterCard was still slow and others argued that people had to attack corporations to get their rights back.

FINANCE AND INFORMATION FAILURE

Ordinary banking networks are also open to everyday manipulation and failure. Research from the firm Global Reviews was reported in January 2011 as stating that workers in call centres for Australian banks could often be persuaded to reveal people's bank account details. When one particular bank was excluded, then two thirds of centre staff would be 'helpful' (Martin 11 January 2011a, b). Some comments on the story allege the report is wrong or exaggerated, or normal. One person wrote:

> I had my wallet stolen a few years ago, and three days after I had told the bank and cancelled my cards [the thief] got my internet banking password re-set and withdrew money from my account. All they had

> to do was provide my drivers license and medicare numbers—not hard
> considering they had stolen my wallet!
>
> (in Martin 2011a)

In other words it is hard to produce information security when we have to carry so much information that identifies us, or when everyone knows (including help centre staff) that things go wrong. Another version of the story about the research (in Martin 2011b) gives further reader responses. One person adds that from their personal experience of working on a bank help line, there are at least two reasons why workers might help fraudulent access:

> [First] improper training . . . I received in total 4 weeks of training—for two different roles. Within such training dealing with situations of fraud in a textual context is mentioned, though actually facing it on the phone and what is required to do was briefly mentioned, and hardly emphasized. Second reason is the job is hard—yes, simply hard, 3 minute calls, over and over 9 hours a day, not one break between a call.

The implication is that costs of training (and perhaps urgency of training) affects thoroughness of training, and that intensity of work leads to workers losing concentration as well as to wanting to finish the call without complaint. Another person pointed out that because businesses constantly ring people up and ask for information:

> A social engineer could call someone up and pretend they're calling from the phone company or bank or whatever. They can say "can I please confirm your name and date of birth" (plus any other details they require). They can then use these details to ring up the bank and pretend to be that person's partner or friend and make up a story.

In general scammers can phone claiming they are from a company and present no evidence that they actually are from that company as this is standard corporate practice. One example is calls, apparently originating in India, claiming to be from 'The Windows Corporation' saying they have found a virus on the victim's computer (Gedda 2009). The common corporate outsourcing of call centres overseas helps the scammers by making it hard to identify where they are. Workers in these organisations may not even be aware that they are engaged in potentially criminal actions; again boundaries are broken. The actions of legitimate organisations in marketing their products, and asking for identification of customers over the phone, allows breaches of identity and security that can then be used against those organisations. Only rarely do marketers enable the customer to identify them as being who they claim to be. Two-way information flow is commonly blocked. Communication is encouraged in the manner that primarily benefits the corporation, and this blockage then threatens corporate security.

On the other hand security can be too tight and automated, causing disorder. As an example, a couple deposited a cheque written in red ink into their bank account, to find that a scanner could not read the cheques with the consequence that their accounts were suspected of fraud and closed down. Their pay cheques could not be deposited and they could not make payments. They "went to the Chase branch in downtown Oakland and spoke to a manager 'who was sympathetic, made some phone calls, but could do nothing about the situation since Chase had already decided to close the account'". The matter was dealt with only after they went to the press (Pender 6 January 2011).

ENISA, the EU's cyber-security agency, issued a report commenting on the steadily rising incidence of personal information disclosure breaches, noting that companies:

> wanted assurances that applying breach notification rules and reporting slips would not result in damaging their brands. The concern is that those that report problems, in compliance with the rules, will be 'punished' by earning a reputation for poor security while those that do nothing will avoid tarnishing their reputation.
>
> (ENISA 2011: 4)

Conflict also emerged because "Regulators want short deadlines whereas service providers wanted to be able to focus their resources on solving the problem, before they dealt with the regulatory fallout of any breach" (ibid: 32). Information that admits problems tends to be suppressed for commercial reasons. As argued previously, information is only valuable if increases profit, is appealing or has an effect. It is not neutral and can be used against the emitter. As a result, ideally the only problems that can be acknowledged are those that have been fixed up and no longer risk anything. Information disorder, rules and errors, vulnerabilities and vagueness accumulate.

OPEN INFORMATION, GOVERNMENT AND CONFUSION

We have previously remarked on the conflict between free circulation of information and commercial value, and this again surfaced in January 2011 when the British Minister for the Cabinet Office, Francis Maude, announced a new Public Data Corporation. He was reported as saying:

> At present many state agencies face a conflict between maximising revenues from the sale of data and making the data freely available to be exploited for social and economic gain. Creating the PDC will enable the conflicts at the least to be managed consistently with a view to opening up access, and at best to be eliminated.
>
> (Rogers 14 January 2011)

The announcement was greeted with considerable suspicion. The article's author guessed this suspicion arose because "no-one knows what it [the PDC] is for"; as usual information and context were unclear. Tom Steinberg of the Public Sector Transparency Board thought that the change could be good or bad depending on the public's actions. Comments on the article suggested standard information paranoia: "This is the government trick to shut [free circulation of government information] down" and "The general implication is that Maude is looking for ways of charging users, and getting the private sector to run the show". The UK government's press release talked about attracting investment, "where charging for data is appropriate to do so on a consistent basis", and making "more data free at the point of use, where this is appropriate and consistent with ensuring value for taxpayers' money". It also wonders if "data held by public bodies could be used in an innovative or entrepreneurial way" (Cabinet Office 12 January 2011). In informationalism any data is always potentially a commodity, and users know this means additional costs.

Governments have many informational problems. Later in January, the UK government announced that the previous government's ID card scheme, which had cost £330 million to establish, would be scrapped at a cost of just £400,000 despite concerns about the security of the data destruction (Fay 20 January 2011). The last of the hard drives containing information was reported as destroyed in February that year. Further problems with British data systems hit the news again when the Information Commissioner's Office reprimanded the NHS Blood and Transplant for wrongly recording organ donation preferences over a decade because of a software error (Laja 21 January 2011). The details of over 400,000 people needed correcting (ICO 21 January 2011). A British Ombudsman's report that month showed that a woman had her details changed in error on one government computer and that the change had spread through the network without check up. As a result personal information was sent to her ex-partner and her government monies were cut back. When she discovered and reported the error it was not corrected, no one would explain what had happened and people were reluctant to change the data until the Ombudsman's office got involved. The point is again, this is not *just* dereliction of duty or inefficiency; this is normal functioning in informationalism. The Ombusdman's report demonstrates the lack of accountability:

> The network of computer systems could not then always locate the source of any errors made . . . By the time we became involved, the audit trail of Ms M's records was no longer available due to the National Insurance Contribution Office's record retention policy, and their records showed no history of the incorrect changes to Ms M's address because the data had been removed without any record or explanation.
>
> (Parliamentary Ombudsman 2011: 10)

Information preserved on computers is only ambiguously permanent and seems relatively easy to hide or to obliterate, compounding the error and hindering attempts at correction or prevention.

The difficulty of containing information was demonstrated by Wikileaks leaking of government documents. Some of these leaks have been credited with beginning the so-called 'Arab Spring' with the revolution in Tunisia, which cumulated in its president fleeing to Saudi Arabia on 14 January 2011. The United Kingdom Information Commissioner Christopher Graham advised governments to publish more information to make the leaks less exciting, saying "From the point of view of public scrutiny, the web and the internet has empowered citizens" (Curtis 30 December 2010). Despite this advice, attempts at containment continued. The White House was reportedly telling U.S. agencies "to create 'insider threat' programmes to ferret out disgruntled workers who may leak state secrets" (BBC 5 January 2011). The U.S. Department of Justice also served subpoenas on Twitter to get information about the tweets of suspected Wikileaks supporters, including those of foreign nationals.

> It includes all mailing addresses and billing information known for the user, all connection records and session times, all IP addresses used to access Twitter, all known email accounts, as well as the "means and source of payment", including banking records and credit cards. It seeks all of that information for the period beginning November 1, 2009, through the present.
>
> (Greenwald 8 January 2011)

Twitter was initially banned from making the order public but early in January they were permitted to do so. Investigative journalist Glenn Greenwald points out that other companies could have complied with the order secretly as requested and not asked for it to be publicised: "[I]t will be a long time before we know, if we ever do, given the prohibition in these orders on disclosing even its existence to anyone" (ibid). This gives more play for speculation and paranoia, which can be useful to the powerful—who knows if what you are doing is being observed or will be observed?

CORPORATE INFORMATION PROPERTY

It is, however, not just governments who have problems with open information and the control of information. There are ongoing disputes about ambiguous property boundaries and hence copyright and patenting. Courts can be used both to make product boundaries and challenge them. For example, on January 25 2011 as part of a long-running dispute, Microsoft filed a complaint with the U.S. International Trade Commission in Washington, accusing TiVo of infringing four patents, and asking that TiVo be barred from importing its set-top boxes into the U.S.

> The four patents in the ITC case relate to program schedules and selection, controlling the interface, and a way to restrict use of the DVR based on the program's rating. Microsoft said the technology is used in its Mediaroom software that runs on competing set-top boxes.
>
> (Decker 25 January 2011)

Microsoft filed the same complaint in a civil lawsuit with the federal court in Seattle (ibid). Almost a week earlier, Apple filed a lawsuit in the High Court in London challenging the validity of a Nokia patent for scrolling technology on touch-screen handsets that Nokia had previously asserted, in a Dusseldorf court, that Apple had violated (Larson 20 January 2011). Other moves can seem like corporate war. Towards the end of January 2011 Finland's Consumer Agency announced that iPhone users who found that the phones would not work in the cold should be entitled to a full refund, despite Apple's small print, as all items sold new should operate in the way they might reasonably be expected to do. The article wondered if this announcement had anything to do with Nokia being a Finnish company and the largest taxpayer in Finland as the writer had found that the phone worked in a Scottish winter (Ray 28 January 2011). Again information is suspected of being used as a weapon.

Open source software faces similar challenges. Its codes and protocols are widely used, as in the software running Google, Amazon, Facebook, Twitter, Wikipedia and various stock exchanges, so it is not merely a theoretical threat to proprietary software. Open source can threaten ideas of information property as enclosure, and the advocacy movement associated with it frequently feels under attack. After the company Novell was taken over by Attachmate for $2.2 billion, patents were to be given to CPTN Holdings, and during January 2011, the Open Source Initiative and the Free Software Foundation alleged that:

> the proposed recipient of Novell's patent portfolio, CPTN, represents a serious threat to the growing use of free/libré and open source software (FLOSS) throughout business, government, academia, and non-profit organizations worldwide.
>
> (OSI & FSF 2011: 1)

Companies affiliated with CPTN (Microsoft, Oracle, Apple and EMC) are generally in competition with open source, while Novell participated in open source. This takeover of Novell's patents could allow companies participating in CPTN to launch patent attacks on open source users (ibid). Later on the U.S. Department of Justice issued a statement saying:

> as originally proposed, the deal would jeopardize the ability of open source software, such as Linux, to continue to innovate and compete in

the development and distribution of server, desktop, and mobile operating systems, middleware, and virtualization products.

(DOJ 2011)

A new agreement was drawn up that seemed to keep the patents open, but disputes continued about what it meant in practical licensing terms (see, for example, the comments on Vaughan-Nichols 2011). So the boundaries on ideas, interrupt ideas.

Software cannot exist if other platforms will not support it, and software value can be perilous and subject to undermining by the fiat of other corporations. On 11 January 2001 Google announced that its web browser Chrome would no longer support the H.264 video codec used by Apple and Microsoft. It would move to the WebM open standard, but still use Adobe's Flash Player, which makes use of H.264. This was seen as a commercial strategy, to limit the access of other companies. Similarly, YouTube, and much advertising, depends on Flash, and Apple did not support Flash on iPhones or iPads (Metz 12 January 2011). A few days later Google announced it would release plug-ins that run WebM for both Internet Explorer and Safari (Metz 15 January 2011). Several days later again, open source advocate Florian Mueller claimed that Google copied at least seven and possibly 43 Android files from Oracle's Java source code. Sun had invented Java, but largely allowed copying, something Oracle was not so keen on after it took over Sun. Mueller's claim could have consequences given that Oracle was in a lawsuit with Google over the use of Java (Metz 24 January 2011).

CONCLUSION

January 2011 was an ordinary month in informationalism's history, and its disorders were writ large across multiple fields of social life. The reportage demonstrates a reflex uncertainty, and also a sense of vulnerability to vested interests, which themselves may be radically destabilised. The wide range of themes, social sectors and concerns are surprisingly unified in terms of the expression of a broadly similar interpretive frame, grounded in what are asserted as broadly similar value claims. Overall, this chapter has discussed the disorder present in ongoing maintenance and infrastructure failure, network collapse and the blurring and ambiguity of boundaries in business, property and government. All of these factors generate an expectation of uncertainty and attack. While computers, networks and software, solve problems, they also open new problems.

Maintenance and infrastructure failure appear to occur largely because they are not considered productive, immediately profitable or glamorous ventures; information society tends to devalue its own material base and attention gets turned in other directions. Consequently, the need for maintenance appears to surprise people, tends to be rushed, dependent on crisis and results in increasing complexity and difficulty of service, due to the accumulation of uncoordinated patches and responses. Increasing complexity suggests increasing conflict over what can be adapted or repaired, and the possibility of increased expense to bring about stability or productive change. As pointed out by Veblen years ago (1915: 130ff.), legacy equipment (he was discussing railways) becomes an increasing burden on what can be done, as well as becoming entangled in politics as vested interests have become built around the equipment and the problems it solves. Change could lead to a loss in their power or wealth. It is likely that vested interests accumulate power in the State and use the State to block changes, and to preserve and increase their existing power relations. Distribution of governance makes areas of responsibility vague, and boundaries can become obstructions, while the removal or erosion of boundaries can cause disruption.

The extension of computer networks has changed the boundaries between people and institutions, making those boundaries sites of battle and suspicion. This is especially the case given the repeated blockage of flows of information, when a system does not work, which then open-up spaces for paranoid fantasy. Corporations are as likely to compete over the definitions of, and boundaries around, intellectual property, as they are to accuse consumers of violating that property. The courts become as important a part of competition as the market. Hacking, or the suspicion of hacking, becomes an everyday affair, and the safety of one's own records, money and identity, or even political action is constantly under threat from actions that could come from anywhere. Again, suspicion is encouraged by fear and by those who profit, and loss of trust, in whatever is identified as potentially hostile, is increased. Disorder, and the fear of disorder, becomes central to everyday life, and to the responses of governmental, corporate and informational institutions.

9 Finance, Crisis and Informationalism

This chapter, again, emphasises disorder, which, as we shall see, is the life-blood of a financial system that feasts on risk and instability. There are three phases in the analysis. After a short discussion of finance and fantasy, we proceed to discuss the general problems of finance as a form of information, focusing on the dynamics of the global financial crisis. Then we introduce a narrative of the rise and effects of information technology in the finance sector with its first 'revolution' in the digitisation of financial value from the 1970s. Finally, we consider what has been characterised, since the mid-2000s, as a 'second revolution' in the sector; the automated digital transactions dubbed 'high frequency trading'.

FINANCE, FANTASY AND SATIRE

On 1 April 2011 the London-based *Financial News* announced that a finance house had bought and sold equities at the speed of light using a particle accelerator, and was looking to 'breach the light barrier' (*Financial News* 1 April 2011). Four days later a retraction was issued, clarifying that this was indeed an April Fools' joke (Schneider 23 September 2011). Later in 2011 the Chicago-based financial data company, Nanex, criticised the presence of apparently inaccurate time stamping of trades in the heart of informational finance, by floating the concept of 'fantaseconds', suggesting that high frequency trading (HFT):

> has reached speeds faster than the speed-of-light, allowing time travel into the future . . . Based on official UQDF/UTDF exchange timestamps, there is unmistakable proof that YHOO trades were executed on quotes that didn't exist until 190 milliseconds later!
>
> (Nanex 2011:1)

In 2013 Nanex clarified that they had been satirically referring to the speed difference between direct trades by HFT machines and other trades, which gives HFT traders the (illegal) advantage of knowing what trades are going to happen, buying first and then selling them to the original buyer at a small markup. This practice is often known as 'front running': Nanex clarified, "if regulations are being followed, we should never see fantaseconds" (Nanex 2013). Coming from a company that itself offers 'real-time streaming' of "over 6,500,000 quotes per second", the spoof had been unintentionally successful:

> What many readers of the paper didn't realize at the time, was our suggestion that somehow high frequency traders figured out how to go faster than light, was satire. It didn't help that just hours later, CERN [European Centre for Nuclear Research] announced the possibility that they detected particles traveling faster than light, and many people conflated the two stories.
>
> (Nanex 2013)

In 2014 the entry on 'Fantasecond' was removed from Wikipedia as 'Patent nonsense, meaningless, or incomprehensible' (any reference to the entry having existed was later deleted; Wikipedia 2014).

The suggestion that the rising speed of financial computing had now brought us into the age of time travel, together with the dissemination of this information beyond those deploying it for ironic effect, reveals something of the role of fantasy (and disinformation) in financial computing. The notion persists in the claim that automated systems "effectively are able to see the future" as they are able to process and aggregate data ahead of rival players (Polansek 10 February 2014). This is 'science fiction capitalism', where "equity changes hands multiple times a second with no reference whatsoever to investment potential or to activity in the real world" (Gower 2011:1). Finance apparently becomes an abstract informational world of its own, with magical properties.

Simultaneous with the time travel fantasy is the persistent economic fantasy that financial market stability is advanced by increased speculation; a fantasy that has persisted even when financial crisis wiped 50% off the value of world stock markets (McNally 2009: 37). Multiple 'inside' observers suggest that the vastly extended speed and scope of today's financial markets is both functional and rational. In 2009 the U.S. Federal Reserve Board conducted several investigations of the period 2005–6, finding there was no causal relation between HFT and market volatility (Chaboud et al. 2009: 26). A 2011 survey of 18 academic studies into HFT from the field of finance economics found only one study that suggested HFT damaged 'market quality' (Gomber et al. 2011: 34). Across these studies there was something of a consensus that the rising speed of trading was inherently desirable, and that automation of financial markets had a generally stabilizing effect. By offering a means of hedging against the risk of price volatility, and of consequent changes in rates of return, it was assumed that financial instruments such as derivatives were beneficial for the global economy.

In 2007, in its influential *Global Financial Stability Report*, the International Monetary Fund argued that speculative 'risk-taking' enabled the spread of risk management and had helped to reduce volatility in share markets, at least between 2000 and 2006 (IMF 2007: 53). The spread of broadly similar automated trading models, though, did threaten to generate a herd mentality where "market price dynamics can be amplified by the models during stressful times" (IMF 2007: 53). Nonetheless, the IMF argued that speculators were the best judges of the risks of these operations: "It is comforting that most risk managers say they understand the shortcomings of their models and believe that they have the latitude to make an independent assessment of their risk-taking during a period of stress" (IMF 2007: 54). With these optimistic claims of understanding amidst complexity, and in the midst of an unfolding global crisis, the IMF advised minimal regulation. It argued there should be no capital adequacy requirements for hedge funds, and that their "freedom to take advantage of the possible herd behavior" should not be constrained by any need to "hold a minimum of economic capital" (IMF 2007: 72).

After the 2008 financial crisis and in the context of rapid automation of finance, the optimism waned. For example Adair Turner, the former chairman of the Financial Services Authority in the United Kingdom, wrote:

> There is no clear evidence that the growth in the scale and complexity of the financial system in the rich developed world over the last 20 to 30 years has driven increased growth or stability, and it is possible for financial activity to extract rents from the real economy rather than to deliver economic value.
>
> (Turner 2010: 6)

Stephen G. Cecchetti and Enisse Kharroubi (2012, 2013) from the Bank of International Settlements have argued that while banking and finance are good for economic and productivity growth at some levels, at the level they are found in many contemporary societies they inhibit such growth. They argue that financial industries come to control and use essential resources that would be better placed elsewhere in the economy, and actually harm the general economy (see also Arcand et al. 2012). Similarly Orthangazi (2008) argues that there is a negative relationship between financialisation and 'real investment', because the increasing size and profitability of financial investment diminishes the finance available for 'real' investment. Other writers suggest that the massive earnings made in finance cripple other 'real' industries by draining talented people from them (Bolton & Scheinkman 2011; Kneer 2013). Similarly the amount of money in finance gives that industry power to tailor political fields to its own purposes. Gerald Epstein, Professor of Economics at the University of Massachusetts, is quoted as pointing to the destabilising network effects of concentration and dispersal in finance:

> The sheer size of the financial sector, plus the increased concentration of it since the financial crisis, means that the economy is more prone to costly asset bubbles where risks get both spread to many actors and,

paradoxically, concentrated at the same time in the large institutions. So, it is the worst of both worlds.

(Steiner 29 January 2014)

Such perspectives suggest the emergence of an inverse, or disruptive, relationship between the success of the finance industry and wider economic development. Information technology has played a central role in this turn-around.

Under informationalism, as we have seen, it can be difficult to separate fantasy and hubris from reality. Undeniably, information technology has been deployed in finance markets to pursue the goal of ever-increased, and hierarchically based, rates of accumulation. These social technologies of finance are a key driver of globalisation, framing and shaping global institutions and policies (Gill 2003). Finance has become reliant on computer software, computer code and associated financial algorithms. Such codes, though, are not simply abstract technological artefacts, but as we have argued earlier are written within social, conflicted, muddled and disinformational domains, which have a disordering outcome for the software and its effects. In this respect, the study of the social basis of 'code', wider 'softwarisation' and the ways that it is routinely disrupted, should form a key element of any attempt to understand the contemporary global political economy.

FINANCE AND CRISIS

Finance is *par excellence* an instance of informationalism. It defines commodities in terms of their relative price, with one investment weighed against another either purely in terms of its rate of return or through the minute momentary price differences in different places and nearby times. Abstracted from the 'real economy', but feeding back into it, finance markets have their own autonomy and speculative (il)logics. Expectations of future return themselves become bankable assets, to be bought and sold as 'futures' or 'derivatives'. Reflecting this, there can be speculative gain in a falling 'bear' market as much as from a rising 'bull' market. The financial sector literally trades information, and is thus subject to all the distortions of information in the capitalist market, including systemic manipulation and deception, as in the infamous sub-prime mortgage market.

At the same time, financial decision-making over where to allocate investment and where to withhold it, shapes livelihood worldwide. For this reason finance can never accurately be defined as an individualised private asset, abstracted from society, to be deployed by its owner at will with no consequences elsewhere. Finance is a social relation whose existence depends on the social conditions of its production; it is a product of society as a whole and an asset of society as a whole. Financial accumulation depends upon a set of class dynamics in which some segments of the population produce wealth and other segments magnify and accumulate it (or turn it into Ruskinian illth). As shown in Chapter 4, the gap between these class groupings is now deeper than at any time in recent human history.

The concrete social conditions of financial accumulation are central to understanding the disorders of finance. The power gulf between the 'one percent' (70 million) who own half the world's wealth and the 3.5 billion who own only 1% of the total wealth (WEF 2012: 18), is amply expressed in the 2008 global financial crisis, and how it was resolved in massive taxpayer funded subsidies for the financial sector, while ordinary people lost jobs and homes. From the 1980s, the relative under-payment of workers around the world, under neoliberalism and under the 'command' economy in China, led to extensive profit-taking, which flooded financial markets with money (McNally 2009). Through the 1980s and 90s these funds increasingly flowed into speculative outlets, boosting the finance sector and making it the largest sector of the economy in terms of transactions (see Chapter 6: 106). With the parallel deregulation and internationalisation of finance markets from the 1980s the gains from speculation became spectacular. Finance companies quickly ascended the corporate league tables: in 1989 none of the world's 50 largest companies were based in the finance sector; in 2003 there were 14 such companies on the list (UNCTAD 2005: 19). In the U.S., finance's share of GDP grew from 2.8% in 1950 to 4.9% in 1980 to 8.3% in 2006 (Greenwood & Scharfstein 2013). These companies can also employ very few people to make huge amounts of money:

> The top 10 hedge funders made $28 billion for clients in the second half of last year. $2 billion more than the net profits of Goldman Sachs, JP Morgan, Citigroup, Morgan Stanley, Barclays and HSBC combined. . . . Even the biggest of the hedge funds have only a few hundred employees, which the six banks employ 1 million between them.
>
> (Mackintosh 1 March 2011)

Financial information workers are not inherently secure either.

When the collapse came in 2008, it violated the orthodox view that deregulated finance markets would always transmit the most accurate assessments of relative value. As argued by the United Nations Conference on Trade and Development (UNCTAD), the orthodoxy denied that finance is a socially distributed phenomenon:

> The standard view in economics in recent years has been that financial innovation can help diversify risk because it can allocate it efficiently to agents who are better suited to bear it. This is, however, misleading, because it does not take account of the fact that at a certain stage, nearly all actors—including the agencies entrusted with rating credit risk—become infected by the euphoria over high returns.
>
> (UNCTAD 2008: 1)

Those entrusted to regulate risk stood to benefit from the high returns, leading to a conflict of interest in supervision. Similarly, through political action, those benefiting from the risks rarely bore the costs of those risks as the costs were shifted to the general population. Market feedback was stripped away, and did not convey painful information/correction to those high in the market. The 'market' was socially and governmentally distributed at its point of failure.

The source of the problem was not in the peripheries, but in the core of global finance, in the U.S. Falling real wages for the working poor in the U.S., together with contracted (but not always visible in the contract) increases in mortgage repayment rates for sub-prime mortgages led to defaults. Initially finance companies were able to sell the defaulted properties into a booming housing market. When U.S. house prices collapsed (because of too many defaults), the failure of sub-prime lenders sparked a worldwide crisis (Lapavitsas 2009). Risky sub-prime investments had been deliberately packaged (via computer programs and models) into bundles, as securities, that could be validated by cooperating credit ratings agencies as low risk. The packaging ('tranching') was too complex for humans to follow, and was validated by players with networked cross-relationships and untested faith in those computerised models, meaning that information was distorted at the heart of the market, and buyers of 'securities' could be unwittingly exposed (Oldani 2008: 67). Players competed to validate and acquire the securities so as not to put themselves at a financial disadvantage, relative to other actors. With the rush to invest in the new financial products by 2008 the global derivative market stood at $680 trillion, with global GDP at about $60 trillion (Lohmann 2010).

The collapse saw the abrupt implosion of several large investment banks. Banks and finance houses used the fear of their failure and the possible resulting collapse of the market as leverage to force governments to bail them out. Defined as 'too big to fail', the banks created a 'moral hazard' for government (and themselves), on an unprecedented scale. Within 12 months the equivalent of 20% of global income, $20 trillion, had been spent on bank bail-outs and economic stimulus (Harvard Business Review 2010: 30–1; Grail Research 2009; McNally 2009). Governments effectively bought the bad credit created by the banks and finance houses, and bankrolled the financial recovery 'on behalf of' ordinary taxpayers.

From 2009 the conversion of private into public debt produced a rapid recovery in the finance sector, paired with a dramatic economic downturn. As a measure of the financial recovery, the number of banks amongst the 50 largest companies by market value fell from 13 in 2007 to eight in 2008, recovering to ten by 2012 (*Financial Times* 2013). While the banks recovered, and their power became further concentrated, governments sought to minimise indebtedness, with a wave of expenditure cuts and increased taxes. This ordering by fiscal austerity produced a further downward spiral in economic activity. Meanwhile, the costs of recession cascaded downwards and all but bypassed corporate players. The 3,000 largest transnational corporations suffered a brief slump in profit from US$1400 billion to $800 billion between 2007 and 2008, recovering to US$1400 billion by 2010 (UNCTAD 2013: 20).

The crisis narrative bears out the underlying drivers of disruption. After 30 years of globalised neoliberalism, under-consumption amongst the global poor had further reduced returns from 'real' commodity production relative to finance markets. The overaccumulation in finance capital led to the massive enrichment of the 'one percent', a new global 'rentier' class living off the proceeds of speculation (Lapavitsas 2009). It also created a global economy where trillions of dollars wash in and out of financial instruments. This tendency to global 'casino capitalism', as identified by Susan Strange in the mid-1980s, with its own elite of 'high rollers', has now become a commonplace (Strange 1986).

The fact that very little regulation was successfully imposed on these corporations in the aftermath of the 2008 crisis bears out the extent to which they were able to convert their financial power into political leverage (see Helleiner & Pagliari 2011). Even the most marginal efforts at delimiting speculation were contested by the finance houses. The issue of food speculation is especially revealing, where an attempt by the Obama administration to impose a limit on financial speculation in food commodities was fiercely resisted. The 'Commodity Futures Modernization Act' had lifted the U.S. ban on food speculation in 2000, and directly led to an inflow of US$14 trillion in speculative funds into food commodities. Rather than make the market orderly and efficient for consumers, this contributed to the doubling of food prices by 2008, which was estimated by the UN to have increased the numbers of those suffering malnutrition by 180 million. In 2010 the UN Rapporteur on the Right to Food warned that "fundamental reform of the broader global financial sector is urgently required" to prevent a recurring food crisis (De Schutter 2010: 1). He was proved right when the financial collapse came and food prices collapsed, only to rise again, higher than previously, with the financial recovery and further speculation. The activities of financial markets produced profit for some and hunger for others. In effect, the imposition of financial order disrupted the order of food supply.

Following the financial crisis, when the U.S. administration proposed limits on food speculation in the Dodd-Frank Wall Street Reform Act 2009–10, the 'Securities Industry and Financial Markets Association' and the 'International Swaps and Derivatives Association', representing, among others, Barclays, Goldman Sachs, JP Morgan and Morgan Stanley, brought a case against the U.S. regulator, seeking to have the limits struck down. Negotiations between these companies and the U.S. Commodity Futures Trading Commission, which is charged with implementing the reforms, dragged on into late 2013 with no sign of resolution (IATP 2013).

FINANCE AND INFORMATION TECHNOLOGY

Financialisation fuelled the boom in global financial speculation, but information technology delivered the means of realising it (Hakken 2010). Finance has always depended upon communication; contemporary reliance on computers intensifies pre-existing problems with financial information. Disordering effects are accentuated as financial transactions are increasingly abstracted and mechanised according to predetermined models. Information technology enables finance to be apparently liberated from the constraints of economic realities. Today, software is critical, as "without code/software the complexity of the modern financial markets would be impossible" (Berry 2012: 278). Before widespread computerisation in 1978 finance flows stood at ten times the value of world trade; in 2000 finance flows were about 50 times the value of world trade, with total flows amounting to $1.5 trillion per day (Palan 2003). With the growing pool of footloose finance there was a fierce 'arms race' to develop new financial technologies, which, in turn, fed the speculative surge (Lohmann 2010).

The relevant features of information technology can be disaggregated into: 'reach', 'extension', 'speed' and 'modelling' through programming, all of which allow further abstraction, and all of which intensify standard factors in trade. The stages of computerised finance can be described as follows.

Reach

ICT allows institutions to extend the geographic range of credit, money supply or transfer, communication and coordination of activities. Finance has always played an internationalising role. Bank credit has its origins in merchant capital in Renaissance Italy, beginning in the fourteenth century, and with the Medici Bank soon becoming Europe's largest (De Roover 1999). These systems of international credit avoided the need for merchants to carry gold or hard cash with them, and risk its loss through theft or accident.

Extension

The extension of reach, information and credit allowed traders to take advantage of geographically spaced price discrepancies. In classical trade, this involves buying something where it is cheap and selling it where the price is higher. The shift from international to global finance comes with the capacity to simultaneously gauge comparative rates of return across national and international contexts, deepening opportunities to discover price discrepancies. Information technology made this possible from the early 1970s by aggregating finance flows and linking finance centres across North America, Europe and East Asia into a 24-hour cycle.

Speed

Through speed, ICT helps users get into an advantageous trade before others do. Again this is a traditional feature of trade: traders compete in getting produce to market, or to bid for a product, and to gain a margin, before others do. Communication is central to trading: financial systems initially relied on telephone lines, then FM radio, satellite and internet data flows, and more recently, direct fibre optic feeds, all with varying speed and reliability. The sources of information regarding likely price movements remained concentrated in the CBDs of financial centres. The speed of trades remained unequal reflecting uneven access to the electronic index; already, by the 1980s, a few seconds could prove critical.

A bidding war to speed up internet connections in the 1990s saw the New York Stock Exchange (briefly and unsuccessfully) impose a modem speed limit of 9.6 Kbaud (Beunza et al. 2006). In the 2000s, traders began to make sure their cables to the exchange were as short as possible, even using microwaves, to ensure they were not beaten to a profitable transaction by microseconds. From 1997 the U.S. government permitted financial institutions to create 'electronic communication networks' to aggregate data, enabling internet-based 'direct market access' and 'electronic real-time price discovery' (Kendall 2007: 71–2). Eventually, the speed required to be on top of transactions became so fast that the times needed for human response and decision-making disrupted the process, and decisions had to become automated.

Modelling

Financial programming enabled the creation of complex models aimed at predicting market behaviour, or finding short-term variations from normal behaviour, and making trades based on those predictions. The models in the software are usually tested on past data, and it is not possible to test for what the result would have been in that past situation if the developing program had been able to act in it. The model itself affects the market and changes its behaviour. With a large number of computerised models in play, the financial system's interactions and effects become even harder to model. Any such model would always be out of date and complex systems tend to be impossible to predict in the long term at all. These models may give advice to human traders or to automated traders; in all cases they represent a simplification and an abstraction.

The financial abstraction process began to intensify when people began trading in temporary discrepancies in the relative prices of currencies across the globe, after the end of the Bretton Woods agreement in 1971. An important modelling innovation was the shift to visualisation, through networked computers, introduced by the Reuters 'Monitor Money Rates Service' in 1973, a system that aggregated trading and pricing data onto a computer screen (Beunza et al. 2006). From 1981 the Reuters service enabled keyboard-based electronic trading, and the terminals reportedly remained in use until 1999 when the Millennium Bug forced their retirement (Berry 2012).

Through the 1980s this visual representation of value, on a trader's computer screen, began to replace the social dynamics of the trading floor. Visual valuation literally abstracted the process of determining value (Beunza & Stark 2012). The price of a commodity, mapped across time, could soon be known globally. A new time-space nexus was made possible by the simulcast of relative commodity values. A 1989 industry book, *24-Hour Trading*, put it this way:

> A picture is truly worth a thousand words, or, perhaps a thousand trades. Graphic presentation of prices, generated by the market during a trading day, allows a trader to make reasonable decisions on several markets . . . the growth in graphic price information translated into the trading floor's dramatic surge in volume.
>
> (Diamond & Kollar 1989: 73)

By the late 1990s investment banks and their networks were competing with each other in using ICT to create new financial products. As part of the modelling process, computers were used to model, divide, share or hide risk in the making of derivatives, collateral debt obligations and other forms of investment. As well as potentially confusing risk and uncertainty, and being taken for reality (not models of reality), these models became so complex that no one understood quite what they were trading, as has been frequently alleged of the financial products traded before the 2008 financial crisis (Das 2006). Thus traders depend on faith, deceit and the valuation of others, for the value and uptake of products. In this aspect finance remains social, no matter how abstract it becomes in other ways.

In derivatives trading, the future is monetised, and a mechanism is created to allow financial expectations to shape 'real' prices. This form of price setting is described by Das as "regarb" or "regulatory arbitrage", where price changes are predetermined by betting on future pricing (Das 2006: 33). Trading models are developed to predict price changes, and then converted into algorithms that can drive computer software, running into problems about predictability. Models feature assumptions based on historical price movements, what variables count as input and on the direction and causality of change: there is always a risk that the choice and mix of variables may lead to "omitted variable bias" and assertion of causality is always vulnerable to "reverse causality" (Das 2006: 209). Furthermore, given the unpredictability of complex interactive systems, past trends have no necessary relation to future trends. Models tested on past data generally cannot give the results of using the models to manipulate that situation, as the data would have been changed by that usage. Hence the models used in trading exist as an appealing, or persuasive 'fantasy' acceptable to whoever is proposing the model and who has authority. As Das argues:

> The irony of trying to model chaos, the finding of order in complete disorder, is not lost on most quants [ie financial analysts] . . . in the end their power is not in the ability to explain phenomena or predict outcomes, it is an ability to engender belief in them and their expectations of the world.
>
> (Das 2006:)

Hakken likewise suggests that being tied to past data sets, these models expressed the "particular ideological presumptions" that the possibility of system failure and disorder could be ignored (2010: 210). In this modality, risk can always be 'rationally' modelled (and distinguished clearly from uncertainty) on the basis of past experience, regardless of how this may build risk upon risk into unpredictability.

These beliefs, entwined with hope and supposition, could be seen as further undermining information accuracy. The inevitable failure to predict events and the consequent under- or overpricing of commodities and financial products is only grist to the mill: barring collapse, such errors simply open up new arbitrage opportunities for traders to exploit, as these markets depend upon volatility and movement for extraction. The bigger the error, the bigger the possible margin.

Overall, ICT demands that most trades become high-speed and automatic to take advantage of reach, extension, speed and of the market and its 'failures'. People not only write programs to guess the market, but also write programs ('algo-sniffers') that attempt to work out what other people's programs are modelling or doing, and take advantage of them (Harford 10 August 2012). Modelling and counter-modelling becomes a form of information warfare, and injects further informational disorder into the market. Furthermore, models may take control of, or disrupt, the finance market, as it is hard to check them, or stop them quickly. Through ICT finance becomes more and more a matter of signs unpredictably interacting with other signs. It has less and less relationship to the 'real' economy that the finance traders depend upon for the activity that fuels the finance market to begin with. Instead of being productive, through its success finance becomes a potentially disruptive parasite, which is politically very hard to dislodge or even reform, due to the massive wealth and political influence it generates until collapse.

HIGH FREQUENCY TRADING

Just as the advent of electronic trading from the 1970s was seen as a revolution in trading, so the latest iteration in automation, trading through automatic computerised algorithms, is described as a 'second revolution'

(Lenglet 2011: 45). The phenomenon is in flux, so is difficult to assess, but there is no doubt it marks an intensification and extension of the practices established under the first wave of financial informationism.

'High frequency trading' (HFT) highlights fictions of money value. With HFT the gaming of values reaches new heights, with mechanised trades almost instantaneously subverting manual trades: a mouse click takes on average half a second, or half a million microseconds when compared to algorithmic trades that are undertaken in half a dozen microseconds or less. HFT machines essentially use a form of time-space compression to anticipate changes in share prices, and it is only possible to gain this edge across spatially distant exchanges, where there is a microsecond delay between a price change in one exchange and a correlated price change in another.

As dramatised in the recent best-selling (and non-fictional) account of HFT, *Flash Boys,* this temporal edge translates into profit in three main ways (Lewis 2014: 172). In the first instance HFT machines do what most traders have always done, which is to profit from price differentials across exchanges. Here HFT exploits 'slow market arbitrage', where there is a microsecond delay in the communication of price movements between exchanges. Second, HFT machines use this advantage to engage in 'electronic front running', to literally profit from other people's purchases. A single offer to buy a large number of shares in a company typically involves multiple purchases automatically routed across a number of exchanges. Once the purchase has been routed to the first exchange, the HFT machines can immediately quote for that company on all other exchanges, forcing the price up. The trader then has to pay the higher price, and the HFT machines pocket the difference. Finally, as different exchanges impose different user fees, HFT machines can make gains by playing one exchange off against another in a form of 'rebate arbitrage'.

As large slow bids lost margin to fast bids, large investors have either tried to deceive the market as to their intentions or they have exited the market into so-called 'dark pools'. Here, transactions could be shrouded from the "aggressive gaming tactics of HFTs", and such dark pools have grown exponentially, to account for as much as one-third of equities trading (Turbeville 2013: 12–13). Whether producing deception or exit, the implications for pricing are far-reaching, as in either case the process disrupts any notion of open, transparent and information-rich markets. Ironically, the large banks that run the dark pools were soon accused of 'front running' on their own clients, by either selling access to HFT companies, or simply running their own HFT outfits (Gapper 2 April 2014). More broadly, HFT is said to have increased the costs of operating for those who are trying to invest in stock market 'fundamentals', and has driven out small investors who find they are constantly being fleeced (Ferguson 30 July 2012; Francis 10 August 2012; Steiner 29 January 2014).

While algorithms were used in the 1970s in finance, and underpin later hedge funds and derivatives, trading was not then automated. Today automation and resulting market disruption is overwhelming. By 2011 more than two-thirds of equity trading in the U.S. was conducted through HFT machines, and from 2014 a majority of European trades were automatic (Reuters 13 March 2014). A key driver mentioned in the report was labour-saving cost-cutting amongst finance houses (ibid); again demonstrating the insecurity of knowledge workers, even in the central institutions of finance (Marshall 2013b: 368–9, 374). Indeed, the reported experiences of these new HFT workers provide some of the most revealing insights into the process.

In 2011 the Dutch anthropologist Joris Luyendijk was given the task of conducting an online anthropology of bankers in the City of London, by the *Guardian* newspaper. In the process he created a series of more than 70 of anonymised portraits, gathered over a three-year period, including one of an HFT analyst. In this portrait the trader talked candidly about the HFT industry, and his role, stating categorically that it defined a new form of financial behaviour

> On any given day, our computers buy and sell shares tens of thousands of times, holding them for very short periods of time, sometimes even less than a minute. No human being, or collection of human beings, could do the volume of trades computers are doing at the moment. . . . This is not stuff that was once done by humans and now taken over by computers. This is something new altogether.
>
> (Luyendijk 15 September 2011: np)

Later in the interview, the analyst clarifies that the HFT process is entirely based on predicted market behaviour, stating "it has nothing to do with analysing a particular company's value or strength. It is about historical patterns of trading which we project on to the future" (this interview drew the most vituperative responses from readers, and led to a re-interview). This latter observation goes to the core of what distinguishes HFT from other forms of trading—it is purely engaged with relative monetary values. As such, it is designed to make a return on extremely small, even accidental, movements in valuation. It does not represent investment, or express the value of a company for raising capital.

The considerable although incalculable investment put into HFT, in the search for ever-faster and more sophisticated means of gaming the system, and indeed the appetite for virtually any form of digestible data that the machines can use to generate their predictions, demonstrates the importance of this sector of financial 'innovation'. This is also shown by the effort put into prosecuting knowledge workers who are suspected of seeking to share or steal its closely guarded algorithms. Profitable information should remain secret. Companies from Goldmann Sachs, to Société Générale, to CME Group, to Citadel have pursued former traders accused of stealing the programs they wrote or used, effectively threatening the free movement of information workers in the sector (Bunge & Or 13 October 2013).

However, the HFT wave has also given rise to a whole new set of financial experts, from the 'quants' who devise the algorithms, to the 'analytics' who mine for data, and the 'informatics' who render it usable for HFT machines, that is, who 'quantise' the information feed (Adler 8 March 2012). However, the institutional barriers, insecurities and power relations amongst these players, of the kind we have discussed earlier, also mean that the models, programing and communication tend to be disrupted and inaccurate to begin with (Marshall 2012). If the models, the data, the assumptions about human behaviour and markets are flawed, and if in the high-pressure world of finance, the programmers are not secure and free to say whether the models are practicable, or given enough time to get them right, then not only might a finance house be affected badly, but the interaction between inadequate programs can produce unexpected results affecting the whole market.

We have already remarked on models being distorted by unrealistic and continually undermined testing procedures and by their persuasiveness as fantasy. One of Luyendijk's interviewees, who is a programmer, blithely comments on the likelihood of computer generated crashes: "Accidents happen, that's how the principle of survival of the fittest operates" (Luyendijk 27 September 2011). As one ex-programmer writes:

> In my experience, software is, almost as a rule, bad in one way or another. And lest I be accused of over-generalising: in more than 20 years I've done work for maybe a dozen companies, almost all of them in the banking industry and many of them household names.
>
> (Mandl 21 December 2012)

Bubbles and crashes are an inherent problem with the financial system as no financier can predict the future and "no level of technology can change this basic fact" (Sornette & Von Der Becke 2011). As the Chair of the U.S. Federal Reserve, Alan Greenspan, stated after the NASDAQ crash in 2002, "it was very difficult to definitively identify the bubble until after the fact, that is, when its bursting confirmed its existence" (quoted in Sornette & Von Der Becke 2011: 17). Computerisation and automation redefine this problem in radically new ways. Given the volume of trading under HFT, the system can now collapse over the space of a few milliseconds, before human traders or regulators have the opportunity to act. Before the event it is impossible to meaningfully assess the likely interactions between automated algorithms that may produce a crash. This was demonstrated by the May 2010 'flash crash', driven by HFT machines, which wiped 1,000 points or 5% off the Dow Jones Index and then restored it 20 minutes later. Smaller-scale crashes generated by HFT have proliferated. In the month of August 2012, Knight Capital lost US$440 million in a few minutes due to a programming bug, and AXA Rosenberg lost US$217 million due to a coding error, paying an extra $25 million penalty for trying to hide the error (Popper 2 August 2012; Eha 9 August 2012; Harford 10 August 2012; Francis 10 August 2012).

As well, HFT can add complications to markets. Machines will routinely test a price by quoting rather than buying a stock. Only when the price moves is the stock purchased, hence overall only about one-tenth of all quotes lead to trades. This large-scale 'quote stuffing', can deceive other HFT machines or slow down trading by clogging the system (Adler 8 March 2012). As a result of HFT, shifts in global market value are now further shrouded in mystery, embedded in the top-secret algorithms that drive the trading machines. The resulting vulnerability and 'turbulence' can undermine long-term confidence in financial markets. Not surprisingly, there has been a rapid shift into multiple dark pools for large investors, and a substantial exodus by individual investors, "motivated by the declining integrity of the market as a result of HFT activity" (Turbeville 2013: 13).

The problems for regulation are exacerbated as ostensible regulators are themselves increasingly dependent on the growth of HFT. Despite the obvious conflicts of interest that arise, many stock exchanges have in recent decades been privatised (London in 1986, New York in 2006, for instance), and have a direct interest in blurring questions of regulation posed by HFT. At the most basic level, the leasing out of spaces for HFT clients seeking to position themselves as close as possible to the exchange, to cut transaction times, creates a hierarchical system of investors in terms of speed of access (Gomber et al. 2011: 35).

Since 2010 the European Commission has debated how to bring HFT under the ambit of regulatory standards that apply to the rest of the industry, especially by limiting the capacity to engage in quote stuffing, as against undertaking transactions (Gomber et al. 2011: 53). In 2014 a broad set of proposals were agreed by the European Council and the European Parliament that would directly regulate HFT and, remarkably, require traders to test algorithms and submit them to regulators (European Parliament 2014). At the same time there is pressure for more extensive dampening of HFT speculation through a Financial Transactions Tax: in 2012 France implemented a 0.2% tax on the purchase of shares and Germany is considering a similar measure (Corkery & Zornada 2012; Gower 2011). A parallel debate in the U.S. led to a series of proposals floated by the Commodity Futures Trading Commission in late 2013. Lobbyists have set about influencing this agenda, notably the Futures Industry Association lauding "market quality improvements that have occurred as markets have become more automated and competitive" (Polansek 10 February 2014).

More broadly, with HFT trading we see ever-extended market 'rationality' eroding the very foundations of market operations. The emergence of dark pools, which are designed to insulate investment from speculation, demonstrates the inherent dangers of market rationalisation. As HFT machines increasingly dominate global finance, it becomes necessary to escape global finance in order to invest. Yet, for the 'true believers' of market rationality, it is the dark pools that are fragmenting and distorting the market by hiding information, and have to be eliminated, not the HFT machines. In 2013 executives from several U.S. exchanges, including the NYSE, met with the U.S. Securities and Exchange Commission, calling on it to rein-in the dark pools, said to by then already account for 37% of total trading (Patterson 17 April 2013).

CONCLUSION

Financial innovation in the area of arbitrage sees the creation of new 'financial products' that further commodify expectations. It also sees the creation of new models, software and machines both to construct these 'securitised' commodities and to enable the increased velocity of circulation in the financial system and to extend that system over the world and into new areas of social life. The speeding-up allows exchanges to occur faster, and further commodifies time, even to the 'nano-second'.

The tendencies in financial transactions also demonstrate a commodification drive into the pre-emptive anticipation of 'forethought'; as Thrift puts it, "capitalism is carpeting expectations and capturing potential" (Thrift 206: 302). There are, of course, still wider implications in the parallel move to reliance on algorithms in other fields of social life. Under informationalism the algorithm has acquired a central role in identifying 'what we need to know', signalling a qualitative change. This is no minor transformation, but rather is (at least) an epochal change, moving us from reliance on "credentialed experts, the scientific method, common sense, or the word of God", to fixed and un-reflexive computerised versions of the past, assumed to be replicated in the present (Gillespie 2014: 167). Key to any algorithm is the process of coding appearances as essences, or habits as attributes, and in the process fixing reality. Once achieved, the code then becomes self-affirming, a tautology that persists, with anything that violates the coded behaviour automatically discounted as anomalous or as unimportant disorder, until that fixing is taken advantage of by others. All of these tendencies are built into the financial algorithms that now 'game' the global financial system with far-reaching effects: they are indeed "codes with consequences" (Gillespie 2014: 194).

Informationalism, in this reading, becomes empowered over human agency, shaping it in often imperceptible and unknowable ways, even though it originates in such agency. Berry outlines how the Reuters trading software progressively gained a life of its own from its birth in 1973 to its demise in 1999 simply due to the fact that its original code, in the software language PDP-11, had been long forgotten and was repeatedly 'patched', plying layer over layer on the original program (Berry 2012). In the era of HFT this constitutive power becomes increasingly generative, in the sense of generating the power of finance capital over society. Machines are increasingly attributed an agency by traders, as if they have their own autonomy (Lenglet 2011), becoming a form of automated distributed governance. Here the extension of "power through the algorithm" embeds the status quo in new ways, and, as a closely guarded commercial secret, it can be rendered free from public scrutiny, governance or criticism (Beer 2009: 994).

However, the order fostered by financial power may be self-disordering. It appears that the size and complexity of the finance sector itself produces economic crises. Finance, after a certain undefined point, reduces real investment and fuels speculation, while concentrating power and distributing instability throughout the network. The system it produces is hyper-complex, volatile and governed by a herd mentality, with firms responding to each other's programs and to unexpected results, because people can never know exactly what other machines will do with their data or what inputs those other programs will feed back to them. There are severe problems in writing predictive software on the basis of past data, which does not reflect how the system would change generally when the model is used. Any attempts at managing the risks associated with this system are inherently limited when the key drivers of the system are commercially secret, and when key players have a financial interest in hiding or obfuscating risk, and selling the risk on. The system thereby is permanently uncertain, rather than quantifiably risky. When trading is automated and incredibly speedy, it is also difficult to oversee what is happening or to apply any brakes if things go wrong.

So far in these markets, the 'front running' enabled by investment in machinery and code does not appear to contribute anything useful to the market; it merely skims off the margins of those who might be thinking of making investments rather than pursuing price fluctuations. The prices generated by high frequency trading bear no relation to actual corporate performance as the machine-generated trading is based on price differentials alone. Dark pools, or other efforts to hide information, and thereby to exit the formal market, appear to have provided only temporary solutions. The overall effect may have been to undermine public confidence in the stock market and the finance industry, as it now seems like an insider game (based on hidden knowledge) and a perilous one at that, and this intensifies the apparent separation of finance from economic 'reality'.

Always, though, the system relies on its rationalisation, that somehow the value of the traded commodities reflects some final instance of 'real' value (Maurer 2006). Certainly, as the 2008 financial crisis demonstrated, there is no such thing as wholly disembedded finance. While money might be an interplay of signs, which allows trading to be possible, it does not have a completely independent and manipulable existence; it depends on systemic confidence and trust. In moments of crisis, incoherence and doubt, as Maurer suggests, "the link between the representation and the reality of money and finance break down, denaturalizing the taken-for-granted monetary order, and place value in question" (2006: 28). Breakdown allows the fictions and fantasies of wealth and order to be questioned. It is no accident that the 'Occupy' movement was, for a while, able to so effectively popularise its slogan, 'We are the 99%', in a context where global financiers were rescued by global taxpayers.

Exposing and re-politicising these power relations, through an under-standing of informationalism as a specific era of accumulation, becomes an urgent priority. A critical factor in enabling this 'return of the political' is the recurrent crisis of confidence that algorithmic ordering creates. Anticipating human agency, enabling pre-emptive judgements and pre-emptive strikes on the social body, is by definition an exercise in hubris. The social field is reflexive, subject to its own rhythms, disorders and melodies, and never preordained. Reportedly, when Isaac Newton lost $20,000 in the South Sea Bubble in 1720 he mused, "I can calculate the motion of heavenly bodies but not the madness of people" (quoted in Das 2006: 210). One wonders how he would have interpreted the current malaise.

10 Disorders of the Commons, Peer-to-Peer

INTRODUCTION

We have already argued profiting from digital 'information' generates critical problems for the orders of informational capitalism. A key feature of information is its non-rivalrous character. Media products "have *always* been a fundamental problem for capitalist economics [as a] person's use of information, unlike tangible goods and services, does not prohibit others from using it" (Foster & McChesney 2011: np, see also Chapter 6). It is easy and usual for information to have multiple possessors. Duplication does not deprive the original holder of their information. Indeed some information increases in its value and effect the more it is distributed. It is hard to prevent people from accessing information without permission, once it is generally available. Similarly, the construction of 'culture' has always depended on people being able to borrow, steal, exchange or elaborate previously existing stories, tropes, characters, themes, images, styles, pieces of music and so on. People continuously share and make culture of previously existing culture. These factors make the boundaries around information property overtly ambiguous. So it should not be surprising that millions of people ('file-sharers' or 'pirates') act as if their right to participate in 'cultural conversations' overrides the restrictive 'legal rights' of corporate copyright holders or the 'moral rights' of artists. Similarly, as mentioned previously, the tools of information distribution, work and piracy are comparable and easily available to knowledge workers and artists. Likewise capitalism encourages instant consumption, and networking sites such as YouTube, Pinterest, Twitter and so on, encourage cultural sharing, for their profit base. Peer-to-peer (P2P) file exchange is 'normal', and exists within a broad scope of legal, illegal or extra-legal practices; from industrial-scale counterfeiting of branded goods, to home recording of radio and free-to-air television. File-sharing is naturalised and supported by the social forces that try to order it away. Given these conditions, the contest over widening, maintaining or excluding access is a key info-battleground between the order of capital and the orders of cultural practice, with both orders disordering each other. There is no necessary harmonious resolution of this struggle; the order/disorder complex is likely to remain a major driver of social processes.

A new 'pirarchical' order/disorder complex emerges from this contestation. At an official level, the piracy debate has largely been framed by the entertainment industries, which have reduced a complex and shifting phenomenon to 'theft' motivated by individual 'greed'. Yet, as media researcher Joe Karaganis (2011: 2) notes:

> Piracy has never had a stable legal definition and is almost certainly better understood as a product of enforcement debates than as a description of specific behavior. The term blurs, and is often used intentionally to blur, important distinctions between types of uncompensated use.

Karaganis describes 'piracy' as the 'ubiquitous, increasingly digital practices of copying that fall outside the boundaries of copyright law' (ibid).

Various internet-based systems of data exchange, which we will describe in more detail later, have enabled strangers to make direct material exchanges with each other, share their enthusiasm about artists and genres, build social relationships and communities via associated online forums, and share their own files, artistic experiments or copyright-violating mash-ups. P2P is sometimes seen by artists as a way they can escape the industry. Even if they do not always get paid, they build reputation and gain a possible market through a combination of the 'long tail' business model of providing hard-to-find 'niche products', and taking advantage of online consumer recommendation systems (Waelbroeck 2013: 393). While this may lead to increased bookings for live performances, talks, residencies or incidental paid work, it simultaneously can reduce their income from recordings or reproductions, etc., and thus threatens while it opens.

P2P file-sharing and other forms of 'unauthorised' and/or 'democratic' media/cultural exchange practices exemplify the inherent tensions and disordering tendencies created by informationalism. The material practices of developers, internet and information activists and self-described 'ordinary' internet users, disturb various interconnected informational regimes, as an unintended part of the ordinary life enabled by these regimes. Each instance triggers an escalation of ordering attempts, not only from within the domain that first produced it, but also from across discrete domains. Unpredictable cross-pollination drives technological and social innovation and failure, as all sides of the deeply polarised 'copyfight' strive to 'enclose' or 'liberate' data and information through legal, political and technological means. Consequently, even the incidental or unintentional pirate becomes an inventor, innovator, exploiter and/or implementer embodying the tension between knowledge, culture and property. A relatively unorganised 'class' of programmers, digital activists and enthusiasts creatively develop information-communication technologies, tools and platforms, enabling a far larger heterogeneous transnational class of 'ordinary users' to participate in alternative circuits for the production and exchange of cultural content. This continuous generative flux means that file-sharing causes perturbations that, along with other forces we highlight in this book, could propel informational capitalism toward multiple points of tension and crisis; resulting in collapse, transformation or incapacitating intensification of its orders. As sovereign governments extend copyright laws at the behest of industry, especially the American entertainment industry, through free trade and IP agreements, popular moves to extend the public commons appear to strengthen.

To understand the P2P phenomenon we chart a course through a series of interconnected domains. After sketching some of file-sharing's technological and social dimensions, we examine some landmark digital copyright court cases, identify trends in online media exchange practices and note the escalation of political/legal attempts to curtail file-sharing. The disruption across various informational domains manifests in disorderly and temporary 'swarm formations', which express a political potential. Although those involved in P2P might be differentiated in terms of ideology, class, geography and so forth, many speak and act as if they believe that the internet and its contents belong to common shared realm. These exchanges are generally normalised to the extent that users perceive them as unremarkable, banal and extendable (da Rimini & Marshall 2014). At the same time, as we have already implied, file-sharing can be a prompt to creative technical and cultural activity.

However, the opponents of file exchange rarely acknowledge this sociality, or creativity. The entertainment industry depicts file-sharing simply as an illegal activity producing economic havoc, and depriving artists (and the industry) of income. By undermining profit margins, P2P is said to destroy creativity. On the other hand, the "increasingly sophisticated industry research enterprise embedded in a lobbying effort with a historically very loose relationship to evidence" has consistently produced spurious or unprovable "headline piracy numbers" (Karaganis 2011: 4). Accuracy of information is secondary to the intended effect of maintaining order in a political and economic field. This partisan view also bypasses the long history of the entertainment industry profiting at the expense of artists, refusing to make existing works readily available and the inverse relationship between copyright and innovation (see, for example, Carrier 2012). These claims of theft seek to legitimise industry attempts to maintain profit from, and control of, the artist's content for longer and longer periods of time.

For example, when Australia signed a Free Trade Agreement with the U.S. in 2004, the agreement demanded the extension of "copyright protection for works (e.g. books, artwork and sheet music), films and sound recordings . . . by an extra 20 years", so that works would "move from the life of the author + 50 years, to life +70" before entering the public domain (Department of Foreign Affairs and Trade 2004). However this intensification and extension of copyright does not guarantee greater financial returns to original creators, as the usual form of contract typically assigns their rights to the publishers, not to them. When the European Council extended the copyright term for sound recordings from 50 to 70 years in September

2011, it was estimated that 72% of the financial benefits would accrue to record labels. Of the 28% earmarked for artists, most would go to 'superstar acts' (Kretschmer 2011). The relationship between artists and media companies is ambiguous, fraught and contested.

Nevertheless, corporations worry about the potential loss of an ordered market that never existed. News Limited Chief Executive Kim Williams (2012: 6) described digital content as a "new hot consumer item", claiming that the scale of its 'theft' by "illegal downloading" made the 2011 London riots "look like children stealing a lolly from a shop". Without acknowledging the very different Elizabethan-era copyright laws, he asks us to "Imagine the great works that are not being produced because the digital bandits are creating virtual pirate Globe Theatres" (ibid: 3). Like many other industry figures Williams argues that the "relentless criminal . . . plunder" of intellectual property must be ameliorated by a "new copyright framework", that is, by a more extreme informational ordering of enclosures that distributes responsibility and cost for enforcement away from the profiting industry to a wider sphere such as Internet Service Providers. Unsurprisingly he did not mention the illegal methods deployed by News Limited in the UK to hack people's phones, steal their private conversations and profit from the stories gathered (Burns & Somaiya 1 May 2012).

Similarly, the International Federation of the Phonographic Industry (IFPI) warned that its members would not "survive" if the market continued to be "massively rigged by piracy", calling for an Internet "guided by the rule of law", and exhorting government to "seize" the opportunity for enforcement (IFPI Digital Music Report 2011: 3). Yet, at the same time, the IFPI (ibid: 3) described a market whose digital revenues had risen "more than 1000 per cent in seven years", driving "new licensing models" including "logical partnerships with ISPs and mobile operators and subscription Internet radio services". In 2010 the digital component of music industry revenues soared to "an estimated 29 per cent" when the film and book industries' equivalent components were "only one and two per cent respectively" (ibid: 8). Over the following two years this market further expanded, with content delivery services like iTunes and Spotify present in more than 100 countries (IFPI Digital Music Report 2013: 5). Moreover, they estimate the revenue from digital music sales was US$5.6 billion, up by 9% from 2011, "accounting for more than a third of total industry revenues" (ibid: 6). The current regime would not seem so bad for the industry, after all, but it does not have total control. Information capitalism wants its order enforced everywhere.

From another perspective, it could be argued that 'the disorders of piracy' have not only created new mass markets from scratch, but also new distribution and delivery modes. For example, the late CEO of Apple, Steve Jobs, recognised that Napster was the "way people wanted to acquire music", inspiring him to design the iPod personal player for shared MP3 music files (Hartley 22 April 2009). This groundbreaking content delivery device coupled with streaming music and TV subscription services created a new 'legitimate' informational order. However, the motivation for this innovation arose from the continual 'illegitimate' expansion of social and technological frontiers. Some amongst the industry have recognised this, such as Ted Sarandos, Chief Content Officer of the video-on-demand platform Netflix, who stated that piracy cannot be combated "legislatively or criminally" but only by "giving good options" for online content delivery (Edwards 1 May 2013).

TECHNOLOGICAL AND SOCIAL DIMENSIONS OF FILE-SHARING

While use of P2P over the internet disturbs relations of power and sets up new conflicts, the results are unclear, as technologies interact with other complex systems, including society. Taking a paradigmatic example, Gutenberg's printing press was a revolutionary information technology, used to mass-produce intellectual commodities following its mid-fifteenth century launch. This interacted with the many sociocultural tensions of the time. Some groups used these commodities, most notably the Bible (in the context of widespread theological debate), to support the prevailing social order, others to agitate for new authoritarian orders, while others used the Bible, and the press, to challenge authority. Often these challenges, and the organisations built around them (and other forces), resulted in bloodshed and war. More peacefully, the press created new industries of printers and censors. It opened the possibility of artists receiving payment from an interested and distant public, while simultaneously enabling works to be printed without authorisation or payment.

Similar claims for revolutionary potential have been made about many contemporary technologies—video cameras, mailing lists, Indymedia, mobile phones, Twitter, Facebook—in specific campaigns, protests and uprisings, often forgetting that all sides of the conflict can use the technology. Clearly we are not claiming file-sharing technologies are inherently radical in their effects. However, by building a fuller understanding of how the phenomenon manifests, and the struggles around it, we can speculate on its social dynamics and effects. Although disruption can become accommodated or enclosed within a social order, it can also trigger societal change and creativity.

P2P Protocols

Peer-to-peer-based file-sharing has been defined as *"the unrestricted duplication of digitised media content between autonomous end-nodes on the Internet"* (Andersson 2010: 13). Similarly, a P2P network's defining feature is that file transfer "is performed directly between users" (Carrier 2012: 901). Different P2P networks employ different communications protocols, but within the global P2P ecosystem, BitTorrent (BT) has been the most commonly used.

BT was not the first such protocol. In 1998 American programmer Shawn Fanning created the Napster system for sharing digitised music tracks over the internet. Napster was a 'hybrid' P2P network because it was partly centralised. Users downloaded the MusicShare software from Napster that, once installed, connected them into the Napster network. They then specified which (music) files situated on their own computers could be shared, and this meta-data was uploaded to Napster "which aggregated the files into one giant index" (ibid: 902). Users "consulted the central server" to find available files, with "peers conduct[ing] the subsequent file transfer between themselves" (ibid). Fanning distributed a beta version to 30 friends in mid-1999, requesting that they keep the software to themselves. But it is hard to confine information for which there is a demand. Within one week 15,000 people had downloaded the software and within six months this had grown to more than two million people (Hartley 22 April 2009). Napster was from the outset a business, albeit one that consciously departed from the music industry's 'moral order'. Its proprietary software was given away to raise stock market interest during the short-lived dotcom boom times. Digital culture researcher Tatiana Bazzichelli argues (2013: 118):

> Napster was able to get so many followers because it managed to absorb their values turning them into its business. . . . Napster opened a (new) cycle of appropriation of values and ethics, transferring them from the so-called underground culture to the business field.

Napster popularised file exchange with an estimated 60 to 80 million people using the system at its peak before a copyright infringement case brought by A & M Records eventually forced its closure in mid-2001 (DeVoss & Porter 2006).

However, a new pirarchical order/disorder complex was now firmly based on, and based in, internet usage. Pirarchy profoundly disordered existing 'legitimate' info-orders by creating new markets hungry for easy access to digitised cultural content. Individuals within these markets would use both the extra-legal and legal distribution systems that flourished in Napster's wake. Thus new info-orders—entangled, intersecting and competing—emerged.

The next significant step occurred when American programmer Bram Cohen developed BitTorrent (BT) in 2001 to overcome the legal vulnerabilities that partially centralised systems like Napster faced. Because the BT system "incorporates no internal search functionality, and creates no single network", the legal liability of BT software providers diminishes (Giblin 2011: 108). The BT protocol exploited the internet's network structure by automatically harnessing the processing power and bandwidth of users' internet connections. It turned a situational 'disadvantage' (that is, the discrepancy between broadband providers' fast download speeds but turgid upload speeds) into an advantage, as the aggregated upload speeds of users enabled everyone to download files more quickly. BT shifted modes of exchange from one-to-one to many-to-many. It breaks up individual files into small data blocks, and transmits the file in random non-contiguous blocks to other users (peers) downloading or 'torrenting' the same file (da Rimini 2013a). The software itself forces users to upload (or 'seed') completed blocks to other peers in the 'swarm' around a file, creating a "virtuous cycle" of exchange (Thompson 2005), with no particular computer being essential to the process.

The P2P swarm is essentially a dynamically changing social phenomenon comprised of connected peers sharing the same desire for a specific cultural item, underpinned by a dynamically changing technological assemblage of peers' computers, P2P software, the BT protocol, the internet and variable bandwidth speeds. Individuals might drop in and out of a swarm by logging in/out of the BT software client, or by starting/pausing a particular download, or by opening/closing their internet connection. But as long as there remains at least one peer seeding a completed version of the file being shared, and one peer accessing that file, the swarm is alive. The ever-shifting and semi-random swarm formations created by P2P networks is mirrored in some of the loose networks that have gravitated around various electronic freedom and digital privacy campaigns in recent years, as we will discuss later.

File-sharers and software application developers rapidly adopted the BT protocol. Due to its efficient use of network resources, mainstream corporate entities also employed the protocol. The British Broadcasting Corporation uses BT to deliver their popular iPlayer platform for catch-up television (Cox, Collins & Drinkwater 2010: 301); commercial streaming television services such as TIVO and Kontiki use it. Other authorised uses include distribution of massive online computer games like World of Warcraft, films, GNU/Linux operating systems and scientific data (Giblin 2011). The Internet Archive (archive.org) has made 1.5 million torrents of its resources available, stating that "distributed nature of BitTorrent swarms" would help "patrons with slower access to the Archive" (Mearian 8 August 2012).

In March 2013 Bram Cohen launched BitTorrent Live, a live video streaming service creating a "direct connection between broadcasters and their viewers, transforming each person tuning in into 'a miniature broadcaster'" (Welch 12 March 2013). Like the original BT protocol, this "disruptive P2P tech" would "offload" most of the data transfer burden to users, with the result that "even with millions of viewers" video streams could be delivered with "only a 5-second delay" (Constantine 13 February 2012). The development could enable independent journalists, filmmakers, activists and educators access to a powerful mass broadcasting medium without having to incur prohibitive infrastructure costs. Commercial operations would pay only a small licensing fee. In Cohn's view the innovation "fits the DNA of what BitTorrent is about because it's open and free" (ibid). As one online commenter noted, the technology would offer independent producers access to an "instant global, monetizable audience . . . which never existed before", allowing "niche content to thrive" (ibid) in direct competition with the established industry, although finding that content amidst the data smog might still be an issue. However this potential freedom threatens the industry, if artists abandon it as their major source of fame and income.

Although, as already pointed out, such claims about the emancipatory power of technology have been made for decades, the diminishing costs of digital technologies plus the scalability of P2P systems and the possibility for spatially disaggregated producers and consumers to directly connect with one another, could threaten older media models based on scarcity and corporate oligopoly. Moreover, while new forms of piratical exchange disorder oligopolistic copyright regimes by making a shared commons, they also offer businesses and cultural institutions new ways of ordering content and service delivery, further underscoring the entangled nature of the order/disorder complex.

Cultural Networks

P2P generates social relationships as its networks, search engines and discussion forums create affinities of usage. These affinities typically take the form of loosely organised networks populated by individuals engaged in the same practices of exchange and holding similar social norms about piracy. The line between community and network is ambiguous. For instance, over 75,000 users of the Pirate Bay, arguably the most infamous and 'resilient' BT search engine (launched in 2003 after gestating as an electronic freedom advocacy project), participated in Lund University's Cybernorms research centre's first study of downloaders' social norms. Over 96,000 people responded to a second online questionnaire, making these the largest surveys conducted within a file-sharing community (Larsson et al. 2012). This level of participation suggests that respondents trusted the Pirate Bay enough to share possibly self-incriminating information and felt some sense of membership of an online community, or loyalty to what appears to be a distributed source/swarm. Indeed, when the Pirate Bay celebrated its tenth birthday in August 2013, its blog announcement underscored the reciprocal nature of the project's "affectionate" relationship with some 34,737,165 participating peers (Pirate Bay 9 August 2013):

> Oh look, we made it.
> A decade of agression [sic], repression and lulz.
>
> We really didn't think we'd make it this far. Not because of cops, mafiaa or corrupt politicians. But because we thought that we'd eventually be to old for this shit. But hey, running this ship makes us feel young.
>
> And we're gonna stay young til we die.
> Thank you for everything. We would not be anything without you.
> Love

Judging by the 264 comments on this posting the 'love' was mutual. Many acknowledged the important role the Pirate Bay had played in meeting the challenges of legal threats, police raids, a major court case and increasing attempts by national governments to block access to the Pirate Bay search engine (see also Larsson 2013).

> We boarded the ship of freedom years ago which took us to the whole world. I cant imagine my life without sailing with u everyday into the vast oceans of knowledge.
>
> With all my love and support.
>
> God bless and happy birthday . . .
>
> (Pirate Bay 9 August 2013, comment #256)

Beyond communities and networks, we suspect that P2P facilitates what we think of as *unintentional societies*. Members of these incidental societies might not necessarily hold consciously articulated anti-copyright or 'open knowledge' positions, but nevertheless their general attitudes and social customs are implicit and built into their downloading habits. Today's techno-social assemblages of software, protocols, search engines, news sites and forums make downloading relatively easy. This sense of normality contributes to building social norms (shared by non-file-sharers also), implying that digital forms of information and culture should be instantly accessible regardless of platform and content type. Whether this be films via the Pirate Bay, encyclopaedia entries via Wikipedia, music clips via YouTube, photographs via Tumblr or news coverage via Reddit, people experience the internet as being simultaneously a content archive and delivery system; a generally free cultural and relational service once access fees are paid.

These 'unintentional societies' appear as periodic swarming formations beyond those more technological swarms produced by P2P software applications. Attempts by governments and corporations to identify illicit internet users and restrict the free flow of information (for example, via supranational anti-piracy treaties like the controversial Anti-Counterfeiting Trade Agreement [ACTA]) or to gather information about internet users (for example, via mass online surveillance programs such as the U.S. National Security Agency's PRISM program), have generated swarms of protest and social activism. Some of these swarms might prefigure or evolve into more organised collective actors, social movements or even political parties. Pirate Parties have brought "IP issues closer to the centre of the parliamentary system", with their electoral campaigns putting candidates into regional parliaments and the European Parliament. Importantly, their success has forced other political parties to "position themselves in relation to the issues raised by the pirate parties" (Haunss 2011: 132). The anti-ACTA campaign found its strongest expression in Europe, bringing together libertarians, anarchists, highly organised activist groups and 'regular' file-sharers, all concerned about clandestine negotiations and the erosion of digital privacy and freedom. Some Polish parliamentarians donned the Guy Fawkes mask associated with the Anonymous network to signify they supported electronic freedom (Olson 27 January 2012). The European Parliament eventually rejected the fiercely contested treaty (Mathews 2012: 1; Sutton 12 July 2012). Similarly, other major national bills and international treaties including the Stop Online Piracy Act (SOPA), PROTECT IP Act (PIPA) and the Trans-Pacific Partnership Agreement (TPP) have generated oppositional swarm formations populated by digital activists, bloggers, network engineers, venture capitalists, members of parliamentary Pirate Parties and others concerned about the "potential for abuse of power through digital networks" (MacKinnon 15 November 2011). Wikileaks released hidden information about this 'public agreement' (the TPP) in late 2013 (see Chapter 6). Other objections centred on electronic privacy, freedom of speech, network logistics and innovation. Predictions included an "eviscerated" legal environment, "pervasive scrutiny and surveillance" of online activities, stunted social media, platforms required to be "content police" and ultimately an "increasingly balkanized Internet" (Howard 2011). Numerous technology companies joined the fight against SOPA. On 18 January 2012, 7,000 websites including Wikipedia joined the Web blackout day, and 7 million people signed Google's online petition (Carrier 2013). The SOPA Bill was withdrawn in the face of this widespread and swarmed public opposition, although the fight is far from over.

Swarms are not inherently democratic or 'progressive', however the customs and habits users have built up around the flow of information effectively blur the 'traditional' capitalist distinctions and imposed boundaries between common and private ownership. File-sharing activities challenge the boundaries of property, by shifting privately owned informational property into the public domain, and highlight the arbitrary boundaries that corporations have declared around cultural property. P2P forum commentary suggests that the original 'seeders' (those who digitise/compress this content and upload the associated addressing information to file-sharing networks), consider both the material and digital versions of their cultural artefacts to be either their own property, or public property, to dispose of as they wish. Even when digital material is bought from a provider, for instance in the form of an e-book, people do not necessarily consider that they have purchased only a 'new' set of limited rights and associated conditions to enjoy that material, but have bought the material itself. Recent restrictions are not curtailments of their rights they ever agreed to, discussed or, in many cases, were even aware of. Instead they believe that, as in the past with a physical book, the commercial transaction grants them the inherent right to do as they like with the content. This includes the right to loan, share or gift it to others, or use as raw material in the creation of new art works.

Others have extensively dealt with the rise of so-called sampling and remix cultures (Lessig 2008; Mason 2008), we will just reiterate a few points. Art, in all its manifestations, depends on those who make it having access to existing works, techniques, processes, knowledges, histories and so forth. The same is true of software, as the free software and open source movements have amply demonstrated (Coleman 2012). The new cannot be separated from the old, nor the informational material from the social world in which it is embedded. Art, science and discussion necessarily demand recombinant and reiterative processes. Through the intensification and extension of copyright law, patents, exclusive licenses and so on attempt to enclose (and increase the enclosure of) cultural output, and deny the instrumental role that unfettered appropriation, quotation, homage, montage and reproduction play in cultural transmission and 'disruptive' innovation. Recognising this, some artists (including established bands such as Radiohead and best-selling author Paulo Coelho) have released versions of selected works on P2P networks, inviting people to either pay what they want or buy professional editions if they choose (Michaels 18 August 2009; Coelho 2008). As we have implied before the artist and the industry's aims and benefits can be conflicted.

In 1998 singer/songwriter Janis Ian (2002) declared: "The Internet, and downloading, are here to stay . . . Anyone who thinks otherwise should prepare themselves to end up on the slagheap of history". She cites her own experiences of renewed interest in her 1975 hit "At Seventeen" and increased album sales at the time when Napster was "running full-tilt". Paulo Coelho (2008) downloaded various translations and audio books of his own work from a popular Russian BitTorrent site, and uploaded them to his own 'Pirate Coelho' website. Although he did not own the translation rights to all editions, he regarded his actions as 'sharing' rather than 'stealing'. His sales subsequently received a "significant boost", reaching over 100 million copies. In late 2012 the Pirate Bay launched the Promo Bay website, inviting creators of music, films, comics, lectures, books, games and applications to send in their demos. Over 10,000 artists responded, with the Pirate Bay periodically highlighting selected clips on their main site (Ernesto 29 November 2012). Each of these examples suggests that fixed boundaries and binary divisions (authorised/non-authorised, commercial/non-commercial, mainstream/independent, private/public, closed/open, amateur/professional) are becoming increasingly blurred, with P2P networks opening up new forms of community, support and connection between artists and aficionados.

FILE-SHARING AND THE LAW

As we have argued, when seeders upload 'their property' into the public realm, the boundaries between different types of ownership are blurred or even decommodified. Information that some have declared restricted becomes public, notwithstanding copyright terms. In response, there have been attempts to strengthen copyright technologically and legally, to recapture some of the drift to the commons.

Some of these attempts are themselves ambiguous. The dovetailing of multi-function set-top boxes with ISP subscriber services, for instance, has further extended delivery options of digital content, which in turns paves the way for more attempts at enclosure via legal means. In 2011 the customers of a French ISP were invited to subscribe to "The Freebox Revolution" a "new-style digital media consumption" package consisting of a hardware player and server offering various services including 300 TV channels and a BitTorrent application enabling games and software to be downloaded directly to the server (Enigmax 12 October 2011). The entrepreneurial ISP recognised a business opportunity in selling a service that combined legal and quite probably extra-legal content streams, engaging renowned designer Philippe Starcke to create the casing (Gobry 14 December 2010). Entertainment industry bodies demanded the ISP remove the BT feature. "This technology is not neutral, it clearly offers illegal downloading of content without a PC", a Syndicat National de l'Édition Phonographique representative reportedly said (ibid). Technology journalist Guillaume Champeau (ibid) countered that a court would have to prove that the ISP had "encouraged its customers to go to BitTorrent sites where pirated movies are indexed", and establish that technical protocols and communications channels are not inherently innocent, which has been an occasionally successful argument in copyright law suits elsewhere. In the Freebox Revolution we see simultaneous processes of deordering and reordering, where contestation redefines the boundaries of technological development and commodification.

Legal attacks on file-sharing systems have targeted other P2P protocols. A classic early case is that of Kazaa (or KaZaA), a proprietary P2P software using the FastTrack protocol. In 2003 Kazaa accounted for "79% of global peer-to-peer file sharing", with the software being downloaded "more than 317 million times" by early 2004 (Giblin & Davison 2006: 75–6, 53). In 2005 Universal Music Australia filed a suit in the Australian Federal Court for copyright infringement against Kazaa's owners, Sharman License Holdings. As with the iiNet case that we discuss later, the U.S.-dominated entertainment industry used Australian courts in their attempt to establish internationally influential legal precedents. We surmise that Australia was a chosen locus for such suits due to both its relationship as a "friend" of the U.S., and its relatively strong copyright laws without flexible 'fair use' provisions. Both 'piracy' and 'copyright' involve shifting international fields, in efforts to find safe places for action. In its landmark decision the Court decided that it was reasonable to "prohibit the continued distribution of a product on the grounds that after its sale it is capable of being used by its purchaser to infringe copyright, even though it may also have non-infringing uses" (ibid: 53). After numerous legal battles Kazaa transformed itself into a legal music subscription service, losing most of its users in the process (ibid: 75). During this period Kazaa also faced allegations that the files it transmitted were full of 'malware'. The firm TruSecure claimed nearly half the files it downloaded were infected. A spokesperson said that:

> the malicious code he found was embedded in program files that are designed to bypass or break copyright protections placed on software files . . . however, music, picture and movie files have not been infected with malicious code, because they aren't executables . . . Organizations need to warn their employees about file-sharing applications and the danger they pose to them at work and at home.
>
> (Zetter 9 January 2004)

Another organisation funded by Google and Sun amongst others:

> listed the Kazaa file-sharing application at the top of a list of noxious software programs that present a threat to business and consumer users. [They said that] Adware and spyware programs that come bundled with peer-to-peer applications present a huge security risk to corporate networks.
>
> (Narraine 21 March 2006)

This kind of report increases people's information paranoia, and suspicions as to who might put this malware online (see Chapter 8). In any case, using file-sharing could have serious consequences. However, this is normal, and Narraine and others such as the Center for Democracy and Technology suggest that "advertising dollars from major, legitimate companies are [also] fuelling the spread of nuisance and harmful adware" (CDT 2006: 1). Indeed, the so-called Intellectual Property Commission has recently recommended that software should be written so that if unauthorised people access the information:

> a range of actions might then occur. For example, the file could be rendered inaccessible and the unauthorized user's computer could be locked down, with instructions on how to contact law enforcement to get the password needed to unlock the account. Such measures do not violate existing laws on the use of the Internet . . .
>
> (IP Commission 2013: 81)

This copyright policing innovation is based on a technique that criminal hackers often use, in which computers are locked down until a ransom is paid. Again, this shows the creative relationship between forces espousing order and those they label as disordering.

In recent years, an increasingly coordinated international approach has brought together various national policing and justice agencies to obliterate significant file-sharing platforms. In December 2011 the U.S. government identified the popular BT tracker and content-indexing site Demonoid as a "notorious market", placing it with other marketplaces that "may merit further investigation" for intellectual property rights infringement. As evidence they cited the website Alexa's ranking of Demonoid as belonging to the 'top 600 websites in global traffic and the top 300 in U.S. traffic' (Office of the United States Trades Representative 2011). For its members, Demonoid was unsurpassed, inhabited by "small groups of people sharing content they all loved" (comment on Andy 8 May 2013):

> users did record and share things like local news shows, to share with expats living abroad etc . . . Maybe only 5 people wanted to download it but it made their day seeing some local news from back home. That's what demonoid thrived at. People sharing unique content. It was the best site for many niche subjects. Spanning all genres of content.
>
> (ibid)

While such remarks ignore many transactions on Demonoid, they show the range of ways such sites were used. In August 2012 three separate law enforcement and justice authorities, one powerful industry body, and the U.S. government, joined to force the closure of Demonoid (which by then had moved its server to Ukraine) (Ernesto 12 February 2013). Retaliation was also networked globally, if not as effectively. Within two days of the site being taken offline, the Anonymous hacktivist network launched its 'OpDemonoid' action conducting Distributed Denial of Service (DDoS) attacks on the websites of three Ukrainian organisations, and releasing a video (BBC 9 August 2012). Shortly after, the British-based International Federation of the Phonographic Industry (IFPI) issued a press release confirming that they had "assisted INTERPOL, the Division of Economic Crimes (DEC) in the Ukrainian police and the investigative arm of the Attorney General of Mexico (PGR)" to effect the site's closure and launch a criminal investigation into Demonoid's owners (allegedly residing in Mexico), resulting in arrests and assets seizures (Jacob 2012). As the U.S. copyright lobby noted in a report "[o]nline copyright thieves have become increasingly peripatetic and can shift their bases with increasing velocity", being "adept at jumping across borders and assuming alternate identities to evade the long arm of the law" (Motion Picture Association of America et al. 2012: 13). Indeed. As indicated above, Demonoid had moved its physical servers from Canada to Ukraine in response to legal threats. It had also pre-emptively changed its .TLD (Top Level Domain) from .com to .me and .ph in 2011, in an effort to protect itself from U.S. authorities terminating its domain name registration. A resurrected Demonoid made a 'glorious comeback' on 30 March 2014, with a new cloud-based server hosting its pre-existing archive of tracker files and user accounts (Ernesto 30 March 2014). The site promises to "respond expeditiously to claims of copyright infringement" reported to its "designated copyright agent", and invites users to "support the site bandwidth and server rental costs" by donating via Bitcoin (Demonoid 2014). The Demonoid story highlights how both control and liberation processes have increasingly shifted to a global level, and how situations originating in policing and legal domains can extend into the social domains of media spectacle and electronic civil disobedience.

The imposition of legal order irrevocably disorders the social swarms around particular P2P platforms, exposing the fragility of the affective ties and social obligation built within each file-sharing system. However, this fragility also enables some resilience; users simply move on to the next available platform, even if they consider it inferior in terms of content or community. In August 2012 file-sharing news site TorrentFreak's breaking news item on Demonoid's closure attracted over 700 comments in the first 24 hours after publication. Many posters declared they would keep torrenting on other P2P sites. Many, again, also vouched that Demonoid had been unsurpassed in terms of niche content, Creative Commons licensed files, sophisticated search categories and a friendly 'community' atmosphere (Enigmax 6 August 2012). Again, for many people Demonoid had other uses than just breaking copyright.

> How are vinyl rips, old radio recordings, and radio show rips infringing on other people's rights? A lot of Demonoid's music/audio content represented a preservation of music culture rather than an infringement upon copyright. . . . Our sites and sharing represent global libraries and should be upheld with the most adamant determination.
>
> (comment on Enigmax 6 August 2012)

Similar comments could be made about YouTube, which seems to survive, perhaps because it is owned by corporate behemoth Google, and therefore wields power far beyond that of relatively tiny projects such as Demonoid.

In recent years major copyright owners have found new staging grounds for the copyfight, pressuring Internet Service Providers directly, often via sovereign governments, to be accountable for 'unauthorised' files transmitted by their customers. The first such case occurred in Australia, when the distributor Roadshow Films and numerous other parties filed a case in November 2008 against iiNet, the country's third-largest ISP, alleging that it knowingly supported its clients' copyright infringements. The primary charge was that iiNet had failed to "take any action (i.e., issue warnings, suspend or terminate) against its users once it was notified by the Australian Federation Against Copyright Theft (AFACT) of the infringing activities via its services" (Eivazi 2012: 458). As it was the first time anywhere that a charge against an ISP had been brought to trial, the case attracted international attention. Evidence of direct political manoeuvring would later surface in two U.S. diplomatic cables to Australian authorities (released in the 2010 Wikileaks 'Cablegate' tranche). These confirmed activists' suspicions that powerful

Hollywood interests had driven the precedent-setting trial. However, the Motion Picture Association of America (MPAA) and its international affiliates had hoped to keep their involvement secret rather than be perceived as Hollywood "bullying some poor little Australian ISP" (McCallum 2008). This marks yet another normal example of information restriction and its failure.

Ultimately (and unexpectedly given the Kazaa result), all three iiNet trials including an appeal and a High Court challenge were decided in iiNet's favour (LeMay 20 April 2012). However, the iiNet litigation has had "significant ramifications" for internet regulation in Australia, with legal scholar Kathy Eivazi (2012: 467) predicting that the government is likely to implement the same kinds of "graduated response" laws (tiered punishments for copyright infringers) initiated (with questionable success) elsewhere. The failure of such laws is demonstrated by the French government's 2013 repeal of its controversial HADOPI law. Although HADOPI had cost millions of Euros to administer since it was enacted in 2009, it had resulted in only two convictions and had no impact on file-sharing practices (Loeffler 1 August 2013). The iiNet saga demonstrates how P2P can trigger interrelated events in specific geopolitical regions (Australia/U.S.) and industry sectors (telecommunications/film), in turn further disordering the informational field by propelling legal innovation and policy development. Certainly ISPs are becoming more involved in drafting industry codes of practice, and many governments are seeking their involvement in reviewing digital copyright legislation. Moreover, given the case highlighted the Australian appetite for cultural materials delivered in desirable formats and in a timely manner, some companies, including ISPs themselves, have offered new legal options of content delivery, such as subscription video-on-demand services (LeMay 3 April 2013).

Evidence suggests that criminal prosecutions and harsh sentences can increase people's resolve to keep capturing and downloading content on principle. In September 2011 U.S. authorities closed down IMAGiNE, a major movie piracy Release Group (RG). In the highly competitive RG scene, which exemplifies another kind of swarm formation, groups strive to be the first to release high quality versions of new cinema releases online, months before DVD versions are commercially available. RG releases are normally only available for download by members of exclusive private "tracker" platforms, who are supposed to adhere to strictly policed house rules including not re-releasing the downloads to open public platforms like the Pirate Bay. RG members 'cam' or 'cap' films in theatres, sometimes capturing the vision and audio separately, recompose the files, and then upload them to their RG platform. This has led to further technological repression and innovation as by analysing the new embedded forensic codes in films' video and audio tracks, intelligence companies can identify which theatres the 'cammers' used, information that then enters the legal chain of evidence.

In the IMAGiNE case both the U.S. Department of Justice (Criminal Division) and the U.S. Immigration and Customs Enforcement (Homeland Security Investigations) were involved, as part of the government's effort to maintain the capitalist informational order of property. The aim was to "combat . . . domestic and international intellectual property crimes, protect the health and safety of American consumers, and safeguard the nation's economic security against those who seek to profit illegally from American creativity, innovation and hard work" (United States Attorney's Office for the Eastern District of Virginia 2012). Subsequently, one IMAGiNE leader who pleaded guilty to conspiracy to commit criminal copyright infringement was jailed for five years, and other American members would also receive some of the "harshest copyright infringement sentences on record" (Andy 6 May 2013). In May 2013, a report by the Toronto-based anti-piracy group Deluxe, whom the studios had hired to 'spy' on IMAGiNE members, revealed that a "decrease of unique pirated English audio sources" occurred immediately after the raid (ibid). However this did not last. In October 2011 there were "more English-language release[s] than each of the nine months prior to the enforcement actions", with Deluxe surmising that the "piracy community re-oriented itself following IMAGiNE's departure". This implication of a rational orderly and unified 'piracy community' is at odds with P2P's disorderly swarms and its creative but uncoordinated play in developing new means to subvert commodification; however it provides further evidence of the paranoia of industry and the difficulty of curtailing file-sharing. Even using the term 'swarm' may give too much sense of order, as it suggests related insects who stay together, but members of the swarms of pirarchy branch off and join other swarms, can be temporary members, have radically different aims and interests, etc. While not completely without the appearance of order, the disordered and temporary quality remains an overt part of their dynamics. Their temporary nature, and formally uncoordinated nature, gives them their capacity to undermine orders the 'members' perceive as hostile or pointless. While the formal order can attack individuals it is hard to attack an organisation that does not exist.

In 2011 network traffic analysis showed that BitTorrent still generated 47.6% of all upstream bytes (uploading), despite real time streamed entertainment and cyberlockers dominating downloading (Sandvine 2011: 8). By the second half of 2012, the overall global picture was changing, mainly due to the increased popularity of streaming options (with commercial video-on-demand service Netflix dominating the U.S. sector, and YouTube the rest of the world).

> In absolute traffic level, BitTorrent has risen in volume by over 40%, but the application continues to exhibit a steady downward trend in overall traffic share, declining to 10.31% of total peak traffic from being 11.30% a half a year ago.
>
> (Sandvine 2012: 7)

Sandvine also remarks that the decline of BitTorrent has influenced the decline of file-sharing, which "since 2010 has seen its traffic share decline from 19.2% to 12.0% of peak period aggregate traffic" (ibid: 7).

The ephemeral quality of streamed data might also add to information-property disorder, as nebulous content flows through devices rather than being downloaded onto them as permanent storable artefacts. Immediate accessibility further dissolves distinctions between the internet as communications infrastructure and as a content repository; means and material become one and the same to the end user. What is being disrupted is the notion that data is something to be downloaded, ordered and stored—or perhaps 'owned' permanently. Rather, data becomes something to move through, and which moves through us. Here its temporal qualities are foregrounded as its spatial ones recede. In this respect the streams through both commercial and decommodified sources mirror disorderly transactions in other informational fields, such as in finance, albeit at a slower space.

CYBERLOCKERS

In August 2011 Google measurements revealed that the "five largest English language websites dedicated to swapping files" were cyberlockers. The most popular of these, 4shared.com, served 2.5 billion page views every month (Ernesto 27 August 2011). Although web analysis companies have been criticised for giving 'guestimates' rather than verifiable snapshots of total internet usage, they do offer a broad picture of trends. The cyberlocker ecosystem includes 'reputable' cloud platforms such as Dropbox and entities such as RapidShare, which originally presented itself as pro-file-sharing (*IFPI Digital Music Report 2010*: 19). Because cyberlockers are web-based they use the HTTP protocol rather than the BitTorrent protocol many P2P networks use. While BT platforms only host the meta-data ('torrents') pointing to a file's location, cyberlockers host the actual data files. People upload files to these centralised repositories, and because each file is assigned a fixed URL others can potentially download them. Typically cyberlockers do not provide search or indexing tools, so downloaders must locate the URLs through distributed announcements on Usenet, private or public file-sharing forums, BBSs or Google. Many cyberlockers were partially funded by hosting advertisements, often for porn or gambling sites. However, as independent film director Ellen Seidler (nd) discovered (and further illustrating the entangled nature of the legal/extra-legal info-orders), many ads on cyberlockers, P2P and streaming platforms are for "legit companies"; and served by devices such as Google's AdSense that "generate their own robust revenue stream by providing the interface for the pirate-site pop-up ads themselves". Unlike most P2P sites, many cyberlockers also sell 'premium' subscriptions offering users fast download times and other benefits unavailable to 'freemium' users. In this way, piracy itself becomes commodified.

THE MEGAUPLOAD CASE AND ITS IMPACT ON
THE CYBERLOCKER ECOSYSTEM

In January 2012 the Megaupload cloud storage site, founded by controversial entrepreneur Kim Dotcom, was taken down in a series of dramatic
multi-country raids, arrests and extradition orders coordinated by the FBI
and the U.S. Department of Justice (DOJ) in conjunction with various local
authorities. Cyberlockers were suddenly the subject of mainstream media
attention. The hacker collective Anonymous promptly retaliated to the raid
by conducting what they called the "largest-ever cyber attack" that temporarily disabled the websites of the DOJ, FBI, MPAA, RIAA and others
(Anderson 20 January 2012; de Neef 2012).

Curiously, a report said to be leaked from the International Federation of the Phonographic Industry (IFPI) claimed that MegaUpload was
an "insignificant" player in the cyberlocker landscape, dwarfed by traffic
on filesonic, wupload and fileserve (Enigmax 25 July 2012). This raises
the question of why authorities had targeted Megaupload. From Dotcom's
perspective, corruption, croneyism and the government/corporate revolv-
ing door, with ex-MPAA and RIAA executives "infiltrating . . . key [U.S.]
government positions", lay at the heart of the matter (Ernesto 14 August
2012). Later, in a release entitled 'Megaupload, the Copyright Lobby, and
the Future of Digital Rights', Dotcom's lawyers argued that the government's attack and assets seizure was "propelled by the White House's desire
to mollify the motion picture industry in exchange for campaign contributions and political support" (Amsterdam & Rothken 2013: 2). Whether
accurate or not, this shows strategic information paranoia in action. This
point was reinforced by Megaupload's principal operatives being indicted
under an act usually applied to organised crime groups, the Racketeer Influenced and Corrupt Organizations (RICO) Act, notwithstanding that the
Federal Court arguably lacks the power to "criminalise secondary copyright
infringement", that is, the behaviour of a company's customers (ibid: 3).
Rhetoric from both sides has been strong, with Dotcom's team drawing
comparisons with the U.S. government's legal case against deceased internet
activist Aaron Swartz, as both cases "evoke a common theme of prosecu-
torial abuse in matters touching upon copyright" (ibid: 12). On the other
hand, copyright lobbyists have described Dotcom and the other "Megaupload conspirators" as "wealthy and arrogant defendants who are leaving no
stone unturned in their efforts to sway public opinion against efforts to hold
them accountable" (Motion Picture Association of America et al. 2012: 27).
In the informational era the media landscape is a crucial, and paranoiac,
battleground for the copyfight.

Immediately following the Megaupload raid major cyberlockers instituted rules around legitimate use, changing their Terms of Service (ToS) to
explicitly forbid users from uploading copyright-infringing material (Enigmax 23 January 2012). For example, the 'House Rules' of 4shared's ToS

warns users not to transmit "any data, message, text, computer file, or other material that infringes any right of a third party and/or any domestic or international law, rule, or regulation, including but not limited to: copyright, trademark, patent, or other proprietary rights" (4shared 2013). The 'Acceptable Use' policy emphasises that 4shared adheres to the U.S. Digital Millennium Copyright Act (DMCA) and "collaborates" with specific industry and governments to "fight against piracy" (ibid).

Similarly, the Swiss-based RapidShare cyberlocker's old website interface had employed graphics and language apparently designed to attract, or at least not repel, file-sharers. Now the company that boasts it "invented Cloud Storage" has repositioned itself as a legitimate cloud hosting service used daily by millions (RapidShare 2013a). With a foot in both camps it pledges to "respect our users' privacy and likewise the legitimate interests of artists, rights holders and publishers". Rapidshare's (2013b) Terms of Use state that it will not "open and view" files users upload, and advises that it "does not provide a search function with which RapidShare's infrastructure can be searched". This implies that it does not overtly facilitate piracy, and, perhaps, that copyright owners are responsible for monitoring (supposedly private) traffic. In a realm in which suspicion flourishes, these terms might seem instruments to defuse legal responsibility, rather than discourage traffic and diminish income from advertising. They also illustrate the tendency within informationalism for the distribution of governance and responsibility to undermine the distinction between public responsibility and private interest. Extending copyright and breaking copyright can both be profit-seeking activities. Intermediaries such as ISPs and cyberlockers on the whole refuse to be held responsible for their clients' activities, with their Terms of Use apparently functioning as risk insurance. Superficial compliance with the official info-order exists concurrently with the creation of an alternative ordering/disordering regime that challenges the status quo.

NEW BUSINESS MODELS AND CROSS-SECTOR ALLIANCES

P2P has clearly driven new commercial business models for digital content delivery. The music industry in particular followed pathways that 'pirate' platforms forged. Again we see the entangled reiterative ordering/disordering processes driving both technological and social innovation. Some entrepreneurial start-ups have pioneered less antagonistic approaches to cultural consumers' demands. Perhaps the entrepreneurs' age and professional backgrounds are relevant to this shift as many are relatively young and come from IT and programming backgrounds (*IFPI Digital Music Report 2011* 2011: 24–7). In contrast, as evidenced by their public pronouncements, members of the older managerial class associated with the MPAA, RIAA and other entertainment industries do not appear to understand the dynamics of digital culture. Start-ups and subsidiaries including We7, Slacker, WiMP, Mflow, Vodafone Music and Spotify have licensed content from the major copyright holders and formed strategic alliances with other companies. They respond to file-sharers' demands for products free from Digital Rights Management (DRM) locks and for platform-transportable media (ibid). Hence they can leverage services that generally lie beyond pirate networks' capacity to match. For instance, Sweden's pioneer music streaming service Spotify not only expanded into new geographical regions, but encouraged people to move "from ownership to access" by developing individuals' music libraries and having playlists shareable via Facebook (ibid: 27). The American internet radio service Pandora offered 75 million users freemium and premium accounts, and in 2010 partnered with Mercedes-Benz and Ford to 'integrate' Pandora into their vehicles (ibid: 24). Telecommunications provider Vodafone combined a subscription service with the "sense of ownership delivered by downloading tracks to keep", bundling selections from millions of tracks that the company had licensed (ibid).

Whether artists have benefited from this new panoply of distribution channels is moot, despite copyright holders arguing that piracy hurts creators financially. For instance, musician Damon Krukowski (14 November 2012) claims that the "ways in which musicians are screwed have changed qualitatively, from individualized swindles to systemic ones", singling out Pandora and Spotify for their miserly reimbursements.

> Galaxie 500's 'Tugboat', for example, was played 7,800 times on Pandora that quarter, for which its three songwriters were paid a collective total of 21 cents, or seven cents each. Spotify pays better: For the 5,960 times 'Tugboat' was played there, Galaxie 500's songwriters went collectively into triple digits: $1.05 (35 cents each).

Moreover, it appears that the companies themselves are unprofitable, with Pandora reporting a "net loss of more than $20 million dollars", in the first quarter of 2012, and Spotify losing 56 million dollars in 2011 (ibid). Krukowski declares these companies "exist to attract speculative capital" as evidenced by Pandora executives selling "$63 million of personal stock in the company" in 2012 (ibid). Other, well-known artists such as Radiohead's Thom Yorke have also exited from Spotify. Yorke claimed that "new artists you discover on Spotify will not get paid. Meanwhile shareholders will shortly be rolling in it" (Arthur 2013). Criticisms from artists (countered by corporate denials) reveal again the tension between, and within, different modes of info-ordering. Technological advances can simultaneously disturb existing social orders and maintain old power relationships. Anti-piracy arguments become less credible as artists desert the new speculative capital ventures for pirarchical and autonomous circuits, further disturbing corporate profit.

CONCLUSION

File-sharing is a social, cultural and technological practice native to internet networks. This is clearest in its peer-to-peer incarnations, in the ebbs and flows, log-ins and drop-outs of constantly changing swarms. Due to the interconnections and cross-pollinations between the fields constituting file-sharing it is impossible to present a neat narrative of straight trajectories. This phenomenon's histories are as reticular as the fields in which it is embedded. Events in one informational domain (legal prohibitions, for example) trigger reactions in another (technological work-arounds, for example) in endless disruptive loops. It seems impossible to chronologically sort the causal order, as code, hardware platforms, network protocols, business models, legal instruments, fan labour and so forth interconnect in ways that are not always immediately apparent. What is clear, though, is that fights over the boundaries of ownership are at the centre of these developments, expressing the co-dependent, confused and interacting relationship between commons and commodification.

The continuous multi-dimensional, multi-sited info-social struggle produces new info-social formations, from peers exchanging files in a P2P swarm, to the nebulous legion of Anonymous hacktivists conducting DDOS attacks on websites symbolising the info-enclosures, to media-savvy masses gathering on the streets to protest against controversial internet laws. In some instances these info-social formations are differentiated culturally or nationally, for example, coalescing as Pirate Parties in the domain of representative politics. Increasingly however, as the forces promoting info-enclosures coordinate their efforts on an international level, so too do the swarms develop strategies, tactics and affective bonds that transcend geo-spatial limits and national concerns, disordering the official orders.

Napster's centralised model made it vulnerable to legal attack, inspiring the creation of an open source protocol, in BT Torrent, enabling a fully distributed peer-to-peer method of file-exchange, harnessing internet users' bandwidth and distributing risk. Not only did BitTorrent help massify digital piracy, but it was also implemented in countless other software programs, network tools, business models and projects outside file-sharing. Ultimately this protocol produced both a more diversified internet ecosystem and a new means of mass engagement with network architecture. The consequent proliferation of P2P activity and code has produced counter-orders of decommodification with their own generative potential in the face of ceaseless commodifying pressures. The result is an entanglement of ordering, disordering and reordering efforts, with globalised social norms possibly tending, at the moment, towards connectivity and openness, regardless of localised legal norms.

File-sharing thereby exposes some of the contradictions and disordering motions inherent in informational capitalism. Because digital content can be easily duplicated, notwithstanding technological locks and legal instruments, its dissemination through black and grey markets and other illicit channels resists external controls. Social norms that treat cultural sharing as vital to participation in everyday life currently trump legal norms perceived to be both anachronistic and favouring a rapacious class of content owners. While it might appear that informationalism is predicated on maintaining and extending regimes of capitalist order, the actions and commitment of millions of info-capital's anarchic constituents have driven the innovation, the new markets and the profits, and spawned new business models for digital content delivery. Consequently, the 'incidental' or 'unintentional' pirate is an inventor, innovator, inspirer and implementer of new techno-social platforms and circuits of exchange, while the industry largely fights rearguard actions. While file-sharing trends are shifting, with P2P forms making way for streaming and cloud services, the realm of piracy is expanding, both spatially as more regions come online, and in terms of genre, as more cultural forms become available in digital formats.

11 Information-Disorder in Academia

The free exchange, sharing and criticism of ideas is the foundation for creative thought and scientific endeavour across all fields. Enclosing ideas as intellectual property disrupts free exchange, locks up knowledge and hampers intellectual creativity and understanding, as well as hindering society's ability to respond to problems and challenges. The order of commodification also devalues most work involved in the production of knowledge, while disordering the creative intellectual project of the public university. The public university was created by the 'modern' State to develop an intellectual commons and support the production of well-informed knowledge workers and administrators, who could contribute to society's well-being. Within this tradition, many (but not all) universities were funded as places free from commercial imperatives and restrictions. This tradition has been hit on two fronts. First, a relatively successful neoliberal politics has put pressure on public provision for universities. Simultaneously intellectual property regimes have strengthened, and organisations have found extensive scope for enclosing the informational commons using digital technology, and for realising monopoly profits from their use. This extension of informationalist and financial order is parasitic on the intellectual commons, and like many parasites, it depends on what it feeds off. Ultimately, if left unchecked, it can kill both its host and itself.

In analysing these processes, it is important not to idealise academic production of knowledge as orderly or unproblematically coherent. Academics live within a reputation economy, and academic publishing is an ordering device whereby academic quality and status is recognised. This recognition leads to promotion, and publication has been far more important to such rewards than (for instance) an ability to teach or inspire students. In some cases publishing can become self-serving, as when the system of peer review breaks down, or when particular journals publish associates or allies of the editors, or the journals follow fads for similar reasons to managers. Books can be so expensive that it is unlikely they are bought outside of academic libraries. The publication can be more important than its availability; indeed publishing popular titles can be viewed negatively. The side-purpose of academic knowledge, of gaining the recognition of peers and career stability, can disorder the production of knowledge. In an era of data smog and insecurity of information work, issues around recognition and gaining a reputation can become even more important.

Digitisation has created the possibility of more open access to the intellectual commons. No longer is it necessary to negotiate access to a library to read the latest research from around the world; information technology theoretically allows it to be 'a click away'. Conversely, digitisation provides scope to impose access requirements across all versions of a document, to impose time limits on access, or to restrict circulation to the individual consumer and their first access. The same mechanisms enable digital surveillance of those violating property restrictions, and exacting punishment. As we have seen, no one knows who is watching, or when they will watch. These opposed features disorder academic research outlets, generating possibilities on all sides. The digital revolution, and the intellectual openness it promised is now locked into a battle with a commodity-based counter-revolution within the revolution, led by journal aggregators and publishers (see Guédon 2001). This chapter explores these contestations, showing how they demonstrate the disordering effects of informationalism at universities, which are still key sites of knowledge production.

Academic publishers have for some time sought to accumulate and assemble journals into a range of specialist offerings. From the 1970s these collections have produced a relatively secure source of subscription income that, publishers argue, has cross-subsidised riskier book sales. With digitisation, 'meta-aggregators' have emerged to draw together publishers' journals into packages of several thousand titles. These aggregators have merged into a small number of providers controlling large numbers of journals. ProQuest for instance, not the largest aggregator, boasted 11,500 serials in 2009, including 1,300 journals in the social sciences (ProQuest 2009). With aggregation, university librarians find journals bundled on a take it or leave it basis (Edlin & Rubinfield 2004). Single journal subscriptions are sold at greatly inflated prices, well above the average cost of a journal as part of an aggregated package. Not surprisingly, the aggregators enjoy monopoly rents: in 2011 the Elsevier division at Reed Elsevier made a profit of €768 million on a revenue of €2,058 million, giving a more-than-healthy return of 37% (Reed Elsevier 2011: 12). Much of this came from the taxpayer, as Reed Elsevier implies in its 2011 Annual Report:

> Given that a significant proportion of scientific research and healthcare is funded directly or indirectly by governments, spending is influenced by governmental budgetary considerations. The commitment to research and health provision does, however, remain high, even in more difficult budgetary environments.
>
> (Reed Elsevier 2011: 12)

THE INFORMATIONALIST UNIVERSITY

Governments and universities themselves have been complicit in this process of commodifying knowledge. From the 1980s public universities in many countries were transformed by corporatised restructuring to meet a growing demand for higher education. In 1991 there were 68 million students worldwide, in 2004 there were 132 million (OECD 2008a: 14). Along with this expansion, in many countries, the public subsidy for higher education and research has been falling on a per student basis, and many countries have re-introduced university fees, whether paid up-front or channelled by student loans agencies. In its 2008 review of tertiary education, the OECD explicitly advocated "cost-sharing between the State and students as the principle to shape the funding of tertiary education" (OECD 2008a: 17). Across the OECD, though, fee for service was still not fully accepted. In 2011 student fees were zero or close to zero in the Scandinavian countries, France, Mexico, Belgium, Spain, Austria, Italy and Switzerland; fees were substantial only in the U.S., Australia, New Zealand, the Netherlands and Japan (OECD 2011). For countries maintaining free tertiary education the OECD recommended in the first instance (perhaps somewhat cynically) a debate about charging 'affluent' students:

> In countries with little tradition of tuition fees, launch a public debate to help clarify whether:
>
> • heavy reliance on public money is sustainable;
> • private benefits are so low as to justify low fees, especially of the more affluent students;
> • higher fees for more affluent students could consolidate the student support system.
>
> (OECD 2011: 1)

In the UK and Australia, fees for all (not just the rich) have become the norm. The goal has been to minimise public expenditure and define tertiary education as a career-enhancing commodity bought by those able and willing to pay for it, and removed from those who cannot pay. As a result, education in informationalism has become a means of maintaining and extending hierarchies of exclusion, and of marking status in informational terms. This move focuses attention on courses that are considered good value for money, in terms of return on fees, or that attract fee-paying students from overseas. Knowledge becomes oriented towards employment and the perceived needs of the corporate sector. Academics frequently lament that most students want qualifications, or recognised markers for the job markets, rather than learning, knowledge or thought itself (Burdon & Heath 2013). As Graeber writes: "now the only justification for knowledge [i]s . . . to facilitate the pursuit of wealth" (2013: 72).

If these university students are to form the up-coming generations of savvy and creative information workers (rather than alienated clerks or the new precariat), then academics should be crucially positioned as providing a foundation for future innovation in information society. Academic work possesses all the basic characteristics of knowledge work or 'immaterial labour'; that is, it is cooperative labour, grounded in the social, depending on communication, which produces (or recombines) information, ideas, symbols, relationships and affects (De Angelis & Harvie 2009: 6; Hardt & Negri 2004: 108). Yet academic labour is increasingly devalued and deskilled: student-teacher ratios have deteriorated, and universities, especially in the OECD Anglophone countries, UK, Canada, Australia and the U.S., have embarked on a dramatic casualisation of the workforce. Contingent teachers and contingent researchers have become the norm, accounting for more than half the teaching in Australian universities (Brown, Goodman & Yasukawa 2010). The American Association of University Professors reported that less than 25% of faculty had tenured or tenure track positions (Curtis & Thornton 2013: 8). As usual most information workers are precarious rather than valued.

The "widespread" trend of "education restructuring" since the 1970s has transformed universities into a "terrain for marketisation agendas" (De Angelis & Harvie 2009: 7). Given the implied role of universities in providing services for business and for the tendency of capitalist ordering to extend, business management is promoted as essential to bridge the difference in cultures, with the business side dominating. This management assumes that academics need managing by corporate methods as they are otherwise inefficient, and that extending corporate order is the only way to make universities viable (see Gallagher 2000). Falling public funding has also led many university managers to become heavily committed to neoliberal flexibilisation strategies (Gould 2003) and to identify as CEOs; an example of an apparently successful form of order in one field being extended without thought (Nelson & Watt 2004: 8). In the UK, it appears that private corporations, or even university managers, will be able to buy existing universities and receive public subsidies for students (Eversheds 2009; Wright 2012). Not surprisingly, the new 'enterprise' university has begun to resemble a flexibilised factory (Marginson & Considine 2000). To attract corporate-style managers, corporate-style pay arrangements are introduced, producing a growing and stark divide between a relatively secure manager class, some supposed 'winner-take-all' 'star' academic performers and administrators and the growing army of casuals, which Berry identifies as the "new class line" in the academy (Berry 2005). Casual contracts commodify and deskill academic labour, as hourly paid intellectual piecework, with no prospect of career advancement (Bryson 2004). Casual academics are relatively precarious workers, with contracts often renewed every semester or term, and large parts of the year unemployed. Continuing academic staff are subjected to managerial whim and are increasingly "proletarianised", disempowered and given more and more administrative work (Callinicos 2006: 26). In this regime management seems remote and ignorant of academia, and a form of disruptive distributed governance is experienced. No one has clear responsibility for events, but the influence of 'impersonal' market power largely seems to benefit certain groups.

The status of higher education as a public good is therefore placed under threat, with entire programs deleted in the context of funding cuts, thereby dramatically redefining and limiting fields of knowledge (Abbas & McLean 2001). Managerial, or student, perception of the reception of a subject by potential employers, or by usefulness to the corporate sector, guides the permanent deletion of branches of knowledge.

As universities deliver student learning on a fee-for-service basis, and actively promote the increased commercialisation of research, and as university work becomes increasingly dependent on ad hoc project funding, the meaning of knowledge is challenged. There is increasing drive for scientific and humanistic knowledge to be defined as property, and turned into property via patents, or business ventures. It could be suggested that it may become increasingly hard to promote and defend an intellectual commons when the key institution that depends on it—the university—is ordered by commercial imperatives alone.

ACADEMIC PUBLISHING

The perceived 'demands of markets' and the changed management culture at universities is reflected in research priorities and publishing trends. Researchers must 'publish or perish,' and so strive to disseminate output via the most prestigious channels, thereby becoming unpaid sources of labour for academic publishers engaged in the "private appropriation of public labour" (Pirie 2009: 32). On top of teaching, academics are supposed to write for free, edit for free and peer review for free, while providing material that is sold to make profit. No one else in the publishing food chain (lawyers, insurers, printers, distributors, clerical support, cleaners and so forth) works for free. The rationale is that payment is returned in the form of academic reputation, which increases employment prospects. This is an increasingly dubious proposition given casualisation and staff reductions. Indeed, the realisation by tertiary students, teaching assistants and interns that their educational debts might never be repaid is contributing to organised globalised and translocally networked rolling waves of university protests and occupations across the world (The Edu-Factory Collective 2009; Graeber 2013: 68, 71). The continuing education debt problem also shows that knowledge and education are not valued as a good in themselves, or as productive in general, only as far as they are owned or serve a strategic use.

Increasingly there is a mobilisation against the commodification of academic knowledge reasserting the intrinsic cultural worth of free public access. Here we describe the 'Cost of Knowledge' campaign, which reaped some ambivalent successes, and demonstrates the difficulties of asserting the intellectual commons as an alternative, rather than as a complement, to commodification dynamics.

THE STANDARD JOURNAL

As already suggested, and as supported by economist Ted Bergstrom, since academic publishers began adopting electronic publishing around 1995 they have increasingly bundled together prestigious and little-wanted journals, and maintained "artificially high prices for pay-per-view and individual subscriptions", (Bergstrom 2010: 8). Title bundling is analogous to the much criticised business model of cable TV where subscribers must pay companies like Foxtel to access hundreds of channels they might not want rather than being able to buy cheaper subscriptions to individual shows or channels. In a significant historical critique, Jean-Claude Guédon tracked how, over the past 50 years, publishers have transformed "scholarly journals—traditionally, a secondary, unpromising publishing venture at best—into big business" (Guédon 2001: 7). In so doing they radically changed the "status of the 'document' and the ways in which individuals may interact", and also "deeply subvert[ed]" the role of libraries (ibid). Publishers have become accustomed to having the upper hand, negotiating individual, highly secretive multi-year 'Big Deal' contracts with each library or national consortia (Gowers 2012: 2), most of which have been unable to lower prices, with a few exceptions like Stanford, Caltech and the University of Wisconsin whose "hard bargaining" forced better deals (Bergstrom 2010: 4, 8). Exacerbating libraries' financial burden has been the compounding annual increase in subscription fees built into the deals. Institutions who signed five-year contracts with Elsevier in 1999, for example, experienced "a 40% increase in the subscription price over the life of the contract" (whereas the U.S. Consumer Price Index rose only by 13%), and they faced "continued annual price increases of between 5% and 6%" (ibid: 4). With "many libraries" now having signed their third round of contracts, upon expiry between 2012–14 these universities will be paying "almost twice as much in real terms as they paid . . . in 1999" (ibid). This production and distribution model based on exploitation of raw materials (human cognitive and communicative capacities), upwardly mobile pricing mechanisms and exclusive copyright licenses, limits the spread of knowledge, which in turns stunts how new knowledge can be developed, and by whom.

In the UK there has been little academic research into developing a "critical political economy" of academic publishing, leaving analysis to "politicians and the major charitable foundations that support scientific enquiry" (Pirie 2009: 32). For example, the Wellcome Trust commissioned a study to compare the models of 'subscriber-pays' and 'author-pays' (where the author/funder/institution pays for the 'publishing services' but where the final paper is published in an online open access journal, for free) (SQW Limited 2004: iii). Wellcome's starting proposition was that an 'organised' and equitable information ordering regime for the "output of scientific endeavour" is an "important activity for any sophisticated society" (ibid: 17). The final report concluded that an author-pays model was a "viable alternative" that could deliver "high-quality, peer-reviewed research at a cost . . . significantly less than the traditional model while bringing with it a number of additional benefits" (ibid: iii). They suggested that the "total cost of producing an article for a good-to-high-quality subscription journal is of the order of [U.S.] $2750 plus a contribution to overheads and profits" whereas a "conservative estimate" of the total costs of an article for author-pays journals "lies in the range $500–$2500" (SQW Limited 2004: 2). However, the economic motifs of self-funding publication can undermine a publication's status because it edges into 'vanity publishing,' a tendency unacknowledged by the report. If the author must pay, then readers may expect that they were published irrespective of quality. This threatens the reputation of OA journals, and potentially increases the status divide between well-endowed and poorer authors.

Academic publishing currently generates a complex dual market. Supply and demand are determined by factors relating to "current research concerns and the reputed quality of output" whereas the associated commercial 'shadow' market is "relatively conventional", with publishers selling a product (journals) to libraries to gain profit (SQW Limited 2004: 1). If a library wants its users to keep up to date with their field's latest developments, it must purchase particular 'name' journals as these are unique goods/sources with a defined status and cachet. For instance, the British medical journal *The Lancet* is nearly 200 years old, making it difficult for a potential rival publication to gain similar visibility or source status, unless there is a collective decision by researchers worldwide to redirect their labour to an agreed replacement journal, which given fragmentation seems unlikely. In this situation, the name of the journal as source guarantees the quality of the article, the status to be given to the writer and the probable likelihood that the article will be referred to. The importance of the journal name conflicts with the idea of openness once the name is owned.

This sets up the question of whether more equitable ways to disseminate new 'reputable' knowledge can be created under informationalism consistent with the academic status regime, similar to say the way the internet-based Gutenberg Project or archive.org disseminate 'old' knowledge and literature (Project Gutenberg 2012). As the SQW report notes, "electronic archiving" online is relatively cheap, and facilitates access to timely research outputs (SQW Limited 2004: 17). The possibility of an electronic archive challenges traditional publishers' relevancy, and SQW suggests that a "*de facto*" open archive offering "very cheap or free document delivery" might emerge organically and become the global "norm" (ibid).

THE RISE OF OPEN ACCESS

The similarities between the digital entertainment usage rights discussed in Chapter 10 and the restrictions imposed by academic publishers illustrate how contemporary struggles around knowledge and property, in different informational domains, are interconnected. Publishers typically charge those not affiliated with a fee-paying university or library between US$30–40 for the right to read one journal paper (frequently placing a time limit of 24 hours access on the paper). Generally this will be a paper where the author, peer reviewers and editors were not paid for their ideas and intellectual labour by the publisher. Such 'economic parasitism' exemplifies "pure rentier capitalism: monopolising a public resource then charging exorbitant fees to use it", as journalist George Monbiot (29 August 2011) argues. However, as with file-sharing, researchers have begun resisting what they consider to be unfair, disruptive and anachronistic monopolies. A growing number are collectively withdrawing their labour and establishing alternative 'open access' (OA) systems of production and exchange that harness internet technologies. The growing quantity of accessible resources linked to the two main OA repositories, OpenDOAR (2012) with 2,195 e-journals, databases and libraries, and ROAR (2012) with 2,924, are testament to how researchers and institutions are changing their own publishing and collecting practices and associated attitudes about research prestige and impact. As with the 'copyfight', these actions have similarly propelled some significant changes in legislation, government policy and corporate business practices.

Moreover, just as file-sharing created new markets for ancillary services such as Virtual Private Networks, so too has the open access movement spawned a market or user base for other services. This is exemplified by projects like SHERPA (2012a) that not only manages OpenDOAR, but also aggregates information about publishers' and funders' (often conflicting) OA policies. The growth of "open-access institutional repositories in universities to facilitate the *rapid and efficient worldwide dissemination of research*" (ibid; emphasis added) signals the formation of new informational flows and orders, which will inevitably experience disordering tendencies themselves. For example, the rapid growth in new OA journals also shows the growing demand by academics for academic publishing venues. This growth makes academic publishing and knowledge even more likely to be lost in the 'data smog' and for new journals to be abandoned after the editorial enthusiasm wears off, leaving the articles 'stranded'. At another level the movement encourages the growth of what have been called 'pseudo-journals', 'pseudo publishers' and 'pseudo conferences', which are journals, publishers and conferences with no reputation or quality control that are apparently set up simply to make money, or to quickly publish theses, using writers' labour and/or finances. Names of such journals and conferences may resemble those with established names. The presence of these publishers also makes it harder for people outside a field to tell what is genuinely peer-reviewed material, and for more 'pseudo knowledge' to flood debate. This reasserts the importance of genuine named sources and potentially disrupts the OA movement (Stafford 2012; Beale 2013; Kolata 7 April 2013). However, even reputable publishers such as Springer and IEEE have been accused of publishing nonsense conference papers thus giving pseudo-conferences a respectable place in the world. The papers were generated by computer programs and apparently peer reviewed. Researcher Cyril Labbé suggests that these publications are "one symptom of a 'spamming war started at the heart of science' in which researchers feel pressured to rush out papers to publish as much as possible" to keep career paths open (Van Noorden 24 February 2014). Likewise, the editors of the established journal *Infection and Immunity* after retracting six papers by one author discovered that, across science journals, retractions were rising and "feared that science had turned into a winner-take-all game with perverse incentives that lead scientists to cut corners and, in some cases, commit acts of misconduct" (Zimmer 16 April 2012). Perhaps the lack of slack in academic life also reduces careful reviewing, as reviewing becomes extra unwanted and unrewarded labour.

Open access can also position itself as a staunch upholder of existing copyright regimes, not as a challenger, as the following statement by the Director of the Harvard Open Access Project, Peter Suber (2012), demonstrates:

> (1) OA is not Napster for science. It's about lawful sharing, not sharing in disregard of law. (2) OA to copyrighted works is voluntary, even if it is sometimes a condition of a voluntary contract, such as an employment or funding contract. There is no vigilante OA, no infringing, expropriating, or piratical OA.

The OA orthodoxy itself appears based upon a strict dogma of property that attempts to allow only one form of partially decommodified access. In this case study we examine a recent example from the field of scientific publishing that highlights some of the antagonisms that continue to fuel the OA movement, and, importantly, presents a snapshot of the affective dimensions to the collective struggle for open forms of knowledge exchange.

DISRUPTIONS TO THE INFO-ORDER: THE COST OF KNOWLEDGE BOYCOTT

On 21 January 2012, eminent Cambridge mathematician Professor Tim Gowers's blog posting on the problems of academic publishing generated a snowball effect, propelling more than 11,000 like-minded academics to withdraw their labour from one bastion of the 'feudal powers' that Monbiot criticises (Chatterjee 2012). The target was Dutch publisher Elsevier.

In 2009, despite the global recession and a "challenging academic budget environment", Elsevier, a subsidiary of Reed Elsevier (which owns the

Scopus citation database service and LexisNexis amongst numerous other holdings), reported revenue of £1,985 million and a profit of £693 million, an increase of 22% on the previous year's figures (Reed Elsevier 2010: 5). By the year ending 31 December 2011 Elsevier's total annual revenue had climbed to £2,058 million, generating an adjusted operating profit of £768 million, an increase of 6% from 2010 returns (Reed Elsevier 2012a: 13). Although it predicted that underlying revenue growth would be "modest", it reported that sales of databases and tools had grown strongly, due to academic research becoming "increasingly interdisciplinary and collaborative across geographies" (ibid). With a portfolio of holdings totalling around 1,250 journals and 700 books in 2011, Elsevier describes itself as the "leading journal publisher in scientific publishing" and hence it expects that it would "attract criticism . . . directed at publishing as a whole" (Reed Elsevier 2012: 13; Hassink & Clark 2012: 833). The tendency of corporations or networks to monopolise and keep growing was demonstrated when by August 2012 Elsevier (2012a) was listing 2,712 journals, 19,838 books and 20 bibliographic databases on its website.

Tim Gowers's (21 January 2012) online article was a *cri de coeur* entitled 'Elsevier—My Part in Its Downfall' (a play on one of comedian Spike Milligan's book titles). In it he expounded the publisher's "heavily criticised" business practices: their exorbitant prices, bundling of indispensable journals with inferior ones, "ruthless" unsubscribing of libraries that attempt to negotiate better deals and support for controversial intellectual property and copyright legislation such as the (now withdrawn) Research Works Act (RWA) in the U.S. that would have outlawed any requirement for taxpayer funded research to be published free of charge "without the publisher's prior permission" (Lancet 2012).

After examining why scholars might be complicit in supporting Elsevier, such as being motivated by a perceived moral obligation to support the mathematics community by reviewing papers for example, and determining that eventually, but not soon enough, the internet itself would bring an end to the "abuses", Gowers decided that he would both "refuse to have anything to do with Elsevier journals" and publicly declare his disavowal. He argued that "the more of us there are, the more socially acceptable [a boycott] becomes", and suggested that someone create a website "where mathematicians who have decided not to contribute in any way to Elsevier journals could sign their names electronically" (ibid). Gowers said "we have much greater bargaining power than we are wielding at the moment, for the very simple reason that we don't actually *need* their services" (ibid), while Elsevier cannot publish mathematical journals without mathematicians. If enough scholars participated in the "powerful gesture" of a boycott it might be "even powerful enough for other sciences to follow suit eventually" (ibid). Gowers did not speak of other informational fields with similar problems, such as the arts and the humanities, although some practitioners from these fields would participate in the proposed boycott. This omission also implies the fragmentation and divides across knowledge workers, which lowers the possibility of collaborative ordering from below.

Gowers's post sparked an immediate online dialogue. As of 21 June 2014, 566 comments had been posted to the blog (most of them immediately following publication) from fellow mathematicians and scientists worldwide, indicating the globalised nature of this particular protest against knowledge enclosures. Indeed, this was not a new problem. Ted Bergstrom (2001: 184–5) had previously compared the costs and reputation of non-profit and commercial journals in the economics field, noting that "while the nonprofits are supplying most of the information used by economists, the commercial presses are absorbing the lion's share of library budgets". Thus intellectual resources that could be considered as belonging to the commons because of their relative affordability were in danger of being abandoned because, although non-profit journals were significantly more cited, they nevertheless did not possess the same "prestige" as the less-cited "price-gouging" commercial journals (ibid: 183, 197). So the academic ordering system also undermines knowledge production and recognition. Bergstrom's solutions involved scholars educating themselves, and then collectively redirecting their intellectual labour and influencing their employing institutions' purchasing decisions. He suggested scholars themselves should expand the number of 'elite' and 'specialised' non-profit journals, supporting the "reasonably priced new electronic economics journals" that had already entered the field, and "punishing overpriced journals" by participating in a "partial boycott" against those identified in Bergstrom's "rogues' gallery" (ibid: 192–4). Such a boycott would include "cancellation of library subscriptions to overpriced journals", "defections by editors and editorial boards", mindful choices by authors of where they would publish and a "referees' boycott" (194–6).

Several years later some of these recommendations were reiterated in the comments posted to Gowers's 2012 blog article, as mathematicians and scientists detailed personal experiences of being exploited, and stated their opposition to "gating scholarly knowledge" (Gowers 21 January 2012, comments). Some commenters posited that the "community of scholars" itself could build a "new style of peer-review", for instance, by applying "some of the technologies and methods used now by many [web]sites to judge comments and replies" (ibid). Others pointed to earlier campaigns within specific countries and disciplines against Elsevier and other major academic publishers including Springer and Wiley. For instance, in 2006 editors had deserted Elsevier's *Journal of Economic Theory* and in its stead launched the low-cost journal *Theoretical Economics,* the venture supported through server space at the University of Toronto (UT), a permanent archive of published articles hosted at the UT Library and typesetting costs covered by authors' "modest" submission fee of US$75 (Theoretical Economics 2012). Similarly, there have been other "mass resignations of entire Elsevier editorial boards over pricing concerns", with the *Journal of Logic Programming*

(1999), the *Journal of Algorithms* (2003) and *Topology* (2006), spurring the mathematical community to found replacement journals such as the *Journal of Topology* (Arnold & Cohn 2012: 828). Such examples demonstrate how disruption of an existing info-order (knowledge enclosure) can have productive effects (knowledge liberation). They also highlight how the first phase of grassroots responses to academia's knowledge enclosures tends to be differentiated and disaggregated, locally coordinated and networked translocally, but uncoordinated across disciplines. Nevertheless, the internet has been a core enabling factor in these scenarios.

On 22 January 2012, within just one day of Gowers's blog posting, mathematician and programmer Tyler Neylon (2012) announced that he had built a website called 'The Cost of Knowledge' as the boycott's electronic headquarters. By 26 January a commenter on another science blog had reviewed the website's signatories, observing that "Very very prominent names in the mathematics community have shown up straight away and in such an extent that the tipping point where refereeing becomes significantly harder in certain subfields might already be within reach". This underscores how professional reputations can tactically enhance online campaigns' impact and scale (comment on Farrell 26 January 2012). As of 21 June 2014, 14,674 researchers "from all subjects" had signed the pledge, with many adding their own commentary on what geologist John Faithfull described as the "appalling swindle" perpetrated on "authors, libraries, the general public, and the bodies who fund public science" (ibid, comments).

Thirty-four distinguished mathematicians published an online statement on 8 February 2012 presenting the issues that "confront the *boycott* movement", analysing the mechanics of academic publishing within the pre-electronic paradigm, including the types of cognitive labour involved in research and its dissemination, and considering the "significant" transformations brought about by the transition to e-publishing (Gowers 2012). So within just over a fortnight an idea shared on a blog had materialised into what some of its most high-profile protagonists described as a 'movement,' albeit a movement that was "anything but monolithic" as participants had "different goals" in the short and long term (ibid: 1, 4). The *Economist* (4 February 2012) warned that "academic publishers might find they have a revolution on their hands" if the boycott grew and transformed into an "Academic spring", referring to the so-called 'Arab Spring' that was often said to have been enabled by digital media. This is protest manifesting as swarm, with both that form's strengths and weaknesses. The main issue might be whether the habit of connecting can be maintained and journals built up, despite the differences and inertia.

The boycotters had focused their "discontent" on Elsevier rather than its competitors because of mathematicians' "widespread feeling" that this corporation was the "worst offender" and "most egregious" on all counts. In its medical titles, for example, it had repackaged sponsored articles from pharmaceutical companies in the guise of bona fide journal papers (Gowers

2012: 2–3; Goldacre 9 May 2009). Profit or connections had undermined impartiality and accuracy. The signatories pointed out that prestigious journals' reputations had been created through the labour of authors, referees and editors who had worked "at no cost to the publishers" over many years. Yet typically the journals' *names* were owned by the publisher, which made it "difficult for the mathematical community to separate this valuable object that they have constructed from its present publisher" (Gowers 2012: 2). This observation alludes to more than the simple corporate *branding* (in this case identification of the brand with a source) that is in itself an important profit driver in informational capitalism. The source/brand's (eg, *Journal X*) reputation is grounded in the materiality of the cognitive and communicative labour through which it had earned its prestige amongst people in the field and elsewhere, that is, through the contributions themselves and the integrity of the evaluation processes, which could then be hijacked, as with the pharmaceutical puff pieces, for profit—and is not legally owned by, or connected to, the people who make the sources' reputation.

The boycott set up a Twitter account tagged 'The Cost of Knowledge' (2012), with Tweets announcing developments in various Open Access and Open Knowledge campaigns. While the Cost of Knowledge website served as the primary online tool for gathering signatures and commentary supporting the Elsevier boycott, the Twitter feed broadened the conversation by highlighting other instances of the digital enclosures such as the Anti-Counterfeiting Trade Agreement (ACTA) mentioned earlier, thereby connecting specific concerns emanating from the fields of education and scientific research to other domains within capitalist informationalism.

Social media can help campaigns to build momentum, attract publicity and forge connections with other relevant counter-movements. A wiki page set up by quantum computing pioneer Michael Nielsen (2012) listed over 120 links to articles in mainstream media as of mid-July 2012, including such sources as *Forbes*, the *New York Times*, *Chronicle of Higher Education* and *der Spiegel*, as well numerous blog articles, some news aggregators and responses by Elsevier. Scholars discussing the boycott on their own blogs attracted further commentary and links. A rich, expanding discursive mesh of information and opinions encompassing print and electronic formats was manifesting in the mediascape, building momentum by keeping the presence of the movement visible and broadening the public conversation to other instances of knowledge enclosures. On the other hand, the relatively small number of tweets to the Cost of Knowledge account (as of 8 October 2012 it had 915 followers and 264 tweets) implied little involvement or interaction.

However, given the swarm formation, sustained consensus was unlikely, and some expressed various reservations about the efficacy of the boycott, putting the case for the existing order as better than none. A neuroscientist, for instance, worried that a "crucial set of publication outlets" could be lost by "embargoing one company based on a handful of misdemeanours", thus "harming science" (Farrell 26 January 2012, comments). Another scientist argued that there was "little value in disorganised science", indicating a belief that publishers were instrumental to the maintenance of quantifiable and recognised informational orders within specific domains of human inquiry (ibid). Some objections pointed to career factors as when another neuroscientist argued that to boycott "1/3 of my field's journals" would be tantamount to "career-suicide" (ibid). Others took a broader view, one for instance pointing out that in starting a journal "from scratch, the hard part is to get a *brand value* to start with, and this is no trivial work" (ibid; emphasis added). Rebellion involves ongoing work and risk.

Much of the online discourse examined the larger issue of the commodification of knowledge. Alok Jha (9 April 2012) reported in *The Guardian* that academic publishers charged British universities around £200 million annually to "access scientific journals, which is almost a tenth of the £2.2bn distributed to them [the universities] by the government" for conducting university research. Moreover, even when the big publishers allowed scholars to lodge copies of their own papers on their universities' archives, rules ensure "that the research cannot be used in any subsequent scientific inquiry without prior permission" (ibid). It certainly "put up barriers for interested members of the public, politicians and patients' groups who need access to primary research" (ibid). Publication could restrict research as it publicised it.

Some months later (probably coincidentally) the Motion Picture Association of America (2012: 20–1) reported that in the first half of 2012 Elsevier had issued more than "78,000 takedown notices regarding infringement of thousands of health sciences and science/technology journal articles". Although over 75% of the time, websites removed the offending articles (albeit sometimes tardily) it was "very common for the same article to reappear quickly, on the same or a related site" (ibid). Obviously Elsevier was ready to take action when it perceived that its own hypothesised profits were being threatened, notwithstanding that, as with 'pirated' entertainment media, it is highly improbable that all, or even many, of the 78,000 papers represented lost sales. Yet as one Elsevier boycotter noted, profits in academic publishing are almost entirely built on "progressively enclosing the research commons, thus effectively stealing from public knowledge" (Neylon 2012, comments). Here, the idea of property/theft had become a key contested term. As always in informational capitalism, social constructions of piracy and theft depend upon who is speaking, and to whom.

Returning to the Elsevier boycott, the mass exodus of scientific contributors generated roll-on effects. Elsevier withdrew its support for the strongly contested Research Works Act (RWA) in the U.S. Congress. The RWA, along with SOPA and PIPA, had been described as an "intellectual land-grab too far" by IT writer Glyn Moody (31 January 2012), the metaphor underscoring how the concept of intellectual enclosure has entered the public imagination. If the bill's own sponsors had not subsequently withdrawn it in light of the "new and innovative model" of open access publishing, the bill would have affected not only American researchers but had the potential to disrupt scholars worldwide because of the internationalisation of research (Howard 27 February 2012).

In the framework of informational capitalism, corporate branding and reputation becomes increasingly important, as stock values can plummet in light of instantly transmitted negative perceptions and rumours (sometimes magnified by automated trading). On 27 February 2012, perhaps astounded by the international momentum the boycott had generated in just one month, Elsevier (2012b) issued an open letter to the mathematics community stating its intention to lower baseline pricing, open the archives of 14 core mathematics journals "from four years after publication" and to withdraw its support for the RWA. Somewhat unconvincingly Elsevier claimed that its RWA withdrawal stemmed from listening not to the boycotters but to those "authors, editors, and reviewers" who continued to work with it, reiterating that they wanted to play a "constructive role" in the "broad discourse right now about how data sets can be made more broadly accessible" (Howard 27 February 2012). In a second open letter dated 2 May 2012 Elsevier (2012b) announced other changes to its publishing and pricing models, including expanding the open archives to 43 journals and increasing sponsored access to research for developing nations. Then in June 2012 two of Elsevier's senior publishing executives, Laura Hassink and David Clark (2012: 833), responded to the mathematics community via a piece in *Notices of the American Mathematical Society*, in which they admitted that the company had not "done a good job communicating what we do" and then addressed the concerns of "Professor Gowers's protest" about pricing, bundling and access (a reductive and personalised framing). Elsevier claimed that its prices were "typically . . . lower than those of other mathematics publishers", bundling was not mandatory and furthermore its disappearance would have a "detrimental impact on access to the research literature", their titles were available in the poorest countries through the Research4Life program, and mathematicians were free to post their manuscripts on the independent open access platform arXiv (834). They also admitted that the community's "critical feedback" on the RWA had been "very sobering" for them (835).

It seems probable that the mobilisation of thousands of scholars triggered by Gowers's original blog posting and facilitated by Neylon's construction of a web platform had played some part in Elsevier's movement towards a (still extremely limited) form of open access. Here, as with some of the P2P facilitating platforms discussed earlier, tools and expertise embedded within the structures and flows of capitalist informationalism had provided the means for new social swarms to coalesce and mobilise. Individuals used internet technology to announce their intentions and create a mass visibility for their proposal to withdraw ideas and labour from one part of the knowledge enclosures. This action had an immediate disordering effect on the domain of academic publishing. This disordering was not without potential cost to the orders that maintained the scholars and their reputations, as they seemed aware. Moreover, and this is significant, unlike some other provocations using the internet (such as the internet blackout days protesting against ACTA and SOPA, or e-petitions), the scholars' actions were theoretically ongoing and could possibly continue to destabilise the old publishing model. The exodus might not be a temporary swarm, but signal a new informational struggle, centred on the disordering problems of information as property. It is still too early to tell how the struggle will work out, and whether the problems of information as property can be worked out in the academic field, or whether the disorder will continue, be suppressed or ignored, or whether the inertia of established forms will win out.

Whatever the case, as Moody (31 January 2012) notes, this was the "most visible revolt in recent years" against publishers' "exorbitant profits" and the restrictions of information under informationalism. At the "dawn of open access" in 2000 the Public Library of Science (PLoS) had issued a comparable call, yet few of the 34,000 signatories would go on to actually boycott offending publishers (ibid). PLoS currently publishes seven peer-reviewed open-access journals, a very small percentage of academic journals, however it is possible that some of its contributors, reviewers and readers have transferred some of their intellectual labour and loyalty to this outlet. However, PLoS contributors pay for publishing, with standard authors' charges ranging between US$1,350 and US$2,900, with exceptions made for writers from 'Low and Lower Middle Income Countries' and also for some individuals who request a fee waiver (PloS 2012). Possibly the costs charged by PLoS have undermined its appeal.

Here is more evidence that the disruptive and disordering tendencies inherent within informationalism produce attempts at new ordering regimes, or the reassertion of ordering regimes, in this case a move to re-monetise intellectual production. Through author payments, these journals offer a new business model for 'open access' informationalism, which creates new hierarchies and social boundaries. This is neither inevitable, nor stable. The new publishing model may overcome the commodification of access, but in the process transforms the author into a consumer who buys journal space for their own work (see Peekhaus 2012). The move, as already noted, creates new contradictions between peer review and pay-for-publication publishing, forcing journals to act less as sites of academic excellence and more as vehicles for monetary gain.

NEW AUSTERITY AND 'OPEN ACCESS'

In May 2012, in a speech to the Publishers Association's annual general meeting, UK Minister of State for Universities and Science, David Willetts (2012), flagged the government's move towards mandating open access policies. He described academic research as resembling not a "sausage machine" but an "ecosystem with subtle and intricate interdependences". It was one of the UK's "greatest economic assets"; 120,000 of the 1.7 million academic articles published worldwide came out of British research, and 400,000 of those articles were published in the UK. Although the UK did not have many academic libraries and research institutes, 5,000 of the world's 23,000 peer-reviewed journals were published in the UK, making journals an "important export industry, with perhaps 80% of their revenues coming from sales abroad". Rather counter-intuitively, he argued that it was such success that had led the Coalition government (an increasingly awkward meshing of the Conservatives and Liberal Democrats) to introduce higher fees and loans that would be "repaid by graduates, despite the intense controversy, to ensure our universities are well funded even as public spending is being cut back" (ibid). The order of exporting information through private publishers was so important that students would have to pay more to sustain it.

We previously mentioned how student debt is tied into the orders of informationalism at many levels. Student debt is now recognised as a societal problem, at least by students and academics if not by universities' upper management and cost-conscious politicians and corporate bodies. In the U.S. it has now passed credit card debt in total volume, according to the think tank Education Sector (Carey & Dillon 2011). In the UK, the privatisation and marketisation of tertiary education has been in train since 1990. The 1998 'reforms' instituted "up-front means-tested tuition fees of £1,200" (Dearden, Fitzsimons & Wyness, 2011: 9). The Higher Education Act 2004 (implemented in 2006) ushered in a new level of expropriation via personal debt, as "variable tuition fees of up to £3,000" were introduced (Callender 2012: 78). Following the government's adoption of the Independent Review of Higher Education Funding and Student Finance's recommendations, annual fees could rise to a maximum of £9,000 from 2012 (Ibrahim 2011: 415). This last economic and social assault sparked "high profile, nationally and locally organised student protests" and a "wide geographical spread" of university occupations around Britain in 2010–11 (ibid: 415, 418).

In the information society, education becomes a marker of class and status, and the extension of this class order can arouse protest from those excluded, whose parents, at least, might have expected them to be amongst the privileged knowledge workers. In the post-Global Financial Crisis period, some national austerity measures also complemented a global "cost-sharing agenda" within higher education, with reforms partially transferring the financial burden of the production of intellectual goods and services away from the State and onto individuals, to the apparent benefit of both corporations (who prosper from research) and government revenues (see Hall & Stahl 2012).

In this situation, perhaps motivated by the wish to deflect criticism around the penury associated with students' mounting debt burden, Willetts (2012) announced the government's commitment to the "principle of public access to publicly-funded research results" so as to "maximise the value and impact" generated by UK research. Moreover, taxpayers (that is, investors) "should not be kept outside with their noses pressed to the window" of an "exclusive" academic space constructed by paywalls. Instead there must be a "right to roam freely" across the publicly funded UK research landscape. Tellingly, Willetts used the example of the music industry to warn academic publishers against clinging onto outdated business models. This industry had "lost out by trying to criminalise a generation of young people for file sharing", whereas companies "outside the music business such as Spotify and Apple, with iTunes" had developed a "viable business model" for online access. Eventually publishers would need to commit to 'green' or 'gold' standards, green being the requirement to "make research openly accessible within an agreed embargo period", and gold meaning that "research funding includes the costs of immediate open publication, thereby allowing for full and immediate open access while still providing revenue to publishers". Philanthropic medical science funder the Wellcome Trust has already adopted the gold standard, and it is anticipated others will follow, while the RoMEO database of publishers' archiving policies currently uses a four-tier system to delineate a more fine-grained set of options (SHERPA 2012b).

The gold standard implies that state, student and philanthropic funds would now directly go to the multi-billion pound publishing oligopoly. So, a question arises of whether we have a change, or an intensification of the old order? Even if the latter, the fact that a right-wing government is responding to key demands of the OA movement is significant. Although we may be inclined to suspect that the UK government might primarily be recognising a new domain of accumulation while encouraging industry to jump in and somehow commodify the decommodification processes currently in train before other agents can successfully liberate knowledge flows.

Evidence exists that institutions themselves are beginning to adopt new modes of accessing and sharing research artefacts, which also requires that they rethink the status markers that "stick" to research and researchers, like prestige, impact and reputation. In April 2012 the Harvard Library announced that academic publishers had made the "scholarly communication environment fiscally unsustainable and academically restrictive", creating an "untenable situation" for the library as its annual journal bill had climbed to US$3.75 million (Harvard Faculty Advisory Council 2012). Without identifying specific culprits by name (and Elsevier would later publicly deny that Harvard had been referring to them), the press release revealed that prices for "online content from two providers" had risen by 145% over the past six years, far exceeding the CPI. In light of such "prohibitive" costs the library would change its subscriptions, and encouraged faculty and students to both lobby for change via their professional organisations, and to adjust their own publication practices in line with OA principles.

Also in April 2012 Open Book Publishers, a small non-profit publisher of peer-reviewed Humanities and Social Sciences books, made its entire catalogue available for free online viewing via Google Books, a landmark in

UK academic publishing (Middleton 24 April 2012). Placing their business decision in the context of the 'academic spring,' they noted that profit-driven publishers overlooked much "valuable research coming from fields not considered to be 'commercially viable'". This commercial restriction not only had an impact on academic jobs but gave the academic presses a "huge amount of power in setting our research agenda", which is a point seldom made in the OA discourse. Giving weight to our assertion that the effective extension of informational regimes of expropriation and accumulation disorders those informational regimes and opens up new avenues for both capitalist exploitation and also experimental anti-capitalist or alternative systems of social relations, Open Book Publishers announced their intention to expand their operations by "moving into academic journals and educational resources".

We should not assume that Open Access is necessarily a socially radical movement. OA may be just be one more system attempting to maintain current order in a changing society, and easily disrupted, or self-disrupted through maintaining that order. As Suber (2012) notes, the OA campaign "focuses on literature that authors give to the world without expectation of payment". That is, the authors generally have other sources of income, thereby excluding other would-be authors. In capitalism, free exchange depends on alternate sources of survival. Suber notes that academics' "disinterested desire to advance knowledge" can come with a "strong self-interest in career-building", and hence in fitting into the system and being published in recognised high status sources (ibid). The orders of OA may be subverted by that needing an income, through troubles with 'pseudo journals' and by people seeking the reputation boost of publishing in high-status sources.

Nevertheless, the mood for change, and the development of coordinated strategies and programs to realise it, is occurring on an international level. For instance, in July 2012 the European Commission's (2012) Science in Society (SIS) Programme released a series of policies on access to scientific information, outlining the EC's vision to "ensure economic growth and to address the societal challenges of the 21st century" by optimising the "circulation and transfer of scientific knowledge among key stakeholders in European research" (ibid). In a similar vein, the Scholarly Publishing and Academic Resources Coalition (SPARC 2012) was formed to "correct imbalances in the scholarly publishing system". Recognising the "unprecedented opportunities created by the networked digital environment to advance the conduct of scholarship" the organisation describes its role as a "catalyst for change", via advocacy, education and business incubation pathways (ibid).

HOSTILITY TO ACADEMIC KNOWLEDGE

In academic tradition knowledge is held to have intrinsic value, whereas informationalism can destroy academic knowledge often to cut costs. As we instanced in Chapter 6, sometimes this destruction has clear information-group-based, political drivers, as in the following case where knowledge focused on environmental concerns has been destroyed, probably to remove any academic obstacles to the imposition of political and commercial priorities, but excused by the benefits of online storage.

In late 2012 "prominent" scientists warned that the conservative government of Canada's closure of "some of the world's finest fishery, ocean and environmental libraries" had been "so chaotic that irreplaceable collections of intellectual capital built by Canadian taxpayers for future generations has been lost forever" (Nikiforuk 23 December 2013). Unique collections have ended up as landfill, paper shreds or ashes in mass acts of what some scientists named "libricide" (ibid). The government stated that useful information had not been lost, as it had been transferred to "digital form", and framed the change as being responsive to consumer demand, stating that:

> More and more Canadians are turning to electronic sources and the Internet to search for resources and information. The growing willingness of Canadians to look online, coupled with an increasing presence of information online, including electronic scientific journals, enable the Department to consolidate its library resources . . . Modernizing our library resources allows for easier search and access to clients no matter their location.
>
> (Department of Fisheries and Oceans 19 December 2013)

This techno-hedge was strongly disputed by scientists who noted that the government's own DFO statistics showed that "only one out of 20 books in the department's 600,000 plus collection" had been digitised. Researchers spoke of feeling "saddened and appalled", "shocked", "demoralised" and "heartbroken" (Nikiforuk 23 December 2013). Rather than expressing a value-free technological rationalism, they viewed the destruction of the "symbolic heart" of research as being ideologically motivated, and executing a "political agenda . . . to reduce the role of government in Canadian society, as well as the use of scientific evidence in making policy" (ibid). A *New York Times* editorial saw this restriction of scientific knowledge circulation as "more than an attack on academic freedom. *It is an attempt to guarantee public ignorance*", to allow the "northern resource rush" to proceed unimpeded (Klinkenborg 21 September 2013; emphasis added). Science librarian John Dupuis (20 May 2013), in his comprehensive chronology of the 'War on Science,' noted many other instances of the "Conservative Canadian government's long campaign to undermine evidence-based scientific, environmental and technical decision-making" and close scientific libraries. As often happens with competing info-orders, Ministerial briefing notes marked 'secret' were leaked online, in which the "rationalisation of library services" was framed as a part of a wide-ranging suite of cost-cutting measures, many of which were linked to the government's pro-business "responsible resource development" (De Souza 27 December 2013).

In informationalism, investigation of accurate information is secondary to establishing filters and building walls around information groups. Groups, including powerful groups, can cultivate ignorance in order to promulgate and reinforce their own views, as those views are clearly correct, bonded to by the group and under threat: attempted control and limiting of information appears vital. Other views come from despised information groups who are seen as 'clearly' political, biased or hostile. Academic research is often condemned as biased, privileged or left wing if it challenges corporate, or other, certainties and this wider movement has the potential to threaten the whole academic venture. Indeed, making the universities more corporately managed, less secure for staff and more dependent on corporate funding for research also intensifies their vulnerability to market discipline. Those empowered by the market define the limits of credible research and what is counted as accepted knowledge. Yet, in threatening to destroy what it feeds off, informationalism produces a crisis of knowledge production, and is deeply contested.

CONCLUSION

Conflicts between knowledge and informationalism are society-wide but are especially sharply posed in academia. Even the most elite academic institutions, and indeed the governments that fund them, have been thrown into a quandary of how to defend the intrinsic value of knowledge against the digital 'monetisation'. As such, the reign of informationalism in academic publishing demonstrates the centrality of commodification and enclosure for 'information society'.

Moroccan social scientist Yousra Afailal Tribak commented on the Cost of Knowledge campaign website that: "The only price to pay to get knowledge have [sic] to be intellectual effort not money" (Neylon 2012). This position, seemingly shared by the thousands of scientists, researchers and other "knowledge workers" who participated in that campaign, is at odds with the priorities of capitalist informationalism that extends its orders of profit by identifying, enclosing and exploiting communicative and intellectual processes that were previously seen as belonging to the commons. A range of technologies and legal instruments are fundamental to these commodification processes. As the academy is a major site of intellectual production, and therefore of enclosure through commodification and the devaluation of knowledge work, it has also become a possible staging ground for social movements dedicated to knowledge liberation, and a key site for seeding wider circuits of discourse and exchange, albeit hampered by academic individualism and dependence on a reputation economy. Protests can be spontaneous and chaotic, or coordinated and highly organised, but also self-undermining.

Certainly there appears to be no overarching proscriptive political program or ideology linking the various movements, although certain digitally enabled possibilities such as 'open access' or 'open knowledge' flow through many of them. However, the info-capital nexus of corporate and State agents can attempt to harness these counter-orders, and co-opt their methods, content and networks. We can see this happening to some extent in the "official" Open Access movement, in which new organisations reap (albeit not large) income from researchers who must still pay for the privilege of publishing in OA journals. It also happens in the government departments established to monitor institutional adherence to the new OA order. Similarly, unscrupulous publishers can use the mechanisms to set up sites to promote vanity publishing as peer-reviewed open access portals.

However, we do not wish to suggest that an exodus from sites of creative and intellectual exploitation is not worth the effort. The order of informationalism is disrupting access to the knowledge that allows it to exist and possibly flourish, and a disordering response is needed. Although each intersecting or parallel ordering of the various informational regimes under the star of info-capital to some extent repeats some of the old limits and constraints, some at least could hold the potential for collective experimentation, social organisation and new knowledge orders, on small and large scales. Both "orthodox" OA and other inchoate and as yet still fluid campaigns like the Cost of Knowledge give agency to those associated with them (however briefly) in that they inspire, and propose changes in the existing informational order. As with file-sharing, when an order is imposed to the point of breakdown, a shift can occur in the ways people imagine, and act out, their claims to access knowledge and cultural production. In that disruption, or potential disruption, the extension of the old order both becomes visible and can be challenged, if not with unanimity or coordination.

12 Communication Technology and the Origins of Global Justice Movements

Throughout the book we have suggested that 'neoliberal' informationalism cannot generate solutions to the disorders and problems it produces. Here we look at how social movements have used the tools of informationalism to challenge domination and pursue alternatives. We focus on the mid-1990s when movements began appropriating ICT to create new kinds of global networks to contest corporate globalisation, and establish new templates for action. At the same time they encountered the disordering limitations of informationalism amidst a remarkable (and historically unprecedented) wave of mass global protest. Clearly, this 'global justice movement', as it came to be known, was, and is, one among many diverse social movements that contest globalising forces, not all of whom share similar politics. It constitutes a focus for us because it established new genres and repertoires in global protest, while demonstrating some of their problems. Furthermore, it certainly laid the groundwork for more recent social movements later such as Occupy, after the 2008 financial crisis (Castells 2012; Graeber 2013).

In the mid-1990s a transnational cycle of contestation enveloped global politics. It is usually claimed the cycle was sparked in Southern Mexico by an indigenous people's movement, the Zapatistas, who acted for solidarity against neoliberal policies. Launched on 1 January 1994, as the North American Free Trade Agreement (NAFTA) came into effect, Zapatismo inspired a new transnational resistance movement calling itself 'Peoples' Global Action' (PGA). The PGA pioneered 'global days of action' against neoliberal institutions and established the political inspiration and template for the subsequent wave of active mobilisations under the 'Global Justice Movement' (GJM) banner. As an early example of globalised network politics, centred on direct action, the PGA relied on email networks and created websites for direct postings and updates. The PGA entered the political stage in 1996 with its 'Global Carnival Against Capitalism', targeting global financial districts. As will be outlined below, the mainstream press heralded the event as the first digitally organised transnational mobilisation. Throughout its existence the PGA questioned its own use of ICT networks and emphasised the centrality of offline social engagement. For the PGA the internet was "an atomiser of social space and a commodified substitute for human association"; for them, "a radical grassroots movement will require the real warmth of human togetherness and the raw 'shout on the street' to make a true social and ecological communications revolution" (PGA 1999). Their approach to ICT was productively ambiguous.

The story of the building of the PGA, and of subsequent movements inspired by their example, demonstrates the growing, but equivocal, importance of information technology, both as a catalyst and as a constraint for social change. The nexus between information technology and emancipatory politics became especially significant in the context of deepened concern about corporate globalisation. ICTs offered a means of advancing corporate interests but also of connecting dissent. This ambivalent dynamic remains in place, 20 years later, as the disorders driven by market globalism, such as climate change, financial crisis or food shortages, still have not been resolved by its governing institutions, only managed (rendered into apparently normal or recurrent 'accidents'), largely ignored and displaced or shifted 'elsewhere'. Crisis management is bound into the power/ignorance nexus as an effort to reinforce the prevailing order. It has no means of resolving problems; rather, by reinforcing the status quo, it invariably exacerbates them (see Goodman & Marshall 2013). Other, perhaps less ordered but more creative responses seek to address the causes of crisis, rather than simply manage its symptoms, and have arisen in the various forms of what we might call 'justice globalism' (see Steger, Goodman & Wilson 2012). This broad orientation has become an important counter-point to the still-dominant logic of market globalism. Protest over the dynamics of market globalism has generated a new set of values and alternatives embedded in concepts of global justice, although this process of moving from reactive opposition to a more proactive counter-force has been fraught with tension.

Cyber-activism itself can be seen as a new venue for transformational politics, for shifting from a defensive or oppositionalist stance, to more proactive, prefigurative or transformative agendas (Van der Donk & Rucht 2003; McCaughey & Ayers 2003). Such transitions are clearly a problem for any social movement, although it is often argued that defensiveness is greatly magnified under informationalism. For example, in Alain Touraine's model, new social movements are engaged in militant battles for self-subjectification, against the objectifying forces of 'programmed society' (Touraine 1971). This tendency to conceptualise networks of movements as being engaged in a process of self-reclamation, rather than transformation, is shared by Alberto Melucci and Jurgen Habermas. For Melucci movements contest the 'master codes' of information society through the expression of autonomy; for Habermas, the movement arises in defence of the 'lifeworld' against cultural incursions (Melucci 1996; Habermas 1988). In these cases, resistance to 'informational power' is seen as primarily a fight to regain meaning, subjectivity and identity, against informational domination. Only on this basis can movements offer the possibility of moving from what Castells calls 'resistance' identities that oppose ruling norms, to 'project' identities where participants seek to redefine "their position in society and, by doing so, seek the transformation of overall social structure" (Castells 2000b: 8). However, significant transformation may never be reached, and certainly not at the scale required, as 'project' strategy can have difficulty in escaping its roots in the autonomy of 'resistance' (Goodman 2001). Despite this failing, the eruption of provisional and contingent resistances, carried through network politics, can politicise and further disrupt informationalism. As highlighted elsewhere in this volume, people, in the course of daily life in informationalism produce alternative spaces and 'commons' beyond commodification. Yet, even so, these zones of autonomy can produce the illusion of transformation, and over time be manipulated to complement commodification (as discussed in Chapters 10 and 11). Furthermore, project identities need not be progressive: 'reactionaries', and other variants, can equally attempt to transformatively redefine their position in society and its overall structure.

The PGA is formative as it inspired, and formed, a networked set of information groups that used IT-mediated networking and embodied protest to bridge 'North' and 'South', and engage in direct action against neoliberal globalism. This combination of the online and offline, and the loosely linked organisational formation that carried it, generated new forms of mobilisation, but also created new dilemmas for transformation. Contingent resistance can make power structures and their failings visible. A second 'proactive' move is marked by the difficulties of establishing emancipatory agendas and producing alternatives that are not totalising or disempowering. As outlined in this chapter, this relationship between resistance and transformation is significantly affected by the emergence and possibilities of ICT use. First, some broader questions of network politics, communication technology, counter-power and class antagonism are addressed. The discussion then proceeds to an account of PGA and its debates about the role of IT in social movement mobilisation.

INFORMATIONALISM AND MOVEMENTS

Capitalist informationalism generates profound global crises. Crises in the dominant order create opportunities for mobilisation around alternatives (see Steger, Goodman & Wilson 2013). Crisis also alters the pace and direction of change. Here, the outcomes of social action are even less predictable: movement capacity changes, social contexts change, actions have unexpected effects and authorities respond surprisingly. But if the social field is contingent and less predictable for movements, then it is also less governable for power-holders. Movements can be potentially less hierarchical and more spontaneous than the authorities, more able to perceive, formulate and communicate the fundamental problems and more able to adapt goals and actions to changing situations. Perhaps, then, social movements can more effectively contend with the disorders of informationalism and with global crisis?

Social movements can be defined by their capacity for sustained collective action to challenge authorities, founded on the building of group identity and solidarity around a common purpose (Tarrow 1998). To be effective, social movements need to constitute themselves as an information group, with shared understandings, sources, internal discussion and relationships to other (opposed) groups. The movement always risks being dispersed when faced with the hostile 'counter-information' presented by mainstream media. Graeber remarks that initially the coverage of the Occupy movement by the U.S. media was dismissive. The *New York Times* wrote nothing for the first five days, and then they mocked it. Violence by the police received little to no coverage (2013: 59–60). The protest was not reported until ICT and social media created a wider audience, especially through video clips of police actions, which could not be ignored.

In this 'movement society', as Tarrow describes it (1998), social movement norms are institutionalised, only to be disrupted and transformed by new waves of mobilisation. Movement 'cycles', of institutionalisation and mobilisation point to the potentially self-disordering nature of movements, as they attempt to survive and gain influence by becoming dependent on the social forms they were attempting to transform. Given this context, social movements are best understood as processes rather than static social objects. Indeed, as a process of collective identification, movements only come to exist by being enacted (Melucci 1996).

In 'movement society' institutionalisation can become a key point of contention. Fominaya, for instance, finds a duality between institutional and autonomous tendencies. Institutionalised movements, Fominaya argues, are founded on a representative and majoritarian political model aiming at a unitary identity and program, with a strong focus on government policy and using an institutionalised repertoire of collective actions (Fominaya 2007). In contrast, autonomous movements use a participatory consensus-based political model and evoke multiple identities and positions; they focus on broad public claims and subsume differences between potential members in counter-culture and direct action (ibid). Organisational form is indispensable to the institutional left but is disposable for more autonomous groups. ICT allows the suspension of movement organisation from relatively hierarchic formations that accrue authority from their representative capacity, to more networked (even swarmed) forms that may not even have formal membership, or collective ideology, such as Occupy and Anonymous.

Autonomous network politics can, however, operationalise the fluidity of identification under informationalism and, in this way, simply deepen diversity and fragmentation. The question of how to enable transformation rather than simply facilitate the experience of contestation or disengagement is central and can become even more elusive. The pursuit of transformation hinges on the possibility of creating counter-hegemonies that make a claim on society and its problems as a whole, rather than simply on some aspect of it (Carroll 2010). Networked, or swarmed, resistance does not necessarily encourage convergence in a common struggle with a shared agenda, and so risks fragmenting into short-term resistance against some particular authority. Movement networks have responded to these problems by seeking to construct strategic capacity through a process of dialogic engagement around shared values and alternatives, rather than by manifesto-building. The obvious example here is the World Social Forum, a yearly gathering of up to 100,000 movement activists meeting from 2001, dedicated solely to constructing global dialogue and global information groups, amidst differences, and against neoliberalism (Conway 2013).

COMMUNICATIONS TECHNOLOGIES AND MOVEMENT ORGANISATION

ICTs have a direct impact on these issues of mobilisation. While the shift to autonomous network politics can seem highly participatory and deinstitutionalised, in practice it can rely on the institutionalisation of network 'nodes' and the accumulation of contacts, and hence can serve to build hierarchy. Certainly, movement elites (or dispersed elites) can attempt to orchestrate, or impose, strategy on the networked movement as a whole. The 'International Forum of Globalisation', for instance, acquired this role by default in the early stages of counter-globalism (Brecher, Costello & Smith 2000). Any abstract mode of network engagement hinges on accumulated reputation. While institutionally fluid, its social structure produces reputational capital and therefore can be highly exclusionary, as individuals and organisations become key nodes of authority, and construct informal hierarchies. As argued earlier, even within horizontally organised networks, issues around elites arise, in this case with the possibility of people feeling that a local movement is being taken over by people from elsewhere, being exploited by others or with the elites not knowing local conditions. As Brecher and Costello have argued, the advent of "global self-organisation from below" enabled a decentralised, fluid and unpredictable swarm that could outflank centralised power but it also created new weaknesses (Brecher et al. 2000: 86). These weaknesses centred on problems of building participation and accountability, while stopping the default to internal (and external) elites. The dilemma reflects the political limitations of internet engagement: openness offers possibilities for broad engagement, at least for those able to access the net, but undermines the process of sustained political strategising.

Networks can also invoke temporary coalitions and alliances, as groups construct common 'convergences'; sometimes away from the rest of the network, risking fragmentation and alienating participants. The delicate goal of convergence is, paradoxically, to create a space for collective action that is not controlled, and is thereby both creative for itself and threatening (or at least unpredictable) to the authorities and perhaps for participants. Participants themselves may not know who is actively involved or who is their audience. Networked movements can, in this sense, be deliberately disorganised and dispersive, moving in response to (and seeking to generate) episodes in consciousness and engagement. Difficulties arise in sustaining the affective engagement beyond such episodes, which may arise and melt away as soon as they emerge; indeed, such 'emotional movements' have become a focus for a number of researchers in social movement studies (Waldgrave & Verhulst 2006). Convergence becomes an episode, not a sustained movement: the existence of the movement, as movement, depends on the power of nodes capable of maintaining engagement between upswings in consciousness and engagement.

It is here that information and communication technology can play a critical role. As with any technology, ICT is not an empty vessel to be 'filled' with content, but rather a product of specific histories, ongoing power conflicts, struggles with 'technical' problems or capacity and tussles with unintended results. The development of information technology mediates and is mediated by social relations and expresses varied ideational and practical responses to capitalism. In the first instance it is bound into structures of connectedness that enable accumulation and communication between globally distributed corporate and state interests. Unintentionally it can enable possibilities for (equally global) networked social movements, which may then add their own structures of communication. In the absence of organisational hierarchy (or at least in a context where 'deep' hierarchy is denied legitimacy), communication technology enables the construction of network hubs that allow the possible formation of common agendas and strategies. The mutual recognition enabled by such nodes may then allow the transformation of communication networks into networks of political solidarity, or dispersal.

These circumstances of mediated network politics give rise to new movement elites who seek to deploy network organising as a mode of participatory engagement. Movements can become increasingly two-tier, with tightly defined 'elite' groups defining the agenda whilst creating spaces for mass digital participation. This is the model for 'distributed' digital campaigns, where mobilisation is networked through social media. In contrast with member-based organisations, which construct representative hierarchies, these networked movement organisations often have no formal membership, and members often do not have a substantive capacity to challenge movement strategy. Promised interactivity is limited, for instance to expressive acts within the frameworks presented. There is no formal accountability in 'the network'. Governance is simultaneously distributed and centralised. One recent example is a '350.org' campaign where people were encouraged to up-load pictures of themselves expressing the demand that greenhouse gas emissions be limited to 350 parts per million.

The tension between elitism and equal participation is a permanent feature of contemporary movements. Movements may claim to reject elite leadership, asserting leadership from 'below': the Zapatista spokespeople, for instance, were anonymised as balaclava-wearing 'subcomandantes' (Cleaver 1994, 1998). However, use of communication technology involves 'representing' the movement to external groups, and this process then acts-back on the movement, to reconstitute it. In the case of the Zapatistas, the poetic political vision of subcomandante Marcos became centrally important to its recognition internationally from 1994, subverting the movement's insistence on non-hierarchy (Routledge 1998). Representation, through communication technology, thus can exercise unintentional power on behalf of the movement, and over it.

The representational and constitutive role of communication technology is not new. Benedict Anderson writes of the role played by printing-press capitalism in the construction of an imagined nationalist political community that built a mass public able to recognise itself as a nation (Anderson 1991). With mass newsprint a new type of political imagination was made possible beyond the face-to-face. Building on Anderson's work, Paul James argues that as communication technology moved from face-to-face encounters to information disseminated by institutions, such as the state or business, we see an enhanced projection of power (James 1996). The state, in issuing a proclamation (whether heard or not), removes dependence on face-to-face assertions for exercising its authority. The more extended the form of communication, the more that power can possibly be projected or diffused across people and places. However, by constituting a national citizenry the state enables reciprocal mobilisation, and gives rise to the possibility of mass national movements such as the republican movements in the Americas and in France in the eighteenth century (Tilly 1979; Calhoun 1993), and, in another political direction, the fascist nationalisms in the twentieth century.

Beyond institutional communication, societies have created progressively more extended modes of communication, first in the form of broadcast technology (radio and television) and then, as digital technology. In capitalist societies communication becomes central to profit-making. The printing press, like the internet, was not simply producing informational artefacts, it was also producing profit for its owners and for its advertisers. As highlighted earlier in this book, the capture and enclosure of everyday social communication for purposes of profit generates struggles online and elsewhere, and creates new technologies, for instance file-sharing, which then generate new waves of accumulation. As with the printing press, digitisation does not fall into a neutral field and, when taken up, has unintended impacts on the character of social and political life. For example, Facebook and Google, are in the first instance, new devices for accumulation, with potentially universal reach, and concomitant and often unperceived power, including the power to disrupt themselves (Kang & McAllister 2011; Kreps

2011). It becomes necessary for people to have a willed active self-immersion in digital interactivity (Dean 2005, 2009), to survive, or maintain their social life, creating a situation in which face-to-face relations appear secondary. With the advent of the 'semantic' web, driven by algorithms that have the capacity to anticipate and shape preferences on a mass global scale, there is further scope for the deepened commodification, and alienation, of social-political life.

CASTELLS AND NETWORK POWER

In his account of *Communication Power* Castells directly addresses this stratificaction of ICT (Castells 2009, 2011: 773). First, 'networking power', is simply gate-keeping the flow of messages in the network; it is an ability to attempt to determine what messages can and cannot flow into the network. Second, 'networked power', is power over nodes in the network, for example, the agenda-setting power exercised by key corporate content sources, or even the elites in social movements. Third, 'network-making' power, encloses the informational 'commons' for commodification, essentially a meta-programming power that attempts to set the preferences of users. And finally, 'network switching' power: the capacity to link networks, across different social fields such as media, finance and politics.

For Castells, this structure of communication power re-orders social life, but at the same time produces the possibility for networked counter-power. Castells posits an exit strategy for social movements in which they create a parallel infrastructure, re-appropriate communication and 'rewire' it for revolution. The insistence that refusal (an unwiring) must always move to a process of constructing the utopia of the commons (a rewiring) reflects the aspiration towards 'counter-', as against 'anti-power' (see an alternative formulation from Holloway 2005). The construction of a 'commons' though does not, in-and-of-itself, enable 'counter-power'. The capacity to create autonomous communication infrastructure does not transform social relations; the mass of the population remains 'wired' to the dominant infrastructure. In this case, the 'rewired' realm can simply become another lifestyle choice. Indeed, collapsing late capitalism into communications power can produce a counter-strategy that replicates the same abstraction process. In this respect 'counter-power' can be seen as mirroring communication power, and lead movements away from embodied contexts of resistance, preventing the construction of emancipatory projects, diverting action into harmless virtual fantasy (Dean 2009).

Here, we would suggest that Castells's model of the communication commons gives too much ground to 'network power'. As we have argued through the book, informationalism is riven with its own internal disorders that destabilise it from within. From this perspective, the disorder is 'inside' informationalism. If there has been an information 'revolution', it has generally been a neoliberal 'revolution from above', which sees the established elites attempting to re-build order in their own interests. Yet that information revolution has produced self-disorderings that open up new possibilities for social movements (Steger, Goodman & Wilson 2013). The subsequent analysis draws these themes of information disorder and network politics into a discussion of the PGA, as an initial configuration between communications technology and counter-globalism.

COUNTER-GLOBALISM AND INFORMATION TECHNOLOGY

From the mid-1990s there was a degree of anxiety amongst policymakers over the impact of digital communication on political protest—a fear, perhaps that the neoliberal revolution was producing discontent. Concerns about the destabilising effect of communication technology surfaced in a project initiated by the U.S. Department of Defense at the RAND Corporation. In 1996 RAND launched the Netwar concept speculating about the disruptive influence of internet movement strategies (Arquilla & Ronfeldt 1996). RAND maintained the project during the following 15 years, with a series of contributions on what came to be called 'cyberwar' (Arquilla & Ronfeldt 2001). On each occasion groups engaged in political violence and global crime were grouped with protest groups, as wreaking global disorder through digital communication. Similar concerns, and the call for governmental counter-moves, were later popularised by Richard Clarke, former staff member at the National Security Council (Clarke & Knake 2010), leading to several attempts at introducing cyber-security legislation through the U.S. Congress (all were opposed on civil liberties grounds, and failed to pass into law). With the revelations leaked by Edward Snowden in 2013, all of these surveillance provisions, and more, were shown to have been implemented (outside the law) by the U.S. National Security Agency, in collaboration with other security agencies and corporations worldwide, to create a potentially global searchable database of all digital communication records (*Observer* ongoing a; Greenwald 2014).

In the mid-1990s the RAND Netwar project positioned the Zapatista movement as the key instance of 'Netwar'. The central technical innovation used in the Zapatista struggle was the electronic mailing list. In 2013 this is an unremarkable (even forgotten) email tool, yet in 1994 its capacity to enable instant mass distribution of user-generated digital text and dialogue was unprecedented. Previously, distribution through print and broadcast media was unidirectional and often inaccessible. Indeed, the use of digital e-lists to disseminate the announcement of the Zapatista uprising against NAFTA in 1994 is often cited as sparking counter-globalism (see Couch 2001). The call for mass refusal of globalised neoliberalism, expressed in the cry 'Ya Basta' (Enough is enough!), resonated amongst people displaced by the marketisation drive, dating back to the 1970s, in rich and poor countries. The call to resist, issued from the jungle of Southern Mexico, was relayed through Listservs based at the University of Texas, spilling out of the local and inspiring a new configuration of forces targeting the globalisation of neoliberalism through institutions such as the World Trade Organisation (which had been launched in 1994) (Cleaver 1994). The international solidarity network that emerged from the Zapatista uprising, fuelled by digital communication, then constructed its own global movement, the Peoples' Global Action (PGA), which went on to spark a new global political cycle of protest against neoliberal globalism.

From at least 1994 email Listservs played a central role in networking around these global issues—notably on the campaign against the OECD's Multilateral Agreement on Investment, which in 1998 was defeated by a loose international alliance of groups sharing strategy across Listservs and websites (Goodman & Ranald 2000). This was only the first manifestation of interactive digital communication in counter-globalism and was quickly superseded by the construction of information hubs, effectively convergence sites, where movement participants could post material, initially text, and later photographs, sound and video. The first of these hubs was built in Sydney, Australia, for the PGA protest against the Birmingham G8 meeting in 1999, discussed later. The program later became the basis for the Seattle 'Independent Media Centre' at the 1999 WTO meeting, a model of software-enabled citizen journalism, and was then disseminated across many cities in the form of 'Indymedia' (Atton 2003).

These convergence sites quickly became places for the development of movement tactics during protests at global summits, and for movement strategising, most intensively from 1999 to 2005. The sites enabled a collective normative engagement, re-grounding and invigorating public spheres, offering new sites of resistance. Internet deliberation of this kind enabled the largest mobilisation in history—the 15 February 2003 protest against the U.S. invasion of Iraq, which attracted ten million people in 600 cities across the world (Strangelove 2005). The digital media hub both extended engagement and offered some compensation for the disorganisation of network politics, enabling forms of mutual recognition, coordination and information group formation, that were more immediate and more widely available than previously (Hackett & Carroll 2006). Anyone with access to an internet connection could send or post-up material that could then be widely accessed, although this openness could now be, and was, disrupted by data smog, overload of responses and deliberate disruption by some participants, leading to activist 'paranoia' and eventual disengagement (Wolfson 2013).

There were similar iterations in mobile digital media, beginning with the use of messaging in the 'SMS revolution' against the Estrada government in the Philippines in 2001 (Shirky 2011). The mass messaging enabled tactical innovation in street protests, out-manoeuvring the authorities. The democratic uprising against the Iranian government in 2009 adopted Twitter to message to the external world as much as to coordinate protests, although clearly it was not enough to force political change. The Occupy protest was inspired by the Arab Spring of 2011, and was characterised as #Occupy reflecting its use of Twitter media (Rane & Salem 2012; Jurgensen 2012). In both the Iranian and Occupy cases visual images of protest actions (and police actions) were conveyed in real time, through corporate-based media like YouTube, Facebook and Twitter, enabling a new sense of immediacy, engagement and spread of information (although they also threatened data smog, loss of clarity, false postings, governmental surveillance and arrests). Occupy took the engagement possibilities a step further by undertaking live streaming of its spokes-council deliberations (Juris 2012). Ironically, by 2012 the U.S. government was seeking to harness the political potential of digital activism to subvert its enemies. In 2012 the U.S. committed $57 million in 'Internet Freedom Grants' to train journalists and activists in encryption and circumvention to enable digital activism, including for instance, against Syria's Assad regime (Newton-Small 13 June 2012). As Graeber suggests, this in turn could rebound and inspire people to use the promoted tactics to attempt to overthrow U.S. client states (2013: 11).

Across these encounters between digital communication technology and social movements we see a process of using and developing digital technology to meet social movement priorities, and sometimes unintentionally to disrupt them. The key challenge for movements, and for their use of communications technology, has been to construct commonalities that (paradoxically) express differences. For transnational movements the apparent contradiction between the universal and the particular has had to be transformed into a mutually reinforcing process. Hardt and Negri characterised a global cycle of struggles, beginning in 1999, as a 'distributed network', where "each struggle remains singular and tied to its local conditions but at the same time is immersed in the common web". This, they argue is "the most fully realised political example we have of the concept of multitude", where the extension of a common field strengthens rather than undermines the singularities of its participants (Hardt & Negri 2004: 217). The assertion of an overarching unity, or singularity, reflects the political logic of contestation, where disunity is a liability. As noted earlier in this volume (Chapters 2 and 4), the assertion directs attention away from both the plurality of competing responses and sources of disunity. While ICT can indeed be a "key facilitator . . . helping to bridge the gap between the different locals" (Washbourne 2001: 102), it can also prevent deeper engagement for common ends, presenting another problem cycle.

One way some of these problems can be overcome is through a more embodied immersion in mobilisation, through mass street protest. Constant dispersion in a net-mediated context accords great symbolic meaning to moments of spatial aggregation, where the transnational movement makes itself visible to itself, and to wider publics. These moments of face-to-face, embodied expression are moments of great significance for participants. This is partly because they offer the only concrete physical evidence of the movement's existence and effect. Inevitably, the moments of aggregation are moments of political drama and public emotion: they form part of a series of engagements linked over time through localised actions and disembodied mediations. At these moments, collective identity is "congealed in...", face-to-face, but highly visible, public gatherings". These moments are especially important for "transnational movements in which subterranean networks are otherwise 'virtual' or stretched very thinly over great distances" (Eschle 2005: 21).

At one level this reflects the central role of offline interpersonal relationships in social movement networks (Diani 2001). At another level it reflects the dramaturgy of movement politics, where urgent mass engagement creates opportunities and transformations in consciousness. Embodied engagements are intensified by the spatial dynamics of street protests or occupations, but are necessarily episodic. We may understand these as 'temporary affective zones', where emotive engagement may be a defining experience that sustains engagement over the intervening period (da Rimini 2013b). Alternatively they may be simply 'out of this world' experiences, which have no connection with the everyday disaggregated individuation. Episodes of intense embodied collective action may therefore be understood as offering a release from the bondage of legitimating identities and a fleeting moment of freedom; a 'catharsis' rather than a mechanism for movement building or sustained problem solving. Transnational movement networks are especially trapped in this cycle. The archives of Indymedia bear this out, with intense periods of activity lapsing into periods of relative inactivity (Sampedro 2004). Meaningful interactions between the expressive everyday contexts and instrumental institutional dimensions seem central to the constitution of ongoing transnational movements (Stammers & Eschle 2005). Without translating experience into political traction, sustained movement challenge is unlikely.

In part this can explain the centrality of embodied direct actions in global protest. These actions must be correlated, at least in the political imagination for them to have symbolic meaning beyond the local, and this has to be done physically and cognitively as well as temporally. The balance between digital networking and immersive expression perhaps can be maintained through a permanent networked immersion, where identification with a transnational movement is sustained through recurring cycles of localised experiences (see MacDonald 2006). To extend the metaphor of thick and thin solidarity (Bamyeh 2009), the thin gruel of digital networking can be greatly thickened by heavily correlated direct actions. The digital and the face-to-face then become mutually reinforcing. To explore these issues in more depth, the following discussion takes the narrative back to the 1990s and to the birth of Peoples' Global Action, progenitor of what today we recognise as justice globalism (Steger, Goodman & Wilson 2012).

'PEOPLES' GLOBAL ACTION'

PGA was not the largest movement network that helped precipitate the Global Justice Movement, but it was one of the most innovative (Rupert 2003). Its importance as an example stems from its organisational character: it was not a child of international NGOs, nor of national political parties, and was not itself a formalised international organisation. At the same time the PGA had strong foundations in active movements, and is best characterised as a transnational grassroots movement network, in contrast with the trend to NGO transnational advocacy networks in the 1990s (Keck & Sikkink 1998). It was weakly institutionalised, and founded on autonomies cast across North and South. Yet it had huge influence (Reitan 2007).

The PGA closely prefigured a global counter-hegemonic bloc, both in terms of scope and purpose. Grounded in North-South 'encounters', the PGA brought together mass movements across North and South. Unlike the counterparts established by NGOs, the PGA is direct action orientated. Reitan's important study of global activism covers four global activist networks: 'Jubilee 2000', 'Our World is not for Sale' (OWINS), 'Via Campesina' and PGA. The four are situated on a spectrum from a 'first generation' expert-based lobbying model, closely aligned with NGOs, to a 'second generation, direct action social justice network' (Reitan 2007: 203). Reitan considers that the PGA most closely embodies the second-generation model, which is much more explicitly concerned with building connectivity across grassroots movements.

Its founding principles state that the PGA is a transnational network of activist groups "based on decentralisation and autonomy" (PGA 1998a). It was one of the first transnational network movements with no organisational leadership, and centred on strengthening relations between autonomous activist groups. It was created in February 1998 to directly reject "capitalism, imperialism and feudalism and all trade agreements, institutions and governments that promote destructive globalisation". It likewise rejected "all forms and systems of domination and discrimination including, but not limited to, patriarchy, racism and religious fundamentalism of all creeds", embracing the "full dignity of all human beings". The PGA adopted a "confrontational attitude", explicitly rejecting lobbying those undemocratic institutions where "transnational capital is the only real policy-maker". Confrontation meant specific calls "to direct action and civil disobedience . . . forms of resistance which maximise respect for life and oppressed peoples' rights, as well as the construction of local alternatives to global capitalism" (PGA 1998a: 1).

PGA practices signalled something of an international 'first' in generating South-North mobilisations against the institutions of capitalist globalisation. The Zapatista National Liberation Army (EZLN) and other Southern organisations, such as the Brazilian landless peasants' movement, the MST (*Movimento Dos Trabalhadores Rurais Sem Terra*), produced the inspiration. Connections had been established through movement media and online during the EZLN uprising against NAFTA in 1994. The international encounters sought to build on these linkages with face-to-face strategising. The first of these, the 1996 'Intercontinental Encounter for Humanity Against Neoliberalism', was the culmination of a series of regional meetings. It signalled a new model of North-South solidarity-building, and called for a new global network of resistance. The 1996 Encounter in Chiapas was followed by a similar event a year later, across a range of squatted spaces in Madrid. The consensus statement issued by this second meeting led to the founding meeting of the PGA in February 1998 in Geneva, where over 300 activists from 71 countries around the world met to plan actions against the World Trade Organisation and the G8, due to celebrate 50 years of free trade in May 1998.

Amongst European groups involved in ecological direct action, such as those against car culture in the case of Reclaim the Streets (RTS), involvement in Zapatista solidarity produced a crucial shift in orientation to link with Southern initiatives. The reversal of North-South internationalism brought with it with a strong transfer Northwards of perspectives and models for direct action learnt in the South. The PGA "took the new political forms, the new ideas about power and the new methods of making things happen that had come out of the Chiapas, and ran with them on a global scale" (Kingsnorth 2003: 74). The model was "gloriously anarchic", centred on "the belief that direct action—taking politics into your own hands—is not simply a lobbying tool, an outlet for frustrations, or a means of pursuing a goal, but an end in itself", with actions organised through consensus decision making, with as much leaderless autonomy and diversity as possible. As Kingsnorth argues, the model was "crucial to understanding the global movement as a whole" (2003: 83). Reflecting this, the anthology of anti-capitalist mobilisations put together by Notes from Nowhere in 2003 explicitly highlighted the importance of South-North linkages emerging out of the Zapatista-MST-RTS-PGA nexus, in the subsequent cycle of transnational protest (Notes from Nowhere 2003). The compliment was extended in political practice: the 'Dissent!' Network, that created an autonomous protest at the 2005 G8 Gleneagles summit and inspired the direct action 'Climate Camp' movement from 2006 to 2010, directly sourced its inspiration from the PGA (Harvie et al. 2005).

From 1994 mobilisations against specific summits had already begun, with the 'Fifty Years Is Enough' demonstration against the World Bank/ IMF meeting in Madrid, and much more extensively, with the mobilisation of Philippine social movements against the 1996 APEC meeting in Manila, followed by the major mobilisation against the 1997 APEC in Vancouver. PGA actions differed in being coordinated across a number of countries in the South as well as the North. The PGA's main legacy is the idea of a decentralised 'global day of action' targeting a global institution or issue, along with the deliberate tactic of symbolically seeking to 'block the summits', first initiated at the WTO in Geneva in 1998. As Graeber notes, "It was an international network called Peoples Global Action that put out the first summons for planet-wide days of action such as J18 and N30" (Graeber 2004b: 204). Kingsnorth likewise stresses the inspiration and initiative offered by the PGA:

> it was the PGA, not PGA alone, by any means, but certainly PGA in the role of inspiration and key player—which helped create the kind of "take on a big summit" action that came to define the first stages of the anti-globalisation movement.
>
> (Kingsnorth 2003: 74)

PGA's first mobilisation on 16 May 1998, against the G8 and the WTO, brought 10,000 people onto the streets in Geneva. PGA assessments of the Geneva events point to both the major difficulties encountered, and to the possibilities that opened up. The attempt to close down WTO negotiations manifested as three days of rolling protests in Geneva, where, along with a 'caravan' of Southern movement representatives that had been convened to tour European capitals, the PGA called for "non-violent civil disobedience . . . with the stated intention of crossing police barriers, entering and stopping the conference" (PGA 1998b). On the first day the PGA reported:

> The people came with the banners of all kinds of struggles against some aspect of globalization: local unions fighting privatizations or austerity, groups of solidarity with the south, squatters, plus many personal banners, musicians, and the caravan tractors towing a huge sound system. Everyone there agreed: stupendous, unbelievable demo . . . the demo moved like a tide of hope through the city.
>
> (PGA 1998b)

The PGA account tells of the protest arriving at a barricaded WTO building, then occupying an intersection for a street party before returning to the city centre. With the bulk of the demonstration dispersed to a campsite, conflicts with the police escalated, the campsite was cleared and running battles continued through the night. Despite the heavy police response, there followed three days of direct actions against corporate headquarters and against the WTO, including a non-violent symbolic move to enter the WTO building by several hundred protesters, some on their knees. Simultaneously with the Geneva protests there were large mobilisations in capital cities across Latin American and Asia (supposedly 50,000 in Brazil; 200,000 in India). In Northern countries the PGA affiliate 'Reclaim the Streets' initiated a 'Global Street Party' across 37 cities in 22 countries. In the UK PGA mobilisations were overshadowed by a large demonstration mounted by the Jubilee 2000 against the G8, calling for the cancellation of Southern debt. In Birmingham, 50–70,000 people arrived to surround the scheduled G8 meeting (which had been moved for security reasons), and later that day 8,000 joined the more anarchic RTS street party.

The protests and attempt at closing down the WTO were successful in their undeclared intention of politicising the institution (which then was still only four years old). The PGA announced "Evaluation: we are happy!!!", claiming that "at one stroke we transformed the WTO from an unknown acronym to a very controversial institution with a very bad public image"; suddenly, they noted, a wide range of agencies not linked to the protests had begun to criticise the WTO (PGA 1998b). The WTO had become visible and contestable.

The PGA looked forward to mobilisations against the Multilateral Agreement on Investment (to be defeated later in 1998), against the January 1999 Davos World Economic Forum (soon to have its counter-organisation in the World Social Forum), a new challenge to the G8 'debt forgiveness' (foreshadowed for the June 1999 G8), and a concerted focus on the proposed WTO Millennium Round and the WTO Seattle meeting in November 1999 (which was to collapse in the face of the protest and a related veto by Southern countries). The PGA had, indeed, taken direct resistance from Chiapas to Geneva, and produced the global cycle of protest that radically reframed globalisation.

Tactically, the May 1998 mobilisations had shown how the carnivalesque street party, traditionally setting aside a place and time for breaking the rules of 'normal life' (Ehrenreich 2007), could be used to protest against global power structures. Developed by Reclaim the Streets in the UK since the early 1990s, the street party model offered a visible means of defying of the authorities, of challenging capitalist culture and asserting alternative values in a spontaneous and creative zone of engagement. With the PGA the device was simply transferred to challenge and politicise global summits, a tactic that laid the groundwork for subsequent forms of protest in the global justice movement (St John 2004b). The reclamation of, and creation of, open spaces, both on the net and in street contexts, allowed for a disorderly creativity: "the creative and unpredictable amalgamation of poetic and pragmatic components . . . triggered uncertain outcomes, potentiating alliances between disparate opponents" (St John 2004a; see also Jordan 1998).

The globally networked mobilisation was repeated, with added force at the June 1999 G8 meeting held in Cologne. Here, Northern and Southern agendas were folded into a generalised 'Carnival against Global Capitalism', which focused its protest on the financial districts of the globe as the key cause of global injustice. While Jubilee and the Stop the Debt movements focused on the G8 meeting itself, PGA protesters sought to close down the financial districts that profited from the debt burden. The leaflet calling for groups internationally to organise actions, aimed to spark the political imagination of a diverse collection of people in terms of liminal carnival. It said, in part:

> IMAGINE financial districts across the world filled not with profit and plunder but with the sounds and rhythms of party and pleasure

IMAGINE replacing the existing social order with a free and ecological society based upon mutual aid and voluntary cooperation
IMAGINE taking your desires for reality

(Do or die 18 June 1999).

In preparation for the mobilisation 500 PGA-affiliated farmers from low income countries toured Europe as an 'Inter-Continental Caravan for Solidarity and Resistance', participating in a range of local direct actions (Reitan 2007). The caravan demonstrated the South-North model of PGA solidarity in being "based on a genuine North-South solidarity model as against the paternalism often lying behind Northern solidarity movements" (Munck 2006: 101). In Cologne, the PGA caravan attempted to mount a 'laugh parade' ridiculing the G8's debt forgiveness as a faux melodrama:

> Now the heads of state of the G7 want to present themselves towards the public as generous world leaders willing to forget and forgive some of these debts in a remarkable charitate gesture. This is a joke!!! We laugh at the Gang of Seven Criminal Hypocrites that are meeting in Cologne. We laugh at their claim that neoliberal policies will bring peace and prosperity for all. We laugh at the corrupt Southern governments for playing their part in this melodrama by paying debts that never existed. We laugh at the so-called 'debt relief' of the G7 — WE DO NOT FORGIVE YOUR DEBTS!!
>
> (PGA 1999)

While the Cologne group was detained by German police, an estimated 10,000 RTS protesters converged on the City of London, embarking on rolling street parties and diversionary tactics, using disorder to disrupt policing and close down the financial district. Despite its ostensible anti-institutionalism, the City of London Police Commissioner stated the protest had reached a "level and sophistication of planning not previously seen at similar demonstrations", and the media commented on the tactic of creating "a 'starburst' in which groups of protesters moved in different directions, creating confusion for the police" (Wilkinson 31 July 1999). Other preparations included a booklet 'Squaring up to the Square Mile', with a map detailing protest targets (Corporate Watch and Reclaim the Streets 1999). This was designed as a tool for on-the-ground actions that included office sit-ins and various forms of property damage, said to have amounted to £2 million over the course of the day (a decade later, in 2009, the protest against the G20 in the aftermath of the 2008 financial crisis, echoed the 1999 event, with its own updated 'Squaring up to the Square Mile'; Indymedia 2009).

The account printed in *Notes from Nowhere* by 'Wat Tyler' (a pseudonym) conveys something of the uncertainty of the prior organisation and also of the surprise and joy at literally closing down much of the City of London, occupying numerous bank headquarters and exchanges. The account ends with an important statement that reflects the kind of idealism and voluntarism that drove the PGA movement, and echoes through the subsequent years:

> Until J18, the idea that there was a global movement against capitalism remained just that. An idea. I hoped it was true, but I couldn't really feel it. Many of us felt the same way. Now, because of J18, it had become tangible and real. Our movement had passed some invisible threshold. Tearing down the barriers that usually keep us apart. While we shut down the City of London, people were doing the same all around the world . . . To feel part of this global movement that transcends boundaries of language, culture, distance, and history, is empowering beyond words.
>
> (Tyler 2003: 96)

Beyond Geneva and London, there were protests in 60 other cities, in 40 countries, from the several hundred who gathered in central Sydney, to the 10,000 people who gathered in Lagos. The global scope of the J18 experiment emboldened U.S. activists who were at that time organising to disrupt the November 1999 WTO Ministerial in Seattle. The second PGA conference, held in Bangalore in August 1999, supported the call for a global day of action against the WTO for November 30, again mounting a caravan to the venue and calling for direct action (Style 2002). From late 1999, with the WTO events, a growing direct action movement focusing on summits overtook the PGA: by then the model had been established.

Although the PGA model inspired subsequent direct action summit protests, including for instance the Dissent! movement (formed in late 2003 to mobilise against the 2005 G8 in Gleneagles; Smith 2005), by November 1999 the PGA itself was subsumed in a much larger broad-based direct action mobilisation. Initially dubbed 'anti-globalisation', this movement for alternative globalisation, 'alter-globalisation', very quickly morphed into a global justice movement claiming a wide and diverse political base extending across international advocacy organisations as well as social movements.

In the UK, where the RTS network had strongly contributed to the J18 event, direct action appeared to decline. The May Day events in 2000 and 2001 attracted diminishing numbers and by 2003 the RTS had effectively wound up. The mantle of global justice was taken on by a 'Trade Justice Movement' of 2001 and the 'Make Poverty History' coalition of 2004 led by development and trade NGOs, with its origins in the Jubilee 2000 coalition from 1997 (Rootes & Saunders 2007). While the PGA went into abeyance, its mobilisation models remained in place. The PGA and its allies had developed new political tactics and organisational formations, and used them to construct mobilisations designed to unmask global power relations. Having polarised the political field, the political agenda increasingly passed from the PGA to other political formations, both autonomous and institutionalised.

The movement's problem-solving energies had been centred on building solidarity and on keeping the diverse and fractured set of movements together. The PGA's approach of creating unity through globally symbolic direct action, channelled its political energy into street protest. Here, the carnivalesque threatened to become a 'ritual of rebellion' (Gluckman 1963), expressing social conflicts but leaving power dynamics unchanged. The temporary egalitarian rule-less community can easily collapse back into structure and hierarchy, or at best maintain its group boundaries as pure and set off from the world (Turner 1969). In this case, issues around sustaining mobilization become key problems, and this was influenced by success as much as failure. Graeber argues the movement had many successes, notably in blocking international agreements of neoliberal governance. He writes:

> We all experienced the infighting and frazzled confusion that followed the first heady years, the crumbling alliances and seemingly endless bitter arguments over racism, sexism, privilege, lifestyle, 'summit-hopping,' process, the lack of ties to genuine communities in resistance . . . And we saw it as the proof of our ultimate fecklessness as a movement, our failure to achieve any of our major goals. The irony is that, really, all these things were a direct result of our success.
>
> (2012: 4)

Perhaps the movements lacked the structural ability to build on success beyond opposition. Success brought the existing fractures to the surface or created them anew.

INFORMATION TECHNOLOGY, J18 AND THE PGA

The J18 event sent shockwaves through the mainstream media, especially in the UK. Many reported it as the first outing of internet-mediated disruption on a global scale. The *Financial Times* announced "Whatever your view, the nature of civil disobedience is being irrevocably transformed by the internet and modern communications" (Wilkinson 31 July 1999). Digital mediation was evident in media-savvy direct actions and stunts, internet coordination and dissemination, the use of mobile phones on demonstrations and, most important, the use of the internet to deepen and broaden engagement, and increase anonymity. The report continued, presciently:

> The Carnival against Capitalism was organised internationally, with protests taking place in several European business centres, although London was the only one that turned nasty. The next focus of protest may occur in Seattle, where the World Trade Organisation is holding a meeting in November.
>
> (Wilkinson 31 July 1999)

The *Independent* argued J18 demonstrated a highly sophisticated political strategy, which focused on the drivers of dispossession, namely the stock markets; it also demonstrated the coming-of-age of the internet as a means of mobilisation. The *Observer* likewise reported that "Virtual Chaos Baffles Police . . . baffled police were yesterday grappling with a new phenomenon—the stealth protest . . . the very beauty of the operation was the apparent lack of organisers, leaders, or any public face" (Observer 20 June 1999). In Australia, the *Financial Review* reported J18 activists had "hitch[ed] a ride on the web", and attacked their use of the internet to "harangue, rave, orate or stand on a soapbox" (Hepworth 19 June 1999). The British *Independent* was more sanguine, stating the protesters were using the "most advanced products of the very global capitalism against which their protests are directed", linking internationally through a technology that was "as good at creating international solidarity as it is for buying and selling shares" (Whittam Smith 21 June 1999). Meanwhile, the *Sunday Times* reported on the J18 "cyber-war" against specific corporate targets in the City of London, using Floodnet, a 'denial of service' program that itself had been created by activists involved in solidarity with Zapatistas in 1998 (Ungoed-Thomas & Sheehan 15 August 1999).

The J18 allowed movement reflection and reframed the global political agenda. The BBC quoted a J18 activist arguing that activists "keep in touch and aware of one another's activities on the Internet. The Internet is empowering, it means that different groups can generate their own media without having it diluted by the mainstream media". It was "a superb vehicle for direct action", and a way of "individuals taking issues into their own hands" (BBC 15 June 1999). Remarkably, it was also with J18 that the mainstream media began to use 'anti-capitalism' to describe the movement, rather than the more pejorative 'anti-globalization'. CNN adopted the movement's own terminology and quipped, "the [J18 web]site's manifesto marries Marx and cyberspace in a spirit of pin-the-tail-on-the-CEO levity" (CNN 18 June 1999). The direct digital reporting caused some genuine curiosity and dismay. J18 media centred on an online media hub—the London Media Centre—as the conduit for a stream of video, sound and text that began with the protest in Sydney. The event used 'active'-code software developed by Sydney's Community Access Technology (CAT), a DIY media centre (that was later to be used as the enabling software used by many other Indymedia projects worldwide, especially in the early years of open publishing). The media centre found itself streamed directly to the *Financial Times*, and was contacted by CNN asking how it had been achieved (Halleck 2004).

As one observer of the early EZLN and PGA process noted in early 1999, a leaderless network with a minimalist institutional structure could hardly have existed without IT. Despite not having much in the way of funds, paid staff or offices, it seemed that:

> a global movement was beginning to crystallize. . . . As the realization dawned that the power of global finance could only be challenged

through global resistance, the Internet proved an ideal medium through which to organize.

(Lynas 1999)

The internet though was not embraced uncritically. There are accounts from the PGA stressing the role of traditional forms of campaigning, along with condemnations of the internet as failing to connect with peoples' needs and desires. In an important commentary on movement media, the PGA announced in 1999 that "the revolution will not be emailed", asserting the marketised nature of net communication and the existence of sharp exclusions, worldwide, in terms of access. More significantly, the PGA argued that even if these issues were addressed, access was sufficient and net space reclaimed, the net would still remain "an atomiser of social space and a commodified substitute for human association"; it continued:

We should of course continue to use the internet for information sharing and for initial contact with like-minded groups but with awareness of its market-led trajectory, its limitations and always alongside more involving and humanising activities. For a radical grassroots movement will require the real warmth of human togetherness and the raw 'shout on the street' to make a true social and ecological communications revolution; and it probably won't be emailed.

(PGA 1999)

The debate also surfaced within a major anthology of reflections on J18 authored by RTS activists (RTS 1999). The accounts demonstrate that the role of IT was only part of the story. The crucial process of conceptualising the movement and its agendas was not digitally mediated. Face-to-face exchanges in the aftermath of the 1998 Street Party, in a variety of settings, are said to have culminated in a proposal to the PGA in September 1998 for a day of direct action to close down financial districts, dubbed a 'Global Carnival Against Capitalism', to be held to coincide with the G8 meeting in June 1999. It was only when that proposal had been endorsed by the international network that a J18 e-list was created. By then, even the non-decision to name the event J18 had been made. That decision, itself, became centrally important in signalling the multiplicity of interpretations of the event, and, reflecting this, the device was subsequently enthusiastically adopted at virtually every subsequent counter-globalist convergence.

Once the event had been defined, the internet played a central role. There was active engagement on the e-list, with 300 people regularly contributing with about 1,000 passing through the list. With a note of wonder, this observer noted:

June 18th could not have happened globally without it [the internet]. The cost of sending letters or making phone calls halfway across the world would have been prohibitive. But it's the way the internet spreads ideas rapidly and in every direction through web sites, discussion lists etc. which is extraordinary. Once a message has gone out, a simple click of a button can send it to thousands of people and each one of these in turn can forward that message within seconds. Ideas spread and multiply at the speed of light.

(Do or Die 18 June 1999)

The net was most enthusiastically embraced as a tool for global solidarity. A good example is the account of the emerging movement that also appeared in a UK eco-activist journal:

International solidarity and global protest is nothing new, from the European revolutions of 1848, the upheavals of 1917–18 following the Russian Revolution or the lightning flashes nearly everywhere in 1968, struggle has been able to communicate globally. But what is perhaps unique to our times is the speed and ease with which we can communicate between struggles and the fact that globalisation has meant that many people living in very different cultures across the world now share a common enemy.

(Do or Die 18 June 1999)

Despite this, the PGA process itself affirmed the centrality of face-to-face exchanges, and the problems of internet mediations. We may say the IT interchanges within PGA reflect the problems of constructing transnational counter-hegemony across autonomous groupings. The PGA linked "militant particularisms" (to use Harvey's term) through informal structures, mediated through face-to-face 'encounters' and IT flows (Harvey 2005). But reliance on internet flows in the longer term proved dysfunctional. In a study of the PGA, Hermann Maiba documents the difficulties generated in terms of lack of accountabilities, centrality of informal face-to-face networks and lack of transnational interlocutors (or what he terms 'spiders'), able to spin and traverse the web of solidarity. The resulting problems of 'entry' for outsiders helped ossify the movement, removing its vitality. Counter-acting these tendencies were the actual face-to-face events, which had the effect of extending and deepening the network (Maiba 2005). Similar conclusions were reached in an anthropological study of global activism, by Stephen Juris, which focuses on PGA-affiliated activists involved in Barcelona's Movement for Global Resistance between 2001 and 2002. Juris' ethnography of anti-globalisation movements and transnational activist networking stresses that direct action is a deliberately spectacular, embodied process that enacts transnational connectivity. Beyond these episodes, connectivity hinges on information technology. Together, these embodied and virtual practices constitute experiments in social relations, social laboratories for alternative lived values and practices (Juris 2008).

CONCLUSION

The self-disordering processes of informationalism provide an opportunity for many different kinds of social movement, some of which are radical and some of which are more 'reactionary'. The PGA was the first radical movement of the new period self-consciously deploying ICT to maximise solidarity and connectivity with the goal of directly challenging the legitimacy of the emerging institutions of neoliberal globalism. A combination of digital networking and face-to-face mobilisation was used to develop a new template of global protest, with great effect. Institutions and ideologies that previously had formed part of the naturalised landscape of globalising neoliberalism were suddenly rendered contestable.

These achievements underpinned much of what later became characterised as the Global Justice Movement. The PGA itself fulfilled a key role in the construction of political community, and as an experiment in solidarity it pointed to new possibilities. As an organisation, though, it fell into abeyance in the early 2000s partly because political energy had flowed elsewhere, especially into the articulation of alternative projects, but also because the network itself was unable to adapt to its own successes and its own disorderings. A key difficulty, as noted, was the problem of maintaining mass participation as a loose distributed network. Problems arose with hierarchy and potential alienation of participants, and in maintaining a large interactive information group not just defined by opposition to power-holders. More generally, protest movements against corporate power holders can be disrupted by their own successes, and by the changing problem field that results. There is also the difficulty of building an explicitly anti-capitalist information group identity, which is able to implement policy, or gain credibility and leverage. However, the PGA belonged to a particular moment in a global movement cycle, and like Occupy, it left powerful legacies that can inspire further action.

Indeed, characterising the PGA as a movement perhaps misses the point—it existed for the purpose of internationalising resistance, as the Zapatistas envisaged it, and in large part it fulfilled that role. The international leaflet promoting the J18 mobilisation centred on building connectivity, not movement building:

> By taking direct action, people make connections, they talk and communicate with each other, they break down the isolation and fragmentation of this alienated society. These connections are now spreading across the globe as people realise that their particular local struggles are part of a wider problem—the global economy.
>
> (PGA 1999)

That connectivity was seen as strengthening existing movements, not replacing them. It helped create "organised popular movements which think things through, which debate, which act, which experiment, which try alternatives, which develop the seeds of the future in the present society" (PGA 1999).

The episodic nature of the PGA, and how it broke the mould of protest, only to pass its legacy onto more institutionalised 'movement society' advocacy campaigns, is symptomatic. The Occupy movement, which erupted in the aftermath of the 2008 financial crisis, again forced new ways of seeing the world, and acting politically onto the global agenda, at least temporarily. The importance of these breaks in 'politics as normal' should not be underestimated, nor should their fragility. As argued here, information technology played in important role in realising the PGA project, as a denormalising moment, and in sparking a global cycle of protest in the late 1990s. At the same time, ICT usage brought its own disordering effects, both intended and unintended, which undermined the movement's capacity to build on its own success. Overall, the PGA should have the last word:

> Since '68 there hasn't been a movement that has grown so fast and beautifully. The success in Switzerland has many people asking, "is this the first flutter of a new global social movement?" After so many years of saying "it's no use resisting here, we would have to organize globally", people are thinking "hey, maybe we can!"
>
> (PGA 1998b)

Conclusion
Disinformation Society

This book has made a series of arguments about the importance of addressing and theorising disorder in relation to intended orders, so as to gain a deepened understanding of informational capitalism. The disorders we have discussed are recurrent and self-generated, not mere accidents or aberrations. The inherent disordering tendencies the book focuses on occur in the contexts of networks, information distribution, software engineering, daily life, management, finance markets, academic publishing, peer-to-peer networking and social movement organisation. We do not address other equally disordered fields in any depth: we have only touched on the ways that informational military order undermines itself, the way that the order of science has disordered itself, the ways that the orders of the information State undermine its ability to act on information or on the co-dependent relationship between economic systems and waste. We have begun a provocation, which we hope will lead to further investigations.

The basic principles we have elaborated are fairly simple. We have suggested that systems of deliberate ordering often, or perhaps always, produce their own disorders, which can undermine the orders being attempted. Ordering efforts are not merely counter-productive in a static sense, but are generative, and form part of a wider social dynamic. This relationship between order and disorder leads us to refer to the intertwined 'order/disorder complex', rather than attempt to separate them, or portray them as universal binary oppositions. The perception of disorder is subjective and socially placed, so that one group's order can be another group's disorder, and thus disorder or the experience of disorder is not uniform or definable in general. Furthermore, people deal with these disorders in different kinds of ways depending on the social and framing contexts they bring to the events.

We have suggested that it is useful to conceive of society as a complex interactive, self-modifying set of systems, which are always in flux and do not have to be harmonious or systematic. Different systems interact in complex ways, with different degrees of mesh, so that the outcomes of actions within those systems are impossible to predict in detail. The constant failure of, or challenge to, attempted order is socially commonplace, and people constantly deal with the unintended effects of their actions. In this regime of disordering and unintended effects, we have pointed to the ways that societies congeal social formations and power relations around apparent solutions to problems, or attempts to solve problems. In these circumstances, difficulties do not only arise through failure, they can arise through the success of particular problem-solving techniques (which are embraced by particular social groups), and the extension of those techniques to perhaps inappropriate fields through attempts to retain or extend power or status differentials, through the inability of successful social groups to receive or process the information that the situations are different or through the overpowering 'virtuous circles' of positive feedback.

We have argued that under (dis)informationalism there are several recurrent responses to these kinds of issues. The systemic causes of informational failure are rarely addressed. More often, problems are ignored, shifted elsewhere, blamed on some particular group or some 'external factor' or 'fixed' by attempting to reimpose the preferred order (even when this exacerbates failure). Contrary to most theories of information society, we have suggested that relatively 'accurate' knowledge, especially public knowledge, is devalued in favour of commodification, secrecy, pre-existing ideology, tailoring information for audiences and assumptions of certainty. Hierarchies also disrupt information flow. In this process, most knowledge workers become devalued. Such devaluations or disruptions of information are not 'accidental' but intrinsic to the social processes of (dis)informationalism.

We have also highlighted another social commonplace, namely that computer programming and the application of software is not an intrinsically successful ordering process. Software is surrounded by difficulties. It has indeed solved many problems for, and generated by, society, but it is also continually disruptive, being open to degrees of failure as well as degrees of success, or oversuccess. The failure of a significant portion of software projects is well documented, as is the cost of those failures, and this is a normal feature of the ordering patterns of disinformation society. In this society people can have a recurrent sense of disorder around their experience of software. If software and associated communication technology do form a technological infrastructure for society, as is commonly argued, that infrastructure is not non-problematic or inherently orderly.

Software development involves implementing a complex software system within a complex social system, with a high probability of producing unexpected meshing effects and unintended disruption. Furthermore the software or automation can be exploited to extend the power, or values, of a particular (often, but not always, dominant) segment of the workspace throughout the workspace, where these values and ideas may not be appropriate and may even interfere with the work to be done. The software therefore can become a source of social conflict and struggle, and that conflict produces different evaluations of effectiveness. Consequently, software problems can be political and social as much as they are technical. Often the plans are constructed, in abstract, by people who may not actually know how the social system works or who do not understand how the software system interacts with other systems. This ignorance arises because of the inevitable disruption of communication and knowledge due to hierarchical, or other cultural or practical divisions, within the workspace.

The features that render communication problematic also make gathering the necessary requirements for software socially difficult. Ambiguity in software user requirements is common. It may not be possible, or practical, for requirements engineers (or project managers) to challenge the assumptions of managerial 'idealists' without risk to their ability to perform their work. Management may further argue that they are not trying to improve current processes but change them completely, so objections based on accurate understandings of current processes are not relevant. Social hierarchies and struggles clash with what might be seen as 'optimal' requirements, or the communication of requirements. Social complexity makes optimisation, and conformity with the requirements within a specific time frame, a matter of first negotiation or politics within the workspace, and second a matter of dealing with the consequences of what has been produced in the available time. Layers of complexity are often added as the software is being written or implemented, when people in different parts of the workspace inevitably ask for modifications, want improvements or find that processes do not work for them. Constant modifications compound issues around unpredictability of results, and magnify the chance of cost blowouts or the difficulties in conforming to artificially enforced deadlines. Changes also may negate earlier planning, as what has been written or designed may not cope with the requested changes, thus leading to confusion, rewriting, extension of deadlines and further conflict. Many of the formal ways of planning software do not solve these well-known problems, or the problems of distributed governance, nor do they address the inevitable difficulties of programming complex functionalities. Research in requirements and software engineering is ongoing. Software can only be as good as our understandings of complex social, political, economic and ecological systems. If informationalism tends to suppress information, then software systems will tend to function unexpectedly and inadequately.

These issues can be compounded as problems with software and electronic networks, while familiar, tend not to be openly acknowledged, and this intensifies both the sense of disruption and people's alienation from, or suspicions of, the systems. Computer and software networks constantly challenge pre-existing boundaries and dismantle them, opening further problems, challenges and apparent threats for social networks. Problems also occur, almost universally in disinformation society, with inadequate maintenance of all kinds of systems. As maintenance tends to be concrete and non-innovative, it also tends to be devalued by both information society theory and profit seeking, and if any system is soon to be out of date why bother overmaintaining it? Systems can be forced to function with very little slack (to cut expenses and wage costs), which does not help them recover from shock, or from the accumulation of bugs, or the fragility resulting from speedy repairs.

We have also suggested, counter to most arguments in information society theory, that networks are not particularly robust or adaptive in general, and not just because of bad maintenance. They can also accumulate vulnerabilities, due to the tendency for well-connected nodes to attract more connections, and the tendency for glitches to spread rapidly through the interconnections. It is relatively hard to isolate or quarantine one section of the network from the rest of the network, so disruptions can spread easily and quickly without directed control. Networks can also distribute governance, so that there can be no definite centre of control. In this context, exercises of power can routinely backfire, as the established pathways of power, trigger unexpected events or resistances, or dissipate. People at any point in the system can feel relatively powerless, and the discovery of patterns of responsibility can become obscured. All of these factors strengthen a sense of living in an uncontrollable system.

However, while networks distribute governance, they can entrench strong hierarchical divisions that further disrupt accurate information flow. In these hierarchical networks income and wealth is inequitably distributed and tax evasion is maximised. The corporations that depend upon States for their trade, security and markets contribute less and less to supporting those States, or the populations of those States, so that wealth is further concentrated in an ongoing 'virtuous circle'. The concentration of wealth may also intensify the financialisation of society, so that financial speculation rather than production becomes the primary form of economic action. The distribution of governance also tends to mean that those people in the lower parts of the hierarchy do not become *one* radical and anti-capitalist 'multitude', they tend to fragment into many small groups, with many different and incompatible experiences or ways of relating to information, and many mutual hostilities. Networks can disorder as well as order, and this must be factored into the sociology of informationalism.

Communication suffers from disorder normally, but these disorders are intensified within informationalism, turning the information society into the disinformation society. Communication depends upon an interplay of order and disorder, and the apparent disorder is reduced by techniques such as 'framing' or bringing in the context, social category, or source status of the emitter, the interpretation of the situation, the understanding (or models) a group has of the world and so on—all of which are open to variability amongst different groups of people and lead to 'misinterpretation'. Communication is further disrupted by hierarchies and incompetence, by political strategy and power relations, by status seeking, by deliberate falsehood or the suspicion of falsehood, by people attempting to belong to a particular information group and so on. These disruptions are normal, and lead to patterns of ignorance throughout any relatively complex social organisation. These normal disruptions are intensified by the data smog of informationalism, the precarity of information workers and the paradoxes generated by the enforcement of boundaries intended to enclose information as capitalist property. Data smog requires filtering. One method of achieving this is through people building loyalty to (and identity from) information groups and sources, and building hostility to 'othered' information groups and sources. This increases the chance that falsifying or complicating information will not be heard, and that people will have a suspicious attitude towards counter-information (which we called 'information paranoia'). The precarity of information workers means that they are less likely to risk speaking truth (as they see it) upwards, and that the information they provide can be destroyed or rendered invisible by those above them.

When information is defined as property, information flow is rendered nigh impossible by the need to profit. Patents and other boundaries disrupt the use of information; technically, scientifically and culturally, and allow power competitions to disrupt innovation. Furthermore, commercially or politically useful (rather than relatively 'accurate') information can be widely circulated, with attempts made to lessen people's knowledge that this information is commercial to help it become accepted. Bad information tends to drive out good. Awareness of these processes increases suspicion of all information and further magnifies information paranoia. All of these issues mean that the information needed to solve new problems can be disrupted, not discovered or not utilised. Here, the system continues to apply problem-solving techniques that do not work, or that generate intensification of the problems that need to be solved. Problems can be perceived as temporary failures of management, government or even human nature, rather than as signalling the need for a more thorough rethink. Neoliberalism, for example, continues to find overwhelming support from authorities, even in the face of financial crisis and precariousness post-2008. This application of superseded techniques (especially by relatively dominant groups) is not just evidenced in the political sphere, but it also permeates the financial and software spheres, and affects the way they function.

The difficulty of privatising information when people believe it should be freely available, and when it is relatively easy to duplicate and distribute with the very tools that are used to produce it, produces an ongoing series of battles that we have described in the chapters on file-sharing and academic knowledge. It almost certainly impossible to forecast the results of these conflicts, but we can see attempts by corporations to monopolise knowledge and culture, and its use, through utilisation of the legal system and apparently also through extra-legal means, with possible system-wide consequences. Protest can form spontaneously in disorderly and non-replicating swarms in the case of peer-to-peer 'pirates', as the legitimacy of free cultural use is reasserted, with some of these protests manifesting in Distributed Denial of Service attacks, in setting up more temporary nodes of resistance, in disorderly technological innovation and counter-innovation and even in offline political parties. Elsewhere, but with a similar dynamics, corporate publishing houses seek to monopolise prestigious academic journals, thus capturing and enclosing intellectual production. Many academics have proposed rejecting intellectual enclosure and embracing open publishing. However some such journals have the danger of being primarily profit-making ventures, charging authors for their work, with all the problems that generates for accuracy of information, proper peer-review and building a valued academic source with a consolidated tradition of innovation and fresh approaches to problems.

Similarly, we find that software applications contribute to a process of dramatic destabilisation in the field of international finance. Software is developed to increase the reach, speed and depth of finance flows, intensifying standard features of trade. These applications are devised in the context of, and contribute to, a growing financialisation of assets and a remarkable explosion in speculative innovation. New financial products create a new flux and flow, producing instability and volatility on an unprecedented scope and scale. Trading has tended to focus on the quickly realisable relative prices of things, rather than in investing in long-term company or economic values. This tendency has built upon the increasing inequalities of wealth, transferring wealth from productive usage to abstract usage, and has led to further systemic instability. Financial uncertainty fuelled by software becomes the life-blood of a speculative system that feeds off risk, but at the same time destabilises itself with booms and crashes, threatens the livelihoods of the general population and vastly increases wealth inequalities.

Finally, we looked at social movements and pointed to their innovative uses of the information and communication technology (ICT) that supports informational capitalism. Again, we found that ICT and networking brings both extensive possibilities and real difficulties into the field of social movement mobilisation. As social movements may be less hierarchical, they may be more able to perceive the problems in disinformationalism and propose solutions to them, than is possible for those heading hierarchies. However, this reflexive capacity is tempered by the inherent limitations of mobilisation through distributed informational networks, as against more institutionalised forms of engagement. These limitations can then translate into a failure of strategic capacity. It is hard to build and maintain a consistent information group with potentially fragmented and differing participants. The problems solved by protest are rarely similar to the problems generated by success. With Peoples' Global Action (PGA) the capacity to bridge online engagement with embodied protest action, as part of a global movement, brought remarkable results. But success ultimately overwhelmed the PGA. With relatively weak institutional structures it became difficult to enable the consensus-forming that was required, or to reduce fragmentation. Deliberation defaulted to cathartic protest, which had diminishing political leverage. The centre of gravity for developing movement agendas shifted elsewhere, into dialogic and face-to-face interactions as part of the World Social Forum and into institutionalised organisations as part of the wider Global Justice Movement.

These disinformational processes suggest that the ruling 'class' is not unified, fixed or particularly well informed. While that class is relatively powerful, every time they assert that power they risk the failure of its pathways or the triggering unexpected effects that might destabilise their power, produce rebels or increase disunity amongst them. Similarly, while social movements are unlikely to be unified without constant effort, even small actions could have systemic consequences, especially if performed regularly. There is a clear benefit in some degree of institutionalisation even though it risks alienating some participants, or being constrained and incorporated into the power structures and losing ground-level knowledge. Non-institutionalisation, and its swarm patterns, while effective in some cases, threatens dispersion, uncoordination, usurpation and uncertain policy. Neither side of the order/disorder complex should be emphasised at the cost of the other, and disordering effects of actions should be expected.

Part of the rationale for this book has been to make the point that the disordering exercise of power, as control and order, inevitably produces resistance and further disordering responses, leading to the possibility of counter-power, counter-counter-power or broader transformation. Power is thus generative, both of disorder and of alternative scenarios, which themselves generate new modes of being, action and power. Taking this approach into the field of informational capitalism and its dynamics, as played out in software applications, we have aimed to demonstrate that disinformational disordering processes lie at the heart of 'information society'. Central to this capitalist 'disinformation society' is a managerialism that is routinely deployed as a means of securing social order for the pursuit of profit. The routinisation of capitalist informational control, and lack of control, is orderly and disorderly but made invisible, woven into the fabric of disinformational existence. Yet, politicisation and contestation over such controls can become socially explosive: their very ubiquity and pervasiveness renders such controls highly vulnerable to self-disordering through intensification, extension and information disruption, or through distributed, swarmed and uncoordinated political challenge. In such contexts we can see something of the generative potential of orderly/disorderly behaviour and processes.

More generally, the book has argued the relatively obvious point that in complex systems (and all social/ecological systems are complex), there is also not just one point of power from which everything flows and which everything obeys. Neither can there be one agreed upon course of action. There are multitudes of agencies, resistances, disturbances, ignorances and knowledges. In these kinds of systems, policies, ideas and practices tend to have unexpected effects, which may increase the instability of the system. Peoples' attempts to produce what they call, or imagine as, order may produce what they call disorder. Rather than suppressing these disorderly effects, or declaring them to be unimportant in the wider scheme of things, or blaming them on others, or explaining them by saying that we have not yet applied our solutions thoroughly and rigorously enough, we should look out for these disordering effects and factor them into our thinking. Otherwise we declare data out of bounds, suppress the feedback provided by others, suppress those people who draw attention to the problems and/or risk making the situation worse by intensifying and extending our orders. We need to understand why our attempts at producing beneficial order do not work as we intend, so as to improve them and adapt to reality. What we call disorder needs to be observed and embraced, and we need to be aware of the ways it and disinformation are generated if we are to have any hope of survival.

Bibliography

Unless otherwise stated all internet references were active in July 2014.

4shared (2013) 4shared Terms of Service. Accessed 11 September 2013. http://wiki.4shared.com/index.php/Terms_of_use

Abbas, A. & McLean, M. (2001) Becoming Sociologists: Professional identity for part-time teachers of University Sociology. *British Journal of Sociology of Education* 22(3):339–52.

ABS (2013) *4602.0.55.005—Waste Account, Australia, Experimental Estimates, 2013*. Canberra: Australian Bureau of Statistics. www.abs.gov.au/ausstats/abs@.nsf/Products/4602.0.55.005~2013~Main+Features~Electronic+and+Electrical+Waste?OpenDocument

Abrahamson, E. (1996) Management Fashion. *Academy of Management Review* 21(1):254–85.

Abrahamson, E. & Freedman, D.H. (2006) *A Perfect Mess: The hidden benefits of disorder*. London: Weidenfeld & Nicolson.

Acaroglu, L. (4 May 2013) Where Do Old Cellphones Go to Die? *New York Times Sunday Review*. www.nytimes.com/2013/05/05/opinion/sunday/where-do-old-cellphones-go-to-die.html

Acohido, B. (5 January 2011) Cyberattacks on Company Websites Intensify. *USA Today*. www.usatoday.com/money/industries/technology/2011–01–05-cyberattacks05_ST_N.htm

Adams, S. (1996) *The Dilbert Principle*. New York: HarperBusiness.

Adler, J. (8 March 2012) Raging Bulls: How Wall Street got addicted to light-speed trading. *Wired*. www.wired.com/2012/08/ff_wallstreet_trading/all/

Adler, T.R. (2000) An Evaluation of the Social Perspective in the Development of Technical Requirements. *IEEE Transactions on Professional Communication* 43(4):386–96.

Agarwal, S., Joseph, D.A. & Padmanabhan, V.N. (2006) Addressing Email Loss with SureMail: Measurement, design, and evaluation. *Microsoft Research: Technical Report MSR-TR-2006–67*. http://research.microsoft.com/pubs/136893/usenix07.pdf

Aguilar, M. (25 September 2013) Your Gmail Was Down Because of a 'Dual Network Failure'. *Gizmodo*. http://gizmodo.com/your-gmail-has-been-messed-up-because-of-a-dual-networr-1377322661

Ahmed, R.E. (2006) Software Maintenance Outsourcing: Issues and strategies. *Computers and Electrical Engineering* 32:449–53.

Aitkenhead, D. (4 January 2014) Rory Stewart: 'The secret of modern Britain is there is no power anywhere'. *Guardian*. www.theguardian.com/politics/2014/jan/03/rory-stewart-interview

Al-Ahmad, W., Al-Fagih, K., Khanfar, K., Alsamara, K., Abuleil, S. & Abu-Salem, H. (2009) Taxonomy of an IT Project Failure: Root causes. *International Management Review* 5(1):93–104.

Albrecht, S. (1996) *Crisis Mangement for Corporate Self-Defense: How to protect your organization in a crisis . . . How to stop a crisis before it starts.* New York: Amacom.

Alford M. (1977) A Requirements Engineering Methodology for Real-time Processing Requirements. *IEEE Transactions on Software Engineering* 3(1):60–9.

Alford M. (1994) Attacking Requirements Complexity Using Separation of Concerns. *Proceedings of the IEEE First International Conference on Requirements Engineering (ICRE94).* Colorado Springs: IEEE Computer Society Press:2–5.

Allard, T. & Kenny, M. (24 October 2013) Contract Riches for Audit Chief. *Sydney Morning Herald.* www.smh.com.au/federal-politics/political-news/contract-riches-for-audit-chief-20131023–2w1w7.html

Allemang, J. (23 August 2008) What Ails the Economy? Too much ownership, author says. *Globe and Mail.* Accessed 10 October 2008. www.theglobeandmail.com/servlet/story/LAC.20080823.GRIDLOCK23/EmailTPStory/Focus

Ames, M. (23 January 2014) The Techtopus: How Silicon Valley's most celebrated CEOs conspired to drive down 100,000 tech engineers' wages. *PandoDaily.* http://pando.com/2014/01/23/the-techtopus-how-silicon-valleys-most-celebrated-ceos-conspired-to-drive-down-100000-tech-engineers-wages/

Amodio, M. (25 January 2011) Virginians Experience Massive Verizon Wireless Outage. *TMCnet.* http://voice-quality.tmcnet.com/topics/phone-service/articles/137982-virginians-experience-massive-verizon-wireless-outage.htm

Amsterdam, R.R. & Rothken, I.P. (2013) Megaupload, the Copyright Lobby, and the Future of Digital Rights. http://kim.com/whitepaper.pdf

Anderson, B. (1991) *Imagined Communities: Reflections on of the origins and spread of nationalism.* London: Verso.

Anderson, N. (24 January 2011) 25% of Files Downloaded from the Pirate Bay Are Fakes. *Ars Technica.* http://arstechnica.com/tech-policy/news/2011/01/25-of-files-downloaded-from-the-pirate-bay-are-fakes.ars

Anderson, N. (20 January 2012) Why the Feds Smashed Megaupload. *Ars Technica.* http://arstechnica.com/tech-policy/news/2012/01/why-the-feds-smashed-megaupload.ars

Andersson, J. (2010) *Peer-to-Peer-Based File-Sharing Beyond the Dichotomy of 'Downloading Is Theft' vs. 'Information Wants to Be Free': How Swedish filesharers motivate their action'.* Thesis. London: Goldsmiths University of London. http://ethos.bl.uk/OrderDetails.do?uin=uk.bl.ethos.523114

Andrews, W., Werner, A. & Dahler, D. (1 October 2013) Healthcare.gov Plagued by Crashes on 1st Day. *CBS News.* www.cbsnews.com/8301–18563_162–57605567/healthcare.gov-plagued-by-crashes-on-1st-day/

Andy (6 May 2013) Busting World's Biggest Movie Pirates Made Piracy Worse. *TorrentFreak.* Accessed 9 September 2013. http://torrentfreak.com/busting-worlds-biggest-movie-pirates-made-piracy-worse-130506

Andy (8 May 2013) 'New' Demonoid D2.vu Quickly Shutdown for Hosting Malware. *TorrentFreak.* http://torrentfreak.com/new-demonoid-d2-vu-quickly-shutdown-for-hosting-malware-130508/

Anon (4 January 2011) Qwest Internet Outage Repaired Service Was Restored To 5,000 DSL Customers Tuesday Night. *KRDO News.* Accessed 20 March 2011. www.krdo.com/news/26370401/detail.html

Anon (13 January 2011) Flood Affects CUA Online Customers. *Illawara Mercury.* www.illawarramercury.com.au/news/local/news/general/flood-affects-cua-online-customers/2046450.aspx

AP (24 February 2009) Gmail Crash Worldwide: Google pays for email outage with 15-day credit. *Huffington Post.* www.huffingtonpost.com/2009/02/24/gmail-crash-worldwide-goo_n_169637.html

APCA (22 June 2011) Media Release: Payments fraud in Australia. www.apca.com.au/docs/2011-media-releases/payments-fraud-statistics-for-calendar-year-2010.pdf

Arcand, J., Berkes, E. & Panizza, U. (2012) Too Much Finance? *IMF Working Paper* 12/161. www.imf.org/external/pubs/ft/wp/2012/wp12161.pdf

Arit, J. (8 October 2013) Now Faulty Private Contractor Software Is the Cause of the Obamacare Glitches. *The Wire.* www.theatlanticwire.com/politics/2013/10/now-private-contractor-error-cause-obamacare-glitches/70313/

Armitage, C. (31 October 2013) Unpicking Psychology of Conspiracy Theories a Dangerous Idea. *Sydney Morning Herald.* www.smh.com.au/nsw/unpicking-psychology-of-conspiracy-theories-a-dangerous-idea-20131031–2wmaf.html

ARN Staff (21 January 2011) Iinet Outage 01–2011–01–23. *ARNET.* www.arnnet.com.au/article/374143/updated_iinet_outage_hits_victorian_nsw_customers/

Arnold, D.N. & Cohn, H. (2012) Mathematicians Take a Stand. *Notices of the American Mathematical Society* 59(6):828–33. www.ams.org/notices/201206/rtx120600828p.pdf

Arquilla, J. & Ronfeldt, D. (1996) *The Advent of Netwar.* Santa Monica: RAND Corporation.

Arquilla, J. & Ronfeldt, D. (2001) *Networks and Netwars: The future of terror, crime, and militancy.* Santa Monica: RAND Corporation.

Arrighi, G., Silver, B.J. & Ahmad, I. (1999) *Chaos and Governance in the Modern World System.* Minneapolis: University of Minnesota Press.

Arthur, C. (13 July 2013) Thom Yorke Blasts Spotify on Twitter as He Pulls His Music. *Guardian.* www.theguardian.com/technology/2013/jul/15/thom-yorke-spotify-twitter

Arthur, C. (20 August 2013) Groklaw Legal Site Shuts Over Fears of NSA Email Snooping. *Guardian.* www.theguardian.com/technology/2013/aug/20/groklaw-shuts-nsa-surveillance

ARUP (2002) The Millenium Bridge—Challenge. http://web.archive.org/web/20020328094351/http://www.arup.com/millenniumbridge/index.html

Arup, T. (19 September 2013) Abbott Shuts Down Climate Commission. *Sydney Morning Herald.* www.smh.com.au/federal-politics/political-news/abbott-shuts-down-climate-commission-20130919–2u185.html

Asay, M. (21 January 2011) Pirates: Good for Microsoft, great for open sourcers. *Register.* www.theregister.co.uk/2011/01/21/the_plusses_of_pirates/

ASCE (2009) *2009 Report Card for America's Infrastructure.* Reston: American Society of Civil Engineers.

Atton, C. (2003) Reshaping Social Movement Media for a New Millennium. *Social Movement Studies* 2(1):3–15.

Ball, J., Harding, L. & Garside, J. (3 August 2013) BT and Vodafone Among Telecoms Companies Passing Details to GCHQ. *Guardian.* www.theguardian.com/business/2013/aug/02/telecoms-bt-vodafone-cables-gchq

Bamyeh, M. (2009) Fluid Solidarities: Affiliations beyond the nation. In P. James & J. Goodman (eds.) *Nationalism and Global Solidarities.* London: Routledge. pp:155–68.

Bano, M., & Zowghi, D. (2013). Users' Involvement in Requirements Engineering and System Success. *Proceedings of the 3rd IEEE International Workshop on Empirical Requirements Engineering (EmpiRE):* 24–31.

Bano, M., Zowghi, D., Ikram, N. & Niazi, M. (forthcoming). What Makes Service Oriented Requirements Engineering Challenging? A qualitative study. *IET Software.*

Barabasi, A. (2002) *Linked: The new science of networks.* Cambridge, MA: Perseus.

Barney, D. (2004). *The Network Society.* Cambridge: Polity.

Barth, F. (1992) Towards Greater Naturalism in Conceptualising Societies. In A. Kuper (ed.) *Conceptualizing Society*. London: Routledge. pp:17–33.

Bartlett, B. (14 December 2012) The Alarming Corruption of the Think Tanks. *Fiscal Times*. www.thefiscaltimes.com/Columns/2012/12/14/The-Alarming-Corruption-of-the-Think-Tanks

Bateson, G. (1972) *Steps to an Ecology of Mind*. San Francisco: Chandler.

Battersby, L. (13 January 2011) Telcos Battle to Maintain Services in Queensland. *Sydney Morning Herald*. www.smh.com.au/technology/technology-news/telcos-battle-to-maintain-services-in-queensland-20110112–19o6w.html

Battersby, L. (14 November 2011) Vodafone Seeks Compo for Network Problems. *Sydney Morning Herald*. www.smh.com.au/business/vodafone-seeks-compo-for-network-problems-20111113–1ndq5.html

Bazzichelli, T. (2013) *Networked Disruption: Rethinking oppositions in art, hacktivism and the business of social networking*. Digital Aesthetics Research Center, Aarhus University. http://disruptiv.biz/networked-disruption-the-book

BBC (15 June 1999) Grunge versus greed. *BBC News*. http://news.bbc.co.uk/2/hi/uk_news/370060.stm

BBC (16 August 2008) Lawsuit Threat to Merrill Lynch. *BBC News*. http://news.bbc.co.uk/2/hi/business/7564630.stm

BBC (5 January 2011) US Urges Action to Prevent Insider Leaks. *BBC News*. www.bbc.co.uk/news/world-us-canada-12117113

BBC (10 January 2011) Microsoft Investigates 'Phantom' Windows Phone 7 Data. *BBC News*. www.bbc.co.uk/news/technology-12152517

BBC (7 March 2011) Cyber Attack on France Targeted Paris G20 Files. *BBC News*. www.bbc.co.uk/news/business-12662596

BBC (18 April 2012) Google Tackles Temporary Gmail Access Failure. *BBC News*. www.bbc.com/news/technology-17748971

BBC (9 August 2012) Demonoid Takedown Prompts Attacks by Anonymous. *BBC News*. Accessed 9 September 2013. www.bbc.co.uk/news/technology-19194467

Beale, J. (2013) Predatory Publishing Is Just One of the Consequences of Gold Open Access. *Learned Publishing* 26(2):79–83.

Beaumont, C. (24 February 2009) Google's Gmail Service Crashes Across World. *Telegraph*. www.telegraph.co.uk/technology/google/4797727/Googles-Gmail-service-crashes-across-world.html

Beck, U. (1992) *Risk Society: Towards a new modernity*. London: Sage.

Beck, U. (2009) *World at Risk*. Cambridge: Polity.

Beck, U. & Lau, C. (2005) Second Modernity as a Research Agenda: Theoretical and empirical explorations in the 'meta-change' of modern society. *British Journal of Sociology* 56(4):525–57.

Beck, U. & Wehling, P. (2012) Politics of Non-knowing. In P. Baert & F. Domínguez Rubio (eds.) *The Politics of Knowledge*. London: Routledge.

Beddoes, Z.M. (13 October 2012) For Richer, for Poorer. *Economist*. www.economist.com/node/21564414

Beer, D. (2009) Power through the Algorithm? Participatory web cultures and the technological unconscious. *New Media & Society* 11(6):985–1002.

Belkin, L. (6 January 2011) Facebook vs. Nursing Moms, Round 2. *NY Times Blogs*. http://parenting.blogs.nytimes.com/2011/01/06/facebook-vs-nursing-moms-round-2/

Bell, A. (7 September 2012) Death by Agile Fever. *InfoQ*. www.infoq.com/articles/death-by-agile-fever

Bell, D. (1971) Technocracy and Politics. *Survey: A Journey of East and West Studies* 17(1):1–24.

Bell, D. (1976) *The Coming of Post-Industrial Society: A venture in social forecasting*. Harmondsworth: Penguin.

Bell, D. (1980) The Social Framework of the Information Society *and* A Reply to Weizenbaum. In T. Forrester (ed.) *The Microelectronics Revolution: The complete guide to the new technology and its impact on society.* Oxford: Basil Blackwell. pp:500–49, 571–4.

Bellegarrigue, A. (1850/2002) *Anarchist Manifesto.* London: Kate Sharpley Library.

Bender, B. (11 August 2013) Many D.C. Think Tanks Now Players in Partisan Wars. *Boston Globe.* www.bostonglobe.com/news/nation/2013/08/10/brain-trust-for-sale-the-growing-footprint-washington-think-tank-industrial-complex/7ZifHfrLPlbz0bSeVOZHdl/story.html

Beniger, J. (1986) *The Control Revolution: Technological and economic origins of the information society.* Cambridge, MA: Harvard UP.

Bennett, K.H. & Rajlich, V.T. (2000) Software Maintenance and Evolution: A roadmap. In A. Finkelstein (ed.) *The Future of Software Engineering.* ACM Press 2000. www0.cs.ucl.ac.uk/staff/A.Finkelstein/fose/finalbennett.pdf

Bergman M., King J.L. & Lyytinen, K. (2002) Large-Scale Requirements Analysis Revisited: The need for understanding the political ecology of requirements engineering. *Requirements Engineering Journal* 7(3):152–71.

Bergstrom, T.C. (2001) Free Labor for Costly Journals? *Journal of Economic Perspectives* 15(3):183–98. http://escholarship.org/uc/item/1wf0r099

Bergstrom, T.C. (2010) Librarians and the Terrible Fix: Economics of the Big Deal. *Serials* 23(2):77–82. http://works.bepress.com/ted_bergstrom/111

Berner, R. (28 May 2006) I Sold It Through the Grapevine. *Business Week.* www.businessweek.com/stories/2006-05-28/i-sold-it-through-the-grapevine

Berry, D. (2012) The Relevance of Understanding Code to International Political Economy. *International Politics* 49(2):277–96.

Berry D.M. (1992) *Academic Legitimacy of the Software Engineering Discipline.* Software Engineering Institute, Carnegie Mellon University, Technical Report CMU/SEI-92-TR-34.

Berry, J. (2005) *Reclaiming the Ivory Tower.* New York: Monthly Review Press.

Besley, T. & 32 others (2009) Letter to the Queen. *British Academy.* www.britac.ac.uk/templates/asset-relay.cfm?frmAssetFileID=9149

Bessen, J., Ford, J. & Meurer, M.J. (2011) The Private and Social Cost of Patent Trolls. *Boston University School of Law Working Paper* No. 11–45. www.bu.edu/law/faculty/scholarship/workingpapers/2011.html

Best, J. (2006) *Flavor of the Month: Why smart people fall for fads.* Berkley: University of California Press.

Beunza, D., Hardie, I. & Mackenzie, D. (2006) A Price Is a Social Thing: Towards a material sociology of arbitrage. *Organization Studies* 27(5):721–45.

Beunza, D. & Stark, D. (2012) Seeing Through the Eyes of Others: Dissonance within and across trading rooms. In K. Knorr-Cetina & A. Preda (eds.) *Oxford Handbook of the Sociology of Finance.* Oxford: Oxford University Press. pp:203–22.

Bezemer, D.J. (2009) 'No One Saw This Coming': Understanding financial crisis through accounting models. *Munich Personal RePEc Archive Paper No. 15892.* http://mpra.ub.uni-muenchen.de/15892/

BIS (2004) Triennial Central Bank Survey of Foreign Exchange and Derivatives Market Activity in April 2004. *Bank of International Settlements.* www.bis.org/publ/rpfx04.pdf

BIS (2012) BIS Quarterly Review: June 2012. *Bank of International Settlements.* www.bis.org/publ/qtrpdf/r_qt1206.htm

Blair, T. (25 October, 1999) Why the Internet Years Are Vital. *Guardian.* www.guardian.co.uk/uk/1999/oct/25/5

Block, L. (2001) Comment on Prendagast's "A Theory of 'Yes Men'". *Quarterly Journal of Austrian Economics* 4(2):61–8.

Bode, K. & Dale, L. (2012) 'Bullshit'? An Australian Perspective; Or, what can an organisational change impact statement tell us about Higher Education in Australia? *Australian Humanities Review* 53. www.australianhumanitiesreview.org/archive/Issue-November-2012/bode&dale.html

Boehm B.W. (1976) Software engineering. *IEEE Transactions on Computers* 25(12):1226–41.

Boehm B.W. (1981) *Software Engineering Economics*. Englewood Cliffs, NJ: Prentice-Hall.

Boehm B.W. (1984) Verifying and Validating Software Requirements and Design Specifications. *IEEE Software* 1(1):75–88.

Boehm B.W. (1988) A Spiral Model of Software Development and Enhancement. *IEEE Computer* 28(5):61–72.

Boehm B.W. & Papaccio P.N. (1988) Understanding and Controlling Software Costs. *IEEE Transactions on Software Engineering* 14(10):1462–77.

Boehm, B. & Turner, R. (2004) *Balancing Agility and Discipline: A guide for the perplexed*. Boston: Addison-Wesley.

Boehm B.W. & Turner R. (2005) Management Challenges to Implementing Agile Processes in Traditional Development Organizations. *IEEE Software* 22(5):30–9.

Bolton, P. & Scheinkman, J. (2011) Cream Skimming in Financial Markets. *National Bureau of Economic Research Working Paper* 16804. www.nber.org/papers/w16804

Bonds, E. (2011) The Knowledge-Shaping Process: Elite mobilization and environmental policy. *Critical Sociology* 37(4):429–46.

Bosker, B. (20 January 2011) Gmail Problems: Users report slow service. *Huffington Post*. www.huffingtonpost.com/2011/01/20/gmail-problems-slow-service_n_811775.html

Botsman, R. & Rogers, R. (2010) *What's Mine Is Yours: The rise of collaborative consumption*. New York: HarperCollins.

Bouc, A. (26 January 2014) Gmail Outage Caused by Software Bug Yahoo Shares on Twitter Apologizes. *Liberty Voice*. http://guardianlv.com/2014/01/gmail-outage-caused-by-software-bug-yahoo-shares-on-twitter-apologizes/

Bowcott, O., Siddique, H. & Sparrow, A. (17 August 2011) Facebook Cases Trigger Criticism of 'Disproportionate' Riot Sentences. *Guardian*. www.guardian.co.uk/uk/2011/aug/17/facebook-cases-criticism-riot-sentences

Brandt, J.R. (1 November 2001) Beware of Bad Buzz. *Chief Executive.net*. http://chiefexecutive.net/beware-of-bad-buzz

Brecher, J., Costello, T. & Smith, B. (2000) *Globalisation from Below: The power of solidarity*. Cambridge, MA: South End Press.

Broad, W.J., Markoff, J.E & Sanger, D.E. (15 January 2011) Israeli Test on Worm Called Crucial in Iran Nuclear Delay. *New York Times*. www.nytimes.com/2011/01/16/world/middleeast/16stuxnet.html

Brooks, F.P. (1987) No Silver Bullet: Essence and accidents of software engineering. *IEEE Computer* 20(4):10–19.

Brooks, F.P. (1995) *The Mythical Man-Month: 20th anniversary edition*. Boston: Addison-Wesley.

Brown, A., Goodman, J. & Yasukawa, K. (2010) Academic Casualisation in Australia: A new class divide? *Journal of Industrial Relations* 52(2):169–82.

Brown, A.K. (2 February 2011) Rolling Outages Affect Most Chilly Texans All Day. *Houston Chronicle*. www.deseretnews.com/article/700106509/Rolling-outages-affect-most-chilly-Texans-all-day.html

Brulle, R.J. (2014) Institutionalizing Delay: Foundation funding and the creation of U.S. climate change counter-movement organizations. *Climatic Change* 122(4): 681–94.

Bruns, A., Burgess, J., Crawford, J. & Shaw, F. (2012) *#qldfloods and @QPSMedia: Crisis communication on Twitter in the 2011 South East Queensland Floods.* Brisbane: ARC Centre of Excellence for Creative Industries and Innovation.

Bryson, C. (2004) What about the Workers? The expansion of higher education and the transformation of academic work. *Industrial Relations Journal* 35(1):38–57.

BSI (nd) Wobbly Start to the Millennium. *BSI Education.* www.bsieducation.org/ Education/downloads/case_studies/Bridges.pdf

Buchanan, M. (2002) *Nexus: Small worlds and the groundbreaking science of networks.* New York: W.W. Norton.

Buldyrev, S.V., Parshani, R., Paul, G., Stanley, H.E. & Havlin, S. (2010) Catastrophic Cascade of Failures in Interdependent Networks. *Nature* 464(April):1025–28.

Bunge, J. & Or, A. (13 October 2013) Ex-Citadel Employee Arrested in Alleged Code Theft. *Wall Street Journal.* http://online.wsj.com/news/articles/SB1000142 4052970203914304576629052474403830

Burdon, P. & Hearth, M. (2013) Academic Resistance to the Neoliberal University. *Legal Education Review* 23(2):379–401

Burnham, J. (1941) *The Managerial Revolution: What is happening in the world.* New York: John Day.

Burns, J.F. & Somaiya, R. (1 May 2012) Panel in Hacking Case Finds Murdoch Unfit as News Titan. *New York Times.* Accessed 6 September 2013. www.nytimes. com/2012/05/02/world/europe/murdoch-hacking-scandal-to-be-examined-by-british-parliamentary-panel.html

Burstein, D. & Kline, D. (1995) *Road Warriors: Dreams and nightmares along the information highway.* New York: Dutton.

Burt, F. (2011) Internet Outage Means Long Lines At AA Ticket Counter: Departing flights may be affected. WESH. Accessed 20 March 2011. www.wesh.com/r/ 26403145/detail.html

CA Technologies (2011) *The Avoidable Cost of Downtime Phase 2.* CA Technologies. Accessed 18 March 2013. www.arcserve.com/us/lpg/~/media/Files/Supporting Pieces/ARCserve/avoidable-cost-of-downtime-summary-phase-2.pdf

Cabinet Office (12 January 2011) Public Data Corporation to Free Up Public Data and Drive Innovation. *UK Cabinet Office.* www.cabinetoffice.gov.uk/news/ public-data-corporation-free-public-data-and-drive-innovation

Calhoun, C. (1993) 'New Social Movements' of the Early Nineteenth Century. *Social Science History* 17(3):385–427.

Callender, C. (2012) The 2012/13 Reforms of Higher Education in England: Changing student finances and funding. In M. Kilkey, G. Ramia & K. Farnsworth (eds.) *Social Policy Review 24: Analysis and debate in social policy.* Bristol: The Policy Press. pp:77–96.

Callinicos, A. (2006) *Universities in a Neoliberal World.* London: Bookmarks.

Cancer Voices SA (2008) RAH Cancer Patient's Radiotherapy Dosing Errors. www. cancervoicessa.org.au/assets/documents/CVSA_radiotherapy_concerns_.pdf

Canfora, G. & Cimitile, A. (2001) Software Maintenance. In S.K. Chang (ed.) *Handbook of Software Engineering and Knowledge Engineering, Vol. 1.* River Edge, NJ: World Scientific. pp:91–120.

Caravanos, J. (2010) Report from Ghana's Agbogbloshie E-Wasteland. *Pollution Blog Blacksmith Institute.* www.blacksmithinstitute.org/blog/report-from-ghanas-agbogbloshie-e-wasteland/

Carey, K. & Dillon, E. (2011) Debt to Degree: A new way of measuring college success. http://staging.completionmatters.org/sites/default/files/debt_to_degree_cyct_release.pdf

Carmichael, H. (26 January 2011) Blame the Cold Weather. *Sudbury Star* www. thesudburystar.com/ArticleDisplay.aspx?e=2947201

Carrier, M.A. (2012) Copyright and Innovation: The untold story. *Wisconsin Law Review* 891(24):891–962. http://wisconsinlawreview.org/wp-content/files/2-Carrier.pdf

Carrier, M.A. (2013) SOPA, PIPA, ACTA, TPP: An alphabet soup of innovation-stifling copyright legislation and agreements. *Northwestern Journal of Technology and Intellectual Property* 11(2):21–31. http://scholarlycommons.law.northwestern.edu/cgi/viewcontent.cgi?article=1179&context=njtip

Carroll, W. (2010) Crisis, Movements, Counter-hegemony: In search of the new. *Interface* 2(2):168–98.

Cast (2011) *The CRASH Report—2011/12: Summary of key findings*. www.castsoftware.com/resources/resource/whitepapers/cast-report-on-application-software-health

Cast (8 December 2011) New Worldwide Software Quality Study from CAST Exposes Millions in Hidden IT Costs. www.castsoftware.com/news-events/press-release/press-releases/new-worldwide-software-quality-study-from-cast-exposes-millions-in-hidden-it-costs

Castells, M. (2000a) *The Rise of the Network Society: The Information Age: Economy, Society and Culture Vol. I*. 2nd Edition. Oxford: Blackwell.

Castells, M. (2000b) *The Power of Identity: The Information Age: Economy, Society and Culture Vol. II*. 2nd Edition. Oxford: Blackwell.

Castells, M. (2000c) *End of Millennium. The Information Age: Economy, Society and Culture Vol. III*. 2nd Edition. Oxford: Blackwell

Castells, M. (2000d) Materials for an Exploratory Theory of the Network Society. *British Journal of Sociology* 51(1):5–24.

Castells, M. (2001) *Internet Galaxy: Reflections on the internet, business and society*. Oxford: Oxford University Press.

Castells, M. (2004) Informationalism, Networks and the Network Society. In Castells, M. (ed.) *The Network Society: A cross-cultural perspective*. Northampton, MA: Edward Elgar. pp:3–47.

Castells, M. (2005) Space of Flows, Space of Places: Materials for a theory of urbanisation in the information age. In Sanyal Bishwapriya (ed.) *Comparative Planning Cultures*. New York: Routledge. pp:45–66.

Castells, M. (2009) *Communication Power*. Oxford: Oxford University Press.

Castells, M. (2011) A Network Theory of Power. *International Journal of Communication* 5:773–87. http://ijoc.org/index.php/ijoc/article/view/1136/553

Castells, M. (2012) *Networks of Outrage and Hope: Social movements in the internet age*. Polity: Cambridge.

CDT (2006) Following the Money: How advertising dollars encourage nuisance and harmful adware and what can be done to reverse the trend. *Center for Democracy and Technology*. 2 May 2006 Update. www.cdt.org/privacy/20060320adware.pdf

Cecchetti, S. & Kharroubi, E. (2012) Reassessing the Impact of Finance and Growth. *BIS Working Paper No. 381*. Basle: Bank for International Settlements.

Cecchetti, S. & Kharroubi, E. (2013) Why Does Financial Sector Growth Crowd Out Real Economic Growth? Paper to the conference: *Finance and the Welfare of Nations, Institute for New Economic Thinking and the Federal Reserve Bank of San Francisco*, San Francisco, 27 September 2013. https://evbdn.eventbrite.com/s3-s3/eventlogos/67785745/cecchetti.pdf

Chaboud, A., Chiquoine, B., Hjalmarsson, E. & Vega, C. (2009) Rise of the Machines: Algorithmic trading in the foreign exchange market. *International Finance Discussion Paper*, Federal Reserve Board, Washington. www.federalreserve.gov/pubs/ifdp/2009/980/ifdp980.pdf

Charette, R.N. (2005) Why Software Fails. *IEEE Spectrum*: 42(9):42–9.

Chatterjee, P. (11 May 2012) Elsevier Versus Wikipedia: Academics revolt against giant publisher. *CorpWatch Blog*. www.corpwatch.org/article.php?id=15725

Chatzoglou P.D. & Macaulay L.A. (1996) Requirements Capture and Analysis: A survey of current practice. *Requirements Engineering* 1(2):75–84.

Chechik, M. & Easterbrook, S.M. (2001) Reasoning About Compositions of Concerns. *Proceedings, Workshop on Advanced Separation of Concerns in Software Engineering, at the 23rd International Conference on Software Engineering (ICSE-01)*, Toronto, Canada.

Cheng, B.H. & Atlee, J.M. (2007). Research Directions in Requirements Engineering. In *2007 Future of Software Engineering*. IEEE Computer Society:285–303.

Cheng, J. (6 January 2011) IE Zero-day Bug Leads to Squabble Between Microsoft, Researcher. *Ars Technica*. http://arstechnica.com/information-technology/2011/01/internet-explorer-zero-day-bug-leads-to-squabble/

Chirgwin R. (12 January 2011) Flood Isolates Internode in Qld. *Register*. www.theregister.co.uk/2011/01/12/qld_floods_internode_down/

Chirgwin R. (27 January 2013) Brisbane Online Flood Maps Woefully Inadequate: No search, no reproduction, and mobile sucks. *Register* www.theregister.co.uk/2013/01/27/brisbane_flood_maps/

Christopher, R. (2003) McKenzie Wark: To the vector the spoils. http://roychristopher.com/mckenzie-wark-to-the-vector-the-spoils

CIA (2012) Field Listing: GDP. *World Factbook*. www.cia.gov/library/publications/the-world-factbook/fields/2195.html

Clarke, R. & Knake, R. (2010) *Cyber War*. New York: HarperCollins.

Cleaver, H. (1994) *Zapatistas! Documents of the New Mexican Revolution*. New York: Autonomedia.

Cleaver, H. (1998) The Zapatista Effect: The Internet and the rise of an alternative political fabric. *Journal of International Affairs* 51(2):621–40.

CNN (18 June 1999) Anti-capitalists Rampage: From Sydney to Senegal: 'J18' activists target big money. *CNN Money*. http://money.cnn.com/1999/06/18/worldbiz/protest/

CNN (24 September 2009) Gmail Service Has Trouble—again. *CNN*. http://edition.cnn.com/2009/TECH/09/24/gmail.crash/index.html

Codd, P. (17 December 2012) Top 10 Software Failures Of 2012. *BCW*. www.businesscomputingworld.co.uk/top-10-software-failures-of-2012/

Coelho, P. (2008) Pirate Coelho. Accessed 8 September 2013. http://paulocoelhoblog.com/2008/02/03/pirate-coelho

Cohn M. & Ford D. (2003) Introducing an Agile Process to an Organization. *IEEE Computer* 36(6):74–8.

Colander, D. (2011) How Economists Got It Wrong: A nuanced account. *Critical Review: A Journal of Politics and Society* 23(1–2):1–27.

Coleman, G. (2012) *Coding Freedom: The ethics and aesthetics of hacking*. Princeton, NJ: Princeton University Press.

Collins, R. (1975) *Conflict Sociology: Toward an explanatory science*. New York: Academic Press.

Collins, T. (23 May 2007) Joe Harley, CIO at the Department for Work and Pensions— Suppliers will give us some home truths in July. *ComputerWeekly blogs*. www.computerweekly.com/blogs/public-sector/2007/05/joe-harley-cio-at-the-departme-1.html

Committee on Indian Affairs (2006) 'Gimme Five': Investigation of tribal lobbying matters. https://web.archive.org/web/20130406170722/http://www.indian.senate.gov/public/_files/Report.pdf

Constantine, J. (13 February 2012) BitTorrent Live: Cheap, real-time P2P video streaming that will kill TV. *TechCrunch*. Accessed 8 September 2013. http://techcrunch.com/2012/02/13/bittorrent-live

ConsumerAffairs (15 March 2005) Merrill Lynch to Pay $10 Million in New Jersey Settlement: Failed to adequately supervise its advisers. www.consumeraffairs.com/news04/2005/nj_merrill.html http://archive.is/8BCY

Consumer Reports (June 2011) House of Cards: Why your accounts are vulnerable to thieves. www.consumerreports.org/cro/magazine-archive/2011/june/money/credit-card-fraud/overview/index.htm

Conway, J. (2013) *Edges of Global Justice: The World Social Forum and its 'others'*. New York: Routledge.

Corkery, J. & Zornada, K. (2012) High-frequency Trading and a Financial Transactions Tax. *Revenue Law Journal* 22(1):1–8.

Corporate Watch and Reclaim the Streets (1999) *Squaring Up to the Square Mile: A rough guide to the City of London*. London: RTS. Accessed 19 November 2013. www.indymedia.org.uk/en/2009/03/425118.html

Coser L.A. (1977) *Masters of Sociological Thought: Ideas in historical and social context*. New York: Harcourt, Brace, Jovanovitch.

Couch, J. (2001) Imagining Zapatismo: The anti-globalisaton movement and the Zapatistas. *Communual/Plural* 9(2):243–60.

Cox, J., Collins, A. & Drinkwater, S. (2010) Seeders, Leechers and Social Norms: Evidence from the market for illicit digital downloading. *Information Economics and Policy* 22(4):299–305.

Craighill, P.M. & Clement, S. (21 October 2013) Poll: Majority believe health-care web site problems indicate broader issue with law. *Washington Post*. www.washingtonpost.com/blogs/the-fix/wp/2013/10/21/poll-healthcare-website-omen-for-broader-problems-most-say/

Credit Suisse (2013) *Global Wealth Report 2013*. http://images.smh.com.au/file/2013/10/09/4815797/cs_global_wealth_report_2013_WEB_low%2520pdf.pdf?

Critical Art Ensemble (1994) *The Electronic Disturbance*. New York: Autonomedia. www.critical-art.net/books/ted

Crockett, R. (1994) *Thinking the Unthinkable: Think-tanks and the economic counter-revolution 1931–1983*. London: HarperCollins.

CTJ (2011) Analysis: 12 corporations pay effective tax rate of negative 1.4% on $175 billion in profits. Citizens for Tax Justice. www.ctj.org/pdf/12corps060111.pdf

Cunnigham, P.W., Cheney, K. & Kenen, J. (8 October 2013) Major Software Failure Caused Obamacare Glitches. *Politico Pulse*. www.politico.com/politicopulse/1013/politicopulse11859.html

Curran, J., Coen, S., Aalberg, T., Hayashi, K., Jones, P.K., Splendore, S., Papathanassopoulos, S., Rowe, D. & Tiffen, R. (2013) Internet Revolution Revisited: A comparative study of online news. *Media Culture Society* 35(7):880–97.

Curtis, J.W. & Thornton, S. (2013) *Here's the News: The Annual Report on the economic status of the profession*. American Association of University Professors. www.aaup.org/file/2012–13Economic-Status-Report.pdf

Curtis, P. (30 December 2010) Ministers Must 'Wise Up Not Clam Up' After WikiLeaks Disclosures. *Guardian*. www.guardian.co.uk/politics/2010/dec/30/wikileaks-freedom-information-ministers-government

da Rimini, F. (2013a) The Tangled Hydra: Developments in transglobal peer-to-peer culture. *Global Networks* 13(3):310–29.

da Rimini, F. (2013b) Re-inscribing the City: Art, occupation, and citizen journalism in Hong Kong. *Globalizations* 10(3):465–79.

da Rimini, F. & Marshall, J. (forthcoming 2014) Piracy Is Normal, Piracy Is Boring: Systemic disruption as everyday life. In M. Fredriksson & J. Arvanitakis (eds.) *Piracy: Leakages from modernity*. Los Angeles: Litwin Press.

Daley, K. (21 January 1999) Olympic Games Report Shows 'Decades of Bribery'. *Independent*. www.independent.co.uk/sport/olympic-games-ioc-report-shows-decades-of-bribery-1075358.html

Daly, E. (1977) Management of Software Development. *IEEE Transactions on Computers* 3(3):229–42.

Darwin, C.R. (1882) *The Formation of Vegetable Mould, Through the Action of Worms, with Observations on Their Habits*. Seventh thousand. Corrected by Francis Darwin. London: John Murray. http://darwin-online.org.uk/content/frameset?itemID=F1364&viewtype=text&pageseq=1

Das, S. (2006) *Traders, Guns & Money: Knowns and unknowns in the dazzling world of derivatives*. Harlow: Prentice Hall and Financial Times.

Davidson, D. & Maher, S. (9 August 2013) NBN is Good for Business: Foxtel unpicks PM's conspiracy theory. *Australian*. www.theaustralian.com.au/national-affairs/election-2013/nbn-is-good-for-business-foxtel-unpicks-pms-conspiracy-theory/story-fn9qr68y-1226693893994

Davis, A., Dieste, O., Hickey, A., Juristo, N. & Moreno, A.M. (2006) Effectiveness of Requirements Elicitation Techniques: Empirical results derived from a systematic review. *Proceedings of Requirements Engineering, 14th IEEE International Conference*: 176–85.

Davis, A.M. (1993) *Software Requirements: Analysis and Specification*. 2nd Edition. Englewood: Prentice Hall.

Davis, A.M. & Hickey, A.M. (2002). Requirements Researchers: Do we practice what we preach? *Requirements Engineering* 7(2):107–11.

Davis, A.M., Jordan K. & Nakajima T. (1997) Elements Underlying the Specification of Requirements. *Annals of Software Engineering, Special Issue on Software Requirements Engineering* 3(1):63–100.

Davis, G.F., Yoo, M. & Baker, W.E. (2003) The Small World of the American Corporate Elite, 1982–2001. *Strategic Organization* 1:301–26.

De Angelis, M. & Harvie, D. (2009) 'Cognitive Capitalism' and the Rat-Race: How capital measures immaterial labour in British universities. *Historical Materialism* 17(3):3–30.

De Carbonnel, A. (30 May 2013) Billions Stolen in Sochi Olympics Preparations-Russian Opposition. *Reuters*. www.reuters.com/article/2013/05/30/us-olympics-sochi-corruption-idUSBRE94T0RU20130530

de la Merced, M. & Story, L. (11 February 2009) Nearly 700 at Merrill in Million-Dollar Club. *New York Times*. www.nytimes.com/2009/02/12/business/12merrill.html

de Neef, M. (2012) Anonymous Launches Largest-Ever Attack in Defence of Megaupload. *Conversation*. Accessed 11 September 2013. http://theconversation.edu.au/anonymous-launches-largest-ever-attack-in-defence-of-megaupload-4989

De Roover, R. (1999) *The Rise and Decline of the Medici Bank: 1397–1494*. Washington: Beard Books.

De Schutter (2010) Food Commodities Speculation and Food Price Crises. *Briefing Note: 2*. Office of the United Nations High Commissioner for Human Rights. www2.ohchr.org/english/issues/food/docs/Briefing_Note_02_September_2010_EN.pdf

De Souza, M. (27 December 2013) Harper Government Cutting More than $100 Million Related to Protection of Water. *Canada.com*. http://o.canada.com/technology/environment/harper-government-cutting-more-than-100-million-related-to-protection-of-water/

Dean, J. (2005) Communicative Capitalism: Circulation and the foreclosure of politics. *Cultural Politics* 1(1):51–74.

Dean, J. (2009) *Democracy and Other Neoliberal Fantasies: Communicative capitalism and left politics*. Durham: Duke University Press.

Dearden, L., Fitzsimons, E. & Wyness, G. (2011) The Impact of Tuition Fees and Support on University Participation in the UK. *Institute for Fiscal Studies Working Papers*. www.ifs.org.uk/wps/wp1117.pdf

Decker, S. (25 January 2011) Microsoft Files Complaint to Stop TiVo From Importing TV Set-Top Boxes. *Bloomberg*. www.bloomberg.com/news/2011-01-24/microsoft-files-trade-case-against-tivo-over-set-top-boxes.html

Delaney, G., Oliver, L. & Coleman, R. (2008) Review of the Radiation Incident at Royal Adelaide Hospital Report 15/08/2008. www.researchgate.net/publication/36722719_Review_of_the_radiation_incident_at_Royal_Adelaide_Hospital_report_15808

Deleuze, G. (1995) Control and Becoming and Postscript on Control Societies. In G. Deleuze *Negotiations 1972–1990*. New York: Columbia UP: 169–82.

Dellarocas, C. (2006). Strategic Manipulation of Internet Opinion Forums: Implications for consumers and firms. *Management Science* 52(10):1577–93.

DeMarco, T. (2001) *Slack: Getting past burnout, busywork and the myth of total efficiency*. New York: Dorest House.

Demonoid (2014) Newspost. Accessed 20 June 2014. www.demonoid.ph

Deneault, A. (2011) *Offshore: Tax Havens and the rule of global crime*. New York: New Press.

Department of Broadband, Communications and the Digital Economy (2012) *Convergence Review Final Report*. Canberra: Commonwealth of Australia.

Department of Fisheries and Oceans (19 December 2013) Libraries FAQ. www.dfo-mpo.gc.ca/libraries-bibliotheques/FAQ-eng.htm

Department of Foreign Affairs and Trade (2004) *Australia-United States Free Trade Agreement—Guide to the Agreement*. Canberra: Commonwealth of Australia. www.dfat.gov.au/fta/ausfta/guide/17.html

Derrida, J. (1973) *Speech and Phenomena and Other Essays on Husserl's Theory of Signs*. Evanston: Northwestern University Press.

Derrida, J (1988) *Limited Inc*. Evanston: Northwestern University Press.

Dervin, B. & Foreman-Wernet, L. (2003) *Sense-Making Methodology Reader*. New Jersey: Hampton Press.

DeVoss, D.N. & Porter, J.E. (2006) Why Napster Matters to Writing: Filesharing as a new ethic of digital delivery. *Computers and Composition* 23(2):178–210.

Diamond, B. & Kollar, M. (1989) *24-Hour Trading: The global network of futures and options markets*. New Jersey: John Wiley and Sons.

Diani, M. (2001) Social Movement Networks, Virtual and Real. In F. Webster (ed.) *Culture and politics in the information age*. London: Routledge. pp:117–29.

Do or Die (18 June 1999) Confronting Capital and Smashing the State. *Do or Die* 8:1–12. www.eco-action.org/dod/no8/j18.html

Dobele, A., Lindgreen, A., Beverland, M., Vanhamme, J. & van Wijk, R. (2007) Why Pass on Viral Messages? Because they connect emotionally. *Business Horizons* 50(4):291–304.

DOJ (2011) CPTN Holdings LLC and Novell Inc. Change Deal in Order to Address Department of Justice's Open Source Concerns. *US Department of Justice*. www.justice.gov/opa/pr/2011/April/11-at-491.html

Dominguez, J. (16 June 2009) The CHAOS Report 2009 on IT Project Failure. *Project Management Hut*. www.pmhut.com/the-chaos-report-2009-on-it-project-failure

Dorling, P. (29 August 2013) Spy Agency Taps Undersea Cables. *Sydney Morning Herald*. www.smh.com.au/national/spy-agency-taps-undersea-cables-2013 0828-2squf.html

Dorling, P. (24 November 2013) New Snowden Leaks Reveal US, Australia's Asian Allies. *Age*. www.theage.com.au/technology/technology-news/new-snowden-leaks-reveal-us-australias-asian-allies-20131124-2y3mh.html

Douglas, M. (1969) *Purity and Danger: An analysis of concepts of pollution and taboo*. London: Routledge and Kegan Paul.

Drucker, P. (1969) *The Age of Discontinuity: Guidelines to our changing society*. New York: Harper & Row.

Drucker, P. (1993) *Post-Capitalist Society*. New York: HarperCollins.

Duff, A.S. (1998) Daniel Bell's Theory of the Information Society. *Journal of Information Science* 24(6):373–93.

Dupuis, J. (20 May 2013) The Canadian War on Science: A long, unexaggerated, devastating chronological indictment. http://scienceblogs.com/confessions/2013/05/20/the-canadian-war-on-science-a-long-unexaggerated-devastating-chronological-indictment/

Durkheim, E. (1982) *The Rules of Sociological Method and Selected Texts on Sociology and its Method*. Edited by S. Lukes. New York: Free Press.

Dyer-Witheford, N. (1999) *Cyber-Marx: Cycles and circuits of struggle in high technology capitalism*. Urbana: University of Illinois Press.

Dynamic Markets Ltd (2007) *IT Projects: Experience certainty*. Independent Market Research Report. Abergavenny: Dynamic Markets Ltd. www.tcs.com/Insights/Documents/independant_markets_research_report.pdf

Eaton, N. (19 January 2011) Microsoft Nails Down Windows Phone 7 Data-Uploading Issue. *Seattle PI: Microsoft blog*. http://blog.seattlepi.com/microsoft/2011/01/19/microsoft-nails-down-windows-phone-7-data-uploading-issue/

Economist (27 November 2004) Special Report: Managing complexity—Software Development; The software-development industry. *Economist* 373(8403):71–3.

Economist (24 April 2011) Garbage in, Garbage out. *Economist Blogs*. www.economist.com/blogs/babbage/2011/04/electronic_waste

Economist (4 February 2012) The Price of Information. *Economist*. www.economist.com/node/21545974

'Editor' (19 January 2011) Inside Kenya's Brutal Mobile Price War. *TechCentral*. www.techcentral.co.za/inside-kenyas-brutal-mobile-price-war/20445/

Edlin, A. & Rubinfield, D. (2004) Exclusion or Efficient Pricing? The 'big deal' bundling of academic journals. *Anti-Trust Law Journal* 72(1):119–57.

Edu-Factory Collective (2009) *Toward a Global Autonomous University*. New York: Autonomedia.

Edwards, H.S. (March/April 2013) He Who Makes the Rules. *Washington Monthly*. www.washingtonmonthly.com/magazine/march_april_2013/features/he_who_makes_the_rules043315.php?page=all

Edwards, L. (1 May 2013) Netflix's Ted Sarandos Talks Arrested Development, 4K and Reviving Old Shows. *Stuff*. www.stuff.tv/netflix/netflixs-ted-sarandos-talks-arrested-development-4k-and-reviving-old-shows/news

Eha, B.P. (9 August 2012) Is Knight's $440 Million Glitch the Costliest Computer Bug Ever? http://money.cnn.com/2012/08/09/technology/knight-expensive-computer-bug/index.html

Ehrenreich, B. (2007) *Dancing in the Streets: A history of collective joy*. New York: Metropolitan.

Eidelson, J. (18 October 2013) Tea Partyers' Grave Fear: Why they disdain young people—even their own! Interview with Theda Skocpol Salon. www.salon.com/2013/10/17/tea_partiers_grave_fear_why_they_disdain_young_people_even_their_own/

Eigenauer, J.D. (1993) The Humanities and Chaos Theory: A response to Steenburg's 'Chaos at the Marriage of Heaven and Hell'. *Harvard Theological Review* 86(4):455–69.

Eilperin, J., Goldstein, A. & Somashekhar, S. (9 October 2013) Many Remain Locked Out of Federal Health-Care Web Site. *Washington Post*. www.washingtonpost.com/national/health-science/many-remain-locked-out-of-federal-health-care-web-site/2013/10/08/be8e71e6-302c-11e3-bbed-a8a60c601153_story.html

Eivazi, K. (2012) Is Termination of Internet Users' Accounts by an ISP a Proportionate Response to Copyright Infringement? *Computer Law & Security Review* 28(4):458–67.

El-Emam, K. & Koru, A.G.A (2008) Replicated Survey of IT Software Project Failures. *IEEE Software* 25(5):84–90.

Elias, N. (1978) *What is Sociology?* New York: Columbia University Press.

Elias, N. (1983) *Court Society*. Oxford: Blackwell.

Ellis, J.M. (1993) *Language, Thought and Logic*. Evanston: Northwest University Press.

Ellis, K. (2008) *Business Analysis Benchmark: The impact of business requirements on the success of technology projects*. IAG Consulting. www.iag.biz/images/resources/iag%20business%20analysis%20benchmark%20-%20full%20report.pdf

Elsevier (2012a) Browse Our Products By Subject. www.elsevier.com/wps/find/subject_area_browse.cws_home

Elsevier (2012b) Open Letters to the Mathematics Community. www.elsevier.com/physical-sciences/mathematics/letters-to-the-community

Elsevier (2012c) Price List 2013. www.elsevier.com/wps/find/journalpricing.cws_home/journal_pricing

Enigmax (12 October 2011) Media Chiefs Want BitTorrent Removed From Home Entertainment Player. *TorrentFreak*. http://torrentfreak.com/media-chiefs-want-bittorrent-removed-from-home-entertainment-player-111012

Enigmax (23 January 2012) Cyberlocker Ecosystem Shocked as Big Players Take Drastic Action. *TorrentFreak*. http://torrentfreak.com/cyberlocker-ecosystem-shocked-as-big-players-take-drastic-action-120123

Enigmax (25 July 2012) Leaked Report Reveals Music Industry's Global Anti-Piracy Strategy. *TorrentFreak*. http://torrentfreak.com/leaked-report-reveals-music-industrys-global-anti-piracy-strategy-120725

Enigmax (6 August 2012) Demonoid Busted as a Gift to the United States Government. *TorrentFreak*. http://torrentfreak.com/demonoid-busted-as-a-gift-to-the-united-states-government-120806

ENISA (2011) Data Breach Notifications in the EU. *European Union Agency for Network and Information Security*. www.enisa.europa.eu/activities/identity-and-trust/library/deliverables/dbn

EPA (2013) Municipal Solid Waste in the United States: 2011 facts and figures. *US Environmental Protection Agency*. www.epa.gov/osw/nonhaz/municipal/pubs/MSWcharacterization_fnl_060713_2_rpt.pdf

Ernesto (27 August 2011) Top 10 Largest File-Sharing Sites. *TorrentFreak*. http://torrentfreak.com/top-10-largest-file-sharing-sites-110828

Ernesto (14 August 2012) Kim Dotcom: MPAA/RIAA corrupted the U.S. government. *TorrentFreak*. http://torrentfreak.com/kim-dotcom-mpaa-riaa-corrupted-the-u-s-government-120814

Ernesto (29 November 2012) Pirate Bay Launches Dedicated 'Promo Bay' Website to Plug Artists. *TorrentFreak*. http://torrentfreak.com/pirate-bay-launches-dedicated-promo-bay-to-help-artists-121129

Ernesto (12 February 2013) Demonoid 'Operator' Released from Jail, Case Stalled. *TorrentFreak*. http://torrentfreak.com/demonoid-operator-released-from-jail-case-stalled-130212

Ernesto (3 June 2013) Sky Broadband Starts Blocking Pirate Bay Proxies. *TorrentFreak*. http://torrentfreak.com/sky-broadband-starts-blocking-pirate-bay-proxies-130603/

Ernesto (30 March 2014) Demonoid Returns, Website Now Back Online. https://torrentfreak.com/demonoid-back-140330

Eschle, C. (2005) Constructing 'The Anti-globalisation Movement'. In C. Eschle & B. Maiguashca (eds.) *Critical Theories, International Relations and the 'Anti-globalisation' Movement*. London: Routledge. pp:17–36.

Espiner, T. (18 May 2007) Failed: Seven out of 10 gov IT projects. *Zdnet*. www.zdnet.co.uk/news/systems-management/2007/05/17/seven-in-10-government-it-projects-fail-39287110/

Estes, M.C. (21 September 2013) Military Scientists Use Yelp and Digg to Test Viral Marketing Skills. *Gizmodo*. www.gizmodo.com.au/2013/09/military-scientists-use-yelp-and-digg-to-test-viral-marketing-skills/

Europa MEMO/11/34 (21 January 2011) Emissions Trading: Q & As following the suspension of transactions in national ETS registries for at least one week from 19:00 CET on Wednesday 19 January 2011. http://europa.eu/rapid/pressReleases Action.do?reference=MEMO/11/34&format=HTML&aged=0&language=EN&guiLanguage=en

European Commission (17 July 2012) *Towards Better Access to Scientific Information: Boosting the benefits of public investments in research.* http://ec.europa.eu/research/science-society/document_library/pdf_06/era-communication-towards-better-access-to-scientific-information_en.pdf

European Parliament (14 January 2014) Deal to Regulate Financial Markets and Products and Curb High-Frequency Trading. *Press Release.* www.europarl.europa.eu/news/en/news-room/content/20140110IPR32414/html/Deal-to-regulate-financial-markets-and-products-and-curb-high-frequency-trading

Evans, I. (2006) Agile Delivery at British Telecom. *Methods & Tools* 14(2):20–7.

Eversheds (2009) *Developing Future University Structures: New funding and legal models.* Universities UK. www.universitiesuk.ac.uk/highereducation/Documents/2009/FutureUniversityStructures.pdf

Fairley, R.E. (2009) *Managing and Leading Software Projects.* Hoboken: John Wiley.

Falkenrath, R. (26 January 2011) From Bullets to Megabytes. *New York Times.* www.nytimes.com/2011/01/27/opinion/27falkenrath.html

Fareed, M. (22 September 2008) China Joins a Turf War. *Guardian.* www.theguardian.com/media/2008/sep/22/chinathemedia.marketingandpr

Farrell, H. (26 January 2012) Friends *Really* Don't Let Friends Publish in Elsevier Journals. *Crooked Timber.* http://crookedtimber.org/2009/05/11/friends-dont-let-friends-publish-in-elsevier-journals

Faulk S.R. (1997) Software Requirements: A tutorial. In R.H. Thayer and M. Dorfman (eds.) *Software Requirements Engineering.* 2nd Edition. IEEE Computer Society Press: 128–49.

Fay, J. (20 January 2011) Gov Will Spend £400k to Destroy ID Card Data. *Register.* www.theregister.co.uk/2011/01/20/id_card_costs/

Fenton N.E. and Lawrence Pfleeger, S. (1997) *Software Metrics, a Rigorous and Practical Approach.* 2nd Edition. London: International Thomson Computer Press.

Ferguson, C.H. (2012) *Predator Nation: Corporate criminals political corruption and the hijacking of America.* New York: Crown.

Ferrara, F. (2003) Why Regimes Create Disorder: Hobbes's dilemma during a Rangoon summer. *Journal of Conflict Resolution* 47(3):302–25.

FCIC (2011) *The Financial Crisis Inquiry Report: Final report of the National Commission on the Causes of the Financial and Economic Crisis in the United States.* Washington: U.S. Government Printing Office.

Ferguson, A. (30 July 2012) The Perils of High Frequency Trading. *Sydney Morning Herald.* www.smh.com.au/business/the-perils-of-high-frequency-trading-20120730-238vn.html

Financial News (1 April 2011) Trading Firm Hits Speed of Light. www.efinancialnews.com/story/2011-04-01/trading-firm-hits-speed-of-light

Financial Times (2013) The Financial Times Global 500 2013. *Financial Times,* London. Accessed 10 March 2014. www.ft.com/intl/indepth/ft500

Floridi, L. (2010) *Information: A very short introduction.* Oxford University Press.

Floridi, L. (2011) *Philosophy of Information.* Oxford: Oxford University Press.

Fominaya, C. (2007) Autonomous Movements and the Institutional Left: Two approaches in tension in Madrid's anti-globalization network. *South European Society and Politics* 12(3):335–58.

Foster, J.B. & McChesney, R.W. (2011) The Internet's Unholy Marriage to Capitalism. *Monthly Review: An Independent Socialist Magazine* 62(10):1–30. http://monthlyreview.org/2011/03/01/the-internets-unholy-marriage-to-capitalism

Foucault, M. (1979) *The History of Sexuality Vol. 1: Introduction*. London: Allen Lane.

Fowler, M. (2005) *The New Methodology*. www.martinfowler.com/articles/new-Methodology.html

Francis, D. (10 Aug 2012) Knight Capital Trading Disaster Portends Frightening Future for Markets. *Financial Post*. http://opinion.financialpost.com/2012/08/10/knight-capital-trading-disaster-portends-frightening-future-for-stocks

Frank, R. & Cook, P.J. (1995) *The Winner Take All Society*. New York: Free Press.

Fraunce, T.A. (4 January 2014) Trans Pacific Partnership Agreement Favours Foreign Investors over Citizens' Rights. *Sydney Morning Herald*. www.smh.com.au/comment/trans-pacific-partnership-agreement-favours-foreign-investors-over-citizens-rights-20140103–309nb.html

Freedlander, D. (19 October 2013) Radio's Mark Levin Might Be the Most Powerful Conservative You Never Heard Of. *Daily Beast*. www.thedailybeast.com/articles/2013/10/19/radio-s-mark-levin-might-be-the-most-powerful-conservative-you-never-heard-of.html

Freedman, D. (1 July 2005) When Technology Runs Amok. *Inc. Magazine*. www.inc.com/magazine/20050701/dfreedman.html

Friedman, T.L. (2005) *The World Is Flat: A brief history of the twenty-first century*. New York: Farrar, Straus and Giroux.

Frum, D. (20 November 2011) When Did the GOP Lose Touch with Reality? *New York Magazine*. http://nymag.com/news/politics/conservatives-david-frum-2011–11/

Fuller, N. (29 January 2011) Three Days After Storm and Some Still without Power: BGE works to restore electricity. *The Baltimore Sun*. www.baltimoresun.com/news/maryland/bs-md-snow-power-outage-20110128,0,3514885.story

Furnham, A. & Taylor, J. (2004) *The Dark Side of Behaviour at Work: Understanding and avoiding employees leaving, thieving and deceiving*. Houndmills: Palgrave Macmillan.

Galbraith, J.K. (2008) *The Predator State: How conservatives abandoned the free market and why liberals should too*. New York: Free Press.

Gallagher, M. (2000) The Emergence of Entrepreneurial Public Universities in Australia. Paper presented at the *IMHE General Conference of the OECD Paris, September 2000*. Department of Education, Training and Youth Affairs. http://vital.new.voced.edu.au/vital/access/services/Download/ngv:4321/SOURCE2

Gapper, J. (2 April 2014) A High-Speed Retreat Keeps Goldman Out of Trouble. *Financial Times*. www.ft.com/intl/cms/s/0/90d700ee-b9b9–11e3-a3ef-00144feabdc0.html

Garg P.K. & Jazayeri M. (1994) Selected, Annotated Bibliography on Process Centred Software Engineering Environments. *ACM SIGSOFT Software Engineering Notes* 19(2):18–21.

Garten, J.E. (2001) *The Mind of the CEO*. New York: Perseus Books Group.

Gatopoulos, D. (3 June 2010) Greek Financial Crisis: Did 2004 Athens Olympics spark problems in Greece? *Huffington Post*. www.huffingtonpost.com/2010/06/03/greek-financial-crisis-olympics_n_598829.html

Gedda, R. (10 August, 2009) Establish Trust First Then Follow Directions over the Phone. *Computerworld*. www.computerworld.com.au/article/314295/windows_event_viewer_phishing_scam_remains_active/

Geneca Consulting (2011) *Doomed from the Start? Why a majority of business and IT teams anticipate their software development projects will fail. Winter 2010/2011 Industry Survey*. Accessed 18 March 2013. www.geneca.com/survey/download.php?file=GenecaSurveyReport.pdf http://bit.ly/1bmBCAK

Georgiakis, S. & Nauright, J. (2012) Creating the 'Scarecrow': The 2004 Athens Olympic Games and the Greek Financial Crisis. George Mason University: *The Center for the Study of Sport and Leisure in Society Sport and Society Working Paper*.

www.academia.edu/1922581/Creating_The_Scarecrow_The_2004_Athens_Olympic_Games_and_the_Greek_Financial_Crisis

Gerges, F.A. (2011). *The Rise and Fall of Al-Qaeda*. Oxford: Oxford University Press.

Gervasi, V. & Zowghi D. (2010) On the Role of Ambiguity in RE. *Proceedings of the 16th International Working Conference on Requirements Engineering, Foundations for Software Quality (REFSQ'10)*: 248–54.

Giblin, R. (2011) *Code Wars: 10 years of P2P software litigation*. Cheltenham: Edward Elgar.

Giblin, R. & Davison, M. (2006) Kazaa Goes the Way of Grokster? Authorisation of copyright infringement via peer-to-peer networks in Australia. *Australian Intellectual Property Journal* 17(1):53–76.

Gill, S. (1995) The Global Panopticon? The neoliberal State, economic life, and democratic surveillance. *Alternatives: Global, Local, Political* 20(1):1–49.

Gill, S. (2003) *Power and Resistance in the New World Order*. Basingstoke: Palgrave Macmillan.

Gillespie, J. & Zweig, D. (2010) *Money for Nothing: How the failure of corporate boards is ruining American business and costing us trillions*. New York: Free Press.

Gillespie, T. (2014) The Relevance of Algorithms. In T. Gillespie, P. Boczkowski & K. Foot (eds.) *Media Technologies: Essays on communication, materiality, and society*. Cambridge: MIT Press. pp:167–94.

Gillies, J. & Cailliau, R. (2000) *How the Web Was Born*. Oxford: Oxford University Press.

Glennan, S.S. (1997) Probable Causes and the Distinction between Subjective and Objective Chance. *Noûs* 31(4):496–519.

Gluckman, M. (1960) *Custom and Conflict in Africa*. Oxford: Basil Blackwell.

Gluckman, M. (1963) *Order and Rebellion in Tribal Africa*. London: Cohen & West.

Gobry, P-E. (14 December 2010) Here's the Awesome TV Box You Can't Buy. *Business Insider Australia*. http://articles.businessinsider.com/2010-12-14/tech/30034511_1_telcos-blu-ray-player-internet-access

Goguen, J.A. (1994) Requirements Engineering as the Reconciliation of Technical and Social Issues. In J. Goguen & M. Jirotka (eds.) *Requirements Engineering Social and Technical Issues*. San Diego: Academic Press Professional Inc. pp:165–99.

Goguen J.A. (1996) Formality and Informality in Requirements Engineering. *ICRE '96 Proceedings of the 2nd International Conference on Requirements Engineering*. IEEE Computer Society: 102–8. http://homepages.laas.fr/kader/Guogen.pdf

Goldacre, B. (9 May 2009) The Danger of Drugs . . . and Data. *Guardian*. www.guardian.co.uk/commentisfree/2009/may/09/bad-science-medical-journals-companies

Goldenberg, J., Han, S., Lehmann, D.R. & Hong, J.W. (2009) The Role of Hubs in the Adoption Process. *Journal of Marketing* 73(2):1–13.

Gomber, P., Arndt, B., Lutat, M. & Uhle, T. (2011) *High Frequency Trading*. Frankfurt: Goethe University and Deutsche Börse.

Goodin, D. (3 January 2011) IE 0day Accidentally Leaked to Chinese Hackers. *Register*. www.theregister.co.uk/2011/01/03/ie_0day_leaked/

Goodin, D. (14 January 2011a) Gamers Raid Medical Server to Host Call of Duty. *Register*. www.theregister.co.uk/2011/01/14/seacoast_radiology_server_breach/

Goodin, D. (14 January 2011b) No Court Order Against PlayStation Hackers for Now. *Register*. www.theregister.co.uk/2011/01/14/no_playstation_hacker_order/

Goodin, D. (18 January 2011) Hackers Eyed Sale of Celebrity iPad Data. *Register*. www.theregister.co.uk/2011/01/18/ipad_data_breach_charges_brought/

Goodin, D. (21 January 2011) EU Halts Carbon Trading After 'Concerted' Hack Attacks. *Register*. www.theregister.co.uk/2011/01/21/carbon_trading_hack_attack/

272 *Bibliography*

Goodin, D. (27 January 2011) Court Orders Seizure of PS3 Hacker's Computers. *Register.* www.theregister.co.uk/2011/01/27/sony_ps3_tro_awarded/

Goodman, J. (2001) Contesting Corporate Globalism: Sources of power, channels for resistance? *International Scope Review* 3(5):1–19.

Goodman, J. & Marshall, J.P. (2013) Crisis, Movement and Management in Contemporary Globalisations. *Globalisations* 10(3):343–53.

Goodman, J. & Ranald, P. (2000) *Stopping a Juggernaut: Public interests vs the MAI.* Sydney: Pluto Press.

Gordon, J. (22 November 2012) When Private Contracts Are a Public Issue. *Sydney Morning Herald.* www.smh.com.au/federal-politics/political-opinion/when-private-contracts-are-a-public-issue-20121121-29q56.html

Gottipati, H.K. (2006) GMail Disaster, Google Confirmed the Mass Email Deletions: Even backups are gone? www.oreillynet.com/xml/blog/2006/12/gmail_disaster_google_confirme.html

Gould, E. (2003) *The University in a Corporate Culture.* New Haven: Yale University Press.

Gower, R. (2011) *Financial Crisis 2: Rise of the machines.* London: The Robin Hood Tax Campaign. http://antigua.ubuntu.upc.edu/docus/Robin_Hood_Tax_Rise_of_the_Machine.pdf

Gowers, T. (21 January 2012) Elsevier—My part in its downfall. *Gowers's Weblog: Mathematics related discussions.* http://gowers.wordpress.com/2012/01/21/elsevier-my-part-in-its-downfall

Gowers, T. (2012) The Cost of Knowledge. http://gowers.files.wordpress.com/2012/02/elsevierstatementfinal.pdf

Graeber, D. (2004a) *Fragments of an Anarchist Anthropology.* Chicago: Prickly Paradigm.

Graeber, D. (2004b) The New Anarchists. In T. Mertes (ed.) *A Movement of Movements: Is another world really possible?* London: Verso.

Graeber, D. (2012) *Revolutions in Reverse: Essays on politics, violence, art and imagination.* London: Minor Compositions.

Graeber, D. (2013) *The Democracy Project: A history, a crisis, a movement.* New York: Spiegel & Grau.

Grail Research (12 September 2009) Bailout/Stimulus Tracker. http://grailresearch.com/pdf/ContenPodsPdf/Global_Bailout_Tracker.pdf

Graybow, M. (5 September 2007) Merrill to Pay $125 Million Settlement to Investors. *Reuters.* www.reuters.com/article/fundsFundsNews/idUSN0519185620070905

Green, A. (13 September 2013) The Preference Deals behind the Strange Election of Ricky Muir and Wayne Dropulich. *ABC Elections.* http://blogs.abc.net.au/antonygreen/2013/09/the-preference-deals-behind-the-strange-election-of-ricky-muir-and-wayne-dropulich-.html

Greenpeace (2012) *Guide to Greener Electronics.* www.greenpeace.org/international/Global/international/publications/climate/2012/GuideGreenerElectronics/Full-Scorecard.pdf

Greenwald, G. (8 January 2011) DOJ Subpoenas Twitter Records of Several WikiLeaks Volunteers. *Salon.* www.salon.com/2011/01/08/twitter_2/

Greenwald, G. (2014) *No Place to Hide: Edward Snowden, the NSA and the US surveillance state.* New York: Metropolitan.

Greenwood, R. & Scharfstein, D. (2013) The Growth of Finance. *Journal of Economic Perspectives* 27(2):3–28.

Gregory, A. (29 January 2010) How to Be Stealth with Undercover Marketing. *Sitepoint.* www.sitepoint.com/undercover-marketing/

Groklaw (27 January 2011) Sony Wins TRO, Impoundment—Updated. *Groklaw.* www.groklaw.net/article.php?story=20110127193058685

Groklaw (20 August 2013) Forced Exposure. *Groklaw.* www.groklaw.net/article.php?story=20130818120421175

Gross, M.J. (2011) Stuxnet Worm: A declaration of cyber-war. *Vanity Fair.* www. vanityfair.com/culture/features/2011/04/stuxnet-201104

Grossman, E. (2006) *High Tech Trash: Digital devices, hidden toxics and human health.* Washington: Island Press.

Grubb, B. (5 January 2011) Vodafone Sets up Taskforce to Fix Network Issues as 9000 Express Interest in Class Action. *Sydney Morning Herald.* www.smh. com.au/technology/technology-news/vodafone-sets-up-taskforce-to-fix-network-issues-as-9000-express-interest-in-class-action-20110105-19fkh.html

Guardian (ongoing a) Edward Snowden. *Guardian.* www.theguardian.com/world/edward-snowden

Guardian (ongoing b) Phone Hacking. *Guardian.* www.theguardian.com/media/phone-hacking

Guédon, J.-C. (2001) *In Oldenburg's Long Shadow: Librarians, research scientists, publishers, and the control of scientific publishing.* Association of Research Libraries. www.arl.org/component/content/article/6/2598

Guglielmo, C. (21 May 2013) Apple, Called a U.S. Tax Dodger, Says It's Paid 'Every Single Dollar' of Taxes Owed. *Forbes.* www.forbes.com/sites/conniegug lielmo/2013/05/21/apple-called-a-tax-dodger-by-senate-committee-apple-says-system-needs-to-be-dramatically-simplified/

Habermas, J. (1988) *The Theory of Communicative Action 2: Lifeworld and System.* Boston: Beacon.

Hackett, R. & Carroll, W. (2006) *Remaking Media: The struggle to democratise public communication.* New York: Routledge.

Hakken, D. (2010) Computing and the Current Crisis: The significant role of new information technologies in our socio-economic meltdown. *TripleC: Cognition, Communication, Co-operation* 8(2):205–20. www.triplec.at/index.php/tripleC/article/download/161/193

Hall, R. & Stahl, B. (2012) Against Commodification: The university, cognitive capitalism and emergent technologies. *Triple C: Cogniton, Communication, Co-operation* 10(2):184–202. www.triple-c.at/index.php/tripleC/article/view/378

Halleck, D. (2004) Indymedia: Building an international activist internet network. *Media Development,* 50(4):Special Issue on Indymedia. Accessed 19 November 2013. www.waccglobal.org/en/20034-indymedia.html

Hardt, M. & Negri, A. (2000) *Empire.* Cambridge: Harvard University Press.

Hardt, M. & Negri, A. (2004) *Multitude: War and democracy in the Age of Empire.* New York: Penguin Putnam.

Hardt, M. & Negri, A. (2009) *Commonwealth.* Cambridge: Harvard University Press.

Harford, T. (10 August 2012) High-frequency Trading and the $440m Mistake. *BBC Radio 4, More or Less.* www.bbc.co.uk/news/magazine-19214294

Harnden, T. (11 June 2011) American Way: Sarah Palin email frenzy backfires on her media antagonists. *Telegraph.* http://blogs.telegraph.co.uk/news/tobyharnden/100091820/american-way-sarah-palin-email-frenzy-backfires-on-her-media-antagonists/

Hartley, M. (22 April 2009) From Culture to Politics, Napster's Impact Is Still Felt Today. *Globe and Mail.* Accessed 6 September 2013. www.theglobeand-mail.com/news/technology/digital-culture/download-decade/thank-you-napster/article1014979/

Harvard Business Review (2010) A Map to Healthy—and Ailing—Markets. *Harvard Business Review* 88(1/2):30–1.

Harvard Faculty Advisory Council (2012) Faculty Advisory Council Memorandum on Journal Pricing. http://isites.harvard.edu/icb/icb.do?keyword=k77982&tabgr oupid=icb.tabgroup143448

Harvey, D. (2005) *A Brief History of Neoliberalism.* Oxford: Oxford University Press.

Harvie, D., Milburn, K., Trott, B. & Wats, D. (2005) (eds.) *Shut Them Down: The G8, Gleneagles 2005 and the movement of movements*. Leeds: Autonomedia and Dissent!

Haslam, S.A., McGarty, C. & Turner, J.C. (1996) Salient Group Memberships and Persuasion: The role of social identity in the validation of beliefs. In J.L. Nye & A.M. Brower (eds.) *What's Social about Social Cognition? Research on socially shared cognition in small groups*. Thousand Oaks: Sage.

Hassink, L. & Clark, D. (2012,) Elsevier's Response to the Mathematics Community. *Notices of the American Mathematical Society* 59(6):833–5. www.ams.org/notices/201206/rtx120600833p.pdf

Hauben. M., & Hauben, R. (1997) *Netizens: On the history and impact of Usenet and the Internet*. Los Alimitos: IEEE Computer Society.

Haunss, S. (2011) Politicisation of Intellectual Property: IP conflicts and social change. *WIPO Journal* 3(1):129–38.

Hearn, L. (11 January 2011) Flock to Facebook for Flood Updates. *Sydney Morning Herald*. www.smh.com.au/technology/technology-news/flock-to-facebook-for-flood-updates-20110111-19mfr.html

Heath, N. (6 September 2012) Agile Development: Five ways it can trip you up. *TechRepublic: CIO Insights*. www.techrepublic.com/blog/cio-insights/agile-development-five-ways-it-can-trip-you-up/

Helleiner, E. & Pagliari, S. (2011) The End of an Era in International Financial Regulation? A postcrisis research agenda. *International Organisation* 65(1):169–200.

Heller, M. (2008) *The Gridlock Economy: How too much ownership wrecks markets, stops innovation and costs lives*. New York: Basic Books.

Henman, P. (1997) Computer Technology—a Political Player in Social Policy Processes. *Journal of Social Policy* 26(3):323–40.

Henman, P. (2004) Targeted! Population segmentation, electronic surveillance and governing the unemployed in Australia. *International Sociology* 19(2):173–91.

Hepworth, A. (19 June 1999) Protesters Hitch a Ride on the Web. *Australian Financial Review*.

Hickey, A.M., Davis, A.M. & Kaiser, D. (2003) Requirements Elicitation Techniques: Analysing the gap between technology availability and technology use. *Comparative Technology Transfer and Society* 1(3):279–304.

Hilbert, M. & Lopez, P. (2011) The World's Technological Capacity to Store, Communicate, and Compute Information. *Science* 332(1st April):60–5.

Hill, A. (27 January 2011) Police Could Use More Extreme Tactics on Protesters, Sir Hugh Orde Warns. *Guardian*. www.guardian.co.uk/uk/2011/jan/27/hugh-orde-police-protest-tactics

Hill, K. (9 August 2013) Lavabit's Ladar Levison: 'If You Knew What I Know About Email, You Might Not Use It'. *Forbes*. www.forbes.com/sites/kashmirhill/2013/08/09/lavabits-ladar-levison-if-you-knew-what-i-know-about-email-you-might-not-use-it

Hindle, T. (2000) *Guide to Management Ideas*. London: Economist Books.

Hodgkins, K. (29 January 2011) Verizon Reports BIS Outage, Affects Sprint, T-Mobile and AT&T [Updated]. *IntoMobile*. www.intomobile.com/2011/01/29/verizon-reports-bis-outage-affects-sprint-t-mobile-and-att/#

Hodgson, G. (1999) *Economics and Utopia: Why the learning economy is not the end of history*. London: Routledge.

Holloway, J. (2005) *Change the World without Taking Power*. 2nd Edition. London/Ann Arbor: Pluto Press.

Holowka, J. (25 January 2014) Gmail, Too Big to Fail? *Guardian Liberty Voice*. http://guardianlv.com/2014/01/gmail-too-big-to-fail/

Holstein, W.J. (2008) *Manage the Media: Don't let the media manage you (Memo to the CEO)*. Boston: Harvard Business School Press.

Hopkins, N. & Reicher, S. (1997) Social Movement Rhetoric and the Social Psychology of Collective Action: A case study of an anti-abortion mobilization. *Human Relations* 50(3):261–86.

Howard, A. (22 November 2011) Congress Considers Anti-piracy Bills that Could Cripple Internet Industries. *O'Reilly Radar*. http://radar.oreilly.com/2011/11/sopa-protectip.html

Howard, J. (27 February 2012) Legislation to Bar Public-Access Requirement on Federal Research Is Dead. *Chronicle of Higher Education*. http://chronicle.com/article/Legislation-to-Bar/130949

Huber, N. (4 November 2003) Hitting Targets: The state of UK IT project management. *Computer Weekly*: 22–3.

Huczynski, A.A. (1993) Explaining the Succession of Management Fads. *International Journal of Human Resource Management* 4(2):443–63.

Huffington Post (17 October 2009) Gmail Down: Here's how to check status. www.huffingtonpost.com/2009/09/01/gmails-down-heres-how-to_n_274350.html

Huffington Post (29 June 2010) Gmail Down? Check gmail outage status here. www.huffingtonpost.com/2010/04/29/gmail-down-check-gmail-ou_n_557351.html

Hugo, P. (2010) A Global Graveyard for Dead Computers in Ghana. *New York Times*. www.nytimes.com/slideshow/2010/08/04/magazine/20100815-dump.html

Hutchings, A. & Knox, S. (1995) Creating Products Customers Demand. *Communications of the ACM* 38(5):72–80.

Ian, J. (2002) *The Internet Debacle: An alternative view*. Accessed 8 September 2013. www.janisian.com/reading/internet.php

IATP (2013) Dodd-Frank Position Limits on Commodity Contracts. *Think Forward Blog*. Institute for Agriculture and Trade Policy. www.iatp.org/blog/201311/dodd-frank-position-limits-on-commodity-contracts-round-2

Ibanez, M. (1996) *European User Survey Analysis*. Technical Report ESI report TR95104, European Software Institute.

Ibrahim, J. (2011) The New Toll on Higher Education and the UK Student Revolts of 2010–2011. *Social Movement Studies: Journal of Social, Cultural and Political Protest* 10(4):415–21.

ICO (21 January 2011) Organ Donation Preferences of over 400,000 People Recorded Inaccurately. London: Information Commisioner's Office. www.ico.gov.uk/~/media/documents/pressreleases/2011/organ_donation_register_news_release_20110121.ashx

IFPI (2010) *IFPI Digital Music Report 2010: Music how, when, where you want it.* London: International Federation of the Phonographic Industry.

IFPI (2011) *IFPI Digital Music Report 2011: Music at the touch of a button.* London: International Federation of the Phonographic Industry.

IFPI (2013) *IFPI Digital Music Report 2013: Engine of a digital world.* London: International Federation of the Phonographic Industry. www.ifpi.org/content/library/DMR2013.pdf

IMF (2007) *Global Financial Stability Report, Financial Market Turbulence: Causes, consequences, and policies.* Washington: International Monetary Fund. www.imf.org/external/pubs/ft/gfsr/2007/02/pdf/text.pdf

iMomus (8 May 2007) Sock Puppets Keep It Shill on YouTube. *Wired*. www.wired.com/culture/culturereviews/commentary/imomus/2007/05/imomus_0508

Indymedia (2009) Squaring up to the Square Mile: The London G20 Map. www.indymedia.org.uk/en/2009/03/425118.html

infosec (18 September 2009) DeepSec 2009 to Focus on Industrial Espionage. www.infosecurity-magazine.com/view/4039/deepsec-2009-to-focus-on-industrial-espionage

infosec (30 March 2011) Hacking No Longer Just About the Money Says Idappcom. www.infosecurity-magazine.com/view/16938/hacking-no-longer-just-about-the-money-says-idappcom

IOC (2012) *Olympic Marketing Fact File*. Lausanne: International Olympic Committee. www.olympic.org/Documents/IOC_Marketing/OLYMPIC-MARKETING-FACT-FILE-2012.pdf

IOC (2013) *The Olympic Charter*. Lausanne: International Olympic Committee. www.olympic.org/Documents/olympic_charter_en.pdf

IP Commission (2013) *The Report of the Commission on the Theft of American Intellectual Property*. NP: The National Bureau of Asian Research. http://ipcommission.org/report/IP_Commission_Report_052213.pdf

Isaac, M. (7 July 2011) Sprint Confirms Text-Message Problems. *Wired: Gadget Lab*. www.wired.com/gadgetlab/2011/07/sprint-sms-text-problem

Isikoff, M. (13 November 2013) HealthCare.gov Targeted 'about 16 times' by Cyberattacks, DHS Official Says. *NBC News*. www.nbcnews.com/news/other/healthcare-gov-targeted-about-16-times-cyberattacks-dhs-official-says-f2D11590309

Jackson M. (1995a) The World and the Machine. *Proceedings of 17th IEEE International Conference on Software Engineering (ICSE17)*. Seattle: IEEE Computer Society Press: 283–92.

Jackson M. (1995b) *Software Requirements and Specifications: A lexicon of practice, principles and prejudices*. Edinburgh Gate, Harlow: Addison-Wesley.

Jackson M. (1997) The Meaning of Requirements. *The Annals of Software Engineering, Special Issue on Software Requirements Engineering* 3:5–21.

Jacob, A. (9 August 2012) IFPI Welcomes Closure of Demonoid. International Federation of the Phonographic Industry. http://ifpi.org/news/ifpi-welcomes-closure-of-demonoid

Jacobsson-Purewal, S. (14 January 2011) Palin E-Mail Hacker Imprisoned Against Judge's Recommendation. *PCWorld*. www.pcworld.com/article/216747/palin_email_hacker_imprisoned_against_judges_recommendation.html

Jacques, P.J., Dunlap, R.E., & Freeman, M. (2008) The Organisation of Denial: Conservative think tanks and environmental scepticism. *Environmental Politics* 17(3):349–85.

James, D. (13 July 2013) Don't Be Fooled by the Jargon. *Sydney Morning Herald*. www.smh.com.au/business/dont-be-fooled-by-the-jargon-20130712-2pvjz.html

James, P. (1996) *Nation Formation: Towards a theory of abstract community*. London: Sage.

Jeffery, D.R. (1992) Software Process Quality: Requirements for improvement from industry. *Rome Air Development Centre Software Quality Workshop*. New York.

Jennings, A. (1996) *The New Lords of the Rings: Olympic corruption and how to buy gold medals*. New York: Pocket Books.

Jha, A. (9 April 2012) Academic Spring: How an angry maths blog sparked a scientific revolution. *Guardian*. www.guardian.co.uk/science/2012/apr/09/frustrated-blogpost-boycott-scientific-journals

Johnson, C. (2004) *Blowback: The costs and consequences of American empire*. 2nd Edition. New York: Henry Holt.

Johnson, C. (2008) *Nemesis: The last days of the American Republic*. New York: Henry Holt.

Jones, P. (12 January 2011a) Floods Cut Brisbane Power and Networks. www.datacenterdynamics.com/focus/archive/2011/01/floods-cut-brisbane-power-and-networks

Jones, P. (12 January 2011b) Argentine Government Suffers Internet Outage. www.datacenterdynamics.com/focus/archive/2011/01/argentine-government-suffers-internet-outage

Jordan, J. (1998) The Art of Necessity: The subversive imagination of anti-road protest and reclaim the streets. In G. McKay (ed.) *DiY Culture: Party and protest in nineties Britain*. London: Verso.

Jowitt, T. (14 December 2012) SQS Identifies Top 10 High Profile Software Blunders of 2012. *Channelbiz*. www.channelbiz.co.uk/2012/12/14/sqs-top-ten-software-blunders-2012/

Jurgenson, N. (2012) When Atoms Meet Bits: Social media, the mobile web and augmented revolution. *Future Internet* 4(1):83–91.

Juris, J. (2008) *Networking Futures: The movements against corporate globalization.* Durham, NC: Duke University Press.

Juris, J. (2012) Reflections on #Occupy Everywhere: Social media, public space, and emerging logics of aggregation. *American Ethnologist* 39(2):259–279.

Kaikati, A.M. & Kaikati, J.G. (2004). Stealth Marketing: How to reach consumers surreptitiously. *California Management Review* 46(4):6–22.

Kallinikos, J. (2005) The Order of Technology: Complexity and control. *Information and Organization* 15:185–202.

Kan, M. (14 January 2011) 'Money Sucking' Phones in China Spur Government Action. *PC World*. www.pcworld.com/businesscenter/article/216657/money_sucking_phones_in_china_spur_government_action.html

Kanalley, C. (17 April 2012) Gmail Down: Google email suffers service disruption. *Huffington Post*. www.huffingtonpost.com/2012/04/17/gmail-down-google-email-s_n_1431918.html

Kang, H. & McAllister, M. (2011) Selling You and Your Clicks: Examining the audience commodification of google. *TripleC* 9(2):141–53. www.triple-c.at/index.php/tripleC/article/view/255/234

Kappelle, L. (13 January 2011) SA Computer Hacker Gets Suspended Sentence. *Sydney Morning Herald*. http://news.smh.com.au/breaking-news-national/sa-computer-hacker-gets-suspended-sentence-20110113-19owd.html

Karaganis, J. (2011) Rethinking Piracy. In J. Karaganis (ed.) *Media Piracy in Emerging Economies*. New York: Social Science Research Council. pp:75–98. http://piracy.americanassembly.org/wp-content/uploads/2011/06/MPEE-PDF-1.0.4.pdf

Karanja, M. (20 January 2011) Safaricom Suffers Cable Cuts. *Capital FM*. www.capitalfm.co.ke/business/Kenyabusiness/Safaricom-suffers-cable-cuts-5321.html

Katz, E. & Lazarsfeld, P.F. (1955) *Personal Influence: The part played by people in the flow of mass communication.* New York: Free Press.

Kay, J. (12 July 2005) An Empty Language for Empty-Headed Executives. Originally from the *Financial Times*. www.johnkay.com/2005/07/12/an-empty-language-for-empty-headed-executives

Keck, M. & Sikkink, K. (1998) *Activists Beyond Borders: Advocacy networks in international politics.* Ithaca: Cornell University Press.

Kendall, K. (2007) *Electronic and Algorithmic Trading Technology: The complete guide.* Burlington: Elsevier Academic Press.

Kerr, O. (13 January 2011) Today's Award for the Silliest Theory of the Computer Fraud and Abuse Act. http://volokh.com/2011/01/13/todays-award-for-the-lawyer-who-has-advocated-the-silliest-theory-of-the-computer-fraud-and-abuse-act/

King, P. (1974) *The Ideology of Order: A comparative analysis of Jean Bodin and Thomas Hobbes.* London: George Allen and Unwin.

Kingsnorth, P. (2003) *One No, Many Yeses: A journey to the heart of the global resistance movement.* London: Free Press.

Kirby, J. & Marsden, P. (2006) *Connected Marketing: The viral, buzz and word-of-mouth revolution.* Oxford: Butterworth-Heinemann.

Klausen, J. (2009) *Cartoons that Shook the World.* New Haven: Yale University Press.

Klein, E. (14 October 2013) Five Thoughts on the Obamacare Disaster. *Washington Post*. www.washingtonpost.com/blogs/wonkblog/wp/2013/10/14/five-thoughts-on-the-obamacare-disaster/

Klein, E. (4 November 2013) The Memo that Could Have Saved Obamacare. *Washington Post*. www.washingtonpost.com/blogs/wonkblog/wp/2013/11/04/the-memo-that-could-have-saved-obamacare/

Kliff, S. (24 October 2013) Everything You Need to Know about Obamacare's Problems. *Washington Post*. www.washingtonpost.com/blogs/wonkblog/wp/2013/10/24/everything-you-need-to-know-about-obamacares-problems/

Klinkenborg, V. (21 September 2013) Silencing Scientists. *New York Times.* www. nytimes.com/2013/09/22/opinion/sunday/silencing-scientists.html

Kneer, C. (2013) The Absorption of Talent into Finance: Evidence from US banking deregulation. *De Nederlandsche Bank Working Paper* 391. www.dnb.nl/en/binaries/Working%20Paper%20391_tcm47–296165.pdf

Kolata, G. (7 April 2013) Scientific Articles Accepted (Personal Checks, Too). *New York Times.* www.nytimes.com/2013/04/08/health/for-scientists-an-exploding-world-of-pseudo-academia.html

Kreps, D. (2011) Social Networking and Transnational Capitalism. *Triple C* 9(2):689–701. www.triple-c.at/index.php/tripleC/article/view/264/319

Kretschmer, M. (2011) Comment on Copyright Term Extension. *Bournemouth University, Centre for Intellectual Property Policy & Management.* Accessed 6 September 2013. http://blogs.bournemouth.ac.uk/research/2011/09/20/comment-on-copyright-term-extension/

Krigsman, M. (10 April 2012) Worldwide Cost of IT Failure (Revisited): $3 trillion. *ZDnet.* http://www.zdnet.com/blog/projectfailures/worldwide-cost-of-it-failure-revisited-3-trillion/15424

Krugman, P. (1995) *The Self-Organising Economy.* New York: Blackwell.

Krugman, P. (2 September 2009) How Did Economists Get It So Wrong? *New York Times.* www.nytimes.com/2009/09/06/magazine/06Economic-t.html

Krukowski, D. (14 November 2012) Making Cents. *Pitchfork.* http://pitchfork.com/features/articles/8993-the-cloud

Laja, S. (21 January 2011) NHSBT Rapped for Incorrect Data on 444,000 Donors. *Guardian.* www.guardian.co.uk/healthcare-network/2011/aug/30/organ-donor-register-nhsbt-dvla-errors

Lakoff, G. (1987) *Women, Fire and Dangerous Things.* Chicago: Chicago University Press.

Lakoff, G. (2010) Why It Matters How We Frame the Environment. *Environmental Communication: A Journal of Nature and Culture* 4(1):70–81.

Lally, K. (28 September 2013) IOC Officials Refuse to Challenge Russia's Anti-gay Laws. *Sydney Morning Herald.* www.smh.com.au/world/ioc-officials-refuse-to-challenge-russias-antigay-law-20130927–2ujh3.html

Lancet (2012) The Research Works Act: A damaging threat to science. *Lancet* 379 (9813):288. www.thelancet.com/journals/lancet/article/PIIS0140–6736%2812%2960125–1/fulltext

Lang, A. (2004) *Email Dependability.* Bachelor of Engineering Thesis. University of New South Wales. http://uluru.ee.unsw.edu.au/~tim/projects/dependable_email/2004/thesis.pdf

Langa, F. (12 January 2004) Email—Hideously Unreliable'. *Information Week.* www.informationweek.com/story/showArticle.jhtml?articleID=1730001.

Lapavitsas, C. (2009) Financialised Capitalism: Crisis and financial expropriation. *Historical Materialism* 17(2):114–48.

Lapham, L. (1998) *The Agony of Mammon: The imperial global economy explains itself to the membership in Davos, Switzerland.* London: Verso.

Larman C. and Basili V. (2003) Iterative and Incremental Development: A brief history. *IEEE Computer* 36(6):47–56.

Larson, E. (20 January 2011) Apple Sues Nokia in London Over Patent for Touch-Screen Scroll. *Bloomberg.* www.bloomberg.com/news/2011-01–19/apple-sues-nokia-in-london-over-patent-for-touch-screen-scroll.html

Larsson, S. (2013) Metaphors, Law and Digital Phenomena: The Swedish Pirate Bay court case. *International Journal of Law and Information Technology* 21(4): 354–79. http://ijlit.oxfordjournals.org/content/21/4/354.full.pdf+html?sid=637 efd19–1609–4e55-bca2-d98b0c7aaf33

Larsson, S., Svensson, M., de Kaminski, M., Rönkkö, K. & Olsson, J.A. (2012) Law, Norms, Piracy and Online Anonymity: Practices of de-identification in the global file sharing community. *Journal of Research in Interactive Marketing* 6(4):260–80.

Latour, B. (1991). Technology Is Society Made Durable. In J. Law (ed.) *A Sociology of Monsters?* London: Routledge. pp:103–31.

Layne, C. (2001) The Unipolar Exit: Beyond the Pax Americana. *Cambridge Review of International Affairs* 24(2):149–64.

Lazarus, D. (6 January 2011) What's to Blame for AT&T Outages? *L.A. Times*. www.latimes.com/business/la-fi-0107-lazarus-20110107,0,3351509,full.column

Lazear, E.P. (2003) The Peter Principle: A theory of decline. *Discussion paper*. Bonn: Institute for the Study of Labor. http://ssrn.com/abstract=403880

Leach, A. (12 December 2012) Worldwide Gmail Crash Was Due to Google Sync Bug. *Register*. www.theregister.co.uk/2012/12/12/gmail_bug_was_actually_chrome_configuration_error/

Lee, A. (1 March 2011) Google Explains Gmail Fail That 'Erased' Users' Emails, Disabled Accounts. *Huffington Post*. www.huffingtonpost.com/2011/03/01/google-gmail-problems-explained_n_829638.html

Lee, A. (3 March 2011) Days-Long Gmail Outage Leads To Fury, Frustration, Mistrust. *Huffington Post*. www.huffingtonpost.com/2011/03/03/google-gmailoutage_n_830229.html

Lehman, M.M. & Ramil, J.F. (2003) Software Evolution: Background, theory, practice. *Information Processing Letters* 88(1–2):33–44.

LeMay, R. (20 April 2012) iiNet Wins High Court Internet Piracy Trial. *Delimiter*. http://delimiter.com.au/2012/04/20/iinet-wins-high-court-internet-piracy-trial

LeMay, R. (3 April 2013) New FetchTV Box + Dervice: Review: It's a game changer. *Delimiter*. http://delimiter.com.au/2013/04/03/new-fetchtv-box-service-review-its-a-game-changer/

Lenglet, M. (2011) Conflicting Codes and Codings: How algorithmic trading is reshaping financial regulation. *Theory, Culture, Society* 28(6):44–66.

Lenskyj, H.J. (2008) *Olympic Industry Resistance: Challenging Olympic power and propaganda*. Albany: SUNY.

Lessig, L. (2008) *Remix: Making Art and Commerce Thrive in the Hybrid Economy*. New York: Penguin.

Leung, R. (11 February 2009) Undercover Marketing Uncovered. *CBS News*. www.cbsnews.com/stories/2003/10/23/60minutes/main579657.shtml

Levin, C. & McCain, J. (2013) Memorandum to Members of the Permanent Subcommittee on Investigations, RE: Offshore profit shifting and the U.S. tax code—Part 2 (Apple Inc.). *US Senate*. www.levin.senate.gov/download/exhibit1a_profitshiftingmemo_apple

Levinson, J.C. & Levinson, J. (2011) *Guerrilla Marketing Remix: The best of guerrilla marketing*. Irvine: Entrepreneur Press.

Levinson, M. (2001) Let's Stop Wasting $78 Billion a Year. *CIO Magazine* 15(2):78–83. www.cio.com/article/30599/SOFTWARE_DEVELOPMENT_Let_s_Stop_Wasting_78_Billion_a_Year

Levy, D. (2008) Information Overload. In K.E. Himma & H.T. Tavani (eds.) *The Handbook of Information and Computer Ethics*. Hoboken: John Wiley. pp:497–515.

Lewis, M. (2014) *Flash Boys: Cracking the money code*. London: Allen Lane.

Leyden, J. (19 January 2011a) Carbon Trading Registry Suspends Ops Following Hack Attack. *Register*. www.theregister.co.uk/2011/01/19/carbon_trading_site_shuts_after_hack_attack/

Leyden, J. (19 January 2011b) Lame Stuxnet Worm 'Full of Errors', Says Security Consultant. *Register*. www.theregister.co.uk/2011/01/19/stuxnet_male_decry_security_researchers/

Leyden, J. (21 January 2011) Facebook Defends Security Strategy. *Register.* www.theregister.co.uk/2011/01/21/facebook_security_analysis/

Leyden, J. (24 January 2011) French President Recovers from Facebook Hack. *Register.* www.theregister.co.uk/2011/01/24/french_pres_facebook_hack/

Leyden, J. (26 January 2011) Zuckerberg's Facebook Page Hacked. *Register.* www.theregister.co.uk/2011/01/26/zuckerberg_facebook_hack/

Library of Congress (2013) *Web Archiving FAQs.* Accessed 10 February 2013. www.loc.gov/webarchiving/faq.html

Lin A. & Silva L. (2005) The Social and Political Construction of Technological Frames. *European Journal of Information Systems* 14(1):49–59.

Linde, F. & Stock, W.G. (2011) *Information Markets: A strategic guideline for the I-commerce.* Berlin: De Gruyter Saur.

Loeffler, T. (1 August 2013) HADOPI Anti-piracy Legislation Officially Repealed by French Government. *Screen Digest.* www.screendigest.com/news/2013_08_hadopi_anti-piracy_legislation_officially_repealed_by_french_government/view.html

Lohmann, L. (2010) Uncertainty Markets and Carbon Markets: Variations on Polanyian themes. *New Political Economy* 15(2):225–54.

Longman, J. (July 24, 2012) Where Even Sausage Rings Are Put on the Chopping Block. *New York Times.* www.nytimes.com/2012/07/25/sports/olympics/2012-london-games-even-sausage-rings-alarm-marketing-police.html

Lorenz, E.N. (1993) *The Essence of Chaos.* Seattle: University of Washington Press.

Luqi & Cooke, D.E. (1995) How to Combine Nonmonotonic Logic and Rapid Prototyping to Help Maintain Software. *International Journal of Software Engineering and Knowledge Engineering* 5(1):89–118.

Luqi & Goguen, J.A. (1997) Formal Methods: Promises and problems. *IEEE Software* January 14(1):73–85.

Luxemburg, R. (1972) The Accumulation of Capital: An anti-critique. In K.J Tarbucjk (ed.) *Imperialism and the Accumulation of Capital.* London: Allen Lane.

Luyendijk, J. (15 September 2011) Voices of Finance: Computer programmer at a trading company. *Guardian Online.* The Banking Blog: Going Native in the World of Finance. www.theguardian.com/commentisfree/joris-luyendijk-banking-blog/2011/sep/15/computer-programmer-high-frequency-trading

Luyendijk, J. (27 September 2011) Capitalism Is Survival of the Fittest, and Sometimes It's Not Pretty. *Guardian Online.* The Banking Blog: Going Native in the World of Finance. www.theguardian.com/commentisfree/joris-luyendijk-banking-blog/2011/sep/26/capitalism-banking-blog-computer-programmer

Lynas, M. (1999) Savages Strike a Blow against Capitalism. *Earth First Journal* 19(7).

Lyon, D. (1988) *The Information Society: Issues and illusions.* Cambridge: Polity.

Lyon, J. (1994) *Electronic Eye: The rise of surveillance society.* Minneapolis: University of Minnesota Press.

MacAskill, E. (1 June 2011) Sarah Palin's Email Exchanges while Alaska Governor to be Released. *Guardian.* www.guardian.co.uk/world/2011/jun/01/sarah-palin-email-exchanges-released

MacDonald, John H.G. (2009) Lateral Excitation of Bridges by Balancing Pedestrians. *Proceedings of the Royal Society* A 8 465(2104):1055–73.

MacDonald, K. (2006) *Global Movements: Action and culture.* Cambridge: Blackwell.

Machlup, F. (1962) *The Production and Distribution of Knowledge in the United States.* Princeton: Princeton University Press.

MacKinnon, R. (15 November 2011) Stop the Great Firewall of America. *New York Times.* Accessed 11 September 2013. www.nytimes.com/2011/11/16/opinion/firewall-law-could-infringe-on-free-speech.html

Mackintosh, J. (1 March 2011) Top 10 Hedge Funds Make $28bn. *Financial Times*. www.ft.com/intl/cms/s/0/24193cbe-4433–11e0-931d-00144feab49a.html

Maiba, H. (2005) Grassroots Transnational Social Movement Activism: The case of People's Global Action. *Sociological Focus* 38(1):41–6.

Mairiza, D., Zowghi, D. & Nurmulian, N. (2010) An Investigation into the Notion of Non-functional Requirements. *Proceedings of the 2010 ACM Symposium on Applied Computing*: 311–17.

Mandeville, B. (1705, 1714, 1732/1988) *Fable of the Bees*. Edited by F.B. Kaye. Indianapolis: Liberty Press.

Mandl, D. (21 December 2012) What Compsci Textbooks Don't Tell You: Real world code sucks. *Register*. www.theregister.co.uk/2012/12/21/financial_software_disasters

Mann, M. (1986) *The Sources of Social Power Vol. 1: A history of power from the beginning to A.D. 1760*. Cambridge: Cambridge University Press.

Marazzi, C. (2011) *The Violence of Financial Capitalism*. New York: Semiotext(e).

Marginson, S. & Considine, M. (2000) *The Enterprise University: Power, governance and reinvention in Australia*. New York: Cambridge University Press.

Marks, S.R. (1974) Durkheim's Theory of Anomie. *American Journal of Sociology* 80(2):329–63.

Markus, O. (2010) *Plan-Driven Methodologies*. https://barelysufficient.org/2010/06/plan-driven-methodologies

Marshall, J.P. (2006a) Negri, Hardt, Distributed Governance and Open Source Software. *Portal: Journal of Multidisciplinary International Studies* 3(1). http://epress.lib.uts.edu.au/ojs/index.php/portal/article/view/122/

Marshall, J.P. (2006b) Categories, Gender and Online Community. *E-Learning* 3(2):245–62. www.wwwords.co.uk/elea/content/pdfs/3/issue3_2.asp#10

Marshall, J.P. (2007) *Living on Cybermind: Categories, communication and control*. New York: Peter Lang.

Marshall, J.P. (2011) Climate Change, Copenhagen and Psycho-social Disorder. *PORTAL Journal of Multidisciplinary International Studies* 8(3):1–23. http://epress.lib.uts.edu.au/ojs/index.php/portal/article/viewArticle/1757

Marshall, J.P. (2012) Information Technology and the Experience of Disorder. *Cultural Studies Review* 18(3):281–309.

Marshall, J.P. (2013a) The Information Society: Permanent crisis through the (dis) ordering of networks. *Global Networks* 13(3):290–309.

Marshall, J.P. (2013b) Communication Failure and the Financial Crisis. *Globalizations* 10(3):367–81.

Marshall, J. & Zowghi, D. (2010) Software and the Social Production of Disorder. In Katrina Michael (ed.) *Proceedings of the 2010 IEEE International Symposium on Technology and Society*. Wollongong. pp. 284–91.

Marshall, P. (1992) *Demanding the Impossible: A history of anarchism*. London: HarperCollins.

Martin, P. (11 January 2011) Bank Call Centre Staff Assist Account Breaches. *Sydney Morning Herald*. a) www.smh.com.au/business/fraud-is-a-cinch—just-ask-your-bank-20110110–19l77.html b) www.theage.com.au/business/bank-call-centre-staff-assist-account-breaches-20110110-19l4f.html

Martin, P. (9 December 2013) Coalition Blocks Senate from Secret Details of Trans-Pacific Partnership Trade Deal. *Sydney Morning Herald*. www.smh.com.au/federal-politics/political-news/coalition-blocks-senate-from-secret-details-of-transpacific-partnership-trade-deal-20131208-2yzh2.html

Martin, P. (10 December 2013) Leaked Memo Reveals 'Weakness' in Trans-Pacific Partnership Delegation's Trade Stance. *Sydney Morning Herald*. www.smh.com.au/federal-politics/political-news/leaked-memo-reveals-weakness-in-transpacific-partnership-delegations-trade-stance-20131209-2z1ul.html

Martin, P. (13 December 2013) Australia 'Stumbling Block' on Tobacco Law. *Sydney Morning Herald*. www.smh.com.au/national/australia-stumbling-block-on-tobacco-law-20131212-2zae7.html

Martin, R.C. (2010) What Killed Waterfall Could Kill Agile. http://cleancoder.posterous.com/what-killed-waterfall-could-kill-agile

Marx, K. & Engels, F. (1968) Manifesto of the Communist Party. In Marx and Engels *Selected Works in One Voume*. Moscow: Progress Publishers.

Mason, M. (2008) *The Pirate's Dilemma: How youth culture is reinventing capitalism*. New York: Free Press.

Masuda, Y. (1980) *The Information Society as Post-Industrial Society*. Washington: World Future Society.

Mathews, D. (2012) The Rise and Fall of the Anti-Counterfeiting Trade Agreement (ACTA): Lessons for the European Union. *Queen Mary University of London, School of Law Legal Studies Research Paper* No. 127/2012. http://papers.ssrn.com/sol3/papers.cfm?abstract_id=2161764

Maurer, B. (2006) The Anthropology of Money. *Annual Review of Anthropology* 35:15–36.

Maxwell, R. & Miller, T. (2012) *Greening the Media*. New York: Oxford University Press.

McAllister, N. (17 August 2013) Google Goes Dark for 2 Minutes, Kills 40% of World's Net Traffic. *Register*. www.theregister.co.uk/2013/08/17/google_outage/

McCallum, R.D. (2008) *Cable 08CANBERRA1197, Film/TV Industry Files Copyright Case Against Aussie ISP*. Wikileaks. Accessed 7 September 2013. http://wikileaks.org/cable/2008/11/08CANBERRA1197.html

McCaughey, M. & Ayers, M. (2003) *Cyberactivism: Online activism in theory and practice*. London: Routledge.

McCracken, D.D. & Jackson, M.A. (1982) Life Cycle Concept Considered Harmful. *ACM SIGSOFT, Software Engineering Notes* 7(2):29–32.

McDonald Gibson, C. & Lichfield, J. (25 May 2014) European Election Results 2014: Far-right parties flourish across Europe. *Independent*. www.independent.co.uk/news/world/europe/european-election-results-2014-farright-parties-flourish-across-europe-in-snub-to-austerity-9434069.html

Mclachlan, G. & Reid, I. (1994) *Framing and Interpretation*. Carlton: Melbourne University Press.

McLean, B. & Nocera, J. (November 2010) The Blundering Herd. *Vanity Fair*. www.vanityfair.com/business/features/2010/11/financial-crisis-excerpt-201011

McManus, J. & Wood-Harper, T. (2007) Understanding the Source of Information Systems Project Failure. *Management Services* 51(3):38–43.

McNally D. (2009) From Financial Crisis to World-Slump: Accumulation, financialisation and the global slowdown. *Historical Materialism* 17: 35–83.

Mearian, L. (8 August 2012) Internet Archive Unleashes 1PB of Data through BitTorrent: Low-budget movies among the most popular downloads. *Computerworld (US)*. Accessed 8 September 2013. www.computerworld.com.au/article/433120/internet_archive_unleashes_1pb_data_through_bittorrent

Melucci, A. (1996) *Challenging Codes: Collective action in the twentieth century*. Cambridge: Cambridge University Press.

Meng, X., Zerfos, P., Samanta, V., Wong, S.H.Y., & Lu, S. (2007) Analysis of the Reliability of a Nationwide Short Message Service. In *Proceedings IEEE Infocom 2007*: 1811–19.

Merton, R. (1993) *On the Shoulders of Giants: A Shandean postscript*. Chicago: University of Chicago Press.

Metz, C. (12 January 2011) Google Axes Jobsian Codec in Name of 'Open'. *Register*. www.theregister.co.uk/2011/01/12/google_pulls_h264_from_chrome/

Metz, C. (15 January 2011) Google Plugins Force-Feed Open Codec to IE and Safari. *Register*. www.theregister.co.uk/2011/01/15/google_does_webm_plugins_for_ie_and_safari/

Metz, C. (24 January 2011) Google Accused of Copying (More) Oracle Java code. *Register*. www.theregister.co.uk/2011/01/24/google_accused_of_copying_oracle_java_code_again/

Metz, C. (26 January 2011) Facebook Offers 500 Million Users SSL Crypto. *Register*. www.theregister.co.uk/2011/01/26/facebook_https/

Metz, C. (29 January 2011) Google to Settle State 'Wi-Spy' Spat out of Court. *Register*. www.theregister.co.uk/2011/01/29/google_connecticut_aggreement/

Mezias, J.M. & Starbuck, W.H. (2003). Studying the Accuracy of Manager's Perceptions: A research odyssey. *British Journal of Management* 14(3):3–17.

Meyrowitz, J. (1985) *No Sense of Place*. New York: Oxford University Press.

Michaels, S. (18 August 2009) Radiohead Officially Release 'These Are My Twisted Words'. *Guardian*. www.theguardian.com/music/2009/aug/18/radiohead-official-release

Middleton, T. (24 April 2012) Open Book Publishers Releases 'The Digital Public Domain'. *Open Knowledge Foundation blog*. http://blog.okfn.org/2012/04/24/open-book-publishers-releases-the-digital-public-domain

Miller, D. & Hartwick, J. (2002) Spotting Management Fads. *Harvard Business Review* 80(10):26–7.

Millar, J. (7 June 2011) Stealth Marketing—the 21st Century Con. http://ethicstechnologyandsociety.wordpress.com/2011/06/07/stealth-marketing-the-21st-century-con/

Milne A., & Maiden N. (2012) Power and Politics in Requirements Engineering: Embracing the dark side? *Requirements Engineering Journal* 17(2):83–98.

Mirowski, P. (2013) *Never Let a Serious Crisis Go to Waste: How Neoliberalism survived the financial meltdown*. London: Verso.

Mitchell, L. (2005) Structural Holes, CEOs, and Informational Monopolies. *Brooklyn Law Review* 70(4):1313–68.

Monbiot, G. (29 August 2011) Academic Publishers Make Murdoch Look Like a Socialist. *Guardian*. www.guardian.co.uk/commentisfree/2011/aug/29/academic-publishers-murdoch-socialist

Moody, G. (2001) *Rebel Code: Linux and the open source revolution*. London: Allen Lane, Penguin Press.

Moody, G. (31 January 2012) Will Academics' Boycott of Elsevier Be the Tipping Point for Open Access—Or Another Embarrassing Flop? *TechDirt*. www.techdirt.com/articles/20120130/13030217589/will-academics-boycott-elsevier-be-tipping-point-open-access-another-embarrassing-flop.shtml

Morgenson, G. (8 November 2008) How the Thundering Herd Faltered and Fell. *New York Times*. www.nytimes.com/2008/11/09/business/09magic.html?pagewanted=all&_r=0

Motion Picture Association of America, National Music Publishers' Association & Recording Industry Association of America (2012) *Joint Submission to the United States Intellectual Property Enforcement Coordinator*. www.mpaa.org/Resources/7960e748-c27e-4745-afe9–1012c85a4755.pdf

Mulgan, G.J. (1991) Communication and Control. Cambridge: Polity.

Mullaney, T. (6 October 2013) Obama Adviser: Demand overwhelmed HealthCare.gov. www.usatoday.com/story/news/nation/2013/10/05/health-care-website-repairs/2927597/

Mullery G.P. (1979) CORE: A method for controlled requirements expression. *Proceedings of the 4th International Conference on Software Engineering (ICSE-4)*. IEEE Computer Society Press: 126–35.

Mullin, J. (23 May 2013) Patent Troll that Wants $1,000 per Worker Gets Sued by Vermont A-G. *ArsTechnica*. http://arstechnica.com/tech-policy/2013/05/patent-troll-that-wants-1000-per-worker-gets-sued-by-vermont-a-g/

Mullin, J. (14 August 2013) Lavabit Founder, Under Gag Order, Speaks Out About Shutdown Decision. *Ars Technica.* http://arstechnica.com/tech-policy/2013/08/lavabit-founder-under-gag-order-speaks-out-about-shut-down-decision

Munck, R. (2006) *Globalisation and Contestation: The new great counter-movement.* London: Routledge.

Naim, M. (2006) *Illicit: How smugglers, traffickers and copycats are hijacking the global economy.* London: William Heinemann.

Nanex (20 September 2011) HFT Breaks Speed-of-Light Barrier, Sets Trading Speed World Record. www.nanex.net/Research/fantaseconds/fantaseconds.html

Nanex (20 December 2013) Nanex ~ Fantaseconds. www.nanex.net/aqck2/4518.html

Napoleoni, L. (2008) *Rogue Economics: Capitalism's new reality.* New York: Seven Stories Press.

Napoleoni, L. (2010) *Terrorism and the Economy: How the War on Terror is bankrupting the world.* New York: Seven Stories Press.

Narraine, R. (21 March 2006) Spyware Trail Leads to Kazaa, Big Advertisers. *E-week.* www.eweek.com/c/a/Security/Spyware-Trail-Leads-to-Kazaa-Big-Advertisers/

National Fraud Authority (2011) *Annual Fraud Indicator.* UK Home Office. www.homeoffice.gov.uk/publications/agencies-public-bodies/nfa/annual-fraud-indicator/annual-fraud-indicator-2011

NCIX (2011) *Foreign Spies Stealing US Economic Secrets in Cyberspace: Report to Congress on foreign economic collection and industrial espionage 2009–2011.* www.ncix.gov/publications/reports/fecie_all/Foreign_Economic_Collection_2011.pdf

Negri, A. (2004) *Negri on Negri: In conversation with Anne Dufourmentelle.* New York: Routledge.

Nelson, C. & Watt, S. (2004) *Office Hours: Activism and change in the academy.* London: Routledge.

Nerur S., Mahapatra R. & Mangalaraj G. (2005) Challenges of Migrating to Agile Methodologies. *Communications of the ACM* 48(5):72–8.

Neumann, P.G. (2007) Widespread Network Failures. *Communications of the ACM* 50(2):112.

Newman, M. (2002) Software Errors Cost U.S. Economy $59.5 Billion Annually. NIST Press Release. http://web.archive.org/web/20090510083405/http://www.nist.gov/public_affairs/releases/n02–10.htm

Newton-Small, J. (13 June 2012) Hillary's Little Startup: How the U.S. is using technology to aid Syria's rebels. *Time.* http://world.time.com/2012/06/13/hillarys-little-startup-how-the-u-s-is-using-technology-to-aid-syrias-rebels/

Neylon, T. (2012) The Cost of Knowledge [website]. http://thecostofknowledge.com

Nielsen, M. (2012) The Cost of Knowledge. *PolyMath* [wiki] http://michaelnielsen.org/polymath1/index.php?title=The_cost_of_knowledge

Nikiforuk, A. (23 December 2013) What's Driving Chaotic Dismantling of Canada's Science Libraries? http://thetyee.ca/News/2013/12/23/Canadian-Science-Libraries/

Notes From Nowhere (2003) *We Are Everywhere: The irresistible rise of global anticapitalism.* London: Verso.

Nurmuliani, N., Zowghi D. & Williams S. (2005) Characterising Requirements Volatility: An empirical analysis. *Proceedings of the 4th International Symposium on Empirical Software Engineering (ISESE).* Noosa: Australia: 427–36.

Oates, J. (14 January 2011) Sainsbury's Techie Jailed for Loyalty Card Scam. *Register.* www.theregister.co.uk/2011/01/14/sainsburys_fraud_prison/

O'Brien, N. (2 October 2011) Dumped Computers Exploited in Overseas Fraud. *Sydney Morning Herald.* www.smh.com.au/technology/security/dumped-computers-exploited-in-overseas-fraud-20111001–1l2rj.html

Observer (20 June 1999) Virtual Chaos Baffles Police. *Observer*: 9.

OECD (2008a) *Tertiary Education for the Knowledge Society: Executive summary.* Paris: OECD. www.oecd.org/edu/skills-beyond-school/41303688.pdf

OECD (2008b) *Funding Tertiary Education Pointers for policy development.* Paris: OECD. www.oecd.org/edu/skills-beyond-school/44124839.pdf

OECD (2011) *Education at a Glance: How much do tertiary students pay and what public subsidies do they receive.* Indicator B5. Paris: OECD. www.oecd.org/edu/skills-beyond-school/48631028.pdf

OECD (2012) *Innovation in Science, Technology and Industry: Global forum on the knowledge economy.* www.oecd.org/innovation/inno/globalforumontheknowledge economy.htm

Office of the United States Trades Representative (2011) *Out-of-Cycle Review of Notorious Markets.* Washington, D.C. www.ustr.gov/webfm_send/3215

Oldani, C. (2008) *Governing Global Derivatives.* Aldershot, UK: Ashgate.

Oliver-Smith, A. (1996) Anthropological Research on Hazards and Disasters. *Annual Review of Anthropology* 25:303–28.

Olson, P. (27 January 2012) Amid ACTA Outcry, Politicians Don Anonymous Guy Fawkes Masks. *Forbes.* Accessed 12 September 2013. www.forbes.com/sites/parmyolson/2012/01/27/amid-acta-outcy-politicians-don-anonymous-guy-fawkes-masks

OMG (2001) The Agile Manifesto. http://agilemanifesto.org

Onnela, J.-P., Saramäki, J., Hyvönen, J., Szabó, G., Lazer, D., Kaski, K., Kertész, J. & Barabási, A-L. (2007) Structure and Tie Strengths in Mobile Communication Networks. *Proceedings of the National Academy of Sciences* 104(18):7332–6.

OpenDoar (2012) The Directory of Open Access Repositories. OpenDOAR. Nottingham: University of Nottingham. www.opendoar.org

Oreskovic, A. (15 April 2014) Google Explains Exactly How It Reads All Your Email. *Huffington Post.* www.huffingtonpost.com/2014/04/15/gmail-ads_n_5149032.html

Orthangazi, O. (2008) Financialisation and Capital Accumulation in the Non-Financial Corporate Sector: Theoretical and empirical evidence: 1973–2003. *Cambridge Journal of Economics* 32(6):863–86.

Osberg, L. (2104) What's So Bad about More Inequality? Keynote Address to *Academy of the Social Sciences in Australia 2013 Annual Symposium,* Canberra, Australia 12 November 2013. www.nuigalway.ie/media/publicsub-sites/economics/news/More-Inequality-Feb-10–2014[1].pdf

OSI and FSF (2011) Position Statement on CPTN Transaction. http://opensource.org/files/CPTN-Position-Final.pdf

Osterhout, J.E. (18 April 2010) Stealth Marketing: When you're being pitched and you don't even know it! *NY Daily News.* www.nydailynews.com/life-style/stealth-marketing-pitched-don-article-1.165278

O'Sullivan, M. & Kearsley, R. (2012) The Global Wealth Pyramid. *Credit Suisse.* www.credit-suisse.com/ch/en/news-and-expertise/news/economy/global-trends.article.html/article/pwp/news-and-expertise/2012/10/en/the-global-wealth-pyramid.html

Ovaska P., Rossi M. & Smolander K. (2005) Filtering, Negotiations and Shifting in the Understanding of Information System Requirements. *Scandinavian Journal of Information Systems* 17(1):31–66

Oxfam (2014) Working for the Few: Political capture and economic inequality. *Oxfam Briefing Paper* 178. www.oxfam.org.au/wp-content/uploads/2014/01/bp-working-for-few-political-capture-economic-inequality-200114-embargo-en.pdf

Ozimek, J.F. (10 January 2011) Facebook Boobs over Breastfeeding Page… Again. *Register.* www.theregister.co.uk/2011/01/10/anger_over_facebook_breastfeeding_group_weekend_shut_down/

Palan, R. (2003) *The Offshore World: Sovereign markets, virtual places and nomad millionaires.* Ithaca: Cornell University Press.

Papows, J. (2011) *Glitch: The hidden impact of faulty software*. Boston: Pearson Education.

Pareto, V. (1901/1968) *The Rise and Fall of the Elites: An application of theoretical sociology*. New Jersey: Bedminster.

Parliamentary Ombudsman (2011) A Breach of Confidence. www.ombudsman.org.uk/__data/assets/pdf_file/0012/6411/PHSO-0108-HC-709-report-final-web-11012011.pdf

Patterson, S. (17 April 2013) Dark Pool Brawl Breaks Out. *Wall Street Journal, Money-Beat*. http://blogs.wsj.com/moneybeat/2013/04/17/nyse-credit-suisse-spat-shines-light-on-dark-pools/

Pear, R., LaFraniere, S. & Austen, I. (12 October 2013) From the Start, Signs of Trouble at Health Portal. *New York Times*. www.nytimes.com/2013/10/13/us/politics/from-the-start-signs-of-trouble-at-health-portal.html

Peckham, M. (1979) *Explanation and Power: The control of human behaviour*. New York: Seabury Press.

Peekhaus, W. (2012) The Enclosure and Alienation of Academic Publishing: Lessons for the professoriate. *Triple C: Cogniton, Communication, Co-operation* 10(2):577–99. www.triple-c.at/index.php/tripleC/article/view/395

Pender, K. (6 January 2011) Chase Misses Checks' Red Ink, Closes Bank Account. www.sfgate.com/cgi-bin/article.cgi?f%3D%252Fc%252Fa%252F2011%252F0 1%252F05%252FBUUJ1H4422.DTL

Penty, A. (1922) *Post-industrialism*. New York: MacMillan.

Perkmann, M. & Spicer, A. (2008) How Are Management Fashions Institutionalized? The role of institutional work. *Human Relations* 61(6):811–44.PGA (1998a) Organisational Principles, Agreed February 1998. www.nadir.org/nadir/initiativ/agp/cocha/principles.htm

Pesek, W. (21 December 2013) Trade Secrets: Why is the US so quiet on the Trans-Pacific Partnership? www.smh.com.au/business/world-business/trade-secrets-why-is-the-us-so-quiet-on-the-transpacific-partnership-20131220–2zqv2.html

Peter, L.J. & Hull, R. (1969) *The Peter Principle: Why things always go wrong*. London: Souvenir Press.

Peterson, I. (1993) *Newton's Clock: Chaos in the solar system*. New York. WH Freeman.

PGA (1998b) Actions of the People's Global Action against the WTO Summit. *PGA Bulletin* 2, June. Geneva: People's Global Action. www.nadir.org/nadir/initiativ/agp/en/pgainfos/bulletin2/bulletin2b.html

PGA (1999) J18: Reflections and analysis. *PGA Bulletin 5*. Geneva: People's Global Action.

Pierceall, K. (3 February 2011) Storm-Related Phone Outages Sign Network Needs Fix, Groups Say. *Press-Enterprise*. www.pe.com/business/local/stories/PE_News_Local_D_telephone04.26f7d84.html

Pigman, G.A. (2007) *The World Economic Forum: A multi-stakeholder approach to global governance*. Oxford: Routledge.

Piller, C. (9 April 2006) How Piracy Opens Doors for Windows. *L.A. Times*. http://articles.latimes.com/2006/apr/09/business/fi-micropiracy9

Pirate Bay (9 August 2013) Happy X! *The Pirate Bay Blog*. http://thepiratebay.sx/blog/232

Pirie, I. (2009) The Political Economy of Academic Publishing. *Historical Materialism* 17(3):31–60.

Plohetski, T., Grisales, C. & Ward, M. (2 February 2011) Cause of Power Shortage in Texas Still Unclear. *American Statesman*. www.statesman.com/news/local/cause-of-power-shortage-in-texas-still-unclear-1229215.html

PLoS (2012) Public Library of Science Publication Fees. www.plos.org/publish/pricing-policy/publication-fees

Polansek, T. (10 February 2014) High-Speed Traders Mount Defense as CFTC Studies Sector. *Reuters.* www.reuters.com/article/2014/02/10/cftc-hft-committee-idUSL2 N0LF1LG20140210

Pollack, A. & Wayne, L. (3 June 1998) Ending Suit, Merrill Lynch to Pay California County $400 Million. *New York Times.* www.nytimes.com/1998/06/03/business/ending-suit-merrill-lynch-to-pay-california-county-400-million.html

Popper, N. (2 August 2012) Knight Capital Says Trading Glitch Cost It $440 Million. *New York Times.* http://dealbook.nytimes.com/2012/08/02/knight-capital-says-trading-mishap-cost-it-440-million/

Porter, C. (17 September 2013) Tony Abbott Has Not Included a Science Minister in New Cabinet. *News.com.au.* www.news.com.au/technology/science/tony-abbott-has-not-included-a-science-minister-in-new-cabinet/story-fn5fsgyc-122672 0375674

Pound, D.W. (1990) *Political Economy and Ideology in the Managerial-Technological Society.* Dubuque: Kendal Hunt.

Prendergast, C. (1993) A Theory of 'Yes Men.' *American Economic Review* 83(4):757–70.

Pressman R.S. (2005) *Software Engineering: A practitioner's approach.* 6th Edition. New York: McGraw-Hill.

Prigogine, I. (1997) *The End of Certainty: Time, chaos and the new laws of nature.* New York: Free Press.

Project Gutenberg (2012) Free eBooks by Project Gutenberg. www.gutenberg.org

ProQuest (2009) Resources Catalogue. www.proquest.com/en-US/products/audience/higheredu.shtml

QFCI (2012) *Final Report.* Queensland Floods Commission of Enquiry. www.flood commission.qld.gov.au/__data/assets/pdf_file/0007/11698/QFCI-Final-Report-March-2012.pdf

Quinn, B. & Sweney, M. (8 June 2013) Tobacco Firm Begins 'Stealth-marketing' Campaign Against Plain Packaging. *Guardian.* www.theguardian.com/society/2013/jun/07/tobacco-firm-stealth-marketing-plain-packaging

Qwest comments (2011) www.topix.net/forum/source/las-cruces-sun-news/TT5ICI MLVU6E1T506

Rachwald, R. (13 November 2008) Hacking—The corporate cover-up. *SC Magazine.* www.scmagazine.com/hacking—the-corporate-cover-up/article/120999/

Rane, H. & Salem, S. (2012) Social Media, Social Movements and the Diffusion of Ideas in the Arab Uprisings. *Journal of International Communication* 18(1):97–111.

Rapidshare (2013a) About Us. Accessed 11 September 2013. https://rapidshare.com/#rsag_about

Rapidshare(2013b)TermsofUse.Accessed11September2013.https://rapidshare.com/#rsag_tou

Ratemo, J. (21 January 2011) Cable Cuts Put Safaricom Subscribers Off Air. *Standard Digital.* www.standardmedia.co.ke/?articleID=2000027149&pageNo=1

Ray, B. (28 January 2011) Finnish Regulator Calls for iPhone Refunds: It's cold in Finland, bloody cold. *Register.* www.theregister.co.uk/2011/01/28/finland_iphone

Rayport, J. (31 December 1996). The Vrus of Marketing. *Fast Company.* www.fastcompany.com/magazine/06/virus.html

Reed Elsevier (2010) Results Announcement 2009. www.reedelsevier.com/mediacentre/pressreleases/Documents/2010/Reed%20Elsevier%202009%20Results%20Announcement%2017%20February%202010%20FINAL.pdf

Reed Elsevier (2011) Annual Report and Financial Statements. http://reporting.reedel sevier.com/ar11

Reed Elsevier (2012) Annual Reports and Financial Statements. http://reporting.reedel sevier.com/staticreports/Reed_AR_2011.pdf

Reich, R. (2007) *Supercapitalism: The transformation of business, democracy, and everyday life*. New York: Random House.

Reitan, R. (2007) *Global Activism*. London: Routledge.

Return Path (2009) The Global Email Deliverability Benchmark Report. www.returnpath.com

Reuters (14 January 2011) Hacker of Sarah Palin's Email Found Guilty. *Brisbane Times*. www.brisbanetimes.com.au/technology/security/hacker-of-sarah-palins-email-found-guilty-20110114–19qef.html

Reuters (13 March 2014) Stock Market Traders Being Replaced by Computers, According to Survey. *Guardian*. www.theguardian.com/business/2014/mar/13/stock-market-traders-replaced-by-computers

Rid, T. (2010) Cracks in the Jihad. *Wilson Quarterly*. 34(1):40–7.

Rifkin, J. (1995) *The End of Work: The decline of the global labor force and the dawn of the post-market era*. New York: G.P. Putnam's Sons.

Riley, C. (July 10 2012) Olympians Face Financial Hardship @CNNMoney. http://money.cnn.com/2012/07/10/news/economy/olympic-athletes-financial/index.htm

ROAR (2012) *Registry of Open Access Repositories (ROAR)*. Southampton: University of Southampton. http://roar.eprints.org

Robinson, J. (2003) *The Sink: Terror, crime and dirty money in the offshore world*. London: Constable & Robinson.

Rogers, S. (14 January 2011) Public Data Corporation: The end of our world, or just the beginning. *Guardian*. www.guardian.co.uk/news/datablog/2011/jan/14/public-data-corporation

Rootes, C. & Saunders, C. (2007) The Global Justice Movements in Great Britain. In D. Della Porta (ed.) *The Global Justice Movement: Cross-national and transnational perspectives*. Boulder: Paradigm Publishers. pp.128–56.

Rosenberg, J. (2000) *Follies of Globalisation Theory*. London: Verso.

Rosenkranz, E.J., Cariello, C.J., Davies, M.S. & Bagdady, J.P. (2013) Amicus Curiae in Highmark v. Allcare Management Systems, in Support of Neither Party. www.americanbar.org/content/dam/aba/publications/supreme_court_preview/briefs-v3/12–1163–12–1184_np_amcu_apple.authcheckdam.pdf

Ross, M.H. (1993) *The Culture of Conflict: Interpretations and interests in comparative perspective*. New Haven: Yale University Press.

Rost J. (2004) Political Reasons for Failed Software Projects. *IEEE Software* 21(6):102–4.

Routledge, P. (1998) Going Globile: Spatiality, embodiment and media-tion in the Zapatista insurgency. In S. Dalby & G. O'Tuathail (eds.) *Rethinking Geopolitics*. London: Routledge. pp.240–26.

Royce W.W. (1970) Managing the Development of Large Software Systems: Concepts and techniques. *Proceedings of IEEE WESCON*: 1–9.

RTS (1999) *Reflections on J18: Discussion papers on the politics, of the global day of action in financial centres on June 18th 1999*. London: Reclaim the Streets.

Rupert, M. (2003) Globalising Common Sense: A Marxian-Gramscian (re-)vision of the politics of governance/resistance. *Review of International Studies* 29(S):181–98.

Rusbridger, A. & MacAskill, E. (18 July 2014) Edward Snowden Urges Professionals to Encrypt Client Communications. *Guardian*. www.theguardian.com/world/2014/jul/17/edward-snowden-professionals-encrypt-client-communications-nsa-spy

Rushkoff, D. (1996) *Media Virus! Hidden agendas in popular culture*. New York: Ballantine.

Ruskin, J. (1907) *Unto This Last and Other Essays on Art and Political Economy*. London: J.M. Dent.

Russell, T. (2010) *A Renegade History of the United States*. London: Simon & Schuster.

Rutherford, T. (20 January 2011) Comcast Internet Outages Concern Huntington City Council. *HuntingtonNews*. www.huntingtonnews.net/987

Sampedro, V. (2004) The Alternative Movement and Its Media Strategy. In F. Polet (ed.) *Globalising Resistance: The state of struggle*. London: Pluto Press.

Sandvine (2011) *Global Internet Phenomena Report, Fall 2011*. Ontario: Waterloo.

Sandvine (2012) *Global Internet Phenomena Report: 2H 2012*. Ontario: Waterloo.

Saran, C. (27 May 2003) Software Failures Damage Business. *Computer Weekly*: 5.

Sauer, C., Gemino, A. & Reich, B.H. (2007) The Impact of Size and Volatility on Software Performance. *Communications of the ACM* 50(11):79–84.

Sawyer P., Sommerville I. & Viller S. (1998) Improving the Requirements Process. *Proceedings of the Fourth International Workshop on Requirements Engineering: Foundation of Software Quality* (REFSQ'98). Pisa: 71–84.

Scheier, R.L. (14 May 2001) Stabilizing Your Risk. *ComputerWorld*. www.computerworld.com/s/article/60298/Stabilizing_Your_Risk

Schiller, D. (1999) *Digital Capitalism: Networking the global market system*. Cambridge, MA: MIT Press.

Schimroszik, N. (6 November 2012) S&P Guilty of Misleading Investors. *Guardian*. www.theguardian.com/business/2012/nov/05/standard-poors-guilty-misleading-investors

Schmidt, E. (2005). Technology Is Making Marketing Accountable. *Google Podium*. www.google.com/press/podium/ana.html

Schneider, D. (23 September 2011) Financial Trading at the Speed of Light. *IEEE Spectrum*. http://spectrum.ieee.org/computing/it/financial-trading-at-the-speed-of-light

Science Daily (3 November 2005) Explaining Why the Millennium Bridge Wobbled. *ScienceDaily*. www.sciencedaily.com/releases/2005/11/051103080801.htm

Secunia (2011) *Yearly Report 2010*. Copenhagen. http://secunia.com/gfx/pdf/Secunia_Yearly_Report_2010.pdf

Seidler, E. (nd) Dirty Money, Who Profits from Piracy? Accessed 9 September 2013. http://popuppirates.com

Sessions, R. (29 October 2009) The Problem with Standish. http://simplearchitectures.blogspot.com.au/2009/10/problem-with-standish.html

Shannon, C. & Weaver, W. (1949) *Mathematical Theory of Communication*. Urbana: University of Illinois.

Shear, M. & Pear, R. (8 October 2013) Health Exchange Delays Tied to Software Crash in Early Rush. *New York Times*. www.nytimes.com/2013/10/08/us/health-exchange-delays-tied-to-software-crash-in-early-rush.html

Shenk, D. (1997) *DataSmog: Surviving the Information Age*. New York: Harper Collins.

SHERPA (2012a) *SHERPA*. Nottingham: University of Nottingham. www.sherpa.ac.uk

SHERPA (2012b) SHERPA's RoMEO: Definitions and terms. www.sherpa.ac.uk/romeo/definitions.php?la=en&fIDnum=|&mode=simple&version=#colours

Shirky, C. (2011) The Political Power of Social Media. *Foreign Affairs* 90(1):1–10.

Siddiqi J. & Shekaran M.C. (1996) *Requirements Engineering: The emerging wisdom*, *IEEE Software* 13(2):15–19.

Simmel, G. (1955) *Conflict and the Web of Group Relations*. New York: Free Press.

Simon, H.A. (1981) *The Science of the Artificial*. 2nd Edition. Cambridge, MA: MIT Press.

Singh, C. & Sprintson, A. (2010) Reliability Assurance of Cyber-physical Power Systems. *Power and Energy Society General Meeting*. IEEE: 1–6. http://ieeexplore.ieee.org/xpls/abs_all.jsp?arnumber=5590189

Slade, G. (2006) *Made to Break: Technology and obsolescence in America*. Cambridge: Harvard University Press.

Slivka, E. (30 September 2013) Resetting Network Settings May Fix iMessages Not Working in iOS 7. *MacRumors*. www.macrumors.com/2013/09/30/resetting-network-settings-may-fix-imessages-not-working-in-ios-7

SMH (19 January 2011) Facebook Halts Plan to Share Contact Information with App Developers. *Sydney Morning Herald*. www.smh.com.au/technology/technology-news/facebook-halts-plan-to-share-contact-information-with-app-developers-20110119-19vmm.html

Smith, A. (1982) *Wealth of Nations*. Indianapolis: Liberty Fund.

Smith, A. (2005) The International Mobilisation to Gleneagles. In D. Harvie, K. Milburn, B. Trott & D. Wats (eds.) *Shut Them Down: The G8, Gleneagles 2005 and the movement of movements*. Leeds and New York: Autonomedia and Dissent!pp:151–62.

Smith, D. (2013) Offshore Shell Games: The use of offshore tax havens by the top 100 publicly traded companies. *US PIRG*. www.uspirg.org/sites/pirg/files/reports/Offshore_Shell_Games_USPIRG.pdf.

Smith, T., Coyle, J.R., Lightfoot, E. & Scott, A. (2007). Reconsidering Models of Influence: The relationship between consumer social networks and word-of-mouth effectiveness. *Journal of Advertising Research* 47(4):387–97.

Snow, D. & Benford, R. (1988) Ideology, Frame Resonance, and Participant Mobilization. *International Social Movement Research* 1:197–217.

Sommer, P. & Brown, I. (2011) Reducing Systemic Cybersecurity Risk. *OECD/IFP Project on 'Future Global Shocks'*. www.oecd.org/dataoecd/57/44/46889922.pdf

Sommerville I. (2010), *Software Engineering*. Ninth Edition. Boston: Addison Wesley.

Sornette D. & Von Der Becke, S. (2011) Crashes and High Frequency Trading, An Evaluation of Risks Produced by High Speed Algorithmic Trading. *Swiss Finance Institute Research Paper* 11(63). http://papers.ssrn.com/sol3/papers.cfm?abstract_id=1976249

Soros, G. (1994) *Alchemy of Finance*. Hoboken: John Wiley.

Soros, G. (2010) *The Soros Lectures at the Central European University*. New York: PublicAffairs.

SPARC (2012) Scholarly Publishing and Academic Resources Coalition (SPARC). www.arl.org/sparc/index.shtml

SQS (2013) SQS Identifies the Highest Profile Software Failures of 2012. www.sqs.com/portal/news/en/press-releases-173.php

SQW Limited (2004) *Costs and Business Models in Scientific Research Publishers*. London: Wellcome Trust.

St John, G. (2004a) Counter Tribes, Global Protests and Carnivals of Reclamation. *Peace Review: A Journal of Social Justice* 16(4): 421–28.

St John, G. (14 November 2004b) Global 'Protestival': Reclaiming the streets and the future. *MC Reviews*. http://reviews.media-culture.org.au/modules.php?name=News&file=article&sid=1903

Stafford, M. (2012) Predatory Online Journals Lure Scholars Who Are Eager to Publish. *Chronicle of Higher Education* 58(27): http://chronicle.com/article/Predatory-Online-Journals/131047/

Stammers, N. & Eschle, C. (2005) Social Movements and Global Activism. In W. de Jong, M. Shaw & N. Stammers (eds.) *Global Activism, Global Media*. London: Pluto Press.

Starbuck, W.H. (1992) Strategizing in the Real World. *International Journal of Technology Management* 8(1–2):77–85.

Steger, M., Goodman J. & Wilson, E. (2013) *Justice Globalism: Ideology, crises, policy*. London: Sage.

Steiner, C. & Coster, H. (13 April 2010) How Facebook Ruined My Career. *Forbes Online*. www.forbes.com/2010/04/13/how-facebook-ruined-my-career-entrepreneurs-human-resources-facebook.html

Steiner, G. (1975) *After Babel: Aspects of language and translation.* Oxford: Oxford University Press.

Steiner, S. (29 January 2014) Does High-frequency Trading Change the Game? *Bankrate. com.* www.bankrate.com/finance/investing/does-high-frequency-trading-change-the-game-1.aspx

Stempel, J. (17 July 2013) Judge Lets U.S. Pursue $5-Billion Fraud Lawsuit Against S&P. *Reuters.* www.reuters.com/article/2013/07/17/us-mcgrawhill-sandp-lawsuit-idUSBRE96G08620130717

Stempel, J. (3 September 2013) S&P Calls Federal Lawsuit 'Retaliation' for U.S. Downgrade. *Retuers.* www.reuters.com/article/2013/09/03/us-mcgrawhill-sandp-lawsuit-idUSBRE98210L20130903

Stiglitz, J.E. (2012) *The Price of Inequality. With a new preface.* New York: W.W. Norton.

Stiglitz, J. (2013) Open Letter to the TPP Negotiators. http://keionline.org/sites/default/files/jstiglitzTPP.pdf

Stolberg, C.G. & McIntyre, M. (5 October 2013) A Federal Budget Crisis Months in the Planning. *New York Times.* www.nytimes.com/2013/10/06/us/a-federal-budget-crisis-months-in-the-planning.html

Story, L. (23 February 2009) Cuomo Has More Questions on Merrill Bonuses. *New York Times.* www.nytimes.com/2009/02/24/business/24cuomo.html

Story, L. (18 March 2009) Cuomo Wins Ruling to Name Merrill Bonus Recipients. *New York Times.* www.nytimes.com/2009/03/19/business/19cuomo.html

Strange, S. (1986) *Casino Capitalism.* Oxford: Basil Blackwell.

Strangelove, M. (2005) *The Empire of Mind: Digital piracy and the anti-capitalist movement.* Toronto: University of Toronto Press.

Strathern, M. (1988) *The Gender of the Gift: Problems with women and problems with society in Melanesia.* Berkeley: University of California Press.

Strogatz, S. (2003) *Sync: The emerging science of spontaneous order.* New York: Hyperion.

Strogatz, S., Abrams, D.M., McRobie, A., Eckhardt, B. & Ott, E. (2005) Theoretical Mechanics: Crowd synchrony on the Millennium Bridge. *Nature* 438:43–4.

Style, S. (1 January 2002) Peoples Global Action. *Z Magazine.* http://zcombeta.org/zmagazine/peoples-global-action-by-sophie-style/

Suber, P. (2012) Open Access Overview. www.earlham.edu/~peters/fos/overview.htm

Sunstein, C.R. (2009) *Going to Extremes: How like minds unite and divide.* New York: Oxford University Press.

Surveillance Studies Network (2006) *A Report on the Surveillance Society: For the Information Commissioner.* Information Commissioner's Office. www.ico.org. uk/~/media/documents/library/Data_Protection/Practical_application/SURVEIL LANCE_SOCIETY_FULL_REPORT_2006.pdf

Sutton, M. (12 July 2012) ACTA's Defeat in Europe and What Lies Ahead. *EFF Deep Links.* www.eff.org/deeplinks/2012/07/acta-victory-europe-and-what-lies-ahead

Swain, V. (8 August 2013) Disruption Policing: Surveillance and the right to protest. *Open Democracy.* www.opendemocracy.net/opensecurity/val-swain/disruption-policing-surveillance-and-right-to-protest

Swan, J. (31 May 2012) Institute Opposing Plain Packaging Funded by Tobacco Company. *Sydney Morning Herald*, p.3.

Tainter, J. (1990) *The Collapse of Complex Societies.* Cambridge: Cambridge University Press.

Tannen, D. (ed.) (1993) Framing in Discourse. New York: Oxford University Press.

Tarrow, S. (1998) *Power in Movement.* Cambridge: Cambridge University Press.

Taylor, D. (nd) Damper Retrofit of the London Millenium Footbridge: A case study in biodynamic design. www.taylordevices.com/papers/damper/damper.pdf

Taylor, J. (1989) *Linguistic Categorization: Prototypes in linguistic theory.* New York: Oxford University Press.

Technology Review (17 September 2013) US Military Scientists Solve the Fundamental Problem of Viral Marketing. www.technologyreview.com/view/519361/us-military-scientists-solve-the-fundamental-problem-of-viral-marketing/

Tetlock, P.E. (2005) *Expert Political Judgment: How good is it? How can we know?* Princeton: Princeton University Press.

Thayer R.H. & Dorfman M. (1997) *Software Requirements Engineering.* 2nd Edition. Los Alamitos: IEEE Computer Society Press.

TheCostOfKnowledge (2012) [twitter account] https://twitter.com/costofknowledge

TheLeakyB@@b (3 January 2011) The Email From Facebook. http://theleakyboob.com/2011/01/the-email-from-facebook/

Theoretical Economics (2012) Theoretical Economics: Journal history. http://econtheory.org/history.php

Thomas, G.M. (2004) Building the Buzz in the Hive Mind. *Journal of Consumer Behaviour* 4(1):64–72.

Thompson, C. (2005) The BitTorrent Effect. *Wired* 13(01). Accessed 8 September 2013. www.wired.com/wired/archive/13.01/bittorrent.html

Thrift, N. (2006) Reinventing Invention: New tendencies in capitalist commodification. *Economy and Society* 35(2):279–303.

Tierney, K.J. (1999) Toward a Critical Sociology of Risk. *Sociological Forum* 14(2):215–42.

Tillet, A. (18 June 2012) Olympic Gold Has a High Price. *West.* http://au.news.yahoo.com/thewest/a/-/news/13974595/olympic-gold-has-a-high-price/

Tilly, C. (1979) *From Mobilization to Revolution.* New York: Addison-Wesley.

Toffler, A. (1980) *The Third Wave.* New York: Collins.

Toffler, A. (1984) *Previews and Premises.* London: Pan.

Toffler, A. (1990) *Power Shift: Knowledge, wealth and violence at the edge of the 21st century.* New York: Bantam.

Touraine, A. (1971) *The Post Industrial Society: Tomorrow's social history, classes, conflicts and culture in the programmed society.* New York: Random House.

Towell, N., Kenny, M. & Bridie Smith (8 November 2013) Razor Taken to CSIRO. *Sydney Morning Herald.* www.smh.com.au/federal-politics/political-news/razor-taken-to-csiro-20131107–2x4fu.html

Trivett, V. (28 June 2011) US Mega Corporations: Where they rank if they were countries. *Business Insider.* www.businessinsider.com.au/25-corporations-bigger-tan-countries-2011–6?op=1#not-all-are-created-equal-26

Turbeville, W. (2013) Cracks in the Pipeline 2: High frequency trading. *Demos.* www.demos.org/sites/default/files/publications/HFT_CracksInThePipeline_Demos.pdf

Turner, A. (2010) What Do Banks Do? Why do credit booms and busts occur and what can public policy do about it? In *The Future of Finance: The LSE Report.* London School of Economics and Political Science: 5–87.

Turner, J., Hogg, M., Oaks, P., Reicher, S. & Wetherall, M. (1987) *Rediscovering the Social Group: A self categorization theory.* Oxford: Blackwell

Turner, V. (1969) *The Ritual Process: Structure and anti-structure.* London: Routledge.

Tyler, W. (2003) Dancing at the Edge of Chaos: A spanner in the works of global capitalism. In Notes From Nowhere (eds.) *We Are Everywhere: The irresistible rise of global anticapitalism.* London: Verso. pp:189–95.

UIA (2014) *Open Yearbook.* Union of International Associations. Accessed 23 June 2104. www.uia.org/ybio/

UML (2012) *Unified Modelling Language.* www.omg.org/spec/UML/

UN (2011) *The Global Social Crisis, Report on the World Social Situation 2011.* UN Department of Economic and Social Affairs. www.un.org/esa/socdev/rwss/docs/2011/rwss2011.pdf

UN (2014) Growth in United Nations Membership, 1945–Present. www.un.org/en/members/growth.shtml

UNCTAD (2005) *World Investment Report 2005: Transnational corporations and the internationalization of R&D*. New York and Geneva: United Nations.

UNCTAD (2008) The Crisis of a Century. *Policy Brief 3*. New York: UNCTAD.

UNCTAD (2013) *World Investment Report 2013 Global Value Chains: Investment and trade for development*. Geneva: United Nations.

Ungoed-Thomas, J. & Sheehan, M. (15 August 1999) Riot Organisers Prepare to Launch Cyber War on City. *Sunday Times*. www.sunday-times.co.uk/news/pages/sti/99/08/15/stinwenws01012.html?999

United States Attorney's Office for the Eastern District of Virginia (2012) *California Member of the Internet Piracy Group 'IMAGiNE' Pleads Guilty to Copyright Infringement Conspiracy*. Accessed 9 September 2013. www.justice.gov/usao/vae/news/2012/05/20120510loveladynr.html

UrbanLegends (nd) Computer Virus Hoaxes. http://urbanlegends.about.com/od/virushoaxes1/Computer_Virus_Hoaxes.htm

Vallee, J. (1982) *The Network Revolution: Confessions of a computer scientist*. Berkeley: And/Or.

Van de Donk, W. & Rucht, D. (2003) *Cyberprotest: New media, citizens and social movements*. London: Routledge.

Van Dijk, J. (2006) *The Network Society: Social aspects of new media*. London: Sage.

Van Knippenberg, D., Lossie, N. & Wilke, H. (1994) In-Group Prototypicality and Persuasion: Determinants of heuristic and systematic message processing. *British Journal of Social Psychology* 33(3):289–300.

Van Lamsweerde, A. (2000) Requirements Engineering in the Year 00: A research perspective. *Proceedings of the 22nd international conference on Software engineering*. ACM: 5–19.

Van Noorden, R. (24 February 2014) Publishers Withdraw More than 120 Gibberish Papers. *Nature.com*. www.nature.com/news/publishers-withdraw-more-than-120-gibberish-papers-1.14763

Vasilyeva, N. (30 May 2013). Russian Critic: Wide corruption at Sochi games. *Yahoo News*. http://news.yahoo.com/russian-critic-wide-corruption-sochi-games-131742967.html

Vaughan, D. (1999) The Dark Side of Organizations: Mistake, misconduct, and disaster. *Annual Review of Sociology* 25:271–305.

Vaughan-Nichols, S.J. (20 April 2011) Microsoft Gets Novell's Patents Rights but Must Share Them with Open-Source Software. *Zdnet*. www.zdnet.com/blog/open-source/microsoft-gets-novells-patents-rights-but-must-share-them-with-open-source-software/8713

Veblen, T. (1915) *Imperial Germany and the Industrial Revolution*. New York: Macmillan.

Victor, D.G. (4 April 2011) Why the UN Can Never Stop Climate Change. *Guardian*. www.theguardian.com/environment/2011/apr/04/un-climate-change

Vitali, S., Glattfelder, J.B. & Battiston, S. (2011) The Network of Global Corporate Control. *PLoS ONE* 6(10). http://arxiv.org/abs/1107.5728

Vodafone (2014) *Sustainability Report*. www.vodafone.com/content/dam/sustainability/2014/pdf/vodafone_full_report_2014.pdf

Vranica, S. (9 February 2005) Getting Buzz Marketers to Fess Up. *Wall Street Journal*. http://online.wsj.com/news/articles/SB110790837180449447

Waelbroeck, P. (2013) Digital Music: Economic Perspectives. In R. Towse & C. Handke (eds) *Handbook of the Digital Creative Economy*. Cheltenham: Edward Elgar. pp:389–98.

Waldgrave, S. & Verhulst, J. (2006) Towards 'New Emotional Movements?' A comparative exploration into a specific movement type. *Social Movement Studies* 5(3):275–304.

Washbourne, N. (2001) Information Technology and New Forms of Organising? Translocalism and networks in Friends of the Earth. In F. Webster (ed.) *Culture and Politics in the Information Age*. London: Routledge. pp:129–42.

Watts, D. (2003) *Six Degrees: The science of a connected age*. New York: W.W. Norton.

Wayne, L. & Pollack, A. (22 July 1998) The Master of Orange County: A Merrill Lynch broker survives municipal bankruptcy. *New York Times*. www.nytimes.com/1998/07/22/business/the-master-of-orange-county-a-merrill-lynch-broker-survives-municipal-bankruptcy.html

WEF (2012) *Global Risks Survey*. Geneva: World Economic Forum.

Weintraub, S. (28 February 2011a) Google Goes to the Tape to Get Lost Emails Back. *CNN*. http://tech.fortune.cnn.com/2011/02/28/google-goes-to-the-tape-to-get-lost-emails-back/

Weintraub, S. (28 February 2011b) Gmail Outage Passes 24 Hours for Some (updated). *CNN*. http://tech.fortune.cnn.com/2011/02/28/gmail-outage-passes-24-hours-for-some/

Weis, A. (24 January 2014) Gmail Temporarily Crashes; Millions Panic. http://guardianlv.com/2014/01/gmail-temporarily-crashes-millions-panic/

Welch, C. (12 March 2013) BitTorrent Live Enters Beta, Uses Peer-to-Peer to Broadcast Video Streams. *Verge*. www.theverge.com/2013/3/12/4093724/bittorrent-live-streaming-beta-uses-peer-to-peer-for-broadcasting

Whimster, S. (2004) *The Essential Max Weber*. London: Routledge.

Whitfield, D. (2007) *Cost Overruns, Delays and Terminations: 105 outsourced public sector ICT projects*, ESSU Research Report No. 3. www.european-services-strategy.org.uk/publications/essu-research-reports/essu-research-report-no-3-cost-overruns-delays/essu-research-paper-3.pdf

Whittaker, Z. (10 December 2012) Gmail in Widespread Outage, Also Caused Chrome Browser Crashes. *Zdnet*. www.zdnet.com/gmail-in-widespread-outage-also-caused-chrome-browser-crashes-7000008568/

Whittam Smith, A. (21 June 1999) The Carnival that Became a Riot Chose the Right Target. *Independent*. www.independent.co.uk/arts-entertainment/the-carnival-that-became-a-riot-chose-the-right-target-1101498.html

Wikileaks (2013) Secret TPP Treaty: Advanced intellectual property chapter for all 12 nations with negotiating positions. http://wikileaks.org/tpp/static/pdf/Wikileaks-secret-TPP-treaty-IP-chapter.pdf

Wikipedia (22 March 2014) 'Fantasecond'. [Deleted by late March]. http://en.wikipedia.org/wiki/Fantasecond

Wilkinson, M. (31 July 1999) The Changing Face of Protest: Idealists or subversives? *Financial Times*, p.12.

Williams, B. (nd) Volcker Overruled? www.ethics.harvard.edu/lab/blog/368-volcker-overruled

Williams, B. & Silverstein, K. (10 May 2013) Meet the Think Tank Scholars Who Are Also Beltway Lobbyists: Why D.C.'s policy shops need to be transparent about who else is paying their scholars. *New Republic*. www.newrepublic.com/article/113158/report-dozens-lobbyists-work-think-tank-scholars

Williams, C. (10 October 2011) BlackBerry Services Collapse. *Telegraph* (UK). www.telegraph.co.uk/technology/blackberry/8818094/BlackBerry-services-collapse.html

Williams, C. (11 October 2011a) BlackBerry Services Collapse Again. *Telegraph* (UK). www.telegraph.co.uk/technology/blackberry/8820075/BlackBerry-services-collapse-again.html

Williams,C.(11October2011b)SecondOutageDeepensBlackBerryCrisis.*Telegraph*(UK). www.telegraph.co.uk/technology/blackberry/8820842/Second-outage-deepens-BlackBerry-crisis.html

Williams,C.(12October2011a)BlackBerryBlackoutEntersDayThree.*Telegraph*(UK). www.telegraph.co.uk/technology/blackberry/8821912/BlackBerry-black out-enters-day-three.html

Williams, C. (12 October 2011b) Compensation Calls as BlackBerry Breakdown Spreads to US. *Telegraph* (UK). www.telegraph.co.uk/technology/blackberry/ 8822525/Compensation-calls-as-BlackBerry-breakdown-spreads-to-US.html

Williams, C. (14 October 2011) BlackBerry Blackout: How it happened. *Telegraph* (UK). www.telegraph.co.uk/technology/blackberry/8825661/BlackBerry-black out-how-it-happened.html

Williams, K. (2012) Keynote Address. Paper presented to the *Australian International Movie Convention*, Gold Coast, Australia, 19–23 August. Accessed 6 September 2013. http://media.news.com.au/fe/2012/08/aimc/doc/AIMC_Keynote_Address_ Kim_Williams_AM.pdf

Willetts, D. (2012) *Public Access to Publicly-funded Research*. UK Department for Business Innovation & Skills. www.bis.gov.uk/news/speeches/david-willetts-public-access-to-research https://www.gov.uk/government/speeches/public-access-to-publicly-funded-research

Wilson, H. (14 December 2012) Banks Are 'Too Big to Prosecute', Says FSA's Andrew Bailey. *Telegraph* (UK). www.telegraph.co.uk/finance/newsbysector/ banksandfinance/9743839/Banks-are-too-big-to-prosecute-says-FSAs-Andrew-Bailey.html

Wilson, R.A. (1980) *The Illuminati Papers*. Berkeley: And/Or Press.

Wittgenstein, L. (1958) *Philosophical Investigations*. Oxford: Basil Blackwell.

Wolf, J. (17 April 2013) Is Gmail Down? 3 ways to survive the Google mail outage. www.policymic.com/articles/7094/is-gmail-down-3-ways-to-survive-the-google-mail-outage

Wolfson, T. (2013) Democracy or Autonomy? Indymedia and the contradictions of global social movement networks. *Global Networks* 13(3):410–424.

Wolin, S.S. (2008) *Democracy Incorporated: Managed democracy and the specter of inverted totalitarianism*. New Jersey: Princeton.

Wolson, T. (2013) Democracy or Autonomy? Indymedia and the contradictions of global social movement networks. *Global Networks* 13(3):410–24.

World Bank (2014) *World Development Indicators 2012*. Washington: World Bank.

WorldWideWebSize.com (7 February 2013). The Size of the World Wide Web (The Internet). www.worldwidewebsize.com [Updated regularly].

Wright, S. (2012) Anthropology and the Imagining of Future European Universities. Paper presented to the *Association of Social Anthropology of Aotearoa/New Zealand conference: Anthropology and Imagination*, 8–10 December 2012.

Xinhua (20 March 2012) Cyber Attacks against China Remain Severe: Report. *People's Daily*. http://english.peopledaily.com.cn/202936/7762737.html

Yaxley, L. (8 November 2013) 21 Committees Scrapped in Fed Govt Savings Drive. *ABC*. www.abc.net.au/news/2013-11-08/21-committees-scrapped-in-fed-govt-savings-drive/5078254

Young, S. (2010) Politics and the Media in Australia Today. *Papers on Parliament No. 50*. www.aph.gov.au/About_Parliament/Senate/Research_and_Education/ pops/~/link.aspx?_id=BBB1EE10832642B4A58C93B92FB39794&_z=z

Zave P. & Jackson, M. (1993) Conjunction as Composition. *ACM Transactions on Software Engineering and Methodology* 2(4):379–411.

Zave, P. & Jackson, M. (1997) Four Dark Corners of Requirements Engineering. *ACM Transactions on Software Engineering and Methodology* 6(1):1–30.

Zdnet (29 May 2012) Gmail Down For Some: Users experiencing problems logging in. *Zdnet*. www.zdnet.com/gmail-in-widespread-outage-also-caused-chrome-browser-crashes-7000008568/

Zetter, K. (9 January 2004) Kazaa Delivers More Than Tunes. *Wired Online*. www.wired.com/techbiz/media/news/2004/01/61852

Zimmer, C. (16 April 2012) A Sharp Rise in Retractions Prompts Calls for Reform. *New York Times*. www.nytimes.com/2012/04/17/science/rise-in-scientific-journal-retractions-prompts-calls-for-reform.html

Zowghi, D. (1999) *A Logic-Based Framework for the Management of Changing Software Requirements*. PhD Thesis, Macquarie University, Sydney, Australia.

Zowghi, D. (2000) A Requirements Engineering Process Model Based on Defaults and Revisions. *Proceedings of the Second International Workshop on Requirements Engineering Process* (REP 2000) in conjunction with DEXA 2000, London.

Zowghi, D. & Gervasi V. (2002). The Three Cs of Requirements: Consistency, completeness and correctness. *Proceedings of 8th International Workshop on Requirements Engineering: Foundation for Software Quality*, (REFSQ'02). Essen.

Zowghi D. & Gervasi V. (2004) On the Interplay Between Consistency, Completeness, and Correctness in Requirements Evolution. *Journal of Information and Software Technology* 46(11):763–79.

Zowghi, D., Gervasi V. & McRae A. (2001) Using Default Reasoning to Discover Inconsistencies in Natural Language Requirements. *Proceedings of the Asia Pacific Software Engineering Conference* (APSEC'01).

Zowghi, D. & Nurmuliani, N. (2002) A Study of Impact of Requirements Volatility on Software Project Performance. *Proceedings of the 9th Asia Pacific Software Engineering Conference*: 38–48.

Zowghi, D., Offen, R. & Nurmuliani, N. (2000) The Impact of Requirements Volatility on the Software Development Lifecycle. *Proceedings of the International Conference on Software, Theory and Practice (ICS2000)*. Beijing: IFIP World Computer Conference.

Index

Printed in the United States
by Baker & Taylor Publisher Services